An Army of Never-Ending Strength

Studies in Canadian Military History

Series editor: Andrew Burtch, Canadian War Museum

The Canadian War Museum, Canada's national museum of military history, has a threefold mandate: to remember, to preserve, and to educate. Studies in Canadian Military History, published by UBC Press in association with the museum, extends this mandate by presenting the best of contemporary scholarship to provide new insights into all aspects of Canadian military history, from earliest times to recent events. The work of a new generation of scholars is especially encouraged, and the books employ a variety of approaches – cultural, social, intellectual, economic, political, and comparative – to investigate gaps in the existing historiography. The books in the series feed immediately into future exhibitions, programs, and outreach efforts by the Canadian War Museum. A list of the titles in the series appears at the end of the book.

CANADIAN WAR MUSEUM
MUSÉE CANADIEN DE LA GUERRE

An Army of Never-Ending Strength

Reinforcing the Canadians in Northwest Europe, 1944–45

Arthur W. Gullachsen

UBCPress · Vancouver · Toronto

30 29 28 27 26 25 24 23 22 21 5 4 3 2 1

Printed in Canada on FSC-certified ancient-forest-free paper (100% post-consumer recycled) that is processed chlorine- and acid-free.

Library and Archives Canada Cataloguing in Publication

Title: An army of never-ending strength : reinforcing the Canadians in northwest Europe, 1944-45 / Arthur W. Gullachsen.

Names: Gullachsen, Arthur W., 1973- author.

Series: Studies in Canadian military history.

Description: Series statement: Studies in Canadian military history, ISSN: 1499-6251 | Includes bibliographical references and index.

Identifiers: Canadiana (print) 20200355368 | Canadiana (ebook) 20200355600 | ISBN 9780774864817 (hardcover) | ISBN 9780774864824 (paperback) | ISBN 9780774864831 (PDF) | ISBN 9780774864848 (EPUB) | ISBN 9780774864855 (Kindle)

Subjects: LCSH: Canada. Canadian Army. Army, First. | LCSH: Canada. Canadian Army. Army, First—Equipment. | LCSH: Canada. Canadian Army. Army, First—Personnel management. | LCSH: World War, 1939-1945—Regimental histories—Canada. | LCSH: World War, 1939-1945—Equipment and supplies.

Classification: LCC D768.153 .G85 2021 | DDC 940.54/1271—dc23

Canadä

UBC Press gratefully acknowledges the financial support for our publishing program of the Government of Canada (through the Canada Book Fund), the Canada Council for the Arts, and the British Columbia Arts Council.

Publication of this book has been financially supported by the Canadian War Museum.

Printed and bound in Canada by Friesens
Set in Helvetica Condensed and Minion by Artegraphica Design Co. Ltd.
Copy editor: Lesley Erickson
Proofreader: Alison Strobel
Indexer: Noeline Bridge
Cartographer: Eric Leinberger
Cover designer: George Kirkpatrick
Cover image: 5th Canadian Armoured Division tanks lined up at Eelde airport, Holland. Lord Strathcona's Horse, Royal Canadian tanks in foreground. 23 May 1945 | LAC 4167256.

UBC Press
The University of British Columbia
2029 West Mall
Vancouver, BC V6T 1Z2
www.ubcpress.ca

To Michele

Contents

List of Figures and Tables / viii

Acknowledgments / xi

List of Abbreviations / xii

Introduction / 3

1 Personnel Reinforcements / 13

2 The Sixty-Day Shortage / 22

3 Vehicles and Weapons / 44

4 Army Doctrine and Losses / 64

5 Formations and Their Units / 93

6 The Normandy Campaign / 101

7 Channel Ports, Scheldt, and the River Mass / 127

8 Veritable, Blockbuster, and War's End / 141

9 An Assessment of Canadian Formations / 167

Conclusion / 172

Appendices / 177

Notes / 200

Selected Bibliography / 227

Index / 231

Figures and Tables

Figures

1.1 Echelons, 21st Army Group Headquarters, France, 1944 / 14

1.2 The personnel delivery system, 1944–45 / 18

1.3 Number of reinforcements dispatched to 21st Army Group, August 1944 to February 1945 / 20

1.4 German battle losses and total replacements, July–August 1944 / 21

2.1 Forecasts versus casualties, June and July 1944 / 34

2.2 Shortages, other ranks, 2nd Canadian Infantry Division, July–September 1944 / 36

2.3 Projected monthly infantry loss rates, normal and intense, 31 August 1944 / 37

2.4 Actual reinforcement holdings versus authorized target strengths, November 1944 / 41

3.1 The equipment losses administrative system / 47

3.2 The AFV replacement system / 49

3.3 Sherman tank strength, 6th CAR, June 1944 / 53

3.4 Panzer IV tank strength, German II/SS Panzer Regiment 12, June 1944 / 53

3.5 Path for "B" vehicle replacement / 57

3.6 Maintenance lines, "A" and "B" vehicles and major weapons systems / 58

3.7 Recovery-and-repair process, "A" and "B" vehicle and major weapons systems, Armoured Division / 59

4.1 Fort Garry Horse two-squadron combined arms tactics with infantry, Louisendorf, 1945 / 72

4.2 Assault on Buron, Operation Charnwood, 8 July 1944 / 75

4.3 Barrage fire plan, Operation Veritable, 8 February 1945 / 84

6.1 Tank strength of 2nd Canadian Armoured Brigade (Sherman, Sherman Firefly, and Stuart) and Panzer Regiment 3 (Panther and Panzer IV), June–August 1944 / 105

6.2 Strength returns versus authorized strengths, 3rd Canadian Infantry Division versus German infantry divisions, August–September 1944 / 111

7.1 2nd Canadian Infantry Division strengths (thousands), July–September 1944 / 128

7.2 German 12th SS Panzer Division strengths (thousands), June–September 1944 / 129

7.3 Strength returns, the Argyll and Sutherland Highlanders of Canada, August 1944 to April 1945 / 139

8.1 Comparison of tank replacement and delivery, 4th Canadian Armoured Division, to German Panzer IV medium tank production for all German land forces, August–December 1944 / 145

8.2 Operational equipment levels of 2nd Canadian AGRA medium regiments, July 1944 to April 1945 / 146

8.3 Battle and nonbattle casualties, 2nd Canadian Infantry Brigade, April 1945 / 151

8.4 Number of Heavy AFVs delivered to the 5th Canadian Armoured Division versus Panther tanks delivered to all German armoured units, March–May 1945 / 159

8.5 5th Canadian Armoured Division, infantry regiment strengths, 31 March 1945 and 5 May 1945 / 161

9.1 3rd Canadian Infantry Division strengths (thousands), 31 July 1944–30 April 1945 / 169

P.1 Personnel working on the index of battle casualties, Canadian Military Headquarters Records Branch, 5 June 1945 / 120

P.2 Regimental Aid Party treating an infantryman, 7 April 1945 / 120

P.3 Wounded infantrymen being helped to cover, ca. 22 April 1945 / 121

P.4 Tank crew with their Sherman Vc Firefly tank, 20 January 1945 / 122

P.5 Personnel with the Sherman tank "Bomb" of the Sherbrooke Fusiliers Regiment, 1945 / 123

P.6 Gunners S.S. Lott and J.G. Spear overhauling a jeep motor, 28 April 1945 / 123

P.7 Brigadier Kenneth Stuart in the first Canadian-built tank, 1941 / 124

P.8 Captain C.H. Davis welcoming an incoming draft to No. 1 Canadian Armoured Corps Reinforcement Unit, 8 August 1944 / 124

P.9 Infantry reinforcements going ashore off the Normandy bridgehead, June 1944 / 125

P.10 W.L. Mackenzie King shaking hands with J.L. Ralston, 7 August 1944 / 126

Tables

I.1 Units and formations, First Canadian Army, 1944–45 / 11
4.1 Infantry small arms, June–August 1944 / 79
A1.1 CAC Armoured Regiment (Armoured Brigade or Division), January 1945 / 179
A1.2 CAC Armoured Car Regiment (Corps Troops), October 1944 / 180
A1.3 CAC Reconnaissance Regiment (Infantry Division), January 1945 / 181
A1.4 CIC Infantry Regiment, January 1945 / 182
A1.5 CIC Motor Battalion (Armoured Division), January 1945 / 184
A1.6 CIC Machine Gun Battalion, January 1945 / 185
A1.7 Towed RCA Field Artillery Regiment (Infantry Division variant), January 1945 / 186
A1.8 Self-Propelled RCA Field Artillery Regiment (Armoured Division), January 1945 / 187
A1.9 Towed RCA Field Artillery Regiment (Armoured Division), January 1945 / 188
A1.10 AGRA RCA Medium Regiment (Army Troops), October 1944 / 189
A1.11 RCA Survey Regiment (Corps Troops), October 1944 / 190
A1.12 RCA Anti-Tank Regiment (Corps Troops), October 1944 / 191
A1.13 RCA Anti-Tank Regiment (Armoured Division), January 1945 / 192
A1.14 RCA Anti-Tank Regiment (Infantry Division), January 1945 / 193
A1.15 RCA Light Anti-Aircraft Regiment (Corps Troops), October 1944 / 194
A1.16 RCA Light Anti-Aircraft Regiment (Infantry Division), January 1945 / 195
A1.17 RCA Light Anti-Aircraft Regiment (Armoured Division), January 1945 / 195
A2.1 Neuro-Psychiatric (NP) Cases October 1944 within the 3rd Canadian Infantry Division after the Scheldt Estuary battles / 197
A2.2 Treatment options that were utilized for NP casualties October 1944 within the 3rd Canadian Infantry Division after the Scheldt Estuary battles / 197
A3.1 Infantry, other ranks, shortages, by division, Northwest Europe, 27 August 1944–28 April 1945 / 198

Acknowledgments

MANY PEOPLE HAVE contributed to this book. First and foremost, I must thank my wife, Michele Connor, for her never-ending support for *An Army of Never-Ending Strength*. I must also thank the late Brock Millman, who sadly passed away in 2018. It was his insight that uplifted my spirit when I was unhappy with the product and pointed me in the direction I needed to go. Next, I must thank the anonymous reviewers who asked me tough questions during the review process at UBC Press. These scholars, recruited by editor Randy Schmidt, were essential to the manuscript editing and revision process. Though I may never learn who you are, your careful review and blunt suggestions took this manuscript to another level. My colleague Asa McKercher at the Royal Military College of Canada helped me identify where the writing could be better. Last but not least, I must acknowledge the diligent work of Canadian Army staff officers at the regimental, brigade, division, corps, and army level during the last year of the Second World War, 1944–45. Without their staff work in the way of carefully drafted orders, reports, memos, and statistical returns, much of which survives today at Libraries and Archives Canada, it would have been difficult to accurately depict the growth of the Army and the challenges it faced in wartime. The First Canadian Army, colossal in size and strength, is something that is completely unimaginable in modern Canada, the most unmilitary of nations, safely bound by oceans. Massively powerful, this army made a significant contribution to the overall Allied victory in 1945.

Abbreviations

A&Q	Adjutant and Quartermaster
AFV	armoured fighting vehicle
AGRA	Army Group Royal Artillery
CAC	Canadian Armoured Corps
CADR	Canadian Armoured Delivery Regiment
CAR	Canadian Armoured Regiment
CBRG	Canadian Base Reinforcement Group
CIC	Canadian Infantry Corps
CMHQ	Canadian Military Headquarters, London
LAA	Light Anti-Aircraft
LAD	Light Aid Detachment
LOD	Line of Departure
NDHQ	National Defence Headquarters, Ottawa
NRMA	National Resources Mobilization Act
OMC	Ordnance Maintenance Company
RCA	Royal Canadian Artillery
RCEME	Royal Canadian Electrical and Mechanical Engineers
RCOC	Royal Canadian Ordnance Corps
REME	Royal Electrical and Mechanical Engineers

An Army of Never-Ending Strength

Introduction

6 JUNE 1944. A day that witnessed the amphibious landing phase of Operation Overlord, the Allied invasion of France. British, Canadian, and American forces pierced German Atlantic Wall defences in five different locations in bitter fighting that lasted most of the morning. By last light on 6 June 1944, the first Canadian formations to invade the continent, the 3rd Canadian Infantry Division and the 2nd Canadian Armoured Brigade, were firmly entrenched in their part of the Allied beachhead. They were the first forces of what would eventually grow into the First Canadian Army, and they had begun what would be a long, costly campaign to liberate northwest Europe, where hostilities concluded with a ceasefire on 5 May 1945.

The Canadian forces' path to eventual victory over the Germans had three distinct phases.[1] The first phase was a bitter campaign of attrition in Normandy, where the Canadian Army prevailed against the strongest German formations. By late August 1944, these enemy forces had been crushed in the Falaise Pocket. The second phase then began with a long pursuit across France that saw the liberation of enemy-held channel ports. This phase concluded with bitter fighting to clear the Scheldt Estuary. They freed the port of Antwerp by November 1944. Following these two costly phases, the Canadian Army assumed defensive positions along the Maas River. It held these static positions from November 1944 to January 1945. The third phase of combat operations began in February. During it, 2nd Canadian Corps reunited with the 1st Canadian Corps, redeployed from Italy. The First Canadian Army now consisted of two complete Canadian corps. Canadian formations within these two corps totalled three infantry divisions, two armoured divisions, two independent armoured brigades, and two army-level artillery groupings.[2] Each of these formations was near full strength in early April 1945, and together they made up the greatest Canadian military force ever assembled in the history of the nation. In the last month of hostilities, this force relentlessly advanced, sweeping aside all opposition.

The Canadian Army had not always achieved this battlefield dominance. Before the German collapse in mid-August 1944, Canadian formations in Normandy faced challenges they had not experienced in Italy in 1943–44. In June, July, and August, they experienced heavy casualties inflicted on them by a seasoned foe equipped with advanced weapons systems. It was a titanic challenge to overcome attrition in personnel, weapons, and equipment. From 6 June through 23 August, casualties in Normandy totalled 18,444, including 5,021 deaths.[3] These losses were the equivalent of a full-strength infantry division.[4] Vehicles and weapons-systems losses also mounted during the summer of 1944. On 11 June, the 6th Canadian Armoured Regiment (1st Hussars, 6 CAR) had fifty-one of its sixty-one 75 mm Sherman and 17-pounder-gunned Sherman Firefly tanks destroyed, a loss rate of 84 percent.[5] The Canadian Army maintained adequate personnel and equipment levels through rapid replacements, which allowed units to remain operational and achieve battlefield victories. This practice preserved units and a formation's combat power. The Canadian Army could not mount offensive operations if there were not enough soldiers or weapons. Strategy, planning, and tactics would be for nought in the absence of reserve resources with efficient administrative systems to sustain the front-line formations.[6]

This book shows that for most of the Canadian Amy's operations in northwest Europe during 1944–45, its three traditional combat arms – infantry, armour, and artillery – were effectively reinforced. Here, *effective reinforcement* is defined as the successful maintenance of units near or at their establishment strengths for vehicles, equipment, and personnel. Reinforcement allowed these units to continue offensive operations despite heavy losses in intense combat. The efficiency of the Canadian Army's personnel- and equipment-reinforcement systems thus allowed it to realize its prime objective: the defeat of the German military by the concentration of superior forces at the decisive points in the theatre.

Historians of the Canadian Army's campaign in Normandy observe that it regularly conducted operations with understrength infantry units.[7] Most critical is the observation of American military historian Russell Hart, who notes the following in his seminal work, *Clash of Arms: How the Allies Won in Normandy:*

> The Battle of the Falaise Pocket witnessed the hardest fighting the Canadians had yet encountered as the enemy fought to escape encirclement. By August a growing infantry shortage undermined Canadian combat effectiveness. With only one division in action during June available replacements covered losses, but by mid-July infantry casualties were 80 percent above forecast. By early August, when the infantry deficit reached 1,900, Crerar acknowledged that the replacement situation had become the most serious problem confronting the Canadians. The heavy losses suffered during TOTALIZE and TRACTABLE increased the shortage: on 15 August Canadian formations were short 2,644 riflemen. Manpower

> shortages thus sapped Canadian offensive drive at the moment when it was put in the unique position of "bagging" the remnants of two German armies in Normandy.[8]

However, the idea that the Canadian Army regularly utilized understrength infantry units to lead an attack during the start of major set-piece operations in the summer of 1944 is a myth.[9] Rather than being half-strength infantry battalions (regiments) struggling to achieve their objectives with a bare minimum of personnel, attacking units were always at or very near their establishment strengths at the start of major operations. While some challenges occurred during the latter half of August and early September 1944, the reinforcement system still functioned. The issue the Canadian Army faced was that the intensity of combat and the sheer number of losses on a weekly basis simply overwhelmed the replacement system for a period of roughly sixty days. Replacements arrived, but the losses were higher and occurred at a much quicker rate than anticipated. Critics who observe that each infantry battalion was not at 100 percent overlook that the First Canadian Army was taking on a major operational role in late August 1944. It was involved in the destruction of two German armies, these containing the majority of the Nazi's military strength in occupied France, and suffering heavy casualties in the process daily.[10]

Canadian military historian Terry Copp states: "It is also important to note that the shortage of infantry replacements had an especially adverse effect on the 2nd Division. By 28 July it was short 1,060 infantrymen; and by 20 August it was reporting a deficiency of 1,840 Infantry Other Ranks."[11] This is the standard view on the Canadian Army's reinforcement capability in the summer of 1944. But it does not consider that the majority of Canadian infantry units were in tolerable shape and capable of operations that would ensure the defeat of the Wehrmacht. Consider that on 28 July 1944 the Essex Scottish Regiment, one of nine infantry battalions in the 2nd Canadian Infantry Division, forwarded a return of 38 officers and 735 other ranks, 96 percent of its establishment strength.[12] Though battalions were understrength at certain points, their strengths changed on a daily basis. If the performance of the Canadian infantry regiments had not been effective, the Falaise Gap would not have been closed, and the decisive victory over the German forces would not have occurred by 21 August 1944.

Make no mistake, during the late summer of 1944 some Canadian infantry regiments were in poor shape, but this situation was remedied largely by mid-September – before major combat operations in the Scheldt Estuary began in October.[13] But even on 31 August 1944, when the Canadian Army's infantry shortage was at its height, the average strength of the twenty-two Canadian infantry battalions was still roughly 77 percent of their establishments. Though reduced, these battalions were still capable of attacking. Considering that these infantry units had just closed the Falaise Gap and were now engaged in high-intensity exploitation operations, their strength returns are indicative of an army at war, not one on the parade ground.[14]

Canada's system of constant reinforcement was in direct contrast to Germany's. Its army suffered continuous losses and was rarely reinforced with new personnel or equipment. The Germans let the strengths of standard infantry formations fall to nothing; they only reinforced a limited number of elite divisions on an ongoing basis. As a result, they had to construct new infantry formations from scratch. Combat formations eventually had to be withdrawn to be reconstituted, re-equipped, and retrained.[15] The Germans did not see the process of constantly reinforcing a division in the field as the most efficient way to maintain a field army's military strength. Often, they allowed near annihilation by attrition to occur before withdrawing a unit for a program of reconstitution. National honour or a unit's history never prevented the destruction of a formation. A recently raised unit with new personnel and equipment would take its place. Because of a lack of reinforcements, corps headquarters perceived German formations as employable tools with a temporary value. This led to their ruthless combat employment by higher command with little regard for their welfare or status.[16] By contrast, during the final year of the war, Canadian divisions were rarely withdrawn from the combat environment and, if so, higher headquarters tasked them with a reserve role near the front line. This constant front-line deployment arguably increased the combat effectiveness of the units within Canadian divisions, as they never ceased operations apart from small breaks.

By offering a detailed statistical analysis of the combat records, this book builds on the existing literature on the Canadian Army's manpower struggles during its last eleven months of operations.[17] Given the lethality and destructive power of modern weapons in 1944–45, an army's ability to rebuild itself was of equal importance to its ability to defeat its enemy. This book, therefore, is as much about the nature of twentieth-century modern warfare as it is about the administrative processes of the Canadian Army.

Detailed statistical studies of the combat records of Canadian units are rare. Operational narratives usually relegate supporting data to limited appendices that are rarely analyzed. The research presented here tracks actual Canadian Army unit strengths and losses and shows how its administrative and logistic organizations successfully reconstituted units during intense operations. The book presents an overview of the operational record of the division or independent brigade to which each combat unit belonged. Within the historiography of Canadian military engagement during the Second World War, historians typically focus on the regiment or combat arms corps rather than on formations such as divisions or brigades. By including data on larger formations and grouping together statistics on all their component combat arms units, *An Army of Never-Ending Strength* presents a more complete picture. As the greatest military force ever created by the nation of Canada, the First Canadian Army's size, strength, and capability were constantly evolving.

Chapters 1 and 2 outline the personnel reinforcement system and how significant challenges in 1944 were resolved. Chapter 3 examines the equipment replacement system and how it maintained the army's military strength. Devoted to battlefield tactics and equipment, Chapter 4 shows why certain losses in personnel and equipment occurred. Chapters 5 through 9 tell the story of how personnel and equipment were replenished in the field. The Conclusion assesses the Canadian Army's replacement practices for both personnel and equipment and how the performance of these essential functions was critical to victory in 1945.

Although the Canadian Army effectively reinforced its three traditional combat arms, it would be incorrect to state that it did so in the most efficient manner possible. *Effectiveness,* as defined in the larger military spectrum, refers to a group successfully producing an intended mission result. *Efficiency* in the same environment is the practice of achieving a mission while keeping wasted or excessive effort to a minimum. The personnel and administration effort required to attain the army's reinforcement goals were at times excessive. As an example, No. 2 Canadian Base Reinforcement Group (No. 2 CBRG), a main cog in the personnel replacement organization, was militarily effective. When well-supplied and given time to establish routine deliveries, it achieved its goal – the timely distribution of personnel to front-line units.[18] But it was excessively bureaucratic in its operations, which hurt its level of efficiency. The five No. 2 CBRG reinforcement battalions that supplied units at the front were holding units. They were beset by the administrative processes to receive, hold, and dispatch soldiers, all of which took time. The skills of soldiers held in these battalions eroded the longer they stayed. To move a replacement soldier from the 21st Army Group reception camp in northwest Europe to his regiment took seven administrative moves between organizations, and two of the destinations were in No. 2 CBRG itself.

It would have been more efficient if each No. 2 CBRG battalion were specialized for a certain trade and their number reduced. Replacements could have been kept nearby in large camp environments where their combat skills could be maintained. Also, the number of administrative moves should have been reduced. This is exactly what occurred in late 1944, when the personnel reinforcement system was reorganized to focus on quickly supplying infantry regiments with replacements.[19] But during the summer and fall of 1944, needless time and resources were spent ensuring that new personnel reached units on a routine schedule.

During the summer of 1944, the delivery of heavy armoured fighting vehicles could also have been more efficient. Operations within the 25th Canadian Armoured Delivery Regiment (CADR) were complicated and overly administrative. Its squadrons duplicated the mechanical and kit inspection process on armoured vehicles at each stop in the delivery process until an "A" vehicle joined a unit.[20] When this vehicle reached the front, it was then checked a final time by the soldiers operating it. The duplication was needless. Again, once the machine was rolling and well supplied with vehicles, large numbers of replacements reached regiments on a regular basis.

As these two examples show, the Canadian Army had an extensive administrative component within its personnel and equipment replacement organizations. Once these organizations were established and well supplied, they achieved their main goals in a satisfactory manner. But they were not streamlined organizations.

Was there a distinct administrative mentality within the Canadian Army that focused on maintaining the strength of combat arms units at the front? The Canadian Army's approach to the replacement of personnel and equipment was similar to that of Britain and the United States. As was the case in their armies, sophisticated and bureaucratic systems ensured that reinforcements and new equipment reached units in the field. From 1939 to 1943, the Canadian Army was not committed to combat apart from two short-lived operations in late 1941 and mid-1942. This nonoperational period led to the establishment of an extensive administrative and training base in England. Administrative structures and systems increased in size and sophistication within what amounted to a peacetime training environment.[21]

Although the Canadian Army took on a major combat role in Italy in 1943–44, it did so with a limited expeditionary force that consisted initially of one infantry division and one independent armoured brigade. Because of the limited number of Canadian formations being deployed, in comparison to the US and British forces, the army could give specialized attention to its personnel and equipment replacement needs. The force eventually became a complete corps of two divisions and one independent brigade, but its losses were still manageable due to breaks in operations. After gaining experience in Sicily and Italy, utilizing existing repair and reinforcement processes already present in the British Army, the army had systems in place for the D-Day landings and beyond that were effective and battle-tested.

The Canadian Army's battlefield doctrine was, for necessary reasons, based on British military philosophy, concepts, and operational art. To attain combat objectives, it focused on the use of equipment and firepower rather than the expenditure of human capital. The Anglo-Canadian emphasis on use of military technology was intended to limit friendly casualties and, simultaneously, cause extreme attrition to occur within the enemy's ranks.[22] This was a "compassionate attritionist" approach. Because of the limited number of Canadian formations engaged in battle, deployed front-line divisions were lavishly equipped with a complete establishment of the latest weapons and equipment in the Commonwealth arsenal. Losses in these inventories were rapidly made good. This allowed the formations to fully utilize a large percentage of their weapons systems on an ongoing basis, continually hammering away at the enemy with a focus on his continued attrition.

It should be mentioned that while Canada suffered severe personnel losses during the disasters at Hong Kong in 1941 and Dieppe in 1942, it never endured the kind of military disasters that befell certain German armies on the eastern front from 1941 to 1945. The possibility that a unit would be destroyed was an eventuality the Canadian Army refused to accept. The reality of total war, practised on a grand scale by nations literally fighting for their national survival, was not a challenge that the Canadian military faced in Europe. It was never involved in a desperate do-or-die struggle with a superior foe in the last year of the war. The Normandy lodgement, for example, was never in danger of liquidation after June 1944. Personnel and equipment challenges could be administratively managed, and no disastrous event equivalent to the German debacle at Stalingrad upset the orderly Canadian management of the war. Also, the Allies' increasing military dominance on the western front from September 1944 onward allowed for a situation where battalion-sized units could be withdrawn into reserve for training, rest, or partial reconstitution. This rotation was completed on a relaxed schedule as determined by 2nd Canadian Corps or First Canadian Army headquarters.

The key factor that led to the fall 1944 Conscription Crisis in Canada was the lack of other ranks (nonofficer) infantry replacements. When discovered, this shortage placed significant political pressure on the Cabinet War Committee of Prime Minister Mackenzie King. This political crisis led to the November 1944 decision to employ home defence conscripts overseas. Prior to this point, during a sixty-day period in August and September 1944, a limited supply of reinforcements had led to serious personnel deficiencies in Canada's infantry regiments. This brief shortage was the result of poor planning for high-intensity operations in Normandy and the Low Countries. Casualty-projection planning at Canadian Military Headquarters (CMHQ), in London, was influenced by the British Eighth Army's recorded casualties by army trade in North Africa during 1941–43. Compared to combat in northwest Europe, warfare in the desert was much more fluid, with the possibility of a logistic and infantry unit suffering similar casualties from wide-ranging German battle groups.[23] As a result, in this mobile armoured warfare theatre, the bulk of Commonwealth casualties in North Africa were not borne exclusively by the infantry. This led Canadian planners to calculate lower levels of infantry replacements than would be required to maintain 100 percent unit strengths in 1944–45. The Canadian government also viewed low casualty estimates favourably because conscription was to be avoided at all costs. But by 1943 the manpower limits of an all-volunteer overseas force were rapidly being reached.

At First Canadian Army headquarters, there were constant returns regarding operational vehicles, vehicles under repair, personnel strengths, and casualties. The most detailed of these were the daily and weekly returns of the Adjutant and Quartermaster (A&Q) war diaries, which tracked the flow of new human and major weapons-systems resources. Using these reports, it is possible to track personnel and material losses and their replacement and to measure the fighting strength of Canadian units at any given time.

There were also organizations within 1st and 2nd Canadian Corps specifically tasked with delivering new ordnance to the field units.[24] Given the value of the assets they were signing for, be it a Sherman Firefly tank or a 25-pounder artillery piece, accurate records were needed for this important job. Tanks, antitank guns, and tracked carriers were examples of equipment that suffered the highest rates of wastage due to their vulnerability to direct enemy fire. While personnel replacement was an all-Canadian affair, the material to equip the British and Canadian armies came from the same common stocks. These stocks consisted of British, Canadian, and American Lend-Lease war material. Depots containing this equipment were located in the United Kingdom or in liberated France. Only a portion of the army's heavy weapons were produced within Canada and then shipped overseas. All major land weapons systems, from artillery pieces to tanks, were found within these common stocks and used to issue replacements to the Commonwealth land forces.

Looking at reinforcement of the three traditional combat arms, *An Army of Never-Ending Strength* does not provide an all-encompassing assessment of the combat effectiveness and tactics of every corps and the resources they each consumed. With the exception of a discussion of the shortage of infantry reinforcements in the last year of the war, it does not address the larger strategic choices made with regard to personnel, equipment, vehicles, or resources.[25] Canadian and German unit-level combat effectiveness – that is, their ability to achieve battlefield objectives – is discussed briefly. But this discussion narrowly focuses on how the army utilized certain tactics to maximize the attrition of the enemy and limit their own losses. While some of these tactics minimized losses in certain areas, they caused higher levels in others. These outcomes in turn influenced the amount of additional resources needed to fill these gaps in specific areas of the reinforcement system.

The focus here is on combat arms units at the regimental level under army-, corps-, and divisional-level command.[26] These infantry, artillery, and armour units were in direct combat with the enemy or operating major weapons systems that were critical to defeating German forces. Table I.1 illustrates the size of regiments (battalions), brigades, and divisions to give an understanding of their composition. Although other Canadian Army trades suffered casualties and required reinforcements, and although they played their part in the final victory, this book focuses on the three combat arms that were in continuous combat and suffered the bulk of the losses. This study does not address consumable resources such as water, petroleum products, and ammunition.[27]

In tracking the replacement, losses, and inventories of vehicles and equipment, this book focuses on major weapons systems. For armoured or artillery regiments, this included heavy armoured fighting vehicles (AFVs) or artillery pieces.

Table I.1

Units and formations, First Canadian Army, 1944–45

Unit/formation	Number of personnel	Composition
Regiment (battalion)	500–900	Three or four companies, squadrons, or batteries
Brigade	2,500–3,000	Three regiments (battalions)
Division	18,000–20,000	Three brigades with separate units attached. Semi-independent brigades often attached in support.

Source: Bouchery, *From D-Day to V-E Day*, 10–16.

For infantry regiments, the major equipment items were medium machine guns, antitank guns, tracked carriers, and mortars. The number of these items held by a unit indicated the army's ability to replenish equipment stocks during the course of high-intensity combat operations.

The focus here is northwest Europe, and the analysis encompasses events and battles in France, Belgium, the Netherlands, and northern Germany. This choice was not made to denigrate Canadian campaigns in Italy or other theatres; rather, it reflects the fact that the Canadian Army's most powerful and complete force was assembled in northwest Europe. Between June and August 1944, this huge force faced the most powerful and concentrated enemy formations on the western front, and the resulting battles led to catastrophic losses for the 2nd Canadian Corps, losses that were without equal in Italy or Sicily.

Despite these losses, the Canadian Army managed to sustain and reconstitute units in its three traditional combat arms. By doing so, it managed to remain in a perpetual state of offensive capability. While major losses did occur, its combat power was never inhibited for an extended period. The Canadian Army's constant state of strength reflected its administrative and logistic capability. Its administrative strength and total combat power contributed greatly to eventual victory.

1 Personnel Reinforcements

The personnel replacement system in the Canadian Army was designed to be a constantly ongoing process for maintaining formations over the long term. Several layers of bureaucracy were necessary to properly administer and control the process. Many control points were needed to ensure that the right number of replacements reached the units in a timely fashion and that the system had the flexibility to divert or increase the flow. In June 1944, staff officers at Canadian Military Headquarters (CMHQ), London, were reasonably confident that they had created a system that could meet any challenges that lay ahead in northwest Europe.[1]

Personnel matters were the responsibility of the Adjutant General's Branch within the Canadian Army and were referred to as "A" branch staff concerns.[2] Logistics matters concerning supplies and war material were handled by "Q" branch, the domain of the Quartermaster General Branch. "Q" matters were more complicated because of the large amounts of war material and consumable supplies required to sustain the Canadian Army in the field. As shown in Figure 1.1, two staff echelons, or groupings, were created to take on these functions at 21st Army Group Headquarters, in France, prior to June 1944's Operation Overlord. Their official titles were 1st or "Q" Echelon (Quartermaster General) and 2nd or "A" Echelon (Adjutant General). These organizations freed First Canadian Army headquarters of all administrative and logistic matters not immediately related to operations. The leadership of Canadian 1st Echelon at 21st Army Group also oversaw and directed Canadian 2nd Echelon activities. Canadian 2nd Echelon's primary focus was personnel administration and replacement.[3]

Canadian 1st Echelon was commanded throughout 1944 by Brigadier A.W. Beament. Following his tenure, Major-General E.L.M. Burns took command in January 1945 after he relinquished command of 1st Canadian Corps in Italy. Both men were very experienced administrators who understood the importance of their responsibilities. The commanding officer of Canadian 2nd Echelon during 1944–45 was Colonel V.S.C. McClenaghan. He was also an officer who had gained experience in administration and planning duties while serving in the Mediterranean theatre. To make all administrative processes with the

Figure 1.1

Echelons, 21st Army Group Headquarters, France

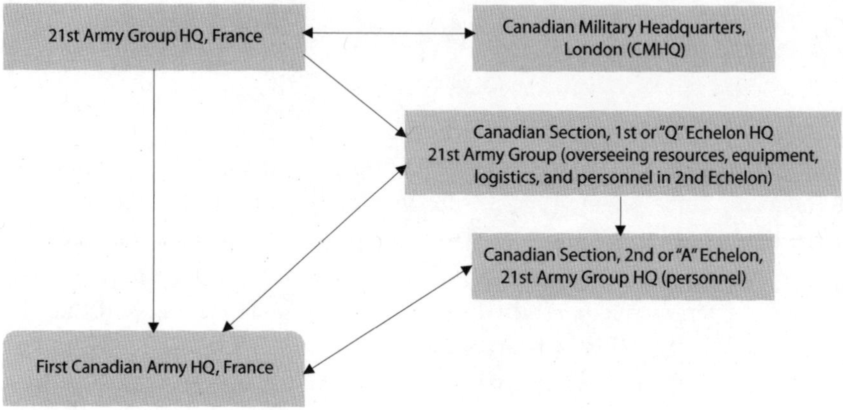

Source: Stacey, *The Official History of the Canadian Army in the Second World War,* vol. 3, *The Victory Campaign.*

21st Army Group seamless, reinforcement practices mirrored those of the British Army. This development was necessary to assist the Canadian reinforcement process in June–July 1944, a period before administrative and headquarters processes were firmly established on the continent.

The principal headquarters for Canada's personnel reinforcement organization was No. 2 Headquarters, Canadian Base Reinforcement Group (CBRG). This headquarters controlled the distribution of reinforcement personnel for all army trades in northwest Europe from 6 June 1944 to the appearance of No. 3 CBRG in March 1945. The No. 2 CBRG was decidedly smaller than its twin reinforcement organization in Italy, the No. 1 CBRG. While No. 1 CBRG had a total of eight reinforcement battalions, No. 2 CBRG had only five.[4] Senior staff were concerned about the deterioration of training levels because less training took place in the holding units the closer personnel were to the front; thus, it was better to have a smaller organization that would hold reinforcements for a shorter period.[5] They planned to hold a two- to three-weeks supply at "intense" casualty rates for the landing forces taking part in the invasion, the 3rd Canadian Infantry Division, and the 2nd Canadian Armoured Brigade. In contrast to the relatively small number of reinforcements available for Normandy, two months' worth of reinforcements had been set aside for Operation Husky, the July 1943 invasion of Sicily. (The Canadian Army's miscalculation concerning projected casualty rates and other personnel challenges is discussed in the next chapter.)

The No. 2 CBRG was under the direct command of 21st Army Group and its echelons, and it later worked closely at all junctures with the headquarters of 2nd Canadian Corps, the First Canadian Army, and CMHQ in London.[6] Its five reinforcement battalions were numbered nine through thirteen.[7] During the last phase of the war it was commanded by three experienced staff officers, the first being Brigadier G. Francoeur. His successor was Brigadier Gostling who was in turn replaced by Brigadier J.G. Spragge by war's end.[8] As soon as the Normandy landings occurred, a forward base was established on the continent. The first battalion to establish itself in France was the 10th, landing on 9 June 1944. Next was the 9th battalion, which came ashore on 13 June. These battalions were soon followed by the 11th and 12th. All four fed a British advance reinforcement battalion, which in turn supplied the 1st British Corps reinforcement company with Canadian replacements until mid-July. It was this company that fed reinforcements forward to Canadian formations in response to daily casualty reports.[9] A representative of the Canadian Section of the 21st Army Group Headquarters, Canadian 2nd Echelon, was attached to this company to control the posting of Canadian personnel. In mid-July, the 2nd Canadian Corps became operational, taking over the leadership and administration of all Canadian formations ashore from the 1st British Corps. The 2nd Canadian Corps was placed under the command of the Second British Army, but this arrangement was short-lived. Early August saw the First Canadian Army become operational, utilizing the 2nd Canadian Corps as one of its two corps. With this act, Canadian control of the personnel reinforcement process became nearly total, with only the 21st Army Group Headquarters maintaining administrative oversight.

The last No. 2 CBRG battalion in France, the 13th, landed on 3 August. Once it was ashore, it based itself forward at the newly operational First Canadian Army road-head staging area.[10] This unit's task was to act as the advance reinforcement battalion, replacing a British Army equivalent battalion in this role. It oversaw the flow of personnel to the 2nd Canadian Corps reinforcement company and the divisional reinforcement companies, which directly fed the infantry and other combat arms regiments to constantly make good their losses. On 2 December 1944, No. 2 CBRG's unit strength was 93 officers and 572 other ranks, and it contained 6,846 reinforcements.[11]

The 1944 reinforcement battalion typically consisted of several categories of personnel in addition to new overseas active volunteers.[12] Personnel could be returning battle (related to enemy action) or nonbattle casualties (nonbattle-related injuries), remusters from another trade, or home defence soldiers formerly conscripted through the National Resources Mobilization Act who volunteered to "go active." Thus, although some were new to the Canadian Army, others had served for some time, possibly years. In view of strains on transportation resources and the necessity of placing personnel where they were needed quickly, a single administrative process was essential. Thus, all personnel, both returning and new reinforcements, were mixed together in one pipeline that stretched from the reinforcement battalion to the divisional reinforcement company.[13]

The process of determining exactly who would be sent where was made as simple as possible. Deficiencies at the unit level were tabulated and reported to Canadian 1st Echelon, which in turn ordered the dispatch of the required replacements from England. By July 1944, a system like the one already in effect in Italy had been created in northwest Europe.[14]

One Canadian Army trade had its own separate reinforcement process. All reinforcement Canadian Armoured Corps (CAC) personnel were split away halfway through the process and attached to 25th Canadian Armoured Delivery Regiment (25th CADR) squadrons. This separation was done in accordance with CAC policy. The 25th CADR delivered all CAC replacements, often as complete armoured fighting vehicle crews, to the armoured regiments. In this way, they were guaranteed to remain with the crews rather than losing their skills during long periods away from their vehicles or during emergency remustering into other trades. Also, if the tanks and the tank crews were isolated from each other, they both lost their combat power.

In January 1945, the No. 2 CBRG was reorganized to improve its effectiveness. One large pool of reinforcements was collected in Ghent, Belgium, to be distributed within First Canadian Army formations. By this point, the transport time for reinforcements reaching the front had been lessened considerably by the opening of the Belgian port of Antwerp. The reorganization began with the disbandment of all companies except one within the 12th Battalion, which was redesignated the 12th Base Reinforcement Battalion. It was placed in charge of supplying rear-area Canadian units. Next, the 10th and 11th Battalions were specialized to feed infantrymen to infantry regiments.[15] The 9th Battalion was reconfigured to feed replacements to divisional-level units, and the 13th took responsibility for replacements to Canadian corps- and army-level units.[16] This reorganization focused on the processing of infantry reinforcements, which was necessary because the majority of all battle casualties were occurring within the Canadian Infantry Corps and relatively few replacements were needed within other trades in comparison.

That same month, 21st Army Group Headquarters directed an advanced divisional reinforcement control officer to radio a list of personnel deficits to

2nd Echelon. During the night, personnel drafts were created in the reinforcement battalions close to the front, and they were dispatched to the divisional reinforcement camps by truck in the morning. Within thirty-six hours, personnel orders had been filled.[17]

In April, the 1st Canadian Corps, whose principal formations included the 1st Canadian Infantry Division and the 5th Canadian Armoured Division, arrived in the Netherlands from Italy and commenced combat operations. The headquarters of the disbanded 12th Canadian Infantry Brigade, a formation that had been created to meet special conditions in Italy, was configured to form a headquarters for 1st Canadian Corps replacements. This group consisted of three reinforcement battalions and was designated the No. 3 Canadian Base Reinforcement Group (No. 3 CBRG). With the creation of this organization, the 1st and 2nd Canadian Corps each had their own reinforcement systems. No. 3 CBRG's battalions were numbered 14 through 16.[18]

The process of arranging for the delivery of required reinforcement personnel was administrative. The infantry regiment headquarters requested reinforcements through weekly officer and other ranks field returns. After evaluating the reinforcement pool and how many reinforcements other regiments required, Canadian 2nd Echelon would decide what could be spared, when, and to what regiment. This decision was often influenced by corps-level general staff, as certain units slated for operations had to be as strong as possible.

Figure 1.2 illustrates the route that reinforcement personnel took to get to their combat arms unit. For example, on arrival in France in July 1944, Canadian general-duty infantry reinforcements were processed through the 21st Army Group reception camp's Canadian section. From there, the soldiers were posted to a No. 2 CBRG reinforcement battalion. They then moved to the No. 2 CBRG advanced reinforcement battalion. From there, they were moved to the corps-level reinforcement company. Following this, they were sent to the divisional-level reinforcement company. Personnel would then be transported to a regiment within a brigade but not to their designated infantry company immediately. The new arrivals spent time either in the regimental "B" Echelon (supply and administration) or Left Out of Battle grouping to allow them to acclimatize to conditions at the front. Following a short period, they would be posted to a platoon within a rifle company. Including shipboard transport from the United Kingdom to Normandy, reinforcement infantry soldiers had a total of eight moves between different camp organizations.[19] At various waypoints within the reinforcement process, a soldier could be redirected if requirements or the situation changed. During the general-duty infantry reinforcement shortage of

Figure 1.2

The personnel delivery system, 1944–45

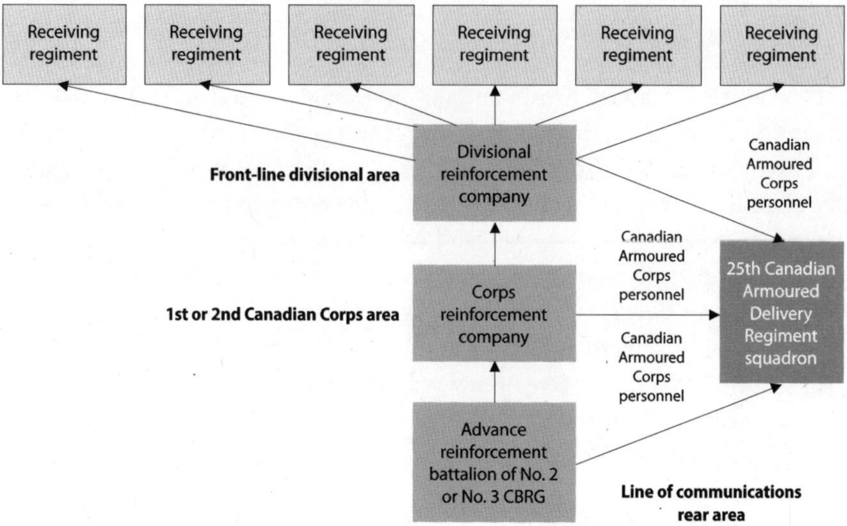

Source: LAC, RG 24, vol. 10,663, "First Canadian Army Plans Diagram of Personnel Replacement and Releases," file 215C1.045 (D12).

the summer of 1944, soldiers from other trades were remustered into infantry regiments after a period of retraining. Nothing else could be done to address the problem in the short term. In fall 1944, remustering of excess noninfantry personnel continued, and reinforcements in the United Kingdom and the continent were retrained to upgrade what infantry skills they had.[20]

Rapid mass transfers were not an everyday occurrence for the No. 2 CBRG. This organization had to consistently maintain a float of personnel should an unforeseen disaster occur, possibly placing several infantry battalions in large deficit positions. If the reinforcement battalions had given away all their personnel at this point, it would have been impossible to respond to such a disaster. They always had to be ready for the possibility that a military reverse could occur. Except for the period near the war's end, this need influenced decisions about the release of reinforcements to front-line units. Aside from the need to keep an emergency reserve of personnel in the reinforcement pool, administrative processes and travel times extended the period before a regiment would receive men at its "B" Echelon.[21] Transfers of over two hundred personnel reinforcements in one day were extremely rare.[22]

To qualify for a large immediate transfer, a regiment's immediate future performance in an upcoming operation had to be in doubt. Once reinforcements joined their units, they were taken on strength by the regimental adjutant. To the higher chain of command, they would then appear as part of the unit on returns for the next day. It is important to note that a transfer of new reinforcements often did not immediately alter the capability of the receiving regiment. Despite urgent requests for new personnel by a receiving regiment, the same unit would often knowingly slow down the "arrival" process, taking time to slowly integrate new soldiers. This action could make the regiment look strong on paper even when it had not fully reorganized itself to absorb its new strength. As noted previously, the new arrivals were often given time to acclimatize themselves within a regiment's "B" Echelon or Left Out of Battle contingents. Acclimatization prevented unnecessary errors in the field that could lead to casualties within hours of arrival.[23]

An important secondary function of the personnel reinforcement system was not one that its designers envisaged. Recovered medical casualties returning to their units were separate from new personnel but part of the incoming reinforcement stream. The return of battle and nonbattle casualties without psychological problems was straightforward; these rehabilitated personnel rejoined their units with minimal delay. However, after intense combat operations, a portion of nonbattle casualties were psychiatric. A segment of these cases could be rehabilitated through a short rest period close to the front line in the battalion regimental aid post; others, however, needed further rest.[24] As part of their medical rehabilitation process, these soldiers were fed directly back into the reinforcement companies.[25] The 2nd Canadian Corps reinforcement company often acted as a tool to extend the rehabilitation period for battle exhaustion cases. This valuable time was used for rest, therapy, and rehabilitation. Also, if an emergency did occur, the soldier in question would be close to the regimental or brigade area of operations.[26]

The capacity of the reinforcement system to deliver personnel was impressive. Figure 1.3 shows the number of Canadian reinforcements dispatched to the 21st Army Group between August 1944 and February 1945. The one blemish on the overall record was the number of personnel sent in August 1944, which did not match demands for reinforcements. This deficit stemmed from poor planning on the part of the Canadian Army's leadership (discussed in the next chapter). The strength of units was adequately rebuilt in September 1944. All units on the eve of the Scheldt fighting were close to their war establishment figures. This rebuilding occurred again in November 1944 following the Battle of the Scheldt.

Figure 1.3

Number of reinforcements dispatched to 21st Army Group, August 1944 to February 1945

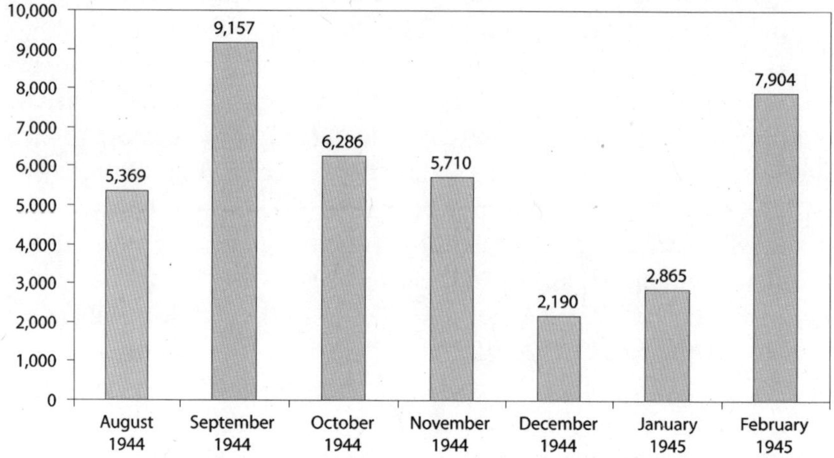

Source: LAC, RG 24, vol. 18,616, "17 March 1945 Report on Canadian Reinforcements Dispatched to 21st Army Group in North West Europe, 5 August 1944–28 February 1945," file 133.035 (D92).

The First Canadian Army was largely inactive during December 1944 and January 1945, with the result that there was low demand for reinforcements other than for ongoing nonbattle losses. Reinforcement numbers spiked again with the resumption of high-intensity operations in February 1945. The Canadian Army's reinforcement ability was superior to that of the German land forces. As shown in Figure 1.4, the German Army, Waffen-SS (the military branch of the SS), and Luftwaffe (air force) ground units were bled white in Normandy, and their losses were not replaced. The two points for every date in the graph chronicle the gulf between losses and replacements. With new losses occurring daily, German units on the front line never had a break to build up their strength. The failure to provide a regular flow of replacements to offset losses meant that units got progressively weaker.

An important question to be addressed definitively is whether the First Canadian Army received sufficient replacement personnel to cope with ongoing battle losses within its formations. Wartime records illustrate that the total number of reinforcements dispatched to keep units at 100 hundred percent of their war establishments was, at first glance, excessive. From August 1944 to February 1945, the 2nd and 3rd Canadian Infantry Divisions, the 4th Canadian

Figure 1.4

German battle losses and total replacements, July–August 1944

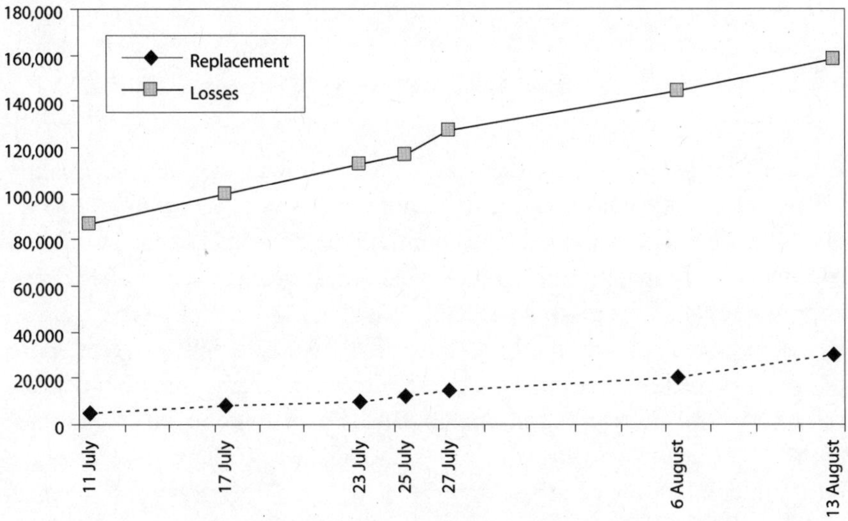

Source: Russell Hart, *Clash of Arms*, 385. Data from Deiter Ose, *Entscheidung im Westen 1944: Der Oberbefelshaber West und die Abwehr der Allierten Invasion*. Stuttgart: Deutsche Verlags-Anstalt, 1982.

Armoured Division and the 2nd Canadian Armoured Brigade sustained 28,277 battle casualties. During the same time period, 36,145 Canadian reinforcements were dispatched to the First Canadian Army. Additional reinforcements were needed due to losses from other causes, including nonbattle casualties, transfers, imprisonment, and AWOL cases. These categories combined constituted an ongoing drain to personnel levels, removing soldiers from units just as effectively as battle losses.[27]

In summary, despite its bureaucratic process, the reinforcement system's production at the CBRG level was continuous, making weekly or twice weekly deliveries at regimental unit "B" Echelons. It was also flexible and could be manipulated to increase the size of personnel replacement deliveries, provided enough replacements were present.

2

The Sixty-Day Shortage

FOR A SIXTY-DAY PERIOD in August and September 1944, the Canadian Infantry Corps had insufficient other ranks reinforcements because of poor strategic planning. Planners had failed to account for the personnel needs of infantry regiments over the long term and allowed other trades to accumulate overly large reinforcement pools that were not needed. As a result, the No. 2 Canadian Base Reinforcement Group (No. 2 CBRG) had a reduced ability to rebuild infantry units engaged in combat operations during the late summer of 1944. The mistakes were serious and somewhat impaired the overall combat effectiveness of the First Canadian Army, which in late August was engaged in some of the most difficult fighting of the Normandy Campaign.[1] This period is a blemish on an otherwise satisfactory record of personnel replacement.

It must be stressed that the shortage of infantrymen was limited to the other ranks. There was no shortage of commissioned infantry officers, subaltern or higher, leading up to the Normandy invasion. This was evidenced by the fall 1943 Can Loan scheme, by which 623 Canadian Infantry Corps officers and 50 Royal Canadian Ordnance Corps officers volunteered to serve within the British Army.[2] Because of the tremendously high rate of casualties suffered by British junior infantry officers, available reinforcements in the form of subalterns began to reach dangerously low levels. The Canadian government thus offered up volunteers. At the time, there was an excessive number of infantry subalterns either at the rank of lieutenant to captain in the reinforcement stream or made surplus by the disbanding of the 7th and 8th Canadian Infantry Divisions, earmarked for home defence in Canada. The first groups of these officers arrived in the United Kingdom in April 1944.[3]

Likewise, once it was clear that there was a shortage of infantry, other ranks, rapid action was taken to correct the problem. Unavoidably, it took time to remuster and retrain surplus troops in other trades, but by early October 1944 Canadian Military Headquarters (CMHQ), London, had significantly reduced deficits in the front-line infantry regiments. The number of remustered personnel totalled ten thousand by December 1944. The period of shortage lasted for less than two months in an eleven-month campaign, and the other combat arms trades, armour and artillery, were unaffected. From early June to late July 1944 and from October 1944 to May 1945, all infantry regiments engaged in combat were kept at adequate personnel strength levels.

The sixty-day shortage was an entirely separate event from the November 1944 Conscription Crisis, which centred on the uncertain supply of infantry reinforcements. But it certainly influenced the crisis. By late October 1944, after the infantry regiments had been rebuilt and a reserve of 16,825 personnel created, the larger problem of maintaining the reserve proved challenging. Prime Minister William Lyon Mackenzie King's War Committee was divided on how to accomplish this goal. Conscriptionists believed the use of National Resources Mobilization Act (NRMA) home defence conscripts was inevitable, while anti-conscriptionists, the prime minister among them, hoped that all future needs could be met with Canadian Army volunteers. But the Canadian Army could not present a viable plan to use only overseas volunteers or personnel converted from NRMA status to cover its reinforcement needs into 1945. Political impasse and pressure from the prime minister led to the forced resignation of Minister of National Defence J.L. Ralston. After the removal of Ralston and the discovery that there were no other viable options, on 23 November the King government decided to deploy conscript personnel overseas.[4]

The origins of the shortage resided in earlier decisions to radically expand the army yet retain its all-volunteer status. From one infantry division in 1940, it expanded to include five divisions and two independent brigades, along with all the necessary support units to sustain them, by August 1944. In fall 1944, these formations formed one complete corps in Italy and a second corps in northwest Europe. Yet evolution in the Canadian Army went past its sheer size. By early 1944, it had also created a completely new trade, the Corps of Royal Canadian Electrical and Mechanical Engineers, and had embraced the latest combat, command, and logistical doctrine of the Commonwealth armies. These practices had evolved as a result of combat experience during campaigns in North Africa, Sicily, and Italy.

During wartime, Ralston managed the size of the army in accordance with decisions made by Prime Minister King and the rest of the War Committee. Political and financial considerations and the needs of the other two services, the Royal Canadian Navy and Royal Canadian Air Force, forced the government to tightly control army expansion. However, during the early months of the war, there was a focus on minimizing Canada's wartime contribution. While the prewar Canadian Army had many plans for expansion, none were firmly endorsed by the government when war broke out. Such was the disarray that in terms of personnel and equipment the army was near its nadir as an organization in 1939. It had no strategic plan that clearly and strictly defined what the eventual size of the Canadian Army should be, how it would be reinforced, and who exactly would equip it.[5]

During the early war years, the other two services, the navy and air force, were also competing for resources, personnel, and funding. The Battle of the Atlantic was in full swing in 1941, and the Luftwaffe was still a powerful force within western Europe. With these two services fully engaged in escorting convoys and embarking on the bomber offensive on occupied Europe, the King government was in no rush to expand the army's role. Furthermore, while defence of the United Kingdom was seen by the Canadian public as important, the government judged that public opinion would not endorse the employment of Canadian forces in North Africa or farther abroad.[6] Heavy combat on land might also force the introduction of conscription, which at the outbreak of war was politically unacceptable to King.[7]

The use of conscription in Canada during the First World War had had a large political impact on the nation. In August 1917, Prime Minister Robert Borden's government enacted the Military Service Act, which aimed to maintain the strength of the Canadian Corps at a time when it was facing a severe shortage of recruits, regardless of success at the front. Over 45,000 personnel conscripted from 1 January 1918 onward reached the front lines by war's end.[8] These men were taken directly from their civilian environment and placed in military training camps. The cost of this decision was national disunity along ethnic lines, with anglophone Canadians being overwhelming proconscription and French Canadians vehemently opposed. Unrest resulted in riots and numerous revolutionary acts in Quebec. Politically, it damaged the Liberal Party's standings in English Canada, reducing Wilfrid Laurier's federal Liberal Party to seats largely within Quebec after the election of 1917. In 1939, King's Liberal government viewed even the proposed use of conscription as a serious matter.

Despite King's caution, following the fall of France his government passed the NRMA on 21 June 1940. The legislation provided human resource planning for Canada's war effort. Its two main areas of focus were employment control and increasing the level of military readiness. Military readiness involved instituting compulsory national registration, restricting employment deemed unnecessary for the war effort, and requiring men to submit to medical treatment so that they might be eligible for military service. It created national service but with very different aims than the conscription legislation of the First World War. The act registered men and women nationwide and moved them into proper employment to aid the war effort. It also mobilized Canadians for military service, some for only a limited thirty-day period. The NRMA established twin Canadian armies. The one for home defence consisted of conscripts; the other was composed of volunteer Canadian Army Active Service Force personnel and was later designated the Canadian Army (Active). Liberal Party supporters of the legislation stressed that there would never be enforced overseas service. While appeasing conscriptionists, the act did not arouse the political ire of anticonscriptionists who opposed overseas military involvement. Extremely aware of the damage that conscription had done to both national unity and his party in 1917–18, King was determined to avoid a repeat.[9]

When King was forced by military necessity to reverse his decision in fall 1944, the damage to national unity was not as great. The servicemen sent were NRMA personnel who had been in the army in some cases for several years instead of new recruits violently stripped from the civilian population. Civilian men who were not in the army in late 1944 did not have their lives affected by this decision. This factor was extremely influential in reducing negative political reaction within Quebec. Furthermore, in 1942 King had put the issue of conscription to the Canadian public in a plebiscite, and voters had overwhelmingly endorsed the idea, giving the government a level of political cover.

Army growth from 1941 to 1944 occurred against a backdrop of political infighting over the issue of conscription. This battle pitted the proconscription minister of national defence, J.L. Ralston, against the anticonscriptionist forces within the War Committee, most notably the prime minister and Minister of Mines and Resources T.A. Crerar. Those in the minister's camp consistently held onto the main goal of resisting conscription to achieve three main goals: retain the Liberal Party's hold on power and political fortunes; avoid nationwide unrest over conscription; and maintain Canada's contribution to the war effort at a manageable minimum level. This was made clear by the War Committee's 29 July 1941 rejection of the army's requests to increase its size by a full two divisions.[10]

By late 1941, Ralston and others within the War Cabinet were under the impression that the army's leadership was not fully committed to the recruitment program for overseas volunteers.[11] Canadian historian Richard Walker argues that this resistance was an intentional move to force the King government into adopting conscription.[12] Conscription would give the army the military might needed to achieve its goals and at the same time make a large force, such as a complete field army, sustainable. Senior army leadership did not endorse the concept of the twin armies, one for overseas personnel and one for NRMA home defence conscripts. At this time, the Canadian Army had the highest standards for acceptance in the world, and all men under nineteen and over thirty-seven were declared ineligible. Furthermore, many thousands of civilians were rejected because of physical standards that were unacceptable in the American and British military recruitment processes.[13]

In August 1941, Canadian Army chief of the general staff Major-General H.D.G. Crerar completed a plan to construct an overseas army of two corps by 1942.[14] To realize this plan, his successor, Major-General Kenneth Stuart, forwarded on 18 November 1941 the proposal, titled *Army Programme, 1942–1943*. The proposal sought to radically enlarge the army and fully utilize available manpower. Ralston endorsed the proposal and supplied data in the form of the Walker-Robinson report, which illustrated that Canada could supply the necessary manpower without damaging national industry. National Defence Headquarters (NDHQ) General Staff in Ottawa also stated that this program could be completed without resorting to conscription, the main issue of resistance in the Liberal government.[15] By late December 1941, Ralston was proving to be susceptible to the advice of the general staff on matters of army expansion and was much shaken by the recent military disaster at Hong Kong, in which two Canadian regiments and a brigade headquarters had been lost.[16] A former army colonel, he began to be perceived by his Liberal Party colleagues as a mouthpiece for army demands and would in time, they believed, eventually endorse conscription to utilize available personnel for overseas service.[17]

Prime Minister King relented to the demands for a larger army on 6 January 1942.[18] He faced political pressure from all sides within Canada for a more robust war effort. The Conservative Party pushed for a coalition government, and powerful Toronto business leaders lobbied for conscription and a more "total war" approach to Canada's contribution. Major-General A.G.L. McNaughton, commander of the Canadian Army (Active) in Great Britain, also aggressively pressed for more intensive Canadian participation in land operations, volunteering Canadian forces for any operation that seemed feasible.[19] McNaughton and other senior army officers also spoke to the press about the perceived challenges the army was facing in sustaining the war effort. Ralston did not stop these transgressions, which continued throughout the war. At this point, he perceived army expansion to be so important to the war effort that it was worth resigning over should King and others rebuff the program. Threatening King with this politically damaging act and acting in cooperation with the army's long-term corporate interests, Ralston divorced himself from his Liberal colleagues to form a proconscription camp within the Ottawa War Committee.

By late 1942, the foundations for what would eventually be the First Canadian Army were laid. What was missing was a strategic reinforcement plan to sustain this colossus, the political will to create a reserve of reinforcements through conscription, and, finally, the means to equip a large army. Concerning the last point, Canada in 1942 still partially lacked a diversified arms industry to supply all its needs in the way of modern weapons systems.[20] The equipment for new units arriving in the United Kingdom simply did not exist, a shortcoming that significantly hindered training well into 1943.[21] Within the army's all-volunteer personnel pool, a reinforcement reserve did not exist to deal with all possibilities, including military disaster on a massive scale.

A primary presupposition held by NDHQ at this point was that it would be politically impossible for the Canadian government to not to sustain a larger army once it was operational in a combat zone. The Liberals' political opponents would not tolerate the army "withering on the vine." It was also clear to senior army leadership that it would be impossible for this large army to be sustained during combat operations without the implementation of conscription, a strategic, if undisclosed, goal of NDHQ. This point was never clearly passed onto the minister of national defence or the prime minister in 1942. National Defence Headquarters was also sure that the British government, grateful for the formations, would equip them with their most modern weapons to ensure success. There were also long-term plans afoot to maintain this creation after the war. Once a larger army was constructed, it was quite plausible that it would be politically difficult to disassemble. Part of Crerar's intent in his plans for a "Big Army" included never revisiting Canada's military insignificance of the 1930s.[22]

A factor that made it even more impossible to sustain the all-volunteer army was its approach to utilizing personnel. Even in November 1944, post Normandy, personnel resources were still being managed poorly despite the shortage of replacements that had occurred during the summer. In comparison to the US Army, the Canadian Army's headquarters units were overstaffed. As historian E.L.M. Burns later noted, in November 1944 only 34.2 percent of all personnel (excluding reinforcements, or 110,147 troops) were part of combat arms units. A disturbing 28.2 percent of personnel, or 90,347 troops, made up Canadian headquarters and other overhead. This compared to 11.6 percent in the US Army in March 1945.[23] As Normandy loomed closer in spring 1944, the army made no attempt to reorganize itself to cope with a possible shortage of infantry replacements. Compounding matters, the army was fully committed to maintaining this bloated establishment.[24] In March 1944, the deputy adjutant and quartermaster general of the First Canadian Army, Major-General A.E. Walford, stated that it was overstrength and could not be sustained. His recommendations to alter its structure were ignored.[25]

What presuppositions did King and the remainder of his War Committee colleagues possess in January 1942? A main assumption was that the "Big Army" program was so massive a request it would be the last of its kind foisted on them for the remainder of the war. King also accepted Major-General Stuart's dubious assurance that it would not be necessary to utilize conscription to supply the enlarged Canadian Army in the future. Though not a military man, it cannot have escaped King's comprehension that to support such a large organization in wartime a large numbers of replacement personnel would be needed. That this point was not clearly conveyed by NDHQ to the War Committee is troubling but understandable. If it had been more clearly stated, this fact would have gradually undermined the ability to ease King and other anticonscription committee members into accepting conscription. It would have also damaged the whole bid for an enlarged army. Finally, it is plausible that King was considering purely political problems at the time of his decision to accept the rapid expansion of the army. His goal, placating the conscriptionist and "total war" political camps, including some within his own War Committee, had to be achieved.

Having dealt with immediate problems, in late January 1942 the prime minister looked to address future issues. Anticipating the need to use conscripts overseas to maintain the war effort, the government conducted a plebiscite to release the government from its previous promise that enforced overseas service would never occur. The 27 April 1942 plebiscite passed, and though the province of Quebec largely voted against it, political resistance was reduced compared to the situation in 1917–18.[26] To mollify Quebec, the government stressed that conscription was not necessary at present and might never be needed.[27] Regardless of what this development meant for the future of the Canadian Army, King had again succeeded politically. Following the January 1942 approval for army expansion, new divisions were raised from large numbers of volunteer Canadian Army (Active) members.

Near the end of this expansion, in July 1943, the Canadian Army's period of relative inactivity in Britain ended with the deployment of one infantry division and one armoured brigade to Sicily. Until this point, the army had not had any experience with large numbers of battle and nonbattle casualties over an extended period of combat operations. Battlefield experience is an essential factor in the successful projection of casualty rates. When operations began in Sicily, projected casualty rates for infantry were extremely unrealistic.

Inaccurate predictions had been made since the establishment of projected losses by the Ottawa War Office in 1939. Sent to CMHQ, London, shortly after the outbreak of war, they erroneously projected monthly infantry losses that, at their worst, could be 20 percent for "intense activity." Since the war had just begun, these rates were purely hypothetical because no one really knew what effect modern weapons or tactics would have. The plan was to keep a reinforcement reserve of three months' worth of losses at "intense rates" on standby in the United Kingdom. This reserve of reinforcements would equal 60 percent of whatever infantry personnel were present in operational units. The reserve would be drawn upon as needed and would be supplemented by one month's worth of personnel placed forward in the immediate theatre of operations, for a total of four months at intense rates.[28]

After the fall of France in 1940, CMHQ, London, perceived that Canadian forces in the United Kingdom would take on a defensive rather than offensive role in the immediate future. The British High Command's priority was defence of the British Isles. In fall 1940, Canadian forces were seen by the British chief of the imperial general staff, General Sir John Dill, as strategically important and best used in their current position as a bulwark against German invasion.[29] As the possibility of immediate German invasion dwindled, it was correspondingly estimated that there would be fewer casualties. It was recommended that the figure for intense monthly losses be lowered to 10 percent, the same figure utilized for "normal" monthly losses. These new levels were approved by NDHQ in August 1940. Three months' worth of reinforcements at normal rates would remain in Canada so as not to build up an excessive amount of reinforcement personnel overseas. Within the United Kingdom, it was believed that, should an invasion occur, the estimated period of fighting would only last a month, in the worst-case scenario.

The Canadian reserve of infantry reinforcements within Britain was then reorganized to contain only three months' worth at the new intense rate. Numbers beyond that would have to be transported from Canada.[30] These rates continued to be in effect until July 1943. Because of this reinforcement strategy, there was no major influx of reinforcements from Canada to build up a large reserve. In both January 1941 and January 1942, the question of rates was examined with reference to the most recent British casualty figures from North Africa.[31] After researching this data, it was decided that the rates would remain unchanged and that the amount of reinforcements kept in the United Kingdom would remain the same.

With Canadian forces set to participate in offensive operations in Sicily and Italy in 1943–44, measures were taken to revise the casualty rates in the face of impending combat. Canadian rates were brought in line with British casualty projections of 20 percent for other ranks infantry.[32] These new rates were brought into effect in July 1943. Because of the relatively small number of forces initially engaged in operations in the Mediterranean – one infantry division and one armoured brigade – any casualties incurred would be easily replaced. Although the number of infantry casualties was out of proportion to other trades, total losses for all trades were manageable and within the July 1943 wastage rates. The eight reinforcement battalions of the No. 1 Canadian Base Reinforcement Group (No. 1 CBRG) were well supplied with two months' worth of replacements and easily replaced losses.[33] But because of the higher infantry casualty rates encountered in these operations, it became obvious that 20 percent was an insufficient number.

The number of reinforcements present in each combat arms trade pool in Italy and England in the spring of 1944 was influenced by the projected casualty figures authorized in July 1943. It was important that these projections be correct or the army would be left with surplus reinforcements in one trade and a shortage of replacements in another. The calculations were adopted from the British and had been influenced by the records of the Eighth Army in North Africa.[34] Because of the fluid nature of the mechanized war in the desert, enemy armoured forces could appear in unexpected places.[35] Artillery, armoured, and infantry casualties had been roughly equal; no trade took significantly more casualties. Rear-area supply services were often just as vulnerable and could be caught off guard by an enemy advance that happened to break through.

The use of these British figures was a miscalculation because it ignored the most recent Canadian Army casualty returns from operations in Sicily and southern Italy in 1943. Constricting terrain, rivers, mountains, weather conditions, and other obstacles made it easy for the German Army to halt Allied advances with well-placed blocking positions at critical points. In difficult terrain, successful offensive operations became dependent on the use of artillery and innovative infantry tactics to root out determined German defenders. This led to increased casualties in the infantry battalions.

Attempts were made by certain staff officers at CMHQ, London, and the Canadian Army in the Mediterranean to raise the issue of miscalculations of the number of infantry reinforcements available. In December 1943, Brigadier A.W. Beament, the officer in charge of the 1st Canadian Echelon in the Mediterranean, noticed that combat casualties were significantly higher for infantry, other ranks, and officers than the projected figures for normal rates of wastage.[36] He came to the conclusion that this wastage would result in a significant shortcoming in reinforcements in the foreseeable future. This deduction led him to argue that personnel in other trades should be forcibly remustered into infantry as soon as possible. National Defence Headquarters and CMHQ, London, refused to validate his view and stuck to the July 1943 revisions.[37] For the time being, Brigadier Beament's concerns were dismissed. This officer recognized that there were enough personnel in the Canadian Army to supply infantry reinforcements, but only if they were managed correctly.

In fall 1943, the pool of reinforcements within the Canadian Army was not being managed properly, both in the United Kingdom and the Mediterranean. Within noninfantry trades, there were miscalculations regarding future casualty figures, which in turn retarded the growth of a reserve of available infantry reinforcements. Projected intense rate losses for the Royal Canadian Ordnance Corps and what would become the Corps of Royal Canadian Electrical and Mechanical Engineers personnel were projected to be nearly 9 percent in July 1943. This was a gross overestimate of the reinforcements that would be required. Actual casualties for both corps in the three worst months of 1944 turned out to be 1 percent of total personnel.[38] In early 1944, reinforcement personnel for these corps continued to be trained on their trades when the time could have been used to effectively remuster them into infantry regiments.

As of 16 March 1944, total Canadian Army reinforcement personnel of all trades within the United Kingdom stood at 3,597 officers and 36,145 other ranks identified as fit soldiers.[39] These totals reflected a surplus of 890 officers and 1,790 other ranks over what was authorized by the July 1943 casualty-projection rates. The number of available reinforcements was never the issue in the spring of 1944. The challenge was allocating the proper number of personnel to the correct corps so that the proper numbers of reinforcements were potentially available – in this case the infantry.

The British Army's pressure on CMHQ prevented the August and September 1944 infantry reinforcement shortage from being far worse. General Bernard Montgomery, 21st Army Group commander, had taken an increased interest in the reinforcement situation in March 1944. During that same month, his headquarters communicated the possibility to CMHQ that casualties from the initial beachhead assault of Operation Overlord might possibly be higher than those forecasted.[40] This caused alarm at CMHQ and NDHQ. Canadian leadership at this point was slowly becoming cognizant of the fact that there were potentially far fewer infantry reinforcements than required. Plans were quickly made to enact a large remustering program. It is troubling that CMHQ was driven into action by the perception that the one-day Normandy beachhead assault – not the extended period of high-intensity warfare that would follow –would be the cause of an upsurge in future casualties.

During further investigations, Montgomery revealed that the Canadian reinforcement units in the United Kingdom had a massive shortfall of infantry, other ranks, when compared with authorized levels.[41] Also, Montgomery observed that a large number of personnel were attached to ad hoc units and training units, a state of affairs that made them less ready to fulfill their reinforcement role. At this time, the chief of staff at CMHQ, Lieutenant-General Kenneth

Stuart, was in hospital. He responded to Montgomery's inquiries by stating that the matter of identifying and preselecting sufficient personnel for remustering was being addressed.[42]

In response to Montgomery's anxious inquiries, in late March 1944 CMHQ forwarded him a report that verified that the total number of reinforcements within Britain was sufficient. However, the content of the reinforcement pool was not satisfactory. Of an authorized level of 23,000 infantry reinforcements (three months' holdings at intense 20 percent rates under the erroneous 1943 figures), the reinforcement organization contained only 14,500 personnel. Of this number, 43 percent were either unfit, serving in ad hoc units in noninfantry roles, waiting to be remustered, or awaiting disciplinary hearings. Thus, the real number of reinforcements ready to be deployed was fewer than 8,000 out of an authorized total of 23,000.[43]

In addition, the practice of dumping unfit or problem soldiers in temporary-holding units was rampant in the Canadian Army. Thus, this report, which stated all was well, masked the great blow that had been done to the capability and strength of the Canadian Infantry Corps. This corps was on the eve of some of the most challenging fighting the Canadian Army would face during the Second World War. By robbing it of a large fluid reserve of infantry, other ranks – the high-ranking officers at CMHQ, London – were condemning it to temporary weakness if large losses occurred at a rapid pace.

The emergency remustering program, begun in late spring 1944 to enlarge the reserve of Canadian infantry reinforcements based in Britain, was hamstrung by the ill-timed creation of further operational units. The 2nd Canadian Corps was still forming the 10th Canadian Infantry Brigade for the 4th Canadian Armoured Division. As of spring 1944, it was filling out the brigade's three infantry regiments with required personnel. In Italy, the 12th Canadian Infantry Brigade was being created for the 5th Canadian Armoured Division. Thus, the authorized ceilings for infantry personnel had grown to 57,592 from 51,083 since January 1944. These building projects, necessary as they were, greatly impaired the creation of an infantry reinforcement reserve pool.[44]

Options never exercised included the possible disbandment of certain combat units to reinforce others, the reduction of the establishment of existing combat units, the reduction in size of headquarters and support units, utilizing excess air force personnel, or relaxing overly strict recruiting standards for volunteers. Concerning this last point, large numbers of able-bodied men were being refused entry on dubious grounds, the exclusion of anyone above the age of thirty-seven and below nineteen being the worst practices.[45]

As Operation Overlord approached, a greater sense of urgency took hold. By the end of March 1944, over 2,000 men had been either voluntarily or forcibly remustered as infantry.[46] April and May saw the deployment of 5,565 personnel to the United Kingdom from Canada, and a further 2,000 were transported in early June.[47] Montgomery and other senior British generals were well aware of the potential consequences of inaction, and, in communications to CMHQ dated 16 March, they categorized the deficit in allocated Canadian infantry reinforcements as "most serious."[48]

In the days following the D-Day landings, Canadian combat arms units needed personnel replacements to cover losses suffered during the amphibious assault and inland combat. No. 2 CBRG units deployed to France immediately began providing reinforcements. Initially, there were no personnel shortages within the Normandy beachhead because of the relatively small number of Canadian units involved. In June, only the 2nd Canadian Armoured Brigade and the 3rd Canadian Infantry Division were deployed, employing a total of three infantry brigades with nine regiments. Replacing losses within these regiments was a relatively small task, and the system appeared to be working with few issues. Casualties to the end of June were significant but not unacceptable.[49] What was disturbing was the percentage of losses taken by the infantry. As shown in Figure 2.1, by 10 July, the infantry had the most battle casualties. The need for a large reservoir of replacements was apparent.

Once other units, such as the 2nd Canadian Infantry Division and the 4th Canadian Armoured Division, became operational, shortages in the number of liquid infantry reinforcements became clear. The scale and intensity of offensive combat operations increased significantly in July and August. All four Canadian formations could not be sustained with the reinforcements on hand. Delays occurred as troop ships had to sail from England to reach the bridgehead, and then the reinforcements had to go through the bureaucratic process of the No. 2 CBRG battalions. No. 2 CBRG did not divest itself of all infantry reinforcements; it retained a small reserve in case some large event occurred.

At 21st Army Group Headquarters, Canadian 1st Echelon's officer in chief, Brigadier A.W. Beament, recently transferred from Italy, observed that his forecasts of December 1943 were coming true. By mid-July, exactly as he had predicted, there were indications of a shortage of general-duty other ranks reinforcements. By 15 July, it was confirmed that there were not enough to meet future demands from all formations.[50] Despite his urgings that by CMHQ resolve the situation quickly, it could not be accomplished overnight. On 17 July, Beament's recommendations for mass remustering were passed to

Figure 2.1

Forecasts versus casualties, June and July 1944

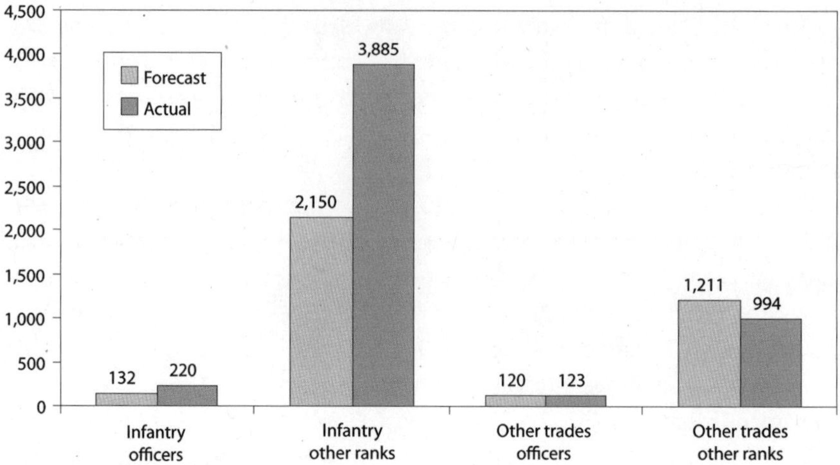

Note: By 30 June 1944, the 3rd Canadian Infantry Division had recorded 2,978 battle casualties.
Source: Stacey, *Arms, Men and Governments*, 434; LAC, RG 24, vol. 10,517, "Daily Record of Casualties for the 3rd Canadian Infantry Division from 6 June 1944," file 215A21.009 (D167).

Major-General Montague, in charge of administration at CMHQ. He communicated them to Lieutenant-General Stuart, who was in Italy. Ironically, Stuart was involved in discussing the creation of a new infantry brigade for the 5th Canadian Armoured Division. Five days passed before Stuart returned to the United Kingdom and then flew to First Canadian Army headquarters to speak with its commander, General H.D.G. Crerar. On 25 July, Stuart finally took drastic corrective action, issuing orders to begin a large-scale remustering of general-duty personnel in other trades. A full 25 percent of all Royal Canadian Artillery (RCA) reinforcements and 60 percent of all Royal Canadian Army Service Corps reinforcements would be remustered as other ranks infantry.

This was the correct course of action, but Stuart arrived at it far too late. On 2 August, during a trip to NDHQ in Ottawa, he spoke with the chief of the general staff, Lieutenant-General J.C. Murchie.[51] Not wishing to appear an alarmist, Stuart failed to communicate the urgency of the problem and how it could be solved. The minister of national defence, J.L. Ralston, would later claim that he was not fully informed of events. In the events of August 1944 and the months leading up to them, General Crerar cannot be accused of extreme negligence. What he must take the blame for, however, is accepting at face value inaccurate wastage rates and tolerating other trades and headquarters that were obviously overstaffed.[52] Despite being pressed to allow partially trained reinforcements forward, Crerar did stand fast on the standard of training: no untrained personnel reached front-line infantry regiments.[53]

At the same time, casualties continued to be incurred at a rapid rate. On 25 July alone, Operation Spring caused roughly 1,500 battle casualties.[54] Despite receiving reinforcements, by 31 July the strength of the 2nd Canadian Infantry Division had dropped by 1,211 personnel.[55] On 4 August, General Crerar stated in a report that the reinforcement situation was the most serious problem facing the First Canadian Army: the deficit hovered at over 1,900 personnel. He went on to state: "It would seriously impair our breakout exploitation tasks" if it were allowed to continue.[56] On 8 August, on the eve of Operation Totalize, the largest Canadian armoured attack of the Second World War, Crerar again pressed for urgent action on reinforcements.[57]

Two days later, Brigadier M.H.S. Penhale of CMHQ visited First Canadian Army headquarters to discuss the situation. It was decided that infantry-training standards would in no way be compromised and there would be no dilution or shortening of training for remustered soldiers. In the following weeks, a significant number of infantry reinforcements did reach the First Canadian Army, but on 15 August the regiments were still 2,644 personnel short. Although Montague estimated that over 3,773 reinforcements could be dispatched by 19 August, casualties continued to mount faster that the rate of replacement by the No. 2 CBRG.[58] Infantry reinforcements sent from the United Kingdom that month numbered 375 officers and 2,831 other ranks.[59] As shown in detail in Appendix 3, by 31 August, shortages in infantry, other ranks, had grown to 4,318, and this was after monthly reinforcements had been accepted. These numbers illustrate that the August replacements did not made a dent in the overall infantry shortage.[60]

The shortage situation reached its nadir on 31 August, when the average personnel deficit within infantry regiments was 206. On 4 September, there were only 731 other ranks infantry reinforcements present in the No. 2 CBRG holdings.[61] From 12 August to 1 September, a total of 4,088 men were remustered and began training to become qualified infantrymen. This did nothing to solve the problem quickly, because these personnel had to complete their training before they could be sent to the front. Figure 2.2 illustrates the infantry, other ranks, shortage in the 2nd Canadian Infantry Division. This formation was the hardest hit by the failure to rapidly replace losses. The totals were spread among its nine infantry regiments and one machine-gun battalion, all of which were largely composed of other ranks infantrymen.

Figure 2.2

Shortages, other ranks, 2nd Canadian Infantry Division, July–September 1944

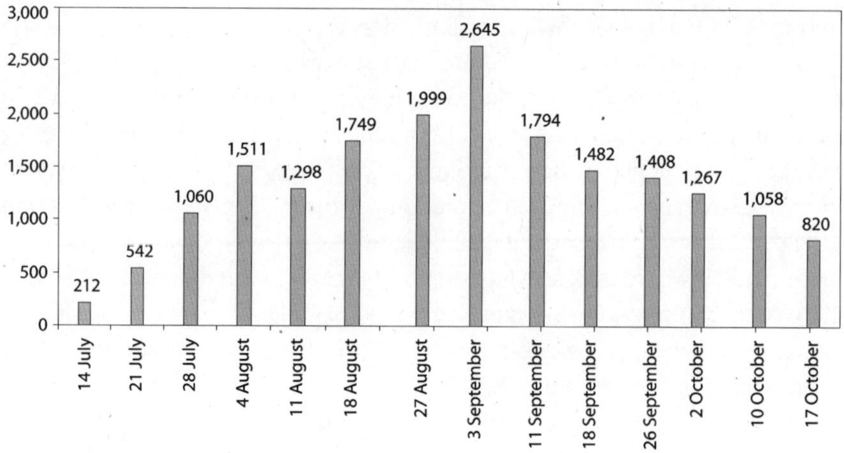

Source: Stacey, *Arms, Men and Governments*, 439.

The infantry reinforcements shortage was particularly difficult for the three francophone infantry battalions in northwest Europe. Le Régiment de Maisonneuve, Le Régiment de la Chaudière, and Les Fusiliers Mont-Royal had all experienced high losses during the July–August battles in Normandy. By late August, their losses still had not been replaced. On 6 June, there were only 348 francophone infantry, other ranks, and reinforcement soldiers – or nearly three infantry companies – within the reinforcement stream in Great Britain. For three infantry regiments about to be engaged in high-intensity combat, this was insufficient. On 23 October, despite some reinforcements being taken on, these three regiments were still short a total of 340 other ranks, the equivalent of an infantry company each.[62]

On 31 August, the same date that the infantry, other ranks, situation reached its low point, an accurate set of casualty projection rates for the Canadian Army was produced. As shown in Figure 2.3, these new rates were in line with the cost of warfare in northwest Europe. They accurately indicated the numbers that should be set aside for monthly reinforcements and that large reserves could be created to cope with losses in the Canadian Infantry Corps. September witnessed a continued remustering effort and the beginning of the end of the shortage problem in the Canadian Army. The situation improved rapidly, but weak rifle companies were given the same tasks as full-strength companies on

Figure 2.3

Projected monthly infantry loss rates, normal and intense, 31 August 1944

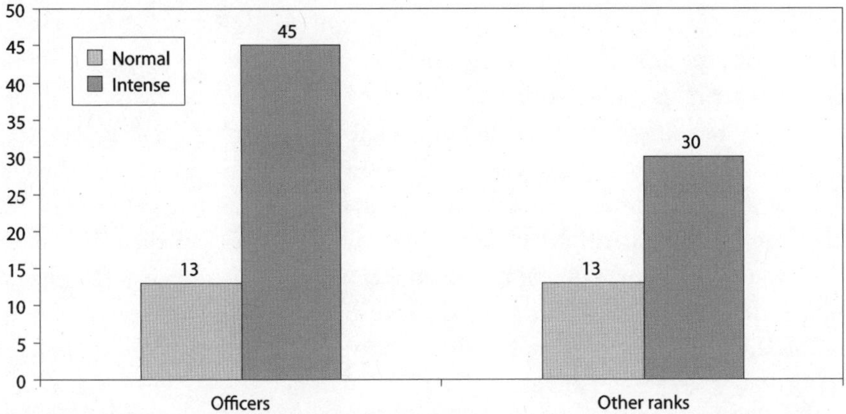

Source: LMH, Terry Copp Papers, Colonel C.P. Stacey, Canadian Army Historical Report No. 134, "Historical Sketch: Rates of Wastage of Personnel, Canadian Army, 1939–1945, Canadian Military Headquarters, London, UK, 5 April 1945," Appendix A, 14.

the battlefield. Throughout the month, a total of 4,720 troops from other trades began infantry training. As weeks passed, the shortage continued to be reduced, and by 24 October it had been reduced to fifty-four soldiers per regiment.[63] But by 5 November, because of losses in the fighting in the Scheldt, it had jumped back up to 100 personnel. While this seems high, no infantry battalion involved in combat operations during the Second World War was maintained at 100 percent of its war establishment, an impossible task without daily reinforcements. By November, the number of personnel that had been remustered was approaching 7,850 troops. At this point, the crisis had passed. Returns for December reflected that 10,000 soldiers had been remustered.

And what was the quality of the remustered, NRMA, or regular replacements that reached the infantry regiments after their often long periods spent as reinforcements? The stereotype of army unit commanders and senior non-commissioned officers never being happy with the training standard of any new replacement soldier is accurate. The oft-recounted story of Ralston questioning the regimental sergeant major of the 48th Highlanders in Italy, who had complained about reinforcement training standards, is an example. When asked by Ralston for the exact names of the seventy-two new reinforcements that had arrived at the regiment, the unit could only provide thirty-two names. All had been in the army for more than a year, a quarter under three years, and some were highly trained specialists. It is highly likely that all had the training needed to take on their new role.[64]

Was this always the case, even in the summer of 1944? Usually, the key determinant was the amount of time the reinforcement had been a designated "infantry, other ranks, reinforcement." If the soldier had been "in the system" for over a year as a rifleman, the likelihood that he would perform at an acceptable level on infantry, other ranks, the battlefield was high. If he had been remustered from other trades, it was likely that large portions of his time had not been spent in infantry training at a high level. Personnel from the Royal Canadian Ordnance Corps and the Corps of Royal Canadian Electrical and Mechanical Engineers remustered in spring and summer 1944 were given crash conversion training.[65] NRMA home defence conscripts, some having been in the army since 1939, were trained to an acceptable standard.[66]

Units that received these personnel often implemented supplementary training to ensure that no one soldier's training standard was overlooked. Receiving units in both Italy and northwest Europe often held new reinforcements for up to four days, but not less than twenty-four hours, during which they would review each soldier's documents, examine his personal equipment, and issue any missing kit. New members were then given a "smartening up drill" consisting of "general tactical hints" and supplementary weapons-handling tests. If there was time, the new soldiers would also be instructed in unit tradition, drill, and saluting practices to instill unit pride and maintain discipline.[67]

How did the personnel replacement record of the Canadian Army compare to those of the British and American armies? Like the Canadian Army, in the last year of the war in northwest Europe, both allies had significant manpower challenges that centred on infantry replacements. While the US Army successfully combatted the effects of attrition in the last year of the war, the British Army did not continue to make good its losses. Britain's replacement system was similar to Canada's, and it was likewise effective in reinforcing units that suffered personnel losses. But like the Canadian system, Britain's was only effective if it was well supplied with new personnel. By mid-1944, the number of new infantry recruits and remustered army personnel designated as deployable infantry was dwindling. At this point, the British Army had two complete field armies fighting the Germans, one engaged in Italy and another in France. Though these field armies contained Commonwealth divisions and separate Commonwealth corps, reinforcements were scarce. Making matters more challenging, these two armies did not encompass numerous British units that made up parts of other British armies in the Far East and Middle East. By 1944, infantry units were taking 80 percent of all combat losses within the British Army. High losses sustained by the British between September 1939 and August 1942 in the Low Countries, France, the Mediterranean, and the Far East had been severe. Over 326,877 troops had become casualties or prisoners of war. British infantry units accounted for 51 percent of this total.[68]

During the Normandy Campaign, the British Army rapidly consumed what was left of its deployable infantry, other ranks, reserve. By the end of August, most of one complete British infantry division, the 59th, had to be broken up to provide reinforcements to other formations. The breakup of this division was followed by a second, the 50th, in late November 1944.[69] The disappearance of these two complete divisions led the British Army to depend increasingly on Commonwealth formations during the last year of the war. Despite its challenges, the Canadian Army never had to break up a single infantry regiment, never mind a full division, to provide replacements.

Military historians such as Carlo D'Este have questioned whether the British military successfully managed its personnel near the end of the war.[70] It had large numbers of personnel attached to training and territorial infantry units throughout the United Kingdom that could have been utilized for replacements.[71] However, the fitness and age of these personnel may have limited their combat capability. Other untapped areas consisted of surplus Royal Air Force and Royal Navy personnel that could have been ruthlessly remustered as infantry. Also, a strict adherence to the territorial and bureaucratic regimental system impaired Britain's employment of personnel where they were needed in the shortest amount of time.

The US Army also suffered heavy infantry losses in northwest Europe; infantry battalions in Normandy suffering 90 percent of their total battle casualties in the bocage terrain.[72] However, the Americans were far more effective than the British in maintaining the strength of infantry battalions engaged in combat operations. Infantry and armoured divisions forming in the United States were cannibalized ruthlessly, destroying what progress they had made in their training programs. Despite this, the number of operational American combat divisions in Europe grew exponentially in the final year of the war. Large surplus reserves of personnel in other trades were raided on a regular basis. Also, there was no adherence to a regimental system that would take personnel from certain regional areas to supply certain regiments. This approach was alien to the corporate personnel management style of the US military.[73] A former casualty returning from hospital from one infantry battalion could easily wind up in another after re-entering the replacement pipeline.[74] The US Army also had no qualms about rapidly utilizing replacements whose infantry skills had eroded due to inactivity following their initial training. This practice resulted in heavy losses, but the main goal of consistently high personnel levels within US infantry line companies was achieved.

Following the successful reconstitution of all its infantry regiments by October 1944, the next hurdle that the Canadian Army (Active) had to jump to stabilize its infantry personnel situation was the creation of a sizable reserve of reinforcements in the United Kingdom and Belgium. This reserve would be maintained so that all ongoing and future infantry attrition could be serviced. Despite the large number of remusters, in 30 November the army still had trouble creating this reserve. As soon as infantry personnel arrived in the reinforcement system they were being dispatched to the regiments. This resulted in a gulf between the authorized reinforcement strength and the actual total reinforcements on hand. Figure 2.4 illustrates the challenge the Canadian Army faced.

When the shortage ended, the Conscription Crisis began in Ottawa. In October 1944, the minister of national defence returned from visiting the Canadian Army in the Netherlands and Italy. Meetings during his travels had raised the concern that if infantry casualties in northwest Europe continued at their current pace or if a large military event occurred, the available reinforcement pools could be extinguished by the end of the year.[75] His concerns were based on uncertainty within the army about whether an adequate reserve could be created from volunteer Canadian Army (Active) personnel.[76] On 13 October, CMHQ Chief of Staff Lieutenant-General Stuart informed the chief of the general staff in Ottawa that 60,000 to 40,000 more losses could be expected in the coming months. Stuart made the immediate request for 16,000 more men in the reinforcement stream. At this stage in the war, it was taking the army nearly four months to give an infantryman basic training. Because of the time needed to get what could only be trained NRMA personnel to the front from Canada, the question of whether they could be used needed an immediate answer.

Ralston felt that his hand was being forced. He had to argue within the War Committee that there was no other option but to supply NRMA soldiers to fill the gap. For him, it was unacceptable that the Canadian Army would run out of personnel it could remuster into infantry reinforcements. After all, there was a large trained NRMA force that was untapped because of the Liberal government's aversion to the overseas deployment of conscripts. After some investigation, Ralston determined that there was no way the army could say it could

Figure 2.4

Actual reinforcement holdings versus authorized target strengths, November 1944

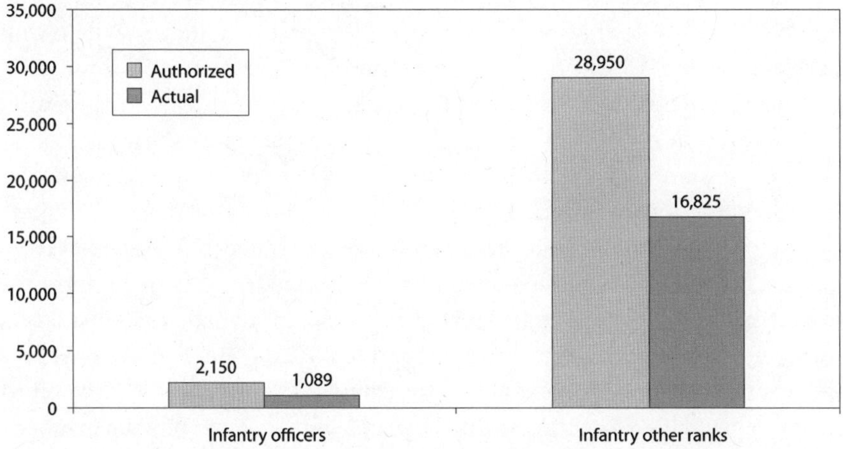

Source: Burns, *Manpower in the Canadian Army*, 97, Figure 14.

fulfill its overseas missions utilizing only volunteers.[77] Members of the proconscription camp in the War Committee judged that the army's needs in wartime were second to the prime minister's desire to maintain national unity. They also believed that King and other opponents of conscription were refusing to come to grips with the reality that NRMA personnel would have to be used. With the War Committee divided over the use of conscripts, Ralston delivered his forced resignation on 1 November. While King and elements of his cabinet accepted Ralston's resignation, the reality of the possibility of heavy combat in spring and summer 1945 remained.

Shortly after the arrival of the new minister of national defence, Andrew McNaughton, a decision was made on 23 November to send 16,000 NRMA personnel overseas: 5,000 in December, 5,000 in January, and then the final 6,000 over the succeeding months.[78] In the end, only a small number reached infantry regiments in the field. Of the 12,908 who reached the United Kingdom, 9,677 went to the continent, and only 2,463 found their way to the front line in time to see combat. Split evenly between regiments, this meant seventy soldiers each, or roughly two platoons worth. The total amount of NRMA casualties suffered in combat was 313, with 69 fatalities.[79] The NRMA men's performance within the infantry regiments was good. If more conscripted men had reached the front, it is highly probable that they would have performed adequately in whatever role was selected for them.

There is no way the leadership of the Canadian Army could have judged in October 1944 whether a large number of infantry reinforcements would be needed for future operations. Given the challenges encountered while trying to create a reinforcement reserve out of remustered personnel in fall 1944, the only feasible option was to dip into the NRMA personnel supply. Furthermore, there were many military uncertainties in late 1944 that made the utilization of NRMA personnel appear to be a necessity.[80] Had Allied operations in the Rhineland not been postponed, had the German military fought on until mid-1945, and had the Netherlands been aggressively liberated, it is likely that large numbers of NRMA personnel would have been needed. A large infantry reinforcement pool needed to be created to sustain all Canadian combat arms units for a possible long-term struggle, and previous attempts using only volunteers had not been successful. The reserve, which had been so difficult to establish, contained 24,500 personnel by late April 1945. Despite the great administrative and political struggle to create it, Germany's surrender meant that the reserve was never needed.[81]

Although the War Committee had approved the rapid growth of the Canadian Army after 1942, both it and NDHQ in Ottawa ignored the need for a detailed plan to reinforce the army when it engaged in combat operations. Both parties understood that the costs of modern warfare would demand potentially large numbers of new personnel to sustain this military entity. The need for conscription was a topic that was politically unacceptable to the Liberal government and one that the Canadian Army did not wish to force because it would endanger its expansion plans. Furthermore, historian Richard Walker argues that the army put no particular emphasis on the need to be efficient in its use of manpower or on pursuing a successful volunteer-recruitment campaign in Canada. It if did, it would have been endorsing the then all-volunteer status of the overseas Canadian Army (Active), a situation of which it did not approve. During the months leading up to Operation Overlord, Lieutenant-General Stuart failed to heed clear indications that a shortage of infantry, other ranks, reinforcements could occur. National Defence Headquarters and CMHQ, London, significantly failed in their responsibility to accurately forecast future infantry casualties for the campaign in northwest Europe. These two headquarters accepted 1943 British infantry-loss projections as accurate when ample operational evidence suggested otherwise. The final failure was a long-term inability to create an adequate reserve of reinforcement infantry in the months leading up to the invasion of Europe, despite having excess Canadian Army (Active) personnel.

because of these failures, infantry units engaged in ongoing combat operations were weakened by a lack of reinforcements to make good their rapid losses.

The shortage of infantry, other ranks, reinforcements only affected the Canadian Infantry Corps in August and September 1944. The situation was resolved in late September because of the earlier implementation of a large-scale remustering program. While this remustering program was temporarily effective, its effects were not rapid, and the shortage persisted over a sixty-day period. It is arguable that a more ruthless management of personnel in the all-volunteer Canadian Army (Active) could have minimized the problems of summer 1944. The crucial decision to create an adequate reserve of infantry reinforcements in spring 1944 was never made, and only half-measures were taken to resolve the situation, allowing the events of August and September 1944 to occur. This reserve, incompetently pursued by the Canadian Army during 1944, was only successfully created after the political decision to insert large numbers of conscript NRMA personnel. Because a limited number of these personnel reached the front, the First Canadian Army maintained its nearly all-volunteer status to the war's conclusion.

3
Vehicles and Weapons

GIVEN THE HIGH INTENSITY of combat operations conducted by the Canadian Army, an effective system of equipment recovery, repair, and replacement was essential. The number of operational vehicles and major weapons systems was critical to keeping the units' offensive and defensive capabilities at a high level.[1] The "A" and "B" categories of vehicle classification, taken from the British Army system, encompassed nearly all vehicles within the Canadian Army in the late war period. The "A" vehicle category included nearly all heavy- and light-armoured combat types, and the "B" classification encompassed all lighter, soft-skinned, wheeled supply and general-service types. If a unit's equipment inventories were significantly below their war establishment levels, its level of military effectiveness was impaired. These establishment levels were the organizational guides for equipping combat arms with personnel, vehicles, equipment, and weapons. Because Canadian units suffered equipment losses for many reasons and often at a rapid rate within infantry, armoured, and antitank regiments, their real strength was often below their establishment levels. How rapidly such losses occurred was determined by unit activity and exposure to enemy action. Accidents and normal wear and tear were also unrelenting, taking vehicles and weapons systems out of action just as effectively as enemy fire.

The First Canadian Army's repair-and-replacement services for "A" and "B" vehicles and major weapons systems were remarkably effective at achieving their main goal: maintaining the combat strength of the Canadian Army (Active). Compared to opposing German forces, new and repaired vehicles and weapons systems reached front-line artillery, armoured, and infantry units at a much faster rate and in larger quantities. Superiority in organizational structure and performance was made possible by the Corps of Royal Canadian Electrical and Mechanical Engineers' (RCEME) repair units being largely separated from the combat arms units they serviced, making them much more effective. In contrast, German divisional-sized formations were largely responsible for the upkeep of their own major weapons systems and vehicles, and because of lack of replacements, they zealously guarded what resources they had, operational or not.

In the early years of the war, because Canada was not fully engaged in war production, Canadian land forces were equipped in a limited manner. Any production that was achieved in way of equipment and munitions was allocated to existing British orders.[2] What little was left went to the Royal Canadian Air Force and the Royal Canadian Navy; the Canadian Army was the last to receive resources. Because Prime Minister King and his government were focused on limiting Canada's involvement in direct front-line combat in what was perceived as a European conflict, the 1st Canadian Infantry Division was largely equipped from British stocks when it arrived in the United Kingdom and partly deployed to France in 1940.

Despite a terribly slow start in 1939, Canadian production levels significantly rose after the fall of France in 1940. While aircraft- and ship-building programs took priority in the early war years, the production of equipment and vehicles for Commonwealth land forces increased significantly as the war proceeded. Levels of production for military vehicles and equipment was very high between 1942 and 1945, far exceeding the army's needs.[3] In total, Canada only utilized 34 percent of its total war production of equipment, of all types: 53 percent went to the United Kingdom, 12 percent went to the United States; and 1 percent went to other wartime allies.[4] Shipments to the United Kingdom for the British Army included 60 percent of Canada's production of armoured vehicles, 67 percent of its artillery pieces, and 70 percent of its rifles.[5] Because of the initial neutrality of the United States and Canada's Commonwealth status, British military vehicles and weapons were taken on as standard for the Canadian Army. When the United States entered the war in Europe in January 1942, the decision was made to stick with supplying the British with equipment and vehicles and to not adopt US standard equipment and weaponry; Canadian officials saw great difficulty in completing such a transformation and little perceived value in adopting American standards.

Like all wartime Commonwealth armies, the Canadian Army was often dependent on the will and ability of the British government to supply it with cutting-edge technology, most notably armoured vehicles.[6] The supply question regarding these vehicles was complicated further by British tank development and production issues that forced the adoption of the American Sherman tank. Thus, Great Britain became dependent on US allocations for its principal tank in all British and Commonwealth armoured regiments. Available stocks went first to Anglo-Commonwealth formations in the field, which were rightly seen as having a higher priority. Up until mid-1943, the vast majority of the Canadian Army (Active) was not involved in continuous combat operations, and it was not until late 1943 that the majority of Canadian units designated for the invasion were properly equipped and training intensively with that equipment.[7]

As the campaign in Normandy raged in summer 1944, the continued stockpiling of large amounts of materiel on the continent was not a great challenge. This stockpile was made possible by Allied success in the Battle of the Atlantic, by Allied economies reaching their full production capacities by mid-1944, and by the securing of the Normandy beachhead. Ample cooperation with the British government and extremely high levels of Canadian war production allowed Canada's military to be equipped and resupplied as needed. As a result, the Canadian Army enjoyed full access to a well-stocked common pool of Canadian, American Lend-Lease, and British produced equipment.

As the larger twin to the personnel replacement organization, the 1st Canadian Echelon within 21st Army Group Headquarters dealt with the equipment and weaponry concerns of the First Canadian Army. The total amount of equipment removed from the strength of combat arms units on the front line because of mechanical failure or enemy action usually amounted to 100 percent of a unit's establishment within several months.

The vehicles of a battalion-sized regiment were spread among its administrative echelons. These three echelons consisted of the "A1" (Fighting) Echelon, which had everything needed to carry out the combat mission; the "A2" Echelon, which had everything needed to immediately resupply the "A1" Echelon; and a small "B" Echelon, which consisted of all supply and stores items not immediately needed and the administrative support elements required to keep a battalion-sized combat grouping functioning. Within the combat arms units, vehicle attrition in the three echelons stemmed from excessive use, enemy action, and travel over harsh terrain. The highest equipment losses occurred during the three months of the Normandy Campaign. Combat in Normandy was more intense and affected a greater number of combat arms units than infantry-oriented battles in the Netherlands and the Rhineland in late 1944 and early 1945. During this time, more enemy heavy weapons and armoured vehicles were encountered due to combat action against multiple German panzer divisions, the Canadian Army's primary opponent from June to August 1944. The fighting power of these armoured formations made a sizable impact on the monthly totals of equipment losses. These totals dropped off markedly once the campaign in Normandy came to a halt in late August and were relatively low on average for the reminder of the war, when German armoured forces were engaged to the south against the British and American armies.

As an example, of the sixty-one Sherman tanks the 6th Canadian Armoured Regiment (1st Hussars) fielded on D-Day, nearly all were lost to enemy action

Figure 3.1

The equipment losses administrative system

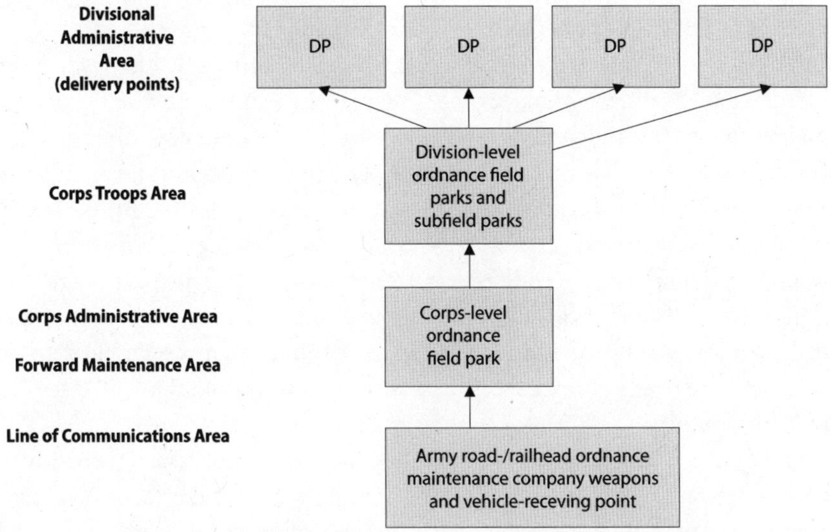

Source: Grodzinski, *Operational Handbook for the First Canadian Army*, 92–93.

or mechanical failure by the end of August. The Hussar Sherman tank "Holy Roller," now a monument in London, Ontario, was the only that remained in the regiment's possession from D-Day until the end of hostilities.[8] There were many noncombat reasons why a vehicle or weapons system might disappear from a regiment's holdings: tanks sent away for heavy maintenance could return with another unit; be replaced by a newer, more technologically advanced models; or be cannibalized if their engine or parts were worn out. The "Holy Roller" was the exception rather than the rule.

The administrative system designed to replace all Canadian equipment losses was sophisticated. As illustrated in Figure 3.1, there were a total of five administrative areas within the First Canadian Army's area of operations. From the front lines to the rear areas, these zones consisted of the Divisional Administrative Area, the Corps Troops Area, the Corps Administrative Area, the Forward Maintenance Area, and the Line of Communications Area.[9] The administrative-control area of Canadian 1st Echelon – which, as mentioned earlier, had control of the supply of major weapons systems and vehicle logistics – began with the Ordnance Maintenance Company (OMC). This unit was much greater in strength than a company-sized organization. It consisted of a headquarters, a regulating station section, a stores section, an ammunition section, and a tank section. It received all manner of supplies, vehicles, and equipment from British-controlled vehicle and ordnance depots located within close transportation distance to the First Canadian Army rail- or roadhead.

Rail- and roadheads were located in the Line of Communications Area and were the logistical start points for the Canadian Army in northwest Europe. In 1944–45, as the front moved forward, there were often multiple rail- and road-heads in existence that included various Service Corps units and numbered supply depots. The OMC distributed what it received from the British Army to Canadian Army–level equipment-storage locations, fuel and ammunition dumps, and vehicle parks. Before anything moved or entered storage, the OMC and road- and railhead personnel worked to prepare all war material for long-term storage or immediate use as required. In a reverse flow, these road- and railheads also received damaged or obsolete equipment removed from the front.[10]

If railroad transport was not available, new vehicles and ordnance were driven forward from the Line of Communications Area depots to the corps-level ordnance field park.[11] By April 1945, there were two ordnance field parks within the First Canadian Army.[12] The corps-level ordnance field park contained everything to support a complete army corps, with the exception of rations, water, and petroleum products. All forms of heavy and light weapons and all types of ammunition and spares for all weapon systems were present. Smaller stores such as small arms, optical, engineering, signals, and workshop equipment were also held. Large parking areas had row upon row of new and repaired "A" and "B" types. Only light "A" vehicles were present, the heavier armoured fighting vehicles (AFVs) having their own separate transport and replacement system. There was a wide variety of specialist "A" and "B" vehicles (command vehicles, wireless trucks, recovery vehicles, and specialist light tracked carriers) present.[13]

This park then fed the forward division-level ordnance field parks and respective armoured or infantry subfield parks. From these parks, deliveries were either made to further supply points or signed for on a need basis by the regimental-level units that required them. For smaller deliverable items that could be pushed forward, these parks contained divisional delivery points. At these delivery points, unit "B" Echelon troops of the combat arms regiments showed up to sign for authorized equipment, vehicles, and weapons and supplies on a need basis.

Heavy AFVs – the major weapons systems of the armoured, armoured reconnaissance, self-propelled field artillery, and antitank units – were the vehicles that required the most logistical resources to transport. As depicted in Figure 3.2,

Figure 3.2

The AFV replacement system

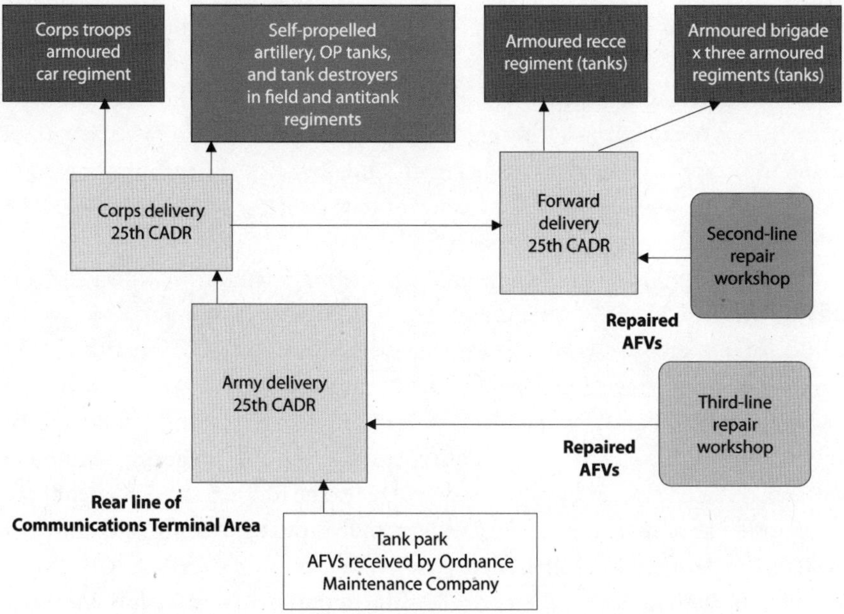

Source: LAC, RG 24, vol. 10,663, "First Canadian Army Plans Diagram of AFV 'A' Vehicle Recovery, Repair and Replacement," file 215C1.045 (D12); and Grodzinski, *Operational Handbook for the First Canadian Army*, 89–90, Appendix E.

AFVs were cut away at the OMC and processed along a separate transport path. Prior to large-scale operations, armoured regiments wanted the number of operational tanks to be as close to the war establishment figures as possible. As an example of maximum serviceability prior to operations, 2nd Canadian Armoured Brigade's strength on 31 January 1945, just prior to Operation Veritable, was 214 tanks against a war establishment figure of 226.[14] Units containing armour reported their replacement needs through an "AFV or tank state" that would be reported on a daily or weekly basis.

These daily and weekly returns from the regimental headquarters of each unit were forwarded up the chain of command. For example, an armoured regiment's AFV state would be a daily summary of whether 75 mm Cruiser tanks (Sherman V), 17-pounder Fireflies (Sherman Ic or Vc with the longer gun), and 37 mm reconnaissance (Stuart Recce) light tanks were fit, not fit, or written off. "Fit" referred to an AFV being fully combat operational. On 1 November 1944, the 4th Canadian Armoured Division fielded 247 fit tanks of all makes and 79 fit scout cars.[15] For Royal Canadian Artillery (RCA) field artillery and antitank units, self-propelled M10 tank destroyers and self-propelled Sexton howitzers were reported as part of their gun state.[16] At the armoured brigade level, the combined states of all armoured regiments would be forwarded to higher command from brigade headquarters. If an armoured unit was short tanks in any of its troops or squadrons, it would be slotted to receive new AFVs at a certain date. These repaired or new replacement tanks would be driven to the front, transported by low-bed trailer or loaded onto rail cars, and then received at the "B" Echelon of the receiving regiment.

The key component of the replacement process for armour was the 25th Canadian Armoured Delivery Regiment (25th CADR). This regiment was divided into a total of eight squadrons, designated "A" through "H."[17] The 25th CADR squadrons in northwest Europe operated a sophisticated and efficient system for supplying new and repaired AFVs to all Canadian Army units that operated them. They also supplied British, Polish, and Czech units operating within the Second British Army and First Canadian Army. The first 25th CADR squadrons that landed in France in June–July were initially under the command of the 1st British Corps. They were then incorporated into the 2nd Canadian Corps and the First Canadian Army when they became operational in mid-July and early August. "C" Squadron landed in Normandy on 7 June and immediately began transferring tanks to the three armoured regiments of the 2nd Canadian Armoured Brigade.[18] On 10 July, "E" Squadron arrived within the beachhead. This squadron was responsible for tank deliveries at the 2nd Canadian Corps level. These two squadrons were followed by "F" Squadron, which landed on 23 July. This squadron would aid in railhead acceptance of AFVs and became responsible for the delivery of vehicles at the First Canadian Army level once the army became operational. In this role, it was also the squadron responsible for sending tanks to British, Czech, and Polish armoured units under the First Canadian Army's command. "D" Squadron landed on 26 July and was responsible for all units within the 4th Canadian Armoured Brigade.[19]

British stocks of replacement AFVs were delivered to large vehicle depots on the continent near roadheads and railheads by the British Army's transport units. The Canadian Army's receiving procedure to accept these vehicles into service was quite comprehensive. From August 1944 onward, the OMC's Tank Railhead Section and the 25th CADR's "F" Squadron worked in tandem. These two groups would receive a shipment of AFVs from a British Army–administered Rear Vehicle Park (Tracked).[20] Once they arrived, the new AFVs would have their documents examined and kit removed and rechecked at the "F" Squadron tank park. Next, the armament would be degreased, and a general cleaning of the fighting compartment would take place. After this, the sprockets, road wheels, and tracks would be adjusted and repaired as required. Following this, a general servicing of weapons, radios, and the power traverse would occur. Any modifications needed would be completed by the 3rd Canadian AFV Support Unit and the 4th Canadian Armoured Troops (third-line maintenance) Workshop, working alongside "F" Squadron. Once this step was concluded, optics, radios, and fragile equipment would be installed or boxed for transport. Next, all onboard stowage of ammunition would be completed in accordance with authorized figures. Finally, the Light Aid Detachment (LAD) attached to "F" Squadron would then recertify all the AFVs to make sure they were mechanically fit. Finally, the tanks were ready to be sent out.[21] If fit tanks were not issued right away, they would be maintained by 25th CADR personnel in the "F" Squadron tank park.

Once an order was received to send tanks forward, the appropriate number would then be driven by rail or tank transporter from "F" Squadron to the 25th CADR's corps delivery squadron.[22] This squadron would then feed the two forward-delivery squadrons of the 25th CADR. Within their operating bases, 25th CADR squadrons operated "tank circuits": staff at each stop in the circuit would check over an area of the tank. This repetitive inspection-and-receiving process at each squadron could take time. While of questionable efficiency, it was effective for resolving issues with newly arrived vehicles and prevented these problems from reaching armoured regiments in the field. At any point, repaired vehicles that had come from the RCEME's facilities could join a 25th CADR squadron.

To meet demands for new AFVs quickly, 25th CADR squadrons usually had an AFV float, or balance, that they could draw from; it was similar to the CBRG's reinforcement units. This float was the percentage of the total AFVs in service with the front-line units that a 25th CADR squadron was designated to support. Though this percentage went up and down with supply and demand, an effort was made to maintain the desired inventory level to deal with emergencies. This allowed the 25th CADR to respond quickly to a recipient unit's requests for large reinforcements. The best example of this rapid-response capability is "D" Squadron's 10 August 1944 delivery of twenty-two fully crewed variants of Sherman tanks to the 28th CAR.[23] This regiment had lost forty-four Shermans (various marks), two Stuart Recce, one Crusader antiaircraft tank, and one scout car in battle on 9 August.[24] The immediate resupply, plus four tanks the regiment had as a reserve Left Out of Battle contingent, gave it a total reinforcement of twenty-six new tanks. This number would theoretically make it capable of immediate combat operations. On 12 August, however, a further sixteen tanks were delivered, bringing up the regiment's new tank deliveries to thirty-eight.[25] The number of tanks and the speed with which they arrived was impressive.

Examining the record of the 27th Canadian Armoured Regiment (the Sherbrooke Fusiliers) over an eighteen-day period in August 1944 illustrates the AFV replacement and repair process within an average Canadian armoured regiment. Over two and half weeks, the 27th CAR lost a significant number of vehicles because of enemy action and mechanical failure. It had participated in Operations Totalize and Tractable and in the initial battles of the Falaise Pocket. Though significantly weakened, after the delivery of new and repaired vehicles, the regiment fielded thirty-eight fit tanks on 18 August. Over the next two days, it repaired two additional tanks within its LAD, for a total of forty fit by 20 August.[26] Though not perfect, this was enough to theoretically field three squadrons of four troops. Each troop could field three tanks each plus four for the headquarters' squadron.

In contrast, within the German Army, tank losses due to combat and mechanical failure were not replaced as efficiently. As an example, the second battalion of the German Panzer Lehr Regiment 130 in Normandy received only eleven replacement 7.5 cm L/48 gunned Panzer IV tanks on 8 July 1944, having received none in June.[27] The effects of combat, mechanical failures, and battle damage on the battalion's operational strength between 1 June and 26 June were severe. Repairs were also slow, as they occurred within the panzer units rather than in specialized, separate repair units. As of 26 June, there were forty-seven Panzer IVs in short- and long-term repair shops, all near the chaos of the front lines.[28]

Over the course of the campaign, the 25th CADR successfully resupplied all Canadian units operating heavy AFVs. This success was due to large levels of production from repair workshops and 25th CADR forward-delivery squadrons being able to maintain large floats. As an example, "D" Squadron delivered a total of 295 new and repaired AFVs to the 4th Canadian Armoured Division in October 1944.[29]

This was enough to nearly re-equip the entire division. As illustrated in Figures 3.3 and 3.4, while Canadian armoured regiments maintained their strength, opposing German units withered. It also certainly helped that Allied forces at this time had total air superiority, large amounts of replacement equipment, and unimpeded vehicle movement and recovery.

The Canadian Army did not use any special delivery squadrons to transport non-AFV major weapons systems and other equipment to a fighting unit. Once past army-level ordnance parks, the weapons and equipment were deposited or driven to corps-level ordnance field parks, as illustrated in Figure 3.1. From

Figure 3.3

Sherman tank strength, 6th CAR, June 1944

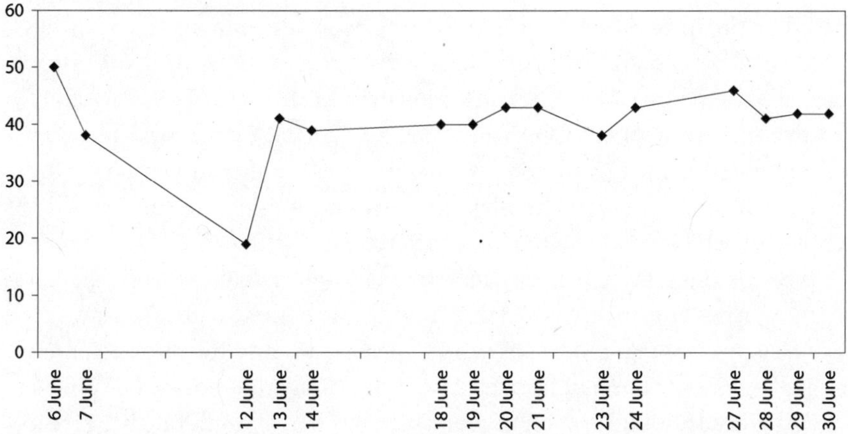

Note: War establishment was fifty Sherman V and 17-pounder Sherman Firefly tanks. Because of the practice of immediately back loading tanks with any deficiencies or damage beyond the repair capabilities of the LAD, all these Shermans must be considered operational.
Source: Jarymowycz, "The Quest for Operational Maneuver in the Normandy Campaign," 336, Appendix E, "Strength Returns for the 2nd Canadian Armoured Brigade in June 1944."

Figure 3.4

Panzer IV tank strength, German II/SS Panzer Regiment 12, June 1944

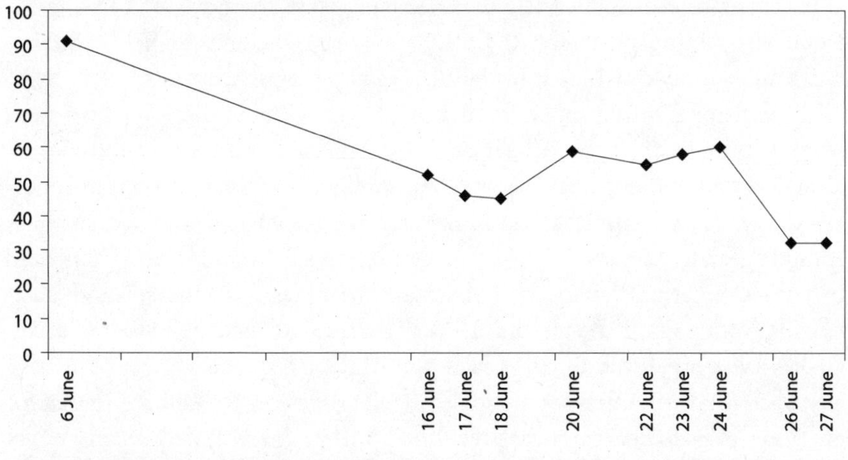

Note: War establishment was 101 Panzer IVs.
Source: Számvérber, *Waffen SS Armour in Normandy*, 234, Appendix 7, "Tank Strength of SS-Panzer Regiment 12, 1 June–11 August 1944."

these locations, the material was then moved to the divisional-level field parks. At the division level, there was a divisional ordnance field park and a corresponding armoured or infantry ordnance subpark.[30] The field parks were numbered by the division number, and the subparks were numbered 201 through 205. For example, the 5th Canadian Armoured Division's ordnance depots consisted of the 5th Canadian Armoured Division Ordnance Field Park and the 205th Canadian Armoured Ordnance Subpark.[31] In these large parks, all manner of equipment, vehicles, and stores were located in a manner similar to the corps-level parks. From these points, divisional units were authorized on a need basis to receive vehicles and equipment to retain their wartime establishments.

RCA medium, field artillery, antitank, and light antiaircraft regiments reported their status in a manner similar to the armoured units. Guns were the primary piece of equipment for artillery regiments, and the number of operational guns and those under repair were constantly monitored. A "Gun State of Ordnance Holdings" report accompanied by an "Ammunition Usage" report was forwarded each day by the artillery regiment's regimental headquarters to higher RCA command. These returns were important, as their data was used to calculate supply requirements and to gauge ammunition usage.[32] The returns made their way up the chain of command, and army-level field ordnance parks would then authorize the release of new equipment to make up for combat and mechanical losses. New replacement artillery equipment was held by army group–level British Army ordnance field parks. The Canadian Army–level ordnance park would then receive new equipment from the OMC and move it to the corps-level ordnance field parks. Repaired and reconditioned equipment would also be transported by RCEME personnel to the division field ordnance parks and subparks, where it would be taken on strength.

The divisional ordnance parks contained everything in the way of new and repaired towed artillery pieces, replacement artillery vehicles, and radios. While all artillery equipment and weaponry was sophisticated, maintaining and operating it was less complicated than maintaining an AFV, which had a motor, running gear, transmission, power turret traverse, sights, and radios. Compared to a 17-pounder antitank gun, a Sherman Firefly tank was much more challenging from a maintenance and delivery perspective, hence the lack of a 25th CADR–type organization exclusively for artillery regiments. In 1944–45, the approach to maintaining sophisticated artillery systems was similar to that for an "A" or "B" vehicle. The successive "lines" within the RCEME's repair system could handle increasingly difficult artillery repairs. Guns constantly required maintenance, which could largely be completed at the regimental level by the LAD. If a gun was worn out or damaged, it could be easily replaced. A new one would be picked up at the field ordnance or subparks by a gun crew with an artillery tractor or tower. New or repaired guns were drawn as needed to replace weapons under repair or lost in battle. A mass draw of new equipment occurred in early August 1944. All three RCA field regiments within the 3rd Canadian Infantry Division drew an entirely new complement of seventy-two towed 25-pounder howitzers, turning in their old self-propelled M7 Priest 105 mm howitzers.[33]

The RCA operated many heavy AFVs within its regiments. These were mainly artillery observation post tanks, self-propelled artillery, tank destroyers, and artillery towers. These vehicles were delivered by the 25th CADR in the same manner as a Sherman Firefly tank was delivered to an armoured regiment. Universal Carriers, T16s (a vehicle similar to a Universal Carrier), and M14 gun tractors were also "A" vehicles, but the delivery of these smaller vehicles was accomplished via tank transporters because of their low weight and small size.

In contrast to the German Army, in 1944–45, the Canadian Army was totally mechanized in all areas that required soft-skinned "B" vehicles. This large motor pool was one of the First Canadian Army's greatest strengths. It allowed Canadian forces to be mobile and carry out all logistic tasks, increasing their military effectiveness. As opposed to occasional "A" combat vehicle shortages, there was never a shortage of soft-skinned transport in Canadian units. The 31 August "B" vehicle return for the 2nd Canadian Infantry Division shows 125 general service 3-ton lorries on strength as opposed to its war establishment number of 104, making it significantly overstrength.[34] In comparison, as of 1 June 1944, the German 12th SS Panzer Division had only 65 percent of its authorized number of trucks operational, and only 33 percent of its gun tractors.[35]

Unsophisticated general service vehicles could be used in multiple roles by virtually any type of unit. Some examples of general service "B" vehicles within the Canadian Army were 3-ton lorries and jeeps. Many were produced in the United Kingdom with a right-hand drive, while others were of North American manufacture. Not being AFVs, they could not sustain damage and had a limited capability to mount weapons. More specialist "B" vehicles included petrol tankers and command caravans that came with assigned drivers to operate them. Documentation for these vehicles had to follow the vehicle from point to point, and their employment and status was monitored constantly.

As shown in Figure 3.5, the British 21st Army Group vehicle depots released "B" vehicles when authorized by 2nd Canadian Corps and later First Canadian Army headquarters. Released "B" vehicles then travelled directly either to the Canadian Corps–level ordnance field park or to a delivery point near the division-level ordnance field park. Unit drivers signed for the new vehicles on a need basis at the delivery point near the divisional ordnance field park. General-service category "B" vehicles repaired by RCEME maintenance units would also go directly to the delivery points near the divisional ordnance field park, where they would also be picked up by unit drivers. New and repaired specialized vehicles such as wreckers, radio vehicles, and ambulances were assembled at the corps-level ordnance field park. From this point, these specialist vehicles could be dispersed to unit delivery points, but only with the proper documentation and the assigned driver. Only 2.5 percent of the corps' total unit holdings of various technical vehicles were held in divisional field ordnance parks and delivery points as replacements.

The Canadian Army's recovery-and-repair systems for maintaining its inventories of vehicles, weapons, and equipment was run by units of the RCEME. Its creation and the recovery-and-repair systems utilized by its units were directly influenced by the introduction of the British Army equivalent, the Corps of Royal Electrical and Mechanical Engineers (REME), formed in October 1942. In October 1941, the British Beveridge Report had identified the need to properly employ large numbers of skilled tradesmen, engineers, and technicians who had hurriedly been put into uniform in the mobilization of 1939.[36] This recruitment had stripped a section of British industry that desperately needed their skills. At the same time, these personnel were not being correctly employed within the military. It was deemed necessary to release some of these personnel for civilian wartime production and to reassign those still needed within the British Army to utilize their technical expertise for maintenance duties.

The subsequent British Sinclair–Weeks–Dunkly Report of February 1942 went further, recommending the creation of a new corps of electrical and mechanical engineers. This corps mainly affected British Royal Ordnance Corps personnel, who were responsible for repair, recovery, and replacement. After royal assent, this corps became REME, and it was officially incorporated into the British Army in the fall.[37] New processes came into effect to allow the recovery and repair of all British Army vehicles, weapons, and equipment in the shortest amount of time.

In May 1942, the commander of the Canadian Army (Active), Lieutenant-General Andrew McNaughton, pointed out the importance of keeping systems for recovery, repair, and maintenance as similar as possible to those of the British Army while minimizing organizational change. As a result, REME processes were officially introduced in January 1943, but personnel affected by these processes remained in the Royal Canadian Ordnance Corps (RCOC). Although two-thirds of all RCOC personnel were involved in maintenance or other

Figure 3.5

Path for "B" vehicle replacement

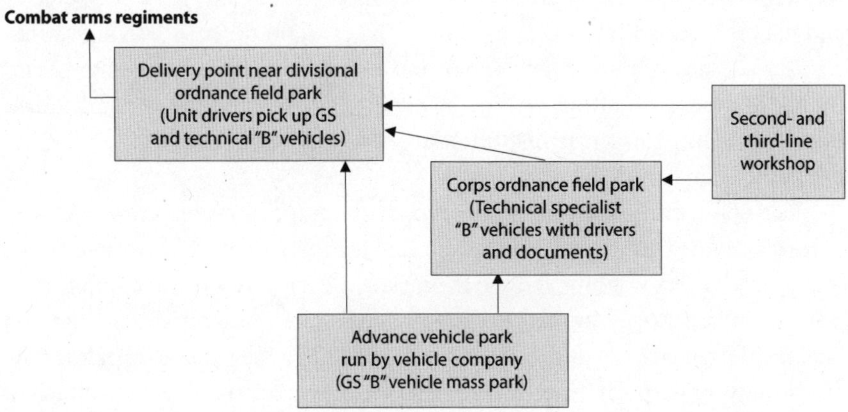

Source: LAC, RG 24, vol. 10,663, "First Canadian Army Plans Diagram of 'B' Vehicle Delivery/Replacement," file 215C1.045 (D12); and Grodzinski, *Operational Handbook for the First Canadian Army*, 93, Appendix D, "Canadian Army System of Supply of Ordnance Stores in the Field Figure, 1944."

engineering roles ("E" Branch) rather than logistic stores roles by 1942, resistance to the creation of a new corps was prevalent within the upper levels of RCOC leadership, made up of senior ("O" Branch) stores officers. Although they had not yet created a new corps, by the time Canadian forces participated in the Sicilian Campaign in summer 1943, REME processes had been fully adopted. Overworked divisional workshops were reorganized into multiple brigade workshops and regimental-level LADs within participating Canadian formations.[38]

Pressure from on-loan REME officers within CMHQ and public debate in the Parliament in Ottawa spurred on by the civilian Canadian Engineering Institute and its publications led the army to again contemplate the creation of a separate corps in spring and summer 1943.[39] Meetings within CMHQ about the operational-planning details of Operation Overlord led to acknowledgment of the need for a separate mechanical-engineering corps within the Canadian Army. Official organizational change to create the Canadian Corps of Electrical and Mechanical Engineers finally came into effect on 1 February 1944, one year and six months after the official incorporation of REME. With royal assent, the corps became RCEME on 2 April 1944, just in time for the Normandy invasion.[40] With this act, virtually the entire "E" Branch of the RCOC was rebadged to become the first members of RCEME.

This transformation put the final administrative and command touches on the maintenance process within a fully mechanized Canadian Army. The system was now more capable than ever of keeping a major percentage of vehicles and major weapons systems operational. The creation of an entirely new army corps and the adoption of new repair-and-recovery processes were significant mileposts in the evolution of the Canadian Army during the Second World War. Overcoming extreme institutional resistance, former RCOC "E" Branch officers had finally prevailed.

When conducting operations, the Canadian Army's recovery-and-repair system was divided into levels so that no one area would be overstressed by its workload. If there was an overload at one level or if a task was too complicated, tasks would be passed to the next successive level, commonly designated as a line. As illustrated in Figures 3.6 and 3.7, RCEME had four lines to repair mechanical faults or battle damage. First line was the organic repair services attached to the combat arms regiments. The lines that followed took on successively more difficult and complicated repair-and-rebuilding assignments. Most of the work

Figure 3.6

Maintenance lines, "A" and "B" vehicles and major weapons systems

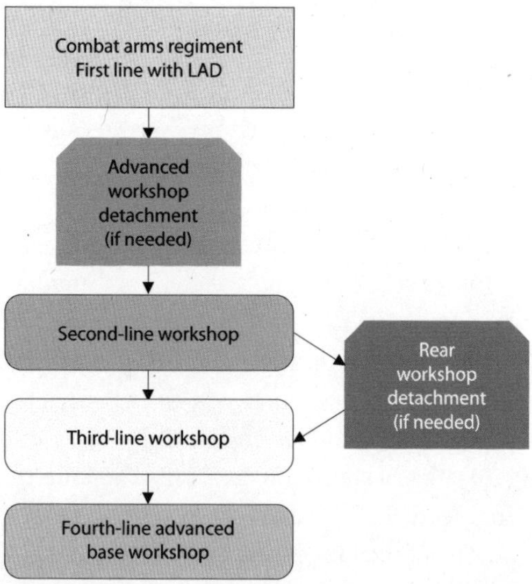

Source: Grodzinski, *Operational Handbook for the First Canadian Army*, 89–90, Appendix E.

Figure 3.7

Recovery-and-repair process, "A" and "B" vehicle and major weapons systems, Armoured Division

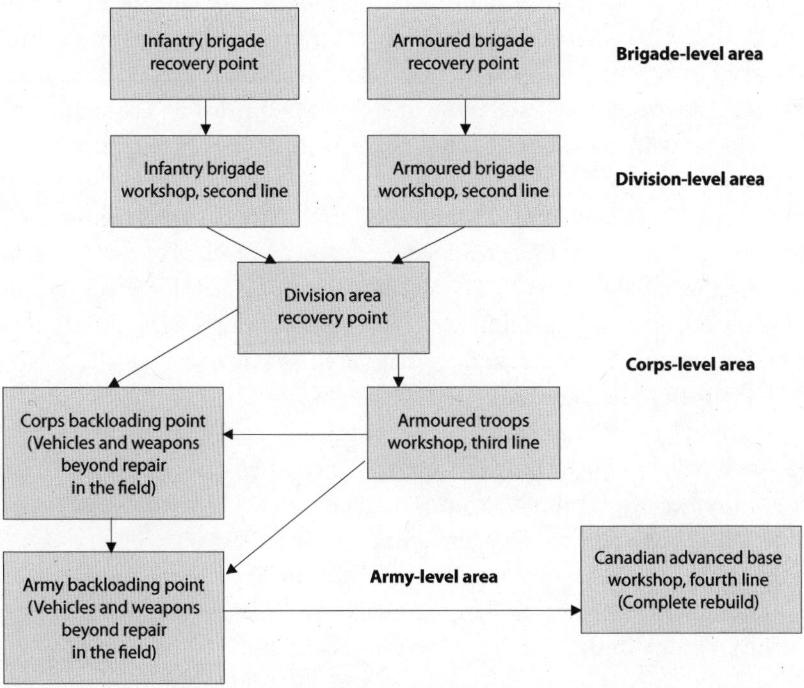

Source: LAC, RG 24, vol. 10,663, "First Canadian Army Plans Diagram of AFV 'A' Vehicle Recovery, Repair and Replacement," file 215C1.045 (D12).

in the RCEME workshops and LADs was done prior to or after combat operations. Enemy action was responsible for only a small percentage of the second line's tasks. Its workload was divided as follows: mechanical breakdowns (95 percent), battle damage (2 percent), and road accidents (3 percent).[41] Each successive line took on more difficult jobs that required more repair hours, more replacement parts, other specialized tools, and more specialized tradesmen to accomplish. This system allowed for the repair and recovery of the maximum number of vehicles in the shortest amount of time.

For example, an "A" vehicle or weapon-repair job that would take more than four hours was immediately backloaded out of a LAD's area of operations (sent to the rear). During a rapid advance, the main body of a brigade-level RCEME workshop could be split into two sections if necessary, establishing rear or forward advanced workshop detachments. These were nonstandard special teams detached from the workshop to meet a temporary need. They could be made as large or small as the tactical situation demanded. These teams were tasked with providing advanced recovery-and-repair services in cooperation with RCEME's first-line maintenance LADs at the regimental level or remaining behind a brigade workshop's main body as it advanced. If needed, the forward advanced workshop could act as the link between the first and second lines of maintenance, with these two lines taking the lion's share of repair, recovery, and maintenance duties.[42]

The first-line maintenance capability within the combat arms regiments was the responsibility of the LAD workshops. One was attached to each RCA and CAC regiment, the infantry LADs being held at the brigade level. For example, the 2nd Canadian Armoured Brigade had the following LADs, each manned by RCEME troops: the 6th Canadian Armoured Regiment contained the No. 54 LAD, the 10th Canadian Armoured Regiment was assigned the No. 55 LAD, and the 27th Canadian Armoured Regiment was issued the No. 85 LAD.[43]

These small, light detachments were designed to be mobile and had a minimum number of personnel, vehicles, and equipment. They dealt with easily correctable problems that AFV and gun crews could aid in resolving within a certain time limit. They put maximum effort into these easier problems and backloaded what could not be handled quickly or was beyond their capabilities. The LADs' main duties were light welding, mechanical repairs, and assisting with maintenance questions. They were spread evenly throughout the regimental administrative ("A1," "A2," "B") echelons of their respective regiment. Vehicles, AFVs, and ordnance backloaded by a regimental LAD for second- or third-line maintenance would be collected by their respective brigade workshops' recovery platoon assets and backloaded to the brigade collection point. This collection point was within the workshop's base of operations or very near it. It also worked closely not only with the three regiments of each brigade but also with divisional troops, such as the field artillery, machine-gun, and antitank regiments. The LADs from these divisional units would be designated to feed a certain brigade workshop in the same manner as one of the armoured or infantry brigade's regimental LADs. An infantry brigade's workshop would collect, repair, or backload all infantry AFVs, vehicles, and ordnance in the same manner as the armoured brigade workshop.

The second line of the RCEME repair organization consisted of the main body of the brigade workshop. For example, the 2nd Canadian Armoured Brigade had the 2nd Armoured Brigade Workshop assigned to it. Despite the misnomer, the brigade workshop operated in what was considered a divisional-level repair area if the workshop in question was part of an infantry or armoured division. The second-line brigade workshop's main bodies in armoured or infantry divisions were located no more than two hours from the location of the LAD. They were not very mobile and had trouble keeping up with the rapid advances of the First Canadian Army in August and September 1944.

This was particularly true of workshops operating within the 4th Canadian Armoured Division. In response, from September 1944, its brigade workshops were sited near the front. The need for a special forward advanced workshop detachment was removed, and the main body of the brigade workshop took on its role. If needed, a rear advanced workshop detachment would remain with less mobile elements, totally reversing the standard procedure. After August 1944, the three infantry brigade workshops within the two Canadian infantry divisions also struggled to remain close to the moving front lines. To mitigate the distances, one workshop's entire main body was always located forward, the other two located farther to the rear or in transit.[44] The 2nd Canadian Corps Troops Workshop was also located in the second-line maintenance structure, providing repair services for corps-level units. The LADs of corps-level combat units would feed the corps workshop using the same process that the infantry and armoured LADs used to feed their brigade workshop.

If an AFV or other equipment was sent off strength as a repair casualty to a second-line maintenance unit, it was taken off the strength of its original regiment. It was now on the strength of the respective RCEME unit, and all further repair work would be completed by RCEME personnel.[45] The repair process was quite flexible, and there was no rule that a tank had to return to its respective squadron or regiment. If a similar tank emerged from the repair-and-recovery pipeline, it would instead take its place and be delivered by the 25th CADR forward squadron.

Despite being titled "infantry" and "armoured," the brigade workshops also worked on AFVs and other ordnance employed by the RCA's field artillery and antitank units. Artillery observation-post tanks, self-propelled howitzers, tank destroyers, and artillery towers broke down and suffered battle damage at the same rate as AFVs employed in infantry and armoured units. If an RCA artillery AFV was repaired, the designated 25th CADR squadron would deliver it to an RCA unit in the same manner as it would to an armoured unit. "E" Squadron was responsible for delivering tracked artillery "A" vehicles directly to the RCA regiments. The "B," "C," "D," and "G" squadrons were responsible for the tank-equipped Canadian armoured brigades.[46]

The third line of RCEME maintenance, under the command of the First Canadian Army's deputy director of mechanical engineering, was designated to complete the rebuilding and reconditioning of equipment. This was not a service available within the first and second lines as shown in Figure 3.7. Rebuilding and reconditioning took a long time and had to be completed in a static factory-like environment. In these locations, detailed and complicated work could take place out of the way of the elements and enemy action. This was their designated role, but most of the work was overflow from second-line maintenance. The corps troops, armoured brigade, and infantry brigade workshops could all feed overflow repair cases directly to third-line units. The No. 2 Tank Troops Workshop was an example of a third-line RCEME asset in the summer of 1944. This facility was used as an overflow catch point for overworked second-line brigade workshops.[47] The third-line maintenance units lacked integral transport and had difficulty remaining at a fixed distance from second-line workshop bases. If one was ordered to move forward, the others stayed in place to take on the moving unit's workload. First Canadian Army fourth-line maintenance was a capability that existed in the form of the No. 1 and No. 2 Advanced Base Workshops. The No. 1 Canadian Base Workshop, as the parent organization of these fourth-line facilities, remained in the United Kingdom. These organizations were commanded by the director of mechanical engineering, 21st Army Group. They were designed to be available at the rate of one per Canadian corps. They also provided factory-like rebuilding and reconditioning services for vehicles and other major pieces of equipment on a higher level than third line. In addition to their designated roles, these groups could also be utilized for special missions. For example, No. 1 Advanced Base Workshop inspected and performed maintenance on over four hundred artillery pieces prior to Operation Totalize in early August 1944. It also rebuilt and repaired large numbers of submerged vehicles recovered from the Juno and Sword Beach landing areas in Normandy.[48] If third-line maintenance assets could not handle a job or were overloaded, these two facilities assisted in rebuilding and reconditioning tasks.[49]

Specialized recovery assets in the army-level Line of Communications Area also existed. The RCEME Canadian Army No. 2 (and, later, Nos. 1 and 3) Recovery Company operated in the strategic route-clearing and vehicle recovery role to the rear of the corps and divisional areas. Prior to August 1944, there was little vehicle and equipment backloading above the regimental and brigade level because of the small area within the Normandy beachhead. As the breakout from Normandy developed in August, these activities increased as broken-down vehicles were littered across northern France.[50]

Once repairs were complete, the vehicle or piece of ordnance would be sent on its way. Using an AFV as an example, once it was deemed fit by a repair line, it was shipped back to the relevant 25th CADR squadron. It would then be sent off strength of the RCEME unit that had worked on it and be taken on the books of the respective 25th CADR squadron. Once the 25th CADR squadron delivered it, the AFV joined the strength of the armoured or RCA unit, and the circle was complete. At its height, in May 1945, the RCEME repair organization was large and extremely capable. A total of 150 RCEME units and subunits existed, from the LAD detachments within combat arms units to fourth-line maintenance facilities located in static locations.

In his seminal 2001 work, *Clash of Arms: How the Allies Won in Normandy*, American military historian Russell A. Hart says of the First Canadian Army's Normandy Campaign: "The rapid but haphazard wartime proliferation of support and service elements further curtailed the Canadian ability to operate independently."[51] This work would like to respectfully present a different appreciation. The armoured and infantry regiments of the First Canadian Army closed the Falaise Gap, sealing the fate of thousands of German troops. This success was due to the fact good service and support services made the combat arms regiments militarily effective.

The Canadian Army (Active) benefitted from adopting what were largely British Army practices that had evolved through trial and error over the course of the war into a very sophisticated system. During the Italian campaign in 1943–44, the army had the opportunity to practise these methods in the field. On its arrival in northwest Europe, familiar practices were put into action with excellent results. Canadian combat arms regiments were never hindered in their operations because of a shortage weapons or vehicles.

4
Army Doctrine and Losses

In theory, the perfect army is tactically flawless in its operations, has clear strategic goals, employs cutting-edge technology, and is well supplied. On the battlefield, it annihilates opposing forces quickly and suffers negligible losses. If an army is not superior to its enemy in all areas, it will face challenges. Exposure to a similar enemy force and its weapons will result in losses in personnel and equipment. This was the case for the First Canadian Army. Although the army had significant strengths that allowed it to methodically defeat the German ground forces – most arguably its vastly superior field artillery tactics – it also had weaknesses.[1] German forces exploited these weaknesses, causing most of Canada's material and personnel losses.

Doctrine is the set of principles that guide how military forces conduct their battles, campaigns, and major operations. *Military tactics* is generally defined as the manner of organizing and employing combat forces on the battlefield; it involves the application of the four battlefield functions: firepower, mobility, defensive measures, and offensive shock action. The three traditional combat arms of the Canadian Army discussed here –the infantry, artillery, and armour – all had distinct roles to play on the battlefield.

The infantry of the Canadian Infantry Corps (CIC), whose main role was to close with and destroy the enemy, carried out its missions on foot because it did not have armoured personnel carriers organic to each of its regiments. Though each regiment contained tracked Universal Carriers, their numbers were small, and they carried a limited number of soldiers. The main unit of manoeuvre for an infantry brigade was the regiment, a battalion-sized unit of four line companies and a support company, which served as its main sub-units. These regiments were the basic building blocks of a battlegroup, to which artillery, armoured, and specialized assets could be added for operations. Using a variety of small arms and organic heavy weapons, each battalion-sized regiment was extremely powerful in that it could capture and hold ground, destroying the enemy in the process.[2]

The role of the armour of the Canadian Armoured Corps (CAC) was to destroy the enemy through fire and manoeuvre. Its main weapons systems were various models of the American Sherman tank. Though inferior to enemy tanks in some aspects of armament and armour, later models remedied many of these shortcomings, and an abundance of these vehicles made the battalion-sized armoured regiment a formidable combat force that could destroy the enemy's armoured, antitank, and infantry forces. Recce units, which were also part of the armoured corps, carried out the role of armoured reconnaissance with both tanks and wheeled armoured cars. While armoured forces could not hold ground alone, they could capture and help hold it in conjunction with infantry and Royal Canadian Artillery (RCA) artillery forces. Though extremely powerful and combat capable, these tanks were vulnerable to enemy antitank weapons when they were not supported by infantry and other assets.[3]

The artillery forces of the Royal Canadian Artillery were divided into four main combat forces: field regiments, medium regiments, antitank regiments and light antiaircraft regiments, Specialist units supported these four main groupings. The field and medium regiments, with their batteries of towed and self-propelled guns and howitzers, provided direct and indirect fire support designed to annihilate and suppress the enemy. The antitank forces, with their towed and self-propelled antitank guns, worked in conjunction with the armour and infantry units to engage and destroy enemy armour. The light antiaircraft units provided defence against enemy ground attack aircraft. Each regiment was equivalent to a battalion and could be broken up and detailed to various infantry regiment-based battle groups. In a large battle space, the numerous and highly sophisticated RCA field and medium regiments under divisional and corps command could have their various batteries engaged in different tasks.[4]

On the battlefield, the force undertaking offensive operations often suffers heavier casualties than the opposing or defending force. Most Canadian personnel casualties in northwest Europe, as discussed in the Chapter 2, were borne by the infantry, which was dismounted and exposed to direct and indirect fire.

In summer 1944, the Canadian Army fought arguably some of the best equipped and experienced enemy formations available in the form of the German Army and Waffen-SS panzer divisions.[5] At times, losses at the unit level were catastrophic. After Normandy, the German forces were never again so consistently strong. Autumn 1944 and spring 1945 saw the Canadian Army facing a primarily defensive opponent, weak in infantry, short of armour, and devoid of continuous artillery and air support. The Germans could launch limited infantry counterattacks, but after August 1944 they did not deploy enough resources or have a strategic plan to conduct large-scale offensive operations against the Anglo-Canadian front. The Allies held the initiative and could choose when and where to attack, fighting the war at their own pace.

The First Canadian Army was one of the last of the great British imperial armies. British and Canadian organization, doctrine, and equipment were intended to be identical. This goal was enhanced by the fact that Canadian units were completely equipped with British and American war material, to the same standard as the British Army. Canadian officers were also influenced by their having been under British corps command during operations in Sicily and in Italy in 1943–44.[6] In the spring before the invasion of France in June 1944, the divisions of the 2nd Canadian Corps had conducted intensive training. These exercises were supervised by the 21st Army Group commander, British General Bernard Montgomery. As part of his role as commander, he sought to ensure that the proper steps in Canadian Army doctrinal evolution took place. This training inculcated the British method of warfare within Canadian corps, divisional, and brigade headquarters staffs. During this period, Montgomery developed capable Canadian officers and culled those he found lacking. He was influential in developing the most promising officers, especially 2nd Canadian Corps commander Lieutenant-General Guy G. Simonds.

In 1941–42, the German Afrika Korps had repeatedly defeated the British Eighth Army in North Africa. The lessons learned and the arrival of General Montgomery as commander in the summer fundamentally changed the way British forces undertook operations. It was these changes that allowed future Anglo-Canadian armies to defeat the German Army in northwest Europe. In spring 1944, Canadian doctrine on UK training grounds was correspondingly transitional. New operational methods stemming from 1943 successes in North Africa were implemented in the United Kingdom as Canadian training mirrored that of the British.

One of the largest changes the British Army made was to its operational method concerning the tactical employment of armour. Between 1939 and 1943, the leadership had encountered serious challenges with design, production levels, transportation to the front, and battlefield performance. British tank design and production methods had stagnated in the interwar years.[7] By 1941, German tanks were more manoeuvrable and had higher speeds and better armament. In comparison, Britain's main gun armament was significantly inferior, and it was slow to catch up to German advances, such as the high-velocity gun equipping the German Panzer IV Ausführung F2.

Expanding wartime tank production took time and significant resources, and the resources allocated to it were inferior to those devoted to warship and aircraft production. This situation did not change much during the war. Skilled labour and precision machine tools, vital for the production of weapons systems such as tanks and artillery, were not present in the United Kingdom in the numbers needed, and the equipment and skilled labour that was present was devoted to the needs of the Royal Air Force and Royal Navy.[8] Also, tanks that could have been employed by the British Army or its Commonwealth allies went to Russia in the decisive period 1941–43. From the outbreak of hostilities until December 1941, only 479 Cruiser-type and 1,375 Infantry-type tanks were produced within British factories.[9] These amounts were insufficient to equip British and Commonwealth forces in the Middle East, meet planned arms shipments to the USSR, and, last but not least, equip Canadian and British formations deployed to defend the United Kingdom.

The tank supply situation changed radically with the entry of the United States into the war in January 1942. It took time for the Americans to reach optimum war production levels, but the US economy began to reach full production capacity in mid-1943. Lend-Lease – a US government program begun in March 1941 to assist the defeat of Germany and Japan through the distribution of fuel, food, and war material – resulted in additional numbers of armoured vehicles and artillery pieces appearing in Britain and the Mediterranean by 1943, equipping new British and Commonwealth formations destined for the invasion of Europe. Also, at this point, the British Cromwell, a new cruiser tank, and the American Sherman tank were beginning to be available in large numbers. As of 1944, 41 percent of the British and Commonwealth armoured vehicle needs and 47 percent of their medium artillery needs were being met by the United States.[10] Although the tank-supply situation had improved significantly, the challenges of 1939–43 had made a huge impact on the doctrine of the British Army and its Commonwealth partners.

The lack of a superior tank design that could defeat German armour and antitank defences on the battlefield led to a high number of Allied losses and battlefield reverses when unsupported armour was utilized as the vanguard. Between 1941 and 1942, these losses could not be replaced rapidly because of the problems of production and getting tanks onto the battlefield. Though these problems were solved by the American entry into the war, British and Commonwealth forces in North Africa began to utilize infantry to lead attacks, with supporting armour following at a distance. In this manner, armoured losses were minimized, and operational success rates were boosted through a combined arms approach. Once the infantry captured an objective, the armour worked closely with powerful artillery and antitank assets to defend it.[11] Where it had once been the dashing and at times solitary vanguard of the attack, after 1942 the Royal Armoured Corps became part of combined arms task forces. Armour properly supported the infantry and worked closely with other assets to use its firepower to defeat strong German resistance or stubborn counterattacks to regain lost defensive positions.

As of May 1944, the Canadian Army had not fought a major armoured engagement in open country or desert terrain, locations where the advantages of long-distance tank gunnery could be utilized to maximum effect. Although Canadians had fought in Sicily and Italy, fluid armoured operations over large distances were a rarity in the hilly and broken terrain of this theatre. And the combat experience gained in Italy remained in Italy, as none of the 1st Canadian Corps armoured units fought in Normandy.

As a result, by spring 1944 Canadian armoured regiments in the United Kingdom had no combat experience advancing as the offensive vanguard. When this was attempted in Normandy, German antitank fire dealt large casualties to Canadian armoured squadrons equipped with inferior technology.[12] Following several intense armoured engagements in June 1944's Normandy bridgehead battles, the armoured regiments were tasked with supporting offensive operations to capture Carpiquet airfield and Caen in early July (Operations Windsor and Charnwood). In these battles, many tanks were destroyed or damaged. Fighting on and around Verrières Ridge south of Caen in late July again led to heavy losses.[13] Here, as in other earlier engagements, the Germans took advantage of good tank country by employing their panzers' long-range main armament and 88 mm antitank guns.

The German Army could capably defeat the Allied armoured attacks because of its experiences in the USSR beginning in 1941. Reverses such as the 6th Canadian Armoured Regiment's failed attack on Le Mesnil-Patry, Normandy, on 11 June, demonstrated the difficulties Canadian armour faced when assaulting prepared German defences.[14] This is not to say that the Canadians did not carry out assaults in a determined manner. Up to the closure of the Falaise Gap on 21 August, Canadian armoured regiments led fifteen major attacks. Some were executed successfully when combined arms tactics were utilized and infantry, antitank, artillery, and air assets were present. But when Canadian armour took a more forward or independent role, it often suffered severe losses due to enemy antitank gun fire.[15]

This issue was especially prominent during the 27th Canadian Armoured Regiment's attempt to capture Carpiquet airfield and the outskirts of Caen on 7 June. In this case, the temporary loss of artillery support significantly contributed to armour's challenges during the mobile tank battle.[16] This was not an exclusively Canadian problem, and strong antitank defences posed a serious obstacle for German, American, and British armoured forces in Normandy and beyond. Because of these challenges, the scope of Canadian armoured objectives in late summer 1944 was limited by the range of the guns and the infantry's ability to keep up. To go beyond the limitations of the First Canadian Army's artillery-based doctrine would risk disaster.

During the later stages of August 1944's Operations Totalize and Tractable, the armoured regiments of the 4th Canadian Armoured Brigade were asked to manoeuvre rapidly in a fluid situation that demanded aggression and initiative from all squadron commanders.[17] The operations were temporarily blocked by weak German armoured forces and held up by traffic jams. The brigade's performance was lacklustre because of inexperience and a large number of officer casualties. During Operation Totalize, when fighting near Rocquancourt-Cintheaux on 9 August, several 22nd Canadian Armoured Regiment command tanks were destroyed. The loss of a squadron commander and two troop leaders at the forefront of the battle significantly degraded command and control.[18] This newly deployed formation was fighting its first battles in August at the vanguard of the First Canadian Army's advance. To ensure success, the Canadian Army needed an abundance of experienced armoured regiments in this role, not ones carrying out their first combat operations.[19]

Without intimate artillery and infantry support, Canadian tanks were vulnerable to all forms of antitank weapons. Canadian Sherman 75 mm and 17-pounder Sherman Firefly variants were susceptible to high-velocity German armour-piercing antitank rounds. The Sherman's armoured plate was not angled enough, hardened enough, or thick enough in its frontal areas. Operational research reports found it took on average 1.63 hits to destroy or knock out a Sherman; 91.2 percent of Shermans with gasoline engines quickly burned out.[20] When German fire hit the internal hull shell racks, it caused catastrophic explosions. Also, the Sherman's profile was too high, and it lacked a 360-degree episcope cupola that the commander could see out of without exposing his head.[21]

The vast majority of casualties for the armoured crews occurred on the assault or in fending off German counterattacks. When not engaged in offensive operations, armoured squadrons were placed in defensive positions or in leaguer, an administrative grouping for refuelling, maintenance, and rearming. Few losses occurred during this administrative tactical grouping. Because of the crew's ability to use the tank as protection, losses from all forms of indirect fire were light.[22] If the tank was hit during combat, CAC crews developed the ability to bail out quickly under fire and shelter behind the burning hulk. With a crew of five, this quick-exit technique limited casualties to only one or two per Sherman destroyed. Despite losing fifty-one Shermans during the attack on Le Mesnil-Patry, the 6th Canadian Armoured Regiment lost only eighty personnel.[23] Given that the total crew strength of the knocked-out tanks numbered 255 potential casualties, the losses could have been higher. Because of the weakness of their tank's armour, crews began to weld on extra track links.[24] If a firefight broke out, commanders were often cautious due to the German ability to destroy a Sherman with one round. This led to a preference for overwatch or ambush tactics rather than an advance to contact; superior numbers of Shermans were arranged to effectively smother a German armoured counterthrust against a newly acquired objective.[25]

In summer 1944, because of shortages, the Canadian Army could only field one Sherman Firefly per three or four tank troops. The 17-pounder Sherman Firefly tank cannon was the only armament that had the penetration power to destroy a German Panzerkampfwagen VI Tiger Ausführung E (Tiger I) or Panzerkampfwagen V Panther A and G (Panther) tank at medium range. It could also destroy a German Panzerkampfwagen IV (Panzer IV) or Sturmgeschütz III assault gun easily at long range. However, the Sherman Firefly also had negative attributes. It had excessive fuel consumption, engine issues, and main gun misfires. The lack of an effective flash suppressor and smokeless powder led to large muzzle flashes when firing, which blinded the gunner as to the location of fall of shot. This made correction difficult, which could be fatal in a tank firefight. Also, the Firefly initially did not fire high-explosive shells, only armour-piercing antitank rounds. This limitation made it near useless in reducing enemy infantry positions. Despite this, other tanks depended on the Sherman Firefly for success in long-range firefights with German 7.5 cm high-velocity cannon-equipped armoured vehicles, as the short-barrelled low-velocity 75 mm–gunned Sherman was not as effective.[26]

Canadian offensive armoured operations in the summer of 1944 could be delayed or halted by the Germans' skilful antitank defence and devastating counterattacks. The apparent inability of Canadian armour to decisively attack and destroy German armour and antitank guns has led some prominent Canadian military historians, such as John English, to label the CAC as the weakest of the Canadian combat arms.[27] This is an exaggeration, but this impression was fuelled by a battlefield doctrine that did not place large numbers of tanks in the vanguard of the attack. The technical inferiority of Allied tanks when compared to their German counterparts also inhibited offensive tactics and forced a reliance on infantry and artillery support in certain tactical situations.[28]

The logical solution to this challenging situation was fielding combined arms teams of armour, infantry, and antitank forces, superbly supported by artillery and air assets. These infantry-led groupings could be used to capture limited objectives, never outstripping supporting indirect assets or the reserves' ability to join the battle. These tactics were more polished after Normandy, and when all elements were adequately represented there was a high chance of success. Later actions near Bergen op Zoom, the Netherlands, and Louisendorf, Germany, in 1944–45 are examples of successful combined arms tactics involving armour. Figure 4.1 illustrates the advance to contact formation for the Fort Garry Horse (10th Canadian Armoured Regiment) while supporting the 4th Canadian Infantry Brigade during operations in the Rhineland. Taking place near Louisendorf, Germany, from 19 to 20 February 1945, it was one of the last tank battles of the war for the Canadian Army, and it destroyed significant numbers of counterattacking German tanks and self-propelled guns of the German Panzer Lehr Panzer Division. In this action, the Canadian combined arms task force seized its objective and then defeated repeated German counterattacks.[29]

Fighting closely with the armoured forces were the infantry foot soldiers of the Canadian Infantry Corps. Allied success in offensive operations in 1944 was often achieved through overwhelming force. However, the more personnel a commander employed in a given area, the higher the probability of casualties. Canadian infantry actions in Normandy and beyond were often characterized by the leadership utilizing minimum infantry force against enemy units deployed in depth. Increased artillery firepower would make up for a lack of infantry numbers and reduce casualties. Rather than a whole brigade attacking with a numerical superiority of at least three to one, a single infantry battalion would assault an objective, often held by a complete enemy battalion. This attack would be made with two companies up front and two to the rear. The battalion's heavy weapons would be held ready should an armoured or infantry counterattack appear. As of October 1944, the support company of an infantry battalion was 7 officers and 184 other ranks; an individual infantry company comprised 5 officers and 120 other ranks. With only two companies up front, the attacking group that made first make contact was not the full weight of the 850 strong battalion but rather 18 percent of combat personnel.[30]

The tactic of the direct-fire firebase, a firm part of modern Canadian Army doctrine, was not often utilized. Tanks concentrated at a right angle to the

Figure 4.1

Fort Garry Horse two-squadron combined arms tactics with infantry, Louisendorf, 1945

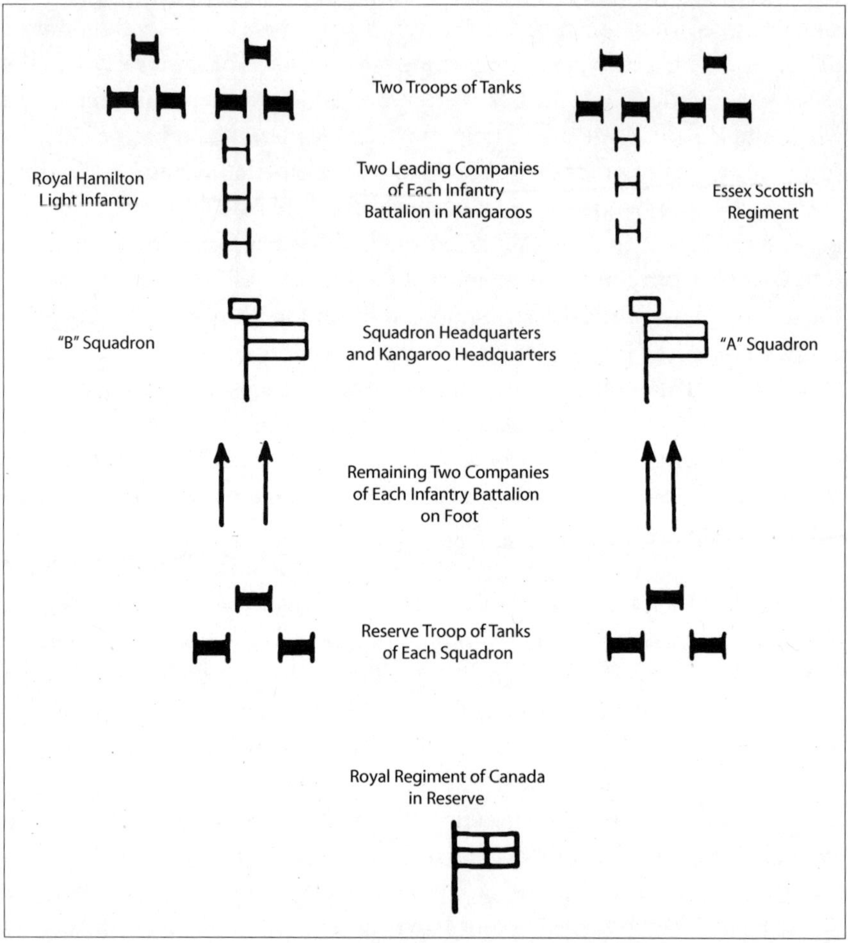

Note: This diagram adequately illustrates the late war final evolution of tank-infantry combined arms tactics.
Source: Fort Garry Horse, *Vanguard,* 100.

infantry assault could use combined firepower to suppress the enemy, but circumstances often hampered this tactic. Poor coordination, tank obstacles, effective German antitank fire, smoke from artillery fire, or other factors conspired to inhibit the effectiveness of the firebase. Regardless of whether the tanks were involved, an artillery rolling barrage commenced at the attack, matched with concentrations on or near the objective. The rolling barrage lifted and moved forward at a set pace per minute towards the enemy lines. Once the artillery fire commenced, the infantry, supported by armour and antitank assets farther back, began to move. The idea was that the infantry would closely follow the barrage, just as it did during the First World War, and establish itself in the enemy trench lines before they could react.

The battlefield could be challenging for Canadian infantry if they were not part of a combined arms team. If the infantry was on its own and the enemy continued to resist when the artillery barrage ended, company and platoon tactics would be used. All light machine guns and mortars would be grouped together to lay down suppressive direct and indirect fire, forming a firebase. The remaining force would infiltrate an enemy flank under an infantry company commander's leadership, forming an assault force. Suppression of the enemy would allow the manoeuvring sections of this force to use fire and movement to eventually reach and destroy the enemy infantry positions. Speed and effective suppression of the enemy were crucial at this stage. If the advance of the assault force was halted or driven back, the attack would likely fail. If enemy armour or self-propelled guns appeared, an unsupported infantry attack could easily falter.

The infantry battlegroup, which had attached armour and antitank assets in supporting roles, was much more effective in operations. Figure 4.2 illustrates a successful Canadian infantry battalion attack supported by armour and British Royal Artillery antitank assets. In this assault, which took place on 8 July 1944, the main infantry force, attacking with two infantry companies forward, fought its way onto its objective, overcoming antitank obstacles and an entrenched enemy. Despite heavy tank losses, the defenders were defeated in detail, and each trench and bunker position in and around the village was captured. Following its consolidation on the successfully captured objective, the assault group was reinforced by antitank assets, namely, British M10 tank destroyers and the support and reserve infantry company of the Highland Light Infantry of Canada. By consolidating its defences on its newly won objective, the Highland Light Infantry, with British Royal Artillery antitank support, could then fight off a German counterattack consisting of Panther tanks sent to drive the Canadians back. This counterattack was defeated with high losses inflicted on the Germans.

The North Nova Scotia Highlanders night attack on Tilly-la-Campagne, Normandy, on 25 July 1944, illustrates the type of reverse that could occur in the absence of combined arms support.[31] Before the assault force could penetrate the village, it was halted by machine gun and tank fire and then counterattacked.

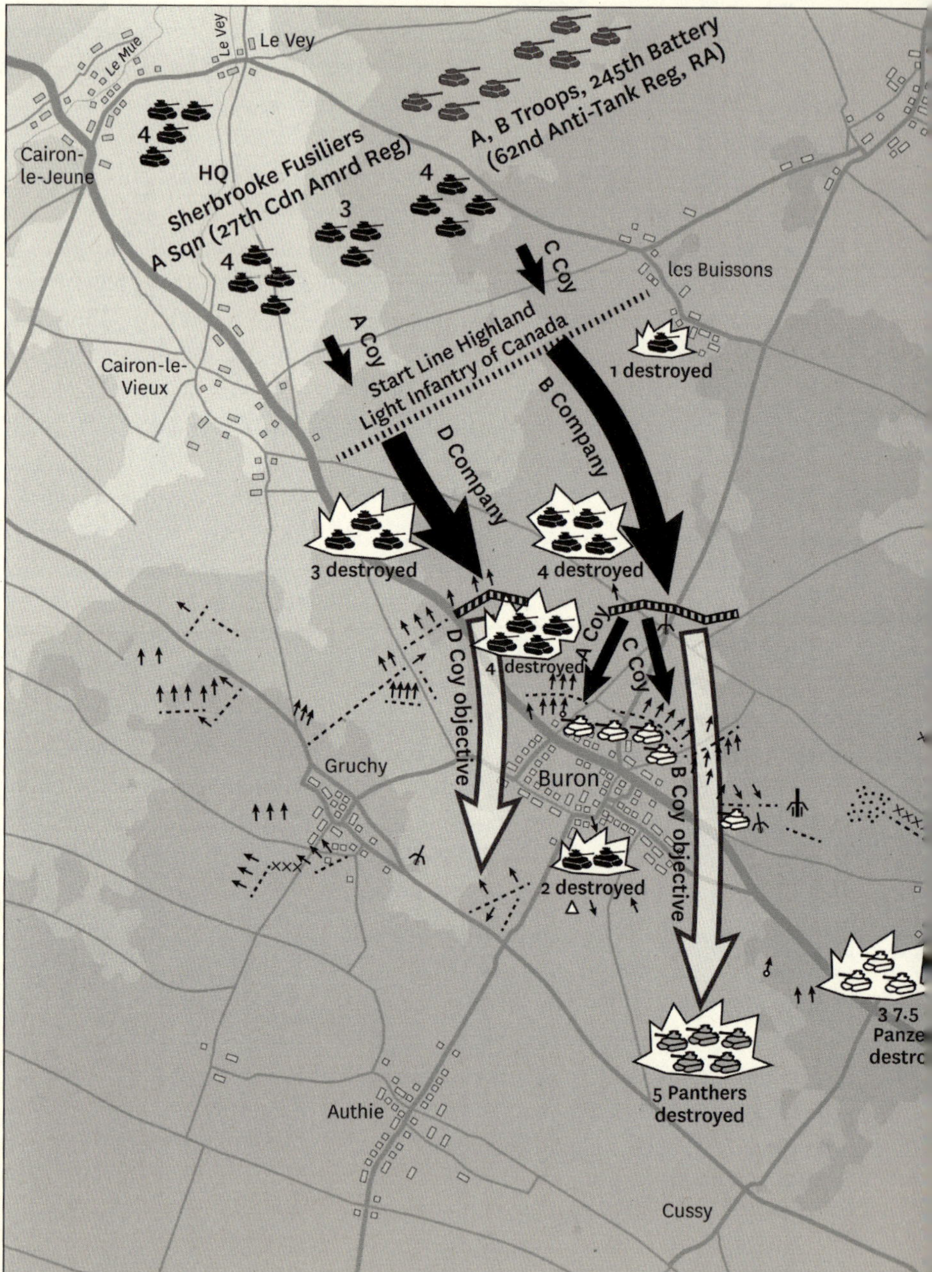
Le Mue
Le Vey
Le Vey
Cairon-le-Jeune
HQ
Sherbrooke Fusiliers
A Sqn (27th Cdn Amrd Reg)
A, B Troops, 245th Battery
(62nd Anti-Tank Reg, RA)
4
3
4
4
C Coy
A Coy
les Buissons
Start Line Highland
Light Infantry of Canada
1 destroyed
Cairon-le-Vieux
B Company
D Company
3 destroyed
4 destroyed
4 destroyed
A Coy
C Coy
D Coy objective
B Coy objective
Gruchy
Buron
2 destroyed
5 Panthers destroyed
Authie
Cussy

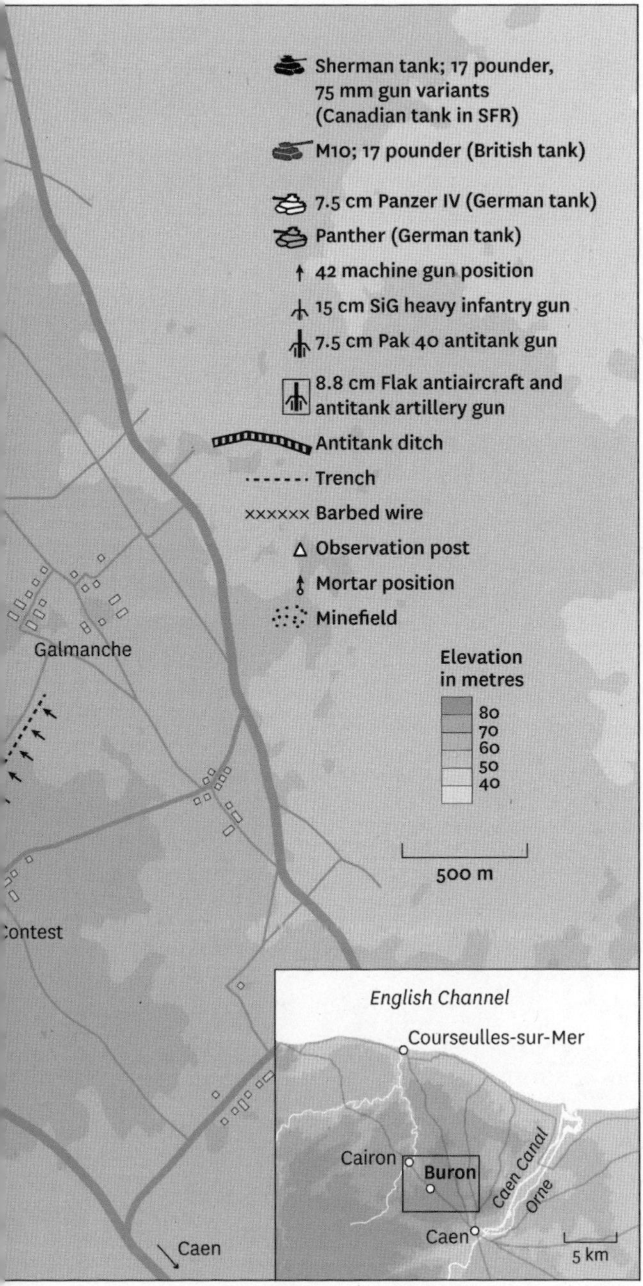

Figure 4.2
Assault on Buron, Operation Charnwood, 8 July 1944. This is an example of a successful Canadian infantry assault supported by armour and artillery assets during the Normandy Campaign.
Source: Barbe, *Charnwood,* 189.

What remained of the companies were driven back to their start lines. Canadian battle casualties in this action were heavy – 139 men.[32] Attacks were more likely to succeed if an assault force of superior numbers could quickly break into the enemy's trench system while the German infantry were suppressed by indirect and direct fire. Using close-quarter techniques, the attacking force would then either destroy the enemy or force them to surrender.

For these infantry tactics to succeed, it certainly helped to have the most advanced weapons and armoured battlefield transport. The latter was crucial for getting an infantry company or platoon onto its objective quickly if it was under fire. But the Canadian Army was weak in this area. Infantry battalions were largely transported around their areas of operation by military-pattern Ford and Chevrolet trucks. In their assembly areas, they debussed and mated up with armour or other supporting assets. They then walked to the start line or line of departure for the assault. At the prescribed time, or "H-hour," they commenced the advance to contact with the enemy. While the Universal (Bren Gun) Carrier platoon rode along and other carriers took the 6-pounder antitank and mortar platoons into battle, the remainder of the battalion was on foot. An infantry company could ride on a tank squadron occasionally, but most of the time they either marched or were trucked along hard-pack roads to their assembly areas. If the battalion was manning the front lines in defensive positions, the carriers and the trucks would be deployed far to the rear of the position.

While Canadian infantry and reconnaissance regiments used their Universal tracked carriers to good effect, the vehicles were small and not designed to carry a fully armed section of infantry into battle.[33] Canadian dismounted infantry regiments did not have the equivalent of a machine gun–armed American White M3 or German SPW 251 half-track armoured personnel carrier. These carriers could carry an infantry section with all its weapons. In summer 1944, the two motor battalions of the 4th and 5th Canadian Armoured Brigades were equipped as such, but only to allow them to follow a rapid armoured advance. These vehicles were limited in their cross-country capability, and having an open top, they offered poor protection from artillery air bursts and sustained heavy machine-gun fire. In the way of positive attributes, half-tracks could provide fire support, increased speed, and some protection to infantry while travelling to the objective. Similar to what occurred during the First World War, Canadian infantry took heavy casualties during their dismounted approach to the objective. What was needed was something that could transport over any terrain while providing armour protection against mortar shrapnel, machine-gun bullets, and near misses from artillery.[34]

A capable infantry-fighting vehicle did not exist in the Canadian inventory until August 1944's Operation Totalize, when a number of Kangaroos (modified Priest 105 mm self-propelled artillery with the guns removed and armour plate added) were made operational. The mounted infantry battalions, which rode into battle using the Kangaroo armoured personnel carriers during Operation Totalize, suffered 63 casualties in comparison to the 260 suffered by dismounted battalions.[35] Because of this success, the 1st Canadian Armoured Personnel Carrier Regiment was formed, frequently used, and expanded.[36] Once the Priest armoured personnel carriers were destroyed or worn out, obsolete Canadian Ram tanks without turrets were utilized. But their numbers were limited, and the Kangaroo regiment was shuffled from battalion to battalion, often in support of British infantry. In December 1944, the CIC's dismounted regiments were still equipped with a single platoon of Universal Carriers per regiment. During the same period, the two motor battalions of the armoured brigades had just fifty-three armoured 15-cwt C15TA trucks per battalion, having exchanged the M3 White half-tracks. As of November 1944, there were only two squadrons of fifty-three Kangaroos each in the 1st Canadian Armoured Personnel Carrier Regiment.[37] These desperately needed carriers were not even fully subordinated to Canadian command, being part of the 79th British Armoured Division.

From fall 1944 onward, the Universal Wasp II flamethrower carrier supplemented the Kangaroo on the battlefield. This fearsome weapon was the flame-throwing version of the tracked Universal Carrier. It could reduce the enemy's infantry positions quickly by killing defenders or forcing them to withdraw. Production challenges encountered in creating an effective three-man vehicle meant that there were virtually none available for the June and July 1944 battles in Normandy. As of 31 August 1944, the Canadian Army in northwest Europe boasted one on strength while its formation's war establishments were authorized a total of 132.[38]

As Table 4.1 illustrates, infantry weapons varied in quality and performance in both the Allied and German forces. Some Anglo-Canadian weapons were not cutting-edge, and this shortcoming arguably influenced the number of casualties. Infantry section Bren light machine guns with 30-round magazines were no equivalent in the sustained fire role of a belt-fed machine gun that fired 200-round belts. To protect the light machine gun, riflemen also needed adequate arms. While the Mark 4 Lee-Enfield bolt action rifle was reliable, its rate of fire was not high. The Sten submachine gun was poorly engineered and cheaply made in comparison to the American Thompson or German 9 mm MP 40 submachine guns. Having the proper weapons to conduct close-quarter fighting at one hundred metres or less was essential. Advancing against a German defender with multiple MG 42 machine guns was a challenging situation. Unless tanks, Wasp II flamethrower carriers, or the heavier British Vickers .303 water-cooled machine guns were brought up, the assault could bog down. If the assault stalled, the chances of casualties multiplied.

German defensive efforts focused on the destruction of dismounted Canadian infantry. As a result, the bulk of Canadian infantry casualties occurred during these types of assaults or when defending against an immediate German counterattack. While harassing mortar or artillery fire caused a few casualties each day, the Germans saved the majority of their artillery resources to repulse Canadian attacks. Casualties often increased rapidly in a very short period of time because of German indirect fire weapons. Since Canadian attacks were usually infantry-led and supported by armour and antitank forces, the infantry nearly always bore the brunt of massed German defensive fires. The Germans realized that if the infantry were beaten back, any armour present would withdraw, being naked without infantry support. If the Canadian Army was conducting offensive operations, an infantry regiment might see four to five days of intensive offensive combat during a thirty-day period. The remainder of the time would be spent patrolling, conducting training, or in defensive positions. Casualties during these inactive phases would be light due to the Germans' inability to launch major offensive operations after August 1944.[39]

Though Canadian armour and antitank forces took a subordinate role in offensive operations, it was important to coordinate them with infantry and artillery prior to battle to ensure their effective participation. Examples from Normandy illustrate that the failure to accomplish this task invited disaster. Attempting to keep in contact with the enemy on 5 August, the Royal Highland Regiment of Canada (the Black Watch) advanced on the village of May-sur-Orne without enough tank and artillery support. On reaching the objective, it suffered heavy casualties from German mortar, machine gun, and tank fire. The officer commanding "A" Company was killed, and his company took heavy losses.[40] The battalion then withdrew back to its start point, St. André-sur-Orne. This action came directly on the heels of a 25 July reverse on Verrières Ridge, which decimated the regiment. Casualties totalled just over three hundred.[41]

In this previous action, the battalion had also attacked without intimate armoured support, attempting to cross a ridgeline devoid of cover. Preparatory artillery fire did not neutralize the defences at the summit, which came to life and annihilated the attackers. Battle casualties could total over two hundred personnel in one day, as evidenced by the Black Watch's experience at May-sur-Orne.[42] Its losses on 25 July were almost exclusively confined to its four

Table 4.1

Infantry small arms, June–August 1944

Army	Type	Make or model	Calibre (mm/inch)	Effective range (m)	Capacity/belt or magazine	Rate of fire (rpms)
American	Rifle	M1 Garand	.30–06	457	clip	40–50
American	Submachine	M1A1 Thompson	.45	150	20 rd magazine	625
American	Light machine	M1918A2 BAR	.30–06	1,300	20 rd magazine	500–650
Anglo–Canadian	Rifle	No. 4 Lee-Enfield	.303	500	10 rd magazine	20–30
Anglo–Canadian	Submachine	Mk V Sten	9	100	32 rd magazine	500–600
Anglo–Canadian	Light machine	Mk 2 Bren	.303	550	30 rd magazine	500–520
German	Rifle	Kar 98K	7.92	500	5 rd magazine	15
German	Submachine	MP 40	9	100–200	32 rd magazine	500–550
German	Light machine	MG 42	7.92	200–2,000	250 rd belt	1,200

Source: Dear and Foot, *The Oxford Companion to the Second World War*, 1014–16.

forward infantry line companies. Because these companies' experienced, highly trained, and effective infantry platoons were the real fighting power of the unit, the Black Watch's combat effectiveness in the immediate aftermath was reduced to nothing. Inexperienced replacements did not perform at the same level as their predecessors, so the Black Watch could not regain its previous combat effectiveness for some time.

It was dangerous for any combat arms unit to launch a new operation after receiving a large number of new replacements. If new personnel were not integrated with appropriate refresher training, heavy losses could occur. This is what befell the Black Watch on 5 August, during its second failed operation at May-sur-Orne. This action involved many new replacement personnel who had not had time to acclimatize themselves, and there was no experienced leadership at the senior noncommissioned officer level.[43] Experienced leadership was vital in that it facilitated refresher training once replacement soldiers arrived at the front. Having a refresher in field craft and effective combat leadership at the ten-man infantry section level was important to overall unit performance and for ensuring that new soldiers did not quickly become casualties.[44]

It was beneficial to slowly acclimatize new personnel to front-line conditions, regardless of the combat arm. Upon arrival, a new infantry replacement would not know any of his fellow platoon members or his section commander. To function as a well-oiled machine in combat, each section member had to possess a certain confidence in his fellow soldiers and his weapons. This came through training and shared experiences, the most valuable but most dangerous being combat itself. And it needed to happen as soon as possible because of the often immediate need to thrust soldiers back into action. However, military necessity and a lack of forces meant this training often did not occur.

Failure to accomplish successful integration could result in poor combat performance and increased casualties within the ranks of the new personnel, especially in the infantry. While a shortage of infantry and constant high-intensity operations from August to November hindered the infantry replacements' ability to integrate, a period of inactivity in winter 1944–45 allowed for unit training and gradual integration.

The US Army's approach to integrating new personnel into infantry units had had negative results from 1943 to 1944. Replacements were thrown into combat with little chance of getting to know their fellow squad members or conduct realistic training prior to reaching the front line. Although it helped maintaining the strength of front-line units, this practice reduced the combat effectiveness of individual companies within American infantry battalions. In fall 1944, this approach changed: new replacements were received in divisional replacement camps that gave refresher training.[45] They were then posted to companies that were out of the front line, giving them additional time to acclimatize themselves.

The re-emergence of the supremacy of concentrated artillery, in which the British Empire had achieved mastery during the First World War, was instrumental in improving the battlefield performance of the British Commonwealth armies in the last years of the Second World War. From the onset, the role of artillery in the Second World War was decisive. It was an artillery war first and foremost, with half of all combat casualties resulting from indirect fire.[46] In the First World War and the interwar period, huge leaps in the technological development of artillery weapons had occurred. Shells, fuses, and the chemistry of propellants had all advanced. The role of artillery in all armies during the Second World War was a basic one: to fire munitions beyond the range and power of the infantry and armoured units' direct-fire weapons.

Following the British defeat in France in 1940, a decentralization of artillery command and control had occurred. During 1940–41, this change resulted in an increased allotment of artillery at the division and brigade level, allowing more artillery to be available to divisional and brigade commanders during a fluid, mobile battle, similar to the German model. British failures in North Africa showed that this dilution of artillery force made it a nonunified organization whose power could not be massed for a serious blow against enemy attacks or defensive positions.[47]

This battlefield reality led to an urgent reorganization of the British Royal Regiment of Artillery, commonly known as the Royal Artillery. This parent organization encompassed all British Army artillery regiments. Command structures such as Divisional Commander Royal Artillery and Corps Commander Corps Royal Artillery were reintroduced, and tactical groupings such as the corps-level Army Group Royal Artillery (AGRA) were reformed. Sophisticated communication nets and synchronized tactics were developed that were superior to anything fielded by the German Army and amazingly destructive.[48]

British Royal Artillery field artillery regiments that used the ubiquitous Ordnance QF 25-pounder howitzer took on two major roles. The first was to engage targets of opportunity with concentrated fire. The second was to carry out fire plans of predicted fire, which were highly sophisticated. One tactic was moving fire, utilizing a creeping or standing barrage, which provided a barrier between attacking infantry and supporting armoured units and the defensive positions of the enemy.[49] Furthermore, all Commonwealth artillery units were entirely mechanized, being either towed or self-propelled, a factor that provided exceptional mobility on the battlefield.[50] Forward observation officers attached to armoured and infantry regiments would direct fire using either tracked Universal Carriers equipped with radios or land lines that connected their positions to the field artillery batteries. By 1943, with a seemingly bottomless supply of ammunition at their fingertips, field artillery regiments could simply batter and suppress German positions with around-the-clock fire plans prior to an assault.

In a departure from the tank-dominated tactics of 1941–42, which often led to failure in the desert war, the British began to see concentrated artillery as essential to all operations, including the use of antitank weapons and all armoured fighting vehicles that came under the artillery arm.[51] If manoeuvring German armour could be dashed against these gun lines, their strength could be whittled away to nothing. German defensive positions that needed to be captured would then be reduced by methodical and concentrated artillery fire, allowing the infantry and supporting armour to invest them. Should the Germans mount a counterattack, these same resources would be at the ready to beat it back, supported this time with newly deployed towed 6- and 17-pounder antitank guns on any captured objectives. Other direct-fire antitank guns were mounted on self-propelled chassis, such as the 3-inch SPM M10 (US Lend-Lease M10 tank destroyer). Combined, indirect and direct Royal Artillery assets would launch such devastating fires on the attacking German infantry and armoured forces that they would have to withdraw or be decimated. As a result, the German counterattack on an attacking British combined arms battlegroup began to be seen not as a cause for alarm but as an opportunity.

Because of these new artillery-centred tactics, British combined arms battlegroups became much more powerful and difficult to defeat. They supported indirect-fire artillery assets and sought to defeat the enemy through attritional means.[52] But there was a price to this operational method: units could only travel at the speed of their infantry formations. Although the British Eighth Army did not attack in a blitzkrieg-type manner, effectively encircling and destroying Rommel's retreating Afrika Korps following its defeat at El Alamein in November 1942, its forces did not suffer any reverses or excessive losses. Although the British had tried to match Germany's rapid armoured tactics earlier in the desert war, they largely abandoned this operational method for a more set-piece–style operations.

Reforms in the Royal Artillery were mirrored within the Royal Canadian Artillery. In 1944, during training exercises in Great Britain, an attacking Canadian division or brigade eschewed any surprise manoeuvres utilizing infantry or armour. Their operational planning corresponded to strict timetables supplied by the divisional or corps RCA fire plan. Lieutenant-General Guy Simonds, 2nd Canadian Corps commander, was himself an artillery officer and often worked out the major features of operational plans in the solitary workspace of his command caravan. He focused on artillery and aerial bombardment as factors on which large operational plans often revolved.[53] As shown in Figure 4.3, Anglo-Canadian artillery-supported operations were extremely sophisticated, well planned, and tied to a strict time figure. Illustrating the barrage fire plan for Operation Veritable, which occurred in February 1945, each line in the figure is a measurement of how far the barrage would lift and move forward after a timed interval. Canadian artillery-centred operational planning was dependent on weight being added in the form of heavier British medium Royal Artillery regiments. In Normandy, the First Canadian Army had at its disposal three medium (5.5-inch) artillery regiments grouped in the 2nd Canadian Army Group Royal Artillery (AGRA). If more force was required, British assets would have to be brought in. This is not to say that the 25-pounder divisional field regiments were inadequate, but larger assets and more of them would certainly increase the odds of success.[54]

After August 1944, the lack of German artillery counterbattery capability, paired with ineffective German Luftwaffe ground attack assets, allowed RCA artillery units to operate with impunity. The enemy's ability to attack and destroy their positions was drastically reduced. Given their location on the battlefield, artillery units were rarely the target for mortar fire in the way infantry units were. Properly deployed and with their fire adjusted, RCA medium and field artillery regiments could pound away at enemy positions with little threat to themselves. This allowed for an excellent ratio of damage done to the enemy versus casualties suffered by these units.[55] During April 1945, the 1st Field Regiment, Royal Canadian Horse Artillery, suffered ten battle and ten nonbattle casualties. This was a small number of losses considering the ferocious bombardments this unit unleashed on the enemy. German forces were simply reduced to digging in deeper, as there was no other defence against the devastating and continuous artillery strikes.[56]

Employment of RCA artillery assets was perceived by the Canadian military leaders as an essential building block of any feasible operational plan in northwest Europe. This combat arm was the most effective tool to attain results while

Figure 4.3

Barrage fire plan, Operation Veritable, 8 February 1945. This fire plan was an evolution of the First World War's moving barrage.

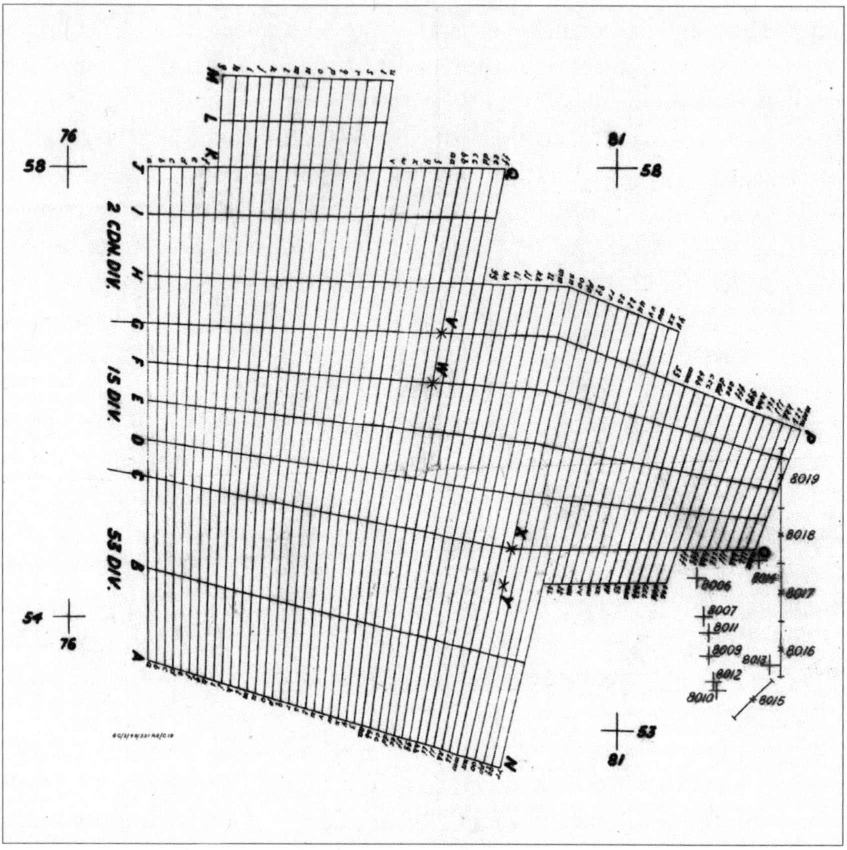

Source: LAC, RG 24, vol. 14,319, "2nd Canadian Army Group Royal Artillery, RCA, War Diary," February 1945.

keeping casualties to a minimum. It could simultaneously destroy enemy fortifications and impede all observed battlefield movement within the combat zone. Its flexibility, speed, and power enabled infantry, antitank, and armoured units to gain their objectives and hold them against enemy counterattack.[57]

The employment of "Uncle," "Victor," "Yoke," and "Mike" fire-plan tactics meant military leaders could coordinate increasing levels of massed firepower for a single purpose in a short amount of time. The Royal Artillery had many different tactics to mass fire during the late war period. A Mike target was a concentration of fire by all guns in an artillery regiment, an Uncle target was a concentration of fire by a division, a Victor target was a concentration by an entire corps, and a Yoke target involved fire by a complete AGRA.[58] Not to be forgotten is the "Stonk" (standard regimental concentration), a brief and sudden bombardment, often used on targets of opportunity or for defensive purposes.[59] This defensive fire concentration, which involved two batteries of a regiment firing on assigned map squares and a third battery superimposed on these squares, was absolutely devastating. It could also be delivered quickly. An RCA field artillery regiment could respond to a call for fire within three minutes, and a corps-level grouping of Anglo-Canadian artillery units (Army Group Royal Artillery) could respond in less than thirty minutes.[60]

Air support is an important factor to consider when reviewing Canadian military operations in northwest Europe. RAF 83 Group and later RAF 84 Group, composite groups of the 2nd Tactical Air Force of the Royal Air Force (RAF), were successful at providing tactical air support for the First Canadian Army in the last year of the war. German logistical and operational movement during daylight hours was terribly inhibited. Air support from the RAF and the Royal Canadian Air Force (RCAF) was also crucial for softening up German defensive positions. The breaching of Dutch dikes by air power was critical to flooding the German Scheldt defences in September and October 1944, making the conquering of this area easier in later battles.

By fall 1944, a sophisticated system for providing tactical on-call air support to First Canadian Army operations was in place.[61] RAF 84 Group – the composite group of Polish, Norwegian, British, and other tactical fighter squadrons flying Spitfire, Typhoon, and Tempest fighters – had its headquarters adjacent to the those of the First Canadian Army. At meetings held the night before an operation, army headquarters staff met with 84 Group staff in a joint conference. The senior representatives of each service discussed the need for air support, reviewed weather reports and other pertinent data, and made decisions about what support would be allocated where and to which operations. On the front lines, an RAF Air Support Squadron Unit and its subordinate forward control pilots would liaise with Canadian Army brigade or battalion headquarters to make on-the-spot decisions regarding the direction of air power assets during the course of the operation.[62]

The ever-present Typhoon fighter bomber was a great asset, not for its rocket- or bomb-carrying capability but for its four 20 mm automatic, wing-mounted cannons. It was these cannons that struck the rear decks of German armour in

Normandy, putting tanks out of action. Soft targets such as trucks and cars could be destroyed, sapping the enemy's morale and ability to move openly in column on roadways in daylight. The German infantry formations were impotent against these attacks, and Canadian morale was boosted greatly by seeing the impact of rockets, bombs, and cannon fire.

The designated role of the RAF's 2nd Tactical Air Force was to fight the air battle and support the 21st Army Group by means of aerial reconnaissance and ground attack.[63] For this purpose, the RAF composite group headquarters and the army headquarters met regularly to discuss support for operations. However, the ties between the RAF, RCAF, and Canadian Army in northwest Europe were not particularly strong. A certain amount of animosity existed between the services regarding the role and utilization of tactical aircraft in support of the ground troops on offensive operations. Air-ground cooperation in the form of an established doctrine was not an institutionalized practice as it is in the modern Canadian Army. Because of this, the potential effectiveness of tactical airpower in support of Canadian ground operations was never reached. If a ground controller was present, this role was usually taken on by a RAF Air Support Signal Unit. These units were RAF-controlled and strictly retained control of RAF and RCAF air activity, regardless of what the Canadian Army wanted or needed.[64]

The practice of embedding RAF and RCAF ground controllers in a manner similar to the artillery forward observation officer in an infantry battalion was accomplished on a limited scale with the use of CAC "contact cars" from September 1944 onward.[65] These were CAC armoured vehicles manned by RCAF and RAF ground signallers with a CAC crew commander and driver. These vehicles were in close contact with the most forward infantry or armoured tactical headquarters but were still subordinate to the Air Support Signal Unit with regard to directing RAF or RCAF ground-attack sorties. Direct communication with air assets by Canadian Army personnel, which could have enhanced the quality of air support, was lacking.[66] Also, terrible instances of fratricide occurred when large numbers of RAF, RCAF, and US Army Air Force four-engined strategic bombers were utilized to destroy in-depth German defences. The danger of this occurring was not something that the Canadian Army recognized or had trained for in the months leading up to Operation Overlord. Reduction of the risk of short bombing and target misidentification was tackled in an ad hoc manner by the Canadian Army as the situation demanded.[67] The Canadian Army's lack of influence in air-support matters offset the excellent support that the RAF and RCAF provided on the battlefield. This led to continued misunderstandings and frustration over friendly fire incidents and cancelled ground-support missions until the end of hostilities.[68]

As a result of combining the combat arms and air support in a dynamic manner, the Canadian Army (Active) in northwest Europe achieved victory during the majority of its offensive operations. By seeking to achieve only limited objectives, aided usually by overpowering air and artillery support, it tried to never push the assaulting forces past their capabilities. At the same time, it took maximum advantage of opportunities to inflict heavy losses on the enemy. The best example of this was the aforementioned defeat of the German 25th SS Panzer Grenadier Regiment in the villages of Buron, Authie, Cussy, and Gruchy, Normandy, on 8 July.[69] In this action, part of Operation Charnwood, the 3rd Canadian Infantry Division's infantry units, along with supporting arms, overran fortified German defences in both villages, attaining all their objectives. They then defeated a powerful German armoured counterattack, inflicting even more casualties on the enemy. This was an impressive victory that reflected an improved level of tactical effectiveness as a result of combat experience gained in June. It was even more impressive considering that the Canadian forces utilized a combined arms method of fighting that had not been perfected during training in the United Kingdom.

Large-scale combined arms training in the United Kingdom for operations in northwest Europe was a challenge. The process of equipping the 2nd Canadian Corps divisions with their full equipment establishments was slow. In March 1944, the 4th Canadian Armoured Division and 2nd Canadian Infantry Division were deemed nonoperational because they had not received enough weapons and vehicles.[70] At this stage, it was critical for both formations to be fully equipped and involved in constant, realistic, and intensive combined arms field exercises.[71] Exercises in tank-infantry cooperation for some Canadian divisions in the United Kingdom were only sporadic in fall 1943.[72] In northwest Europe, the utilization of RCA forward observation officers to call down timely artillery support was necessary to consistently defeat German counterattacks.[73] The skill of summoning and maintaining artillery support had not been perfected in infantry and armoured regiments despite the long period of time spent training in the United Kingdom from 1940 to 1944. To make matters worse, Canadian D-Day assault formations had focused training solely on the one-day amphibious assault. They were in as bad shape as the follow-on divisions regarding combined arms training.

While the RCA field artillery regiments were equipped with superb weapons, the CAC and CIC were not. While it would have been advantageous for the

Canadian Army to increase allotments of certain types of vehicles or weapons systems, or more effective variants, it had limited ability to influence these matters. The British Army was largely in control of what and how much the First Canadian Army received in northwest Europe, and the 21st Army Group had strict regulations on what would be contained in the establishment of each type of combat arms regiment. The British argument for this approach was that uniformity in unit establishment was essential to the proper reinforcement of personnel and the maintenance of equipment inventories. While the minute details of these unit establishments were modified on a monthly basis, general orders enforced these changes on all units of the same type within the 21st Army Group. An example of the enforcement of these regulations was the rapid reorganization of arriving Canadian formations from Italy in 1945 to conform with the standards in effect.[74]

Commonwealth nations such as Canada, New Zealand, and Australia were dependent on Great Britain or the United States for the design of their most advanced weapons systems.[75] There were exceptions, of course, such as the Canadian-produced Sexton 25-pounder self-propelled gun, but for the most part their vehicles and weapons were British or of US origin. While it was desirable to have more Wasp Mk II flamethrower Universal Carriers, Ram Kangaroo armoured personnel carriers, and larger numbers of advanced small arms, the availability of these items was limited, and it took time for these items to reach the front. While Canadian units certainly wanted better technology and more of it, so did every other Commonwealth army.

Canadian armoured-vehicle and heavy-weapons-systems losses resulted in a similar reduction in unit combat effectiveness, regardless of how quick a replacement piece of equipment was allocated. Given the relative abundance of Allied armoured vehicles and heavy weapons in comparison to limited numbers of replacement infantry personnel, units were rarely short of equipment. But how effectively heavy weapons systems such as tanks and artillery pieces were used depended on the team performance of the crews operating them. For example, if a tank was knocked out, usually one or two crew members would be lost. Given the tight-knit camaraderie of tank crews, a reduction of combat effectiveness would be expected until new members were acclimatized to combat conditions and the leadership of their tank commander. For the Canadian Army after Normandy, losses of artillery pieces were rare because of the German Army's inability to engage in sustained counterbattery fire or air strikes. As was the case with US artillery crews, the combat effectiveness of the RCA artillery regiments increased over time.[76] Their team performance increased with experience, and artillery battery cohesion was not destroyed by heavy losses and the constant need to integrate and train new personnel.

Compounding these disadvantages was the lack of recent combat experience within the divisions about to be deployed to northwest Europe. Lessons learned from Italy and Sicily in the form of reports on operations and enemy tactics were not passed down rapidly or effectively to British-based Canadian units in early 1944.[77] Once in Normandy, the British practice of keeping units forward did not allow Canadian regiments to be easily removed from the line for retraining in the field. Mated with the erosion of Canadian infantry strength in the summer of 1944 was the arrival of inexperienced remustered replacements. These factors led to occasional performance issues in the fall.[78] Problematically, experienced Canadian personnel remained in Italy while green units were used in Normandy.[79] When employed against powerful German units with advanced weapons and veteran officers, losses were often heavy.

Despite initial operational challenges during June and August, Canadian formations had achieved sufficient combat experience to allow offensive performance levels to rise in September.[80] When an all-arms combat team well versed in assault tactics was employed with heavy artillery support, good results could be achieved. Infantry platoons with intimate armoured support assaulted the objective while other tanks suppressed the enemy in a firebase role. The tanks would move at an infantry pace, following the artillery barrage and using their machine guns to suppress the enemy. Supplementary artillery tactics accompanied the rolling barrage, such as surprise concentrations, air bursts, and bombardments of all suspected armoured assembly areas and antitank positions. Intensive counterbattery fire was placed simultaneously on all suspected enemy artillery and mortar positions. Once the assault force reached the objective, the tanks could churn up the trenches by turning on their tracks and firing directly into bunkers and dugouts. They would knock out German antitank guns and machine-gun positions, protecting the infantry until they were literally on top of the objective. At this point, the tanks were vulnerable to enemy infantry antitank teams, so friendly infantry had to be close at hand. All gains would immediately be fortified by the infantry and their supporting arms, as the German counterthrust would be expected at any moment. This was a second victory waiting to happen, as the new defenders would crush the German counterattack and inflict heavy casualties.

Canadian Army strategy in northwest Europe was not focused on being constantly on the offensive. The transition phase between offensive operations was defensive: the focus was on creating "fortress" and "firm base" positions.

In both Italy and northwest Europe, once an objective was captured, an evolved version of First World War "bite and hold" tactics was utilized. Antitank, armoured, and mortar assets were rushed in to help to create an infantry battalion or brigade "fortress."[81] In Normandy, there was initially a real risk that powerful German formations would attack and liquidate the Allied beachhead. It was onto these fortresses that the German land forces were enticed to shatter themselves in failed counterattacks. This was an opportunity for Canadian and British artillery forces to expend the full weight of their defensive fires on the enemy with coordinated Mike and Uncle targets. These RA and RCA tactics utilized massive amounts of on-call firepower on a point or area target, tactics that largely pushed the German 12th SS Panzer Division Hitlerjugend onto the defensive in June 1944, crushing its counterattacks and attempts to gain the initiative.[82] This practice was successful in destroying German counterattacks in June but with the caveat that it led to static warfare. Periods of inactivity when the Allies were between offensive operations in Normandy gave the Germans time to fortify in-depth defensive zones that could be conquered only with major losses. They were so strong, in fact, that the Allies turned to massive aerial and naval bombardments, using four-engine bombers and the guns of battleships on occasion.[83]

Following the collapse of the German front in Normandy due to attrition, from September 1944 to May 1945, the Canadian Army was primarily infantry oriented. Infantry-led offensive operations were tied to elaborate artillery fire plans designed to annihilate dug-in German defenders. While there were some operations that were led by armour, set-piece attacks by infantry units with supporting arms and extensive artillery support were the standard. To be fair, the flooded Dutch polders and peninsulas of the Scheldt Estuary restricted armour movement terribly. Individual Canadian armour squadrons were assigned to support attacking infantry battalions rather than operating together in regimental strength. Limited objectives were bitten off and defended in a hold manner until Canadian units were ready for the next bite. The defensive hold was supported by tanks, mortars, and antitank guns, which were hurried onto the objective to stave off the inevitable German counterattack. The destruction of the enemy by encircling mechanized pincer movements was not envisaged, and the terrain rarely allowed for it. This methodical approach by Anglo-Canadian formations led to repeated set-piece operations, even against poor-quality German forces during the last two months of the war. For example, even though German defences on the IJssel River in April 1945 were weak, lengthy preparations were made for attacking them.[84]

Anglo-Canadian doctrine in northwest Europe was the opposite of tactics being used on the eastern front in 1944 and 1945. In this theatre, armour dominated the attack, and Red Army infantry often specialized in riding on the engine decks of the Russian T34 tanks. The Soviet commanders conducted the deep armoured battle, one of extreme penetration and manoeuvre based on available logistics, opportunities, and attacking the enemy at its weakest point. Strong artillery fire was present on the eastern front but on a much smaller scale and between intervals, the guns taking a long time to catch up with the tanks.

On the Anglo-Canadian front, the opposite was true. Armour and infantry were always within reach of the guns, and a pattern of long-range mechanized manoeuvre warfare did not occur. Troop density in Normandy and the Netherlands stood in stark contrast to the eastern front. The limited size of the area of operations meant that movement was always observed by the enemy. These factors in Normandy severely limited the Canadian Army's ability to find a weak spot in German defences and achieve tactical surprise.[85] Periods of inactivity would allow each side to build defences in depth, making it difficult for the opposing force to achieve a breakthrough. Every factor was multiplied in an ongoing campaign of attrition, and artillery and armour resources from each side could quickly be brought to bear on the battle.

To summarize, Anglo-Canadian "bite and hold" tactics, with specific objectives allotted per infantry battalion, allowed the campaign to proceed at a slow, steady grind. This grind slowly defeated the Germans in Normandy and beyond with limited Canadian casualties. The casualties that were suffered were mainly in the infantry regiments, and they occurred during offensive operations. There were two main reasons for this situation. First, because of their role as the vanguard of the attack, infantry drew the most fire. Second, infantry were vulnerable to all types of German weaponry while they advanced in open ground. Noninfantry RCA and CAC regiments suffered significantly fewer casualties because of their role, tactics, position on the battlefield, and because of the enemy's ability to attack them.

The Canadian Army quickly learned to maximize it strengths and minimize its weaknesses while in combat. Following initial challenges in Normandy in June and July 1944, necessary modifications were made to place greater emphasis on indirect firepower and combined arms tactics. Armour would take on a reduced role and operate within the limits of the infantry and artillery units. Once these modifications were made, infantry-led combined arms teams executed assaults with better cooperation and achieving improved results. In adopting this method, the Canadian Army sacrificed armoured manoeuvre in return for the set-piece limited attack with overpowering indirect fire support. Weakened German formations in late 1944 and spring 1945 had limited assets in which to defeat these assaults. Devastating firepower from the RCA, operating with impunity, reduced resistance and crushed all German counterattacks.[86] Canadian infantry with plentiful armoured and antitank support would then capture and consolidate their objectives, taking an acceptable number of casualties on average in the process.[87]

5
Formations and Their Units

DURING THE COURSE of the campaign, the Canadian Army fielded three infantry divisions, two armoured divisions, two independent armoured brigades, two corps-level artillery groupings, and over a dozen independent units held at the corps and army level. The personnel, vehicles, and equipment that these regiments were authorized are listed in Appendix 1.

Created from both permanent force regiments and militia units, the 1st Canadian Infantry Division had been authorized to begin forming soon after hostilities broke out in September 1939. Deployed to the United Kingdom later that year, large parts of the division were not properly equipped or combat ready. In June 1940, the 1st Canadian Infantry Brigade arrived in France but was evacuated shortly afterward as the British position became hopeless.[1] Elements of the 2nd Canadian Infantry Brigade took part in Operation Gauntlet, from 25 August to 3 September 1941, and successfully denied German occupation forces coal and weather reports from the island of Spitzbergen, located close to the Arctic Circle.[2] Some personnel were detached to serve in the British First Army in 1943, gaining valuable experience in the final fighting in North Africa.[3] From late 1941 until mid-1943, the division performed garrison duties and conducted training exercises. From 1943 to early 1945, it fought in Italy as part of the British Eighth Army, forming part of the 1st Canadian Corps. In January 1945, the entire corps began a planned redeployment to northwest Europe. The overall aim of Operation Goldflake was uniting the corps with the First Canadian Army. The 1st Canadian Infantry Division began the move to Belgium in late February 1945, travelling by sea from Livorno, Italy, to Marseilles, France.[4] From there, it moved north by road through France's Rhone Valley. It took until late March 1945 to reorganize, re-equip, and concentrate the infantry brigades and other divisional units.[5]

As of April 1945, the division's commanding officer was Major-General H.W. Foster. The division comprised the 1st, 2nd, and 3rd Canadian Infantry Brigades. The 1st Canadian Infantry Brigade consisted of the Royal Canadian Regiment, the Hastings and Prince Edward Regiment, and the 48th Highlanders of Canada. The 2nd Canadian Infantry Brigade consisted of the Princess Patricia's Light Infantry, the Seaforth Highlanders of Canada and the Loyal Edmonton

Regiment. The 3rd Canadian Infantry Brigade consisted of the Royal 22nd Regiment, the West Nova Scotia Regiment, and the Carleton and York Regiment. Divisional troops consisted of the 4th Canadian Reconnaissance Regiment (4th Princess Louise Dragoon Guards) and the Saskatchewan Light Infantry (Machine Gun). The reconnaissance regiment had been converted to an infantry regiment during its service in Italy in 1944 and was assigned to the 12th Canadian Infantry Brigade, part of the 5th Canadian Armoured Division. This brigade was disbanded because all Canadian formations joining 21st Army Group in northwest Europe had to conform to established divisional standards for resupply and logistics. Thus, on its arrival, the regiment was ordered to reconvert back to a reconnaissance regiment. It carried out this task throughout April 1945 and was not committed to operations. Divisional artillery units consisted of the 2nd and 3rd Field Regiments (RCA), the 1st Field Regiment Royal Canadian Horse Artillery, the 1st Anti-Tank Regiment (RCA), and the 2nd Light Anti-Aircraft Regiment (RCA).[6]

Formed in May and June 1940, the 2nd Canadian Infantry Division was organized on regional lines from militia units located in Ontario, Quebec, and the Prairie provinces. Prior to 1942, the division saw limited action, conducting garrison duties in Iceland before being deployed to the United Kingdom. Two of its three brigades took part in the disastrous August 1942 raid on Dieppe, France, Operation Jubilee. The regiments involved suffered catastrophic losses and were completely rebuilt.[7] The division trained continuously throughout 1943 to spring 1944 in preparation for its upcoming role in the Allied invasion of the continent. It did not land on D-Day as part of the initial assault force, instead arriving during the first week of July 1944. With other Canadian formations, it formed part of the 2nd Canadian Corps.

As it commenced combat operations in Normandy, its commanding officer was Major-General Charles Foulkes. The main combat fighting components of the division were the 4th, 5th, and 6th Canadian Infantry Brigades. The 4th Canadian Infantry Brigade consisted of the Royal Regiment of Canada, the Royal Hamilton Light Infantry, and the Essex Scottish Regiment. The 5th Canadian Infantry Brigade's main components were the Royal Highland Regiment of Canada (the Black Watch), Le Régiment de Maisonneuve, and the Calgary Highlanders. The 6th Canadian Infantry Brigade was made up of Les Fusiliers Mont-Royal, the Queen's Own Cameron Highlanders of Canada, and the South Saskatchewan Regiment. Divisional units consisted of the 8th Canadian Reconnaissance Regiment (14th Canadian Hussars) and the Toronto Scottish (Machine Gun) Regiment. Artillery units consisted of the 4th, 5th, and 6th Field Regiments, the Royal Canadian Artillery, the 2nd Anti-Tank Regiment (RCA), and the 3rd

Light Anti-Aircraft Regiment (RCA).[8] A significant problem within the division was an initial lack of self-propelled antitank capability in the 2nd Anti-Tank Regiment. In contrast with the antitank regiment in the 3rd Canadian Infantry Division, it was not authorized any self-propelled antitank guns.[9] Taking into consideration future combat encounters with enemy armour in July 1944, the presence of these armoured fighting vehicles could have strengthened the division significantly.

The 3rd Canadian Infantry Division was activated in Canada in spring 1940. It spent the following year assembling its component brigades. The regimental units were drawn from the Prairie, central, and eastern provinces.[10] During the winter of 1940–41, one of its regiments, the Cameron Highlanders of Ottawa (Machine Gun), formed part of the Allied garrison in Iceland. Transported to the United Kingdom in fall 1941, the division embarked on a three-year period of training and further garrison duties. While the 2nd Canadian Infantry Division participated in the 1942 Dieppe Raid and the entire 1st Canadian Corps deployed to Italy in 1943–44, the 3rd Canadian Infantry Division remained in Britain. In July 1943, the division was designated as one of the amphibious assault formations for Operation Overlord.[11] As a result, its training focused on successfully assaulting the beaches and defending the initial lodgement. Arguably, this specialized training for a temporary role was conducted at the expense of offensive combined arms training to defeat German armoured formations after the landing.[12]

From 31 May 1944, the 3rd Canadian Infantry Division's commanding officer was Major-General Rodney Keller. Its main infantry formations were the 7th, 8th, and 9th Canadian Infantry Brigades.[13] The regiments of 7th Canadian Infantry Brigade were the Royal Winnipeg Rifles, the Regina Rifle Regiment, and the Canadian Scottish Regiment. The 8th Canadian Infantry Brigade consisted of the Queen's Own Rifles of Canada, Le Régiment de la Chaudière, and the North Shore Regiment. The 9th Canadian Infantry Brigade's was made up of the North Nova Scotia Highlanders, the Stormont, the Dundas and Glengarry Highlanders, and the Highland Light Infantry of Canada. Divisional field artillery units consisted of the 12th, 13th, and 14th Field Regiments (RCA). An additional field artillery regiment, the army-level 2nd Canadian Army Group Royal Artillery's (AGRA) 19th Army Field Regiment (RCA) was temporarily attached. This addition gave the division a total of four Canadian field artillery regiments, as well as other British Royal Artillery field and medium regiments temporarily attached for Operation Overlord.[14] Antitank and antiaircraft units consisted of the 4th Light Anti-Aircraft Regiment (RCA) and the 3rd Anti-Tank Regiment (RCA). Nonartillery divisional units were the 7th Canadian

Reconnaissance Regiment (the 17th Duke of York's Royal Canadian Hussars) and the Cameron Highlanders of Ottawa (Machine Gun).

The 4th Canadian Infantry Division was ordered to begin forming in spring 1940. Established from units located in central and western Canada, in early 1942 it was reorganized as an armoured division. Prior to its deployment overseas, its development was slowed by the diversion of some units to what would become the 5th Canadian Armoured Division. In fall 1942, the division was deployed to the United Kingdom and arrived in several convoys. Like the 3rd Canadian Infantry Division, it did not to take part in combat operations prior to its 1944 deployment to Normandy. Administrative and supply problems during winter 1942–43 caused some delays in equipping the division with armoured fighting vehicles and other pieces of equipment. These delays interrupted its training schedule, and the division did not conduct battalion-level exercises until fall of the latter year.[15] On the eve of its deployment to Normandy, in late July 1944, as part of the 2nd Canadian Corps, its commanding officer was Major-General George Kitching. The main combat formations within the division were the 4th Canadian Armoured Brigade and the 10th Canadian Infantry Brigade.[16] The armoured brigade was composed of the 28th Canadian Armoured Regiment (the British Columbia Regiment), the 21st Canadian Armoured Regiment (the Governor General's Foot Guards), and the 22nd Canadian Armoured Regiment (the Canadian Grenadier Guards). Its infantry component was the Lake Superior (Motor) Regiment. This last regiment was mechanized and equipped with M3 and M5 half-tracks so it could keep up with the tanks as motorized infantry.

The 10th Canadian Infantry Brigade was the dismounted infantry force of the division and close in composition to an infantry brigade within an infantry division.[17] While the division's armoured brigade was designed to make armoured breakthroughs through the enemy's main line of resistance, the infantry brigade could hold these gains and launch attacks of its own. It consisted of three infantry regiments and an independent machine-gun company. The three regiments within the brigade were the Lincoln and Welland Regiment, the Argyll and Sutherland Highlanders of Canada, and the Algonquin Regiment. Rather than a full battalion as in an infantry division, support was provided by an independent machine-gun company – the 10th Independent Machine Gun Company (the New Brunswick Rangers). The role of reconnaissance within the division was taken up by a fourth armoured regiment, the 29th Canadian Armoured Reconnaissance Regiment (the South Alberta Regiment). Divisional antitank and antiaircraft assets consisted of the 5th Anti-Tank Regiment (RCA) and the 5th Light Anti-Aircraft Regiment (RCA). The RCA divisional field artillery was made up of two regiments, the 15th Field Regiment (self-propelled)

(RCA) and the 23rd Field Regiment (RCA), which operated 25-pounder howitzers.

Raised in February 1941 and initially named the 1st Canadian Armoured Division, the 5th Canadian Armoured Division was composed of units from across Canada. After building up its strength by incorporating units of the nascent 4th Canadian Infantry Division, the division deployed to the United Kingdom in fall 1941. It was initially organized with two armoured brigades in accordance with the 1941 British armoured division organizational structure. In January 1943, it was reorganized with one infantry brigade and one armoured brigade. The division saw action in Italy from January 1944 to early January 1945 as part of the 1st Canadian Corps. Operating with an additional infantry brigade from July 1944 onward, the division in Italy had a much different structure than armoured divisions fighting in northwest Europe. Ordered to northwest Europe as part of Operation Goldflake, the division moved by road to Livorno, Italy, in early February 1945. It was then transported by ship to Marseille, France, and by road and rail to Belgium, arriving in late February. After reorganizing itself and being re-equipped, the division took part in combat operations in northwest Europe from 31 March until the end of hostilities.[18] The division's commanding officer was Major-General Bertram Hoffmeister. The two main fighting components of the division were the 11th Canadian Infantry Brigade and the 5th Canadian Armoured Brigade. The armoured brigade consisted of the 2nd Canadian Armoured Regiment (Lord Strathcona's Horse) (Royal Canadians), the 5th Canadian Armoured Regiment (the 8th Princess Louise's [New Brunswick] Hussars), and the 9th Canadian Armoured Regiment (the British Columbia Dragoons). The mechanized infantry component of the brigade was the Westminster Regiment (Motor).

The 11th Canadian Infantry Brigade contained the Perth Regiment, the Irish Regiment of Canada, and the Cape Breton Highlanders. The 11th Independent Machine Gun Company (the Princess Louise Fusiliers) was available to provide support for the infantry regiments. Like the 4th Canadian Armoured Division, the 5th Canadian Armoured Division did not possess a machine-gun battalion. Divisional reconnaissance was provided by a fourth armoured regiment, the 3rd Canadian Armoured Reconnaissance Regiment (the Governor General's Horse Guards). The two Royal Canadian Artillery field artillery regiments within the division were the 17th Field Regiment and the 8th Field Regiment (Self-Propelled). Antitank and antiaircraft assets were provided by the 5th Light Anti-Aircraft Regiment, RCA, and the 4th Anti-Tank Regiment, RCA.

The 1st and 2nd Canadian Armoured Brigades were independent armoured formations consisting of three armoured regiments each. These brigades were designed to mate with and support Canadian infantry divisions rather than act independently or form their own battle groups based on their armoured regiments. While the brigade headquarters provided an administrative support function, the regiments were parcelled out, one to each infantry brigade, for various operations.

Raised in 1941, the 1st Canadian Army Tank Brigade was originally one of two armoured brigades that formed part of the 1st Canadian Armoured Division, which was subsequently renamed the 5th Canadian Armoured Division. One of its three armoured regiments, the Calgary Regiment, participated in the disastrous Dieppe Raid. Following a reorganization of the division in early 1943, the brigade became an independent formation. In its new role, its regiments were to provide support to infantry brigades in battle. Following another training period in the United Kingdom, the brigade took part in the Sicilian Campaign in July and August 1943. Near the conclusion of this campaign, the brigade was renamed the 1st Canadian Armoured Brigade. Service in Italy continued until January 1945, and the brigade successfully supporting several different Allied formations in multiple operations.[19] When the brigade was given its new title in August 1943, its regiments were renamed the 11th, 12th, and 14th Canadian Armoured Regiments on top of the regimental titles already present. At this point, the brigade consisted of a headquarters squadron, the 11th Canadian Armoured Regiment (the Three Rivers Regiment), the 12th Canadian Armoured Regiment (the Ontario Regiment), and the 14th Canadian Armoured Regiment (the Calgary Regiment). Like all Canadian armoured brigades, it also had a Royal Canadian Electrical and Mechanical Engineers second-line armoured brigade workshop attached.[20] In mid-February 1945, the brigade was redeployed to Belgium with the rest of the 1st Canadian Corps as part of Operation Goldflake. On its arrival in northwest Europe, its commanding officer was Brigadier General W.C. Murphy. Utilizing the same route as the 1st Canadian Infantry Division and the 5th Canadian Armoured Division, the brigade arrived in Belgium in mid-March 1945.[21]

Raised in January 1942, the 2nd Canadian Army Tank Brigade was established with units that were formerly part of the 4th Canadian Infantry Division. At the time, the division was reorganizing itself as an armoured division and had to shed excess units. Deployed to the United Kingdom in July 1943, it was renamed the 2nd Canadian Armoured Brigade. The 3rd Canadian Army Tank Brigade, also an independent formation, was already present in the United Kingdom. Concerned about the Canadian Army's ability to sustain a third independent armoured brigade, Canadian Military Headquarters, London, broke up the original three regiments of the 2nd Canadian Army Tank Brigade for reinforcements. The three more experienced regiments from the former 3rd Canadian Army Tank Brigade took their place. From fall 1943 to spring 1944, the brigade, renamed the 2nd Canadian Armoured Brigade, conducted training exercises for its upcoming amphibious role in Operation Overlord. With Brigadier General R.A. Wyman in command, the brigade consisted of a headquarters squadron and three armoured regiments: the 6th Canadian Armoured Regiment (the 1st Hussars), the 10th Canadian Armoured Regiment (the Fort Garry Horse), and the 27th Canadian Armoured Regiment (the Sherbrooke Fusiliers). Structured like the 1st Canadian Armoured Brigade, the brigade also had its own armoured brigade workshop.[22]

Corps- and army-level combat arms units under the command of the First Canadian Army headquarters and the 1st and 2nd Canadian Corps were independent of Canadian divisions and independent brigades. These units were made available to corps and divisional commanders, who could attach them to their formations on a need basis. These units could increase the combat power of a division during offensive operations or strengthen its defensive front. Most of them were part of RCA, and their indirect firepower was utilized to help implement the artillery-based doctrine of the Canadian Army in the late war period.

The higher command structures that allocated these units included the First Canadian Army headquarters, which was formed in April 1942 when the number of Canadian divisions in the United Kingdom reached the strength of two corps. It became operational in Normandy on 31 July 1944, and the army's commander for the duration of the campaign in northwest Europe was General H.D.G. Crerar. The 2nd Canadian Corps headquarters was established in the United Kingdom in January 1943 to command excess Canadian formations not controlled by 1st Canadian Corps, then destined for the Mediterranean. On becoming active in Normandy during the first week of July 1944, its commander for the balance of the campaign in northwest Europe was Lieutenant-General Guy Simonds. The 1st Canadian Corps headquarters was transferred back to northwest Europe from the Italian front in early 1945. Under corps commander Lieutenant-General Charles Foulkes, it was operational for the final April–May 1945 phase of fighting.[23]

The First Canadian Army in the last month of hostilities employed multiple battalion-sized army-level and corps-level units. As of April 1945, the 1st Canadian Corps contained the following corps-level units: the 1st Light Anti-Aircraft Regiment (RCA), the 7th Anti-Tank Regiment (RCA), the 1st Survey Regiment (RCA), and the 1st Armoured Car Regiment (the Royal Canadian Dragoons).[24] At the same point in time, the 2nd Canadian Corps contained the following corps-level units: the 6th Light Anti-Aircraft Regiment (RCA), the 6th Anti-Tank Regiment (RCA), the 2nd Survey Regiment (RCA), and the 18th Armoured Car Regiment (the 12th Manitoba Dragoons).

Canadian Army–level units were allocated to corps commanders as needed, but these commanders did not have the luxury of controlling them permanently. These regiments consisted of six medium and two army field artillery regiments, divided evenly into two Army Group Royal Artillery (AGRA) formations. These formations, the 1st and 2nd Canadian AGRA, held an awesome concentration of firepower that allowed for the facilitation of the Canadian Army's artillery-based doctrine. The 2nd Canadian AGRA was placed in support of the 2nd Canadian Corps, and the 1st Canadian AGRA was place in support of the 1st Canadian Corps in operations in northwest Europe.[25] The 1st Army Group (RCA) consisted of the 11th Field Regiment (RCA) and the 1st, 2nd, and 5th Medium Regiments (RCA). The 2nd Army Group (RCA) consisted of the 19th Field Regiment (RCA); the 3rd, 4th, and 7th Medium Regiments (RCA); and the 2nd Heavy Anti-Aircraft Regiment (RCA) (Mobile). There were other miscellaneous RCA units at the battery level.

The AGRA medium regiments were initially equipped with 5.5-inch medium guns, and the Army Field Regiment was equipped with M7 Priest 105 mm self-propelled artillery pieces. These units contained a total of seventy-two artillery pieces, the same amount of artillery contained in an infantry division. But two-thirds of the pieces in the AGRA grouping were the heavier medium 5.5-inch guns. Because of the lack of any super heavy Canadian artillery units, the three 5.5-inch medium regiments were the most powerful artillery regiments in the Canadian Army.

All formations, both those dispatched to partake in the Normandy invasion and those redeployed from Italy in 1945, were fully operational and combat-ready for the entirety of their deployments to northwest Europe. The organization, assembly, equipping, and training process for each formation had been a long and at times challenging ordeal. But when all were finally united within two army corps in April 1945, they were the greatest combat force ever assembled by Canada, superbly equipped with both personnel and the most advanced military equipment available within the British Empire.

6
The Normandy Campaign

The First Canadian Army's reinforcement ability faced its greatest test during the Normandy Campaign of June–August 1944. The intensity of combat and losses sustained was extremely high. The Canadian Army's ability to make losses in personnel good was pushed to the absolute limit. A crippling shortfall in infantry manpower in late summer 1944 was avoided only through the crash remustering of Canadian personnel in other army trades in the UK reinforcement pools to other ranks infantry. The First Canadian Army was also fortunate to face an opponent coming to grips with one of its worst defeats during the war as it barely accomplished an organized withdrawal during its ejection from Northern France in late August. These circumstances mitigated any lack of capability on the part of the First Canadian Army, whose biggest challenge at the end of the campaign was pursuing the remnants of the defeated German Army.

On the eve of the invasion, in June 1944, every Canadian division in southern England was fully equipped or very near to it in accordance with war establishment figures for personnel, vehicles, and equipment.[1] Assigned to carry out the actual beach assaults, the 3rd Canadian Infantry Division was significantly better equipped in personnel, vehicles, and weaponry than the other two Canadian infantry divisions in England, and it thus had a greater level of combat power. The major difference in manpower and weaponry stemmed from the attachment of the 19th Army Field Regiment, Royal Canadian Artillery (RCA), and additional British Royal Artillery regiments. To provide added mobility, all four Canadian field artillery regiments were equipped with M7 105 mm Priest self-propelled artillery pieces rather than towed variants. The RCA Anti-Tank Regiment included a battery of M10 3-inch self-propelled tank destroyers.[2] These additions gave the division an extensive mobile, self-propelled artillery and antitank component that could rapidly disembark from landing craft and support a quick armoured advance if required.

On D-Day, four infantry regiments of the 3rd Canadian Infantry Division successfully assaulted Juno Beach. With significant armoured, air, naval, and engineer support, they cleared the beaches of German defenders. These regiments suffered a large number of battle casualties; the greatest number were in the Regina Rifle Regiment, which lost forty-five men, and the Queen's Own Rifles of Canada, which lost sixty-one.[3] The division immediately pushed inland, consolidating its area of the beachhead and landing the remainder of its units in the next few days.

The fighting of 7–11 June resulted in a consolidated, static front for the invasion force. An important defensive success was achieved in this period, with all German armoured counterattacks against the beachhead being defeated.[4] However, infantry and armoured forays to the south against Le Mesnil-Patry, Carpiquet, and Carpiquet airfield failed with heavy losses. Attempting to take Carpiquet airfield and the adjoining village on 7 June, a 9th Canadian Infantry Brigade task force initially made good progress but then suffered a sharp reverse in the afternoon, when the Germans unleashed an armoured counterattack that the Canadians stopped only at the cost of heavy infantry casualties.[5] The 7th Canadian Infantry Brigade's operations to the east on 8–9 June had better results, capturing the villages of Bretteville-l'Orgueilleuse and Putot and holding them against frequent armoured and infantry attacks. The 7th Canadian Infantry Brigade prevailed because of excellent defensive combined arms tactics and effective artillery support. These previous successes were tempered on 11 June, when the Queen's Own Rifles of Canada took heavy losses while supporting a failed 2nd Canadian Armoured Brigade armoured attack against Le Mesnil-Patry.[6] Following these battles and the successful Allied defence of the beachhead, the fighting turned static for the remainder of the month.

During June, the 3rd Canadian Infantry Division received large numbers of reinforcements to bring its regiments back up to strength. The record keeping for this period was incomplete because of the chaotic nature of the initial bridgehead battles and landings, but some data was recorded. For example, the Royal Winnipeg Rifles, the 7th Canadian Infantry Brigade regiment that had sustained some of the highest casualties, received 449 new personnel, which, by 30 June, brought its strength to 37 officers and 790 other ranks, 97 percent of establishment.[7]

Landing on D-Day, the 2nd Canadian Armoured Brigade faced some of its most difficult fighting of the war during the Normandy Campaign. Prior to the landings, armoured-fighting-vehicle and personnel strengths within the brigade had been satisfactory. The brigade was 23 percent overstrength in vehicles, with 245 tanks on hand versus its authorized number of 199.[8] Personnel returns for the regiments were also adequate prior to the invasion of the continent. The 10th Canadian Armoured (the Fort Garry Horse) Regiment's field return of 3 June reported a strength of 36 officers and 665 other ranks, 2 percent overstrength.[9] On 6 June, elements of the brigade successfully assaulted Juno Beach and drove inland. Further bridgehead battles with German armoured battle groups led to heavy casualties in personnel and tanks. From 6 to 30 June, battle casualties totalled 331 personnel.[10] During this phase, the brigade's three regiments were instrumental in providing armoured support to defend the bridgehead. This success was tempered by two significant reverses on 7 and 11 June, when the regiments attempted to take a more forward role in offensive operations. An operational pause in late June and early July allowed the regiments to train, receive new tanks, and take on reinforcements. On 10 June, British Army forward-delivery squadrons delivered twenty-six armoured fighting vehicles (AFVs) to the 1st Hussars, twenty-one to the Fort Garry Horse, and twenty-seven to the Sherbrooke Fusiliers. These vehicles were delivered through the British replacement organization, and specific types are not mentioned.[11]

In early July, the 3rd Canadian Infantry Division's infantry brigades again assaulted the German defences west and north of Caen. Operation Windsor, the 4 July assault on Carpiquet village and airfield, was only partially successful. Operation Charnwood, the 8 July operation against German forces north of Caen, met all its objectives.[12] Heavy infantry casualties were sustained in each operation. Moving south to support the British Operation Goodwood on 18 July, the division took the southern industrial portion of Caen in its part of the Canadian Operation Atlantic. Following this initial success, the newly arrived 2nd Canadian Infantry Division took over the advance and attacked southward towards Verrières Ridge. Its assaults were repulsed, resulting in heavy casualties and limited gains. Following the mixed results of Operation Atlantic, on 25 July the 3rd Canadian Infantry Division participated in Operation Spring. During this operation, the 9th Canadian Infantry Brigade suffered severe casualties while attempting to take the village of Tilly-la-Campagne. These reverses on or near the tactically significant Verrières Ridge stemmed from the aggressive use of German armour, which was too strong for any breakthroughs to take place or significant objectives to be taken.[13] Despite terrible casualties, a majority of the division's infantry regiments were still maintained at satisfactory levels of strength in late July. As an example, the Stormont, Dundas, and Glengarry Highlanders of the 9th Canadian Infantry Brigade recorded a strength return of 34 officers and 727 other ranks on 28 July, 89 percent of its war establishment strength.[14]

This was not the case with all infantry regiments. For instance, the North Nova Scotia Highlanders of the 9th Canadian Infantry Brigade's strength stood at 29 officers and 572 other ranks on its 29 July 1944 return, putting its strength at 70 percent of its war establishment.[15] It should be noted that when this return was submitted, the unit was involved in heavy fighting. This figure highlights the losses the regiment had sustained in late July and in its failed attack on Tilly-la-Campagne on 25 July, when it took 139 casualties on a single day.

July 1944 was also a month of intense operations in Normandy for the 2nd Canadian Armoured Brigade. During this time, its regiments supported both infantry divisions in their offensive operations against German positions. Operations Windsor and Charnwood saw the armoured regiments support the eventual capture of Carpiquet airfield and the city of Caen. Operations Atlantic and Spring were only partial successes as the armoured regiments struggled against strong German positions on Verrières Ridge. All these operations involved costly tank engagements that resulted in large tank and crew losses. As of 31 July, all three regiments had been brought back up to strength in battle tanks but were short of personnel.

The 25th Canadian Armoured Delivery Regiment's (25th CADR) "C" Squadron effectively carried out its role of resupplying the 2nd Canadian Armoured Brigade with new and repaired AFVs throughout summer 1944. During June and July, the brigade received a total of 129 new and repaired battle tanks from this squadron.[16] Returns for 31 July show 295 battle tanks on strength versus its authorized total of 199, the brigade being 48 percent overstrength in this category.[17] As shown in Figure 6.1, the brigade's AFV strength remained high while a comparable German unit's strength dwindled, the Germans being starved of new panzers and forced to repair damaged ones near the front lines. The figure reflects only operational Canadian tanks. There were others on strength that were repairable within one to two days by the LAD in each regiment, boosting its numbers even higher.

Due to the intensity of combat, personnel losses in Canadian armoured regiments increased rapidly in July 1944. The regiments were still combat effective but not near their war establishment strengths in terms of personnel. For example, the 6th Canadian Armoured Regiment had been reduced to 38 officers and 522 other ranks, 81 percent of its authorized strength. The 25th CADR reinforcement organization would rectify these losses, but the process took time. Because of the constant steam of losses sustained in ongoing operations, it was difficult to maintain these units perfectly at their establishment levels. These personnel deficits would only be rectified in fall 1944, when the number of the armoured engagements during operations fell.

Mid-July saw the deployment of a second Canadian infantry division to the Normandy front. Once it was deployed to the front lines on 16 July, the strength of the 2nd Canadian Infantry Division stood at 933 officers and 17,425 other ranks.[18] Despite some minor shortages, all combat arms regiments within the

Figure 6.1

Tank strength of 2nd Canadian Armoured Brigade (Sherman, Sherman Firefly, and Stuart) and Panzer Regiment 3 (Panther and Panzer IV), June–August 1944

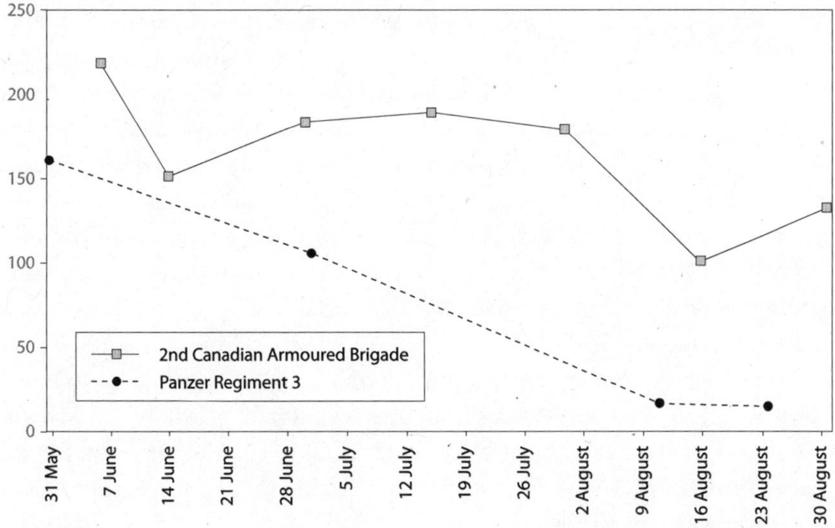

Source: Jarymowycz, "The Quest for Operational Maneuver in the Normandy Campaign," Appendix E, "2nd Canadian Armoured Brigade Tank States, June–August 1944," 336–38; and Zetterling, *Normandy 1944*, 315.

division were at or close to their authorized personnel strengths during the early part of the month. The strengths of two of its infantry regiments taken were as follows. On 1 July, Les Fusiliers Mont-Royal contained 36 officers and 809 other ranks, 99 percent of its authorized strength.[19] The Calgary Highlanders personnel strength on 9 July was also very high, with 37 officers and 806 other ranks, also 99 percent of its war establishment. [20] All divisional RCA artillery regiments were also strong. On 15 July, the 4th Field Regiment contained 38 officers and 633 other ranks, 99 percent of its authorized strength.[21] On 1 July, the 3rd Light Anti-Aircraft Regiment consisted of 43 officers and 802 other ranks, or 98 percent of its war establishment.[22]

With regard to vehicles and weaponry, the division was not equivalent to the 3rd Canadian Infantry Division. Most noticeably, as of July 1944 it did not contain any self-propelled artillery pieces or self-propelled antitank guns. The 21st Army Group's "'A' & 'B' Consolidated Vehicle Position Report" does not contain a return for 30 June, but one exists for 31 May.[23] At this point, the division was entering its final work-up phase before deploying to the continent to join the invasion forces. As of 31 May, the division contained 643 combat "A" vehicles versus a war establishment of 593, making it 8 percent overstrength. Some "A" vehicle shortages did exist at the beginning of June 1944. Only thirty-six of the sixty authorized medium machine-gun tracked carriers had been issued to the machine-gun battalion. There were only seventeen Humber armoured cars present against the authorized number of twenty-nine. This shortcoming was offset by the unauthorized presence of nine Fox armoured cars, but the division was still short three. There were thirty-two tracked 4.2-inch mortar carriers on the war establishment figures, but none had been issued. Against an authorized number of fifty-four Wasp II tracked flamethrower carriers, none had been issued. This last "A" vehicle was a very valuable infantry support weapon. Its employment with other Canadian divisions would prove to be effective, especially against entrenched infantry. Twenty-First Army Group's monthly returns for nonvehicle equipment for the division do not exist for 31 May or 30 June.[24] The first return with the division's equipment listed is for 31 July, which was after a significant period of combat had occurred. However, in evaluating the war diaries from the division's regiments there is no mention of severe shortages in any major weapons systems.

Once the 2nd Canadian Infantry Division's component brigades, including all their vehicles and weapons, were concentrated on the continent in mid-July, they participated in Operation Atlantic on 19–21 July. In this, their first combat operation since the Dieppe Raid, they were badly mauled, suffering large losses from German armoured counterattacks.[25] Poor execution of combined arms tactics left the battalions highly vulnerable to direct German AFV fire. The dismounted infantry were not adequately supported by other arms during assaults, particularly by armour, and this led to catastrophic losses. After Operation Atlantic, the division participated in Operation Spring on 25 July, again taking heavy casualties for very limited gains.[26]

Though there were significant personnel losses in August, the bulk of the casualties inflicted on the division during the Normandy Campaign occurred in July. As a result of Operations Atlantic and Spring, by 31 July the division's overall strength had fallen by over 1,261 men. To compound the damage, this figure was recorded after all of July's personnel reinforcements had been accepted.[27] The Royal Highland Regiment of Canada (the Black Watch) of the 5th Canadian Infantry Brigade suffered 307 battle casualties on 25 July alone.[28] The extent of the damage to the regiment is reflected in a 27 July strength return. The regiment on this date contained 32 officers and 415 other ranks, 53 percent of its war establishment.[29]

Because of the division's back-to-back participation in two major operations in late July 1944, its infantry brigades lost a large number of personnel in a short amount of time. These deficits would not be reduced significantly until just prior to the Battle of the Scheldt in mid-September. The infantry regiments were still combat ready, but they had reduced capabilities. Every time they received reinforcements, they were immediately engaged in new combat operations, losing even more personnel. In this manner, the strength of the regiments was slowly but steadily reduced during late July and early August.

In response to these heavy losses, replacements were sent to the 2nd Canadian Infantry Division, but they did not arrive quickly enough or in significant enough numbers to mitigate ongoing losses. The main challenge was that personnel losses were occurring in much higher volumes and much more quickly than the reinforcement system could handle. After Operation Atlantic, there were not enough replacement infantry officers and general duty infantrymen allocated to the division to rectify the shortcomings. A 22 July 1944 letter to the 2nd Canadian Corps commander, Lieutenant-General Guy Simonds, from Corps Deputy Adjutant and Quartermaster General Brigadier H.V.D. Laing, spells out the main obstacles to reinforcing the division:

1. GOC 2nd Infantry Division phoned me at approximately 2100 hours that he anticipated the following shortages as a result of operations of the last 24 hours. Replacements required: Officers 8, Other Ranks 750–1,000.
2. The above mention reinforcements are applicable very largely to the infantry of the division, and in particular, to the SSR, the Essex Scottish and the Fusiliers Mont-Royal, but to the latter battalion only to a small degree.
3. The reinforcement situation in the Rft Battalions, according to the latest information given to the DAQG on the 21 July, 1944, is, in brief, that there are approximately 26 officers and 150 other ranks available, the ORs being, of course, general duty.
4. In the division forward battalion there are 6 officers and 120 other ranks.[30]

It also should be noted that on 20 July the division had just received an allotment of reinforcements, depleting the float of available reinforcements set aside for it. General duty (other ranks) infantry were available, but in mid-July a large number of them were located in reinforcement organization bases in England. The personnel shortages could be remedied but not immediately. In the meantime, ongoing losses due to combat conditions continued. In these circumstances, the division could not meet the challenge of maintaining its war establishment personnel strength in July and August.

The same letter later states:

> 8. It is understood that 550 general duty personnel were to have sailed from the United Kingdom on 21 July 1944, and that 2,000 are scheduled to sail on the Tuesday next. This should make 550 available by Sunday and the balance by the Thursday next – in both cases, provided the sailings and landings are carried out as scheduled.[31]

The 2nd Canadian Infantry Division's weapons and vehicles losses from 20 to 23 July had also been considerable. A large effort was made to replace these losses, which included 11 T16 tracked gun tractors, 23 tracked Universal Carriers, 3 3-inch tracked mortar carriers, 21 6-pounder antitank guns, 4 17-pounder antitank guns, 3 25-pounder howitzers, 47 2-inch mortars, and 153 Bren .303 light machine guns.[32]

The 2nd Canadian Infantry Division was successfully re-equipped by the end of the month, as evidenced by its 31 July returns for both major weapon systems and combat "A" vehicles.[33] At this point, it contained 627 combat "A" vehicles compared to a war establishment level of 616, 2 percent over its authorized strength. There were no serious shortages in nonvehicle weapons at the end of the month. The division at this point possessed 90 percent of its war establishment inventories for these items. This percentage was largely the result of a temporary shortage in the area of 2-inch infantry mortars. There were only 226 on hand versus an authorized strength of 283.

The costly battles endured by the 3rd Canadian Infantry Division in July were followed by the division's participation in Operation Totalize on 8–13 August. The removal of some German formations from the front and a massive airstrike by Allied four-engined strategic bombers allowed for a successful night attack by Anglo-Canadian divisions on 7–8 August. After this night attack, a further large bomber airstrike occurred that saw some regiments of the division take losses from inaccurate Allied bombing runs.[34] Making contact with the enemy on 10 August, the 8th Canadian Infantry Brigade advanced towards its objective, the Quesnay Wood. Two regiments attacked on the right flank of the 4th Canadian Armoured Division but failed to capture the wooded area in difficult fighting. Further participation by the division's brigades in Operation Tractable on 13–21 August saw the division's regiments reach the outskirts of Falaise on 16 August.[35] Up to 22 August, the final Falaise Gap fighting led to major German personnel and equipment losses as the encirclement closed around them. Intense combat with German forces seeking to break out resulted in more casualties for the division as all remaining escape routes were cut off.[36]

Battle casualties up to 26 July had been high within the 3rd Canadian Infantry Division. There were 6,481 killed, wounded, or missing.[37] Despite these losses and others in August, the reinforcement organization had kept the infantry regiments combat ready. The 30 August strength returns for two infantry regiments indicate the infantry strength within the division. The North Nova Scotia Highlanders, a regiment that had been in poor shape at the end of July, possessed 40 officers and 757 other ranks, 93 percent of its war establishment.[38] The regiment had suffered considerably, with a total of 881 battle and 241 nonbattle casualties occurring during the campaign.[39] Reinforcements assigned to the regiment numbered 1,069, sufficient for roughly eight complete new infantry companies.[40] The North Shore Regiment in late August was also reasonably strong, with 35 officers and 725 other ranks on strength, 89 percent of its authorized strength. This regiment had sustained 821 battle and 233 nonbattle casualties to this point.[41] It had been very well reinforced by approximately 964 replacements during the June–August fighting.[42] Both of these regiments had suffered 100 percent losses during this period and had been completely rebuilt to near their authorized strengths.

Battle casualties for the RCA units in the division in July and August had been light. Total RCA battle casualties for all five regiments in the division totalled 561 killed, wounded, or missing.[43] On a day-to-day basis, it was rare for any one regiment to suffer a large number of casualties. As an example, the war diary for the 12th Field Regiment reported only light casualties during its involvement in Operation Totalize, despite some German shelling.[44]

As of 4 August, personnel reinforcements for the 3rd Canadian Infantry Division revealed that the cost of battle was being borne by the infantry to a large degree. Total Canadian Infantry Corps reinforcements sent to the division numbered 269 officers and 5,618 other ranks, an astounding total equivalent to forty-nine new infantry companies. Other arms within the division received a total of 52 officers and 1,045 other ranks.[45] Not only was the 3rd Canadian Infantry Division exceptionally outfitted for battle in Normandy, it was also exceptionally reinforced while in the field.

Major weapons systems and AFV losses suffered by the division were continually made good during the campaign.[46] On 31 August the division was in a satisfactory state with regard to its combat "A" vehicles and weaponry. However, it was in a state of transition with regard to the number of combat "A" vehicles within its RCA field artillery regiments. The three field regiments had exchanged their self-propelled artillery vehicles for towed artillery, which was superior for indirect fire tasks.[47] The fourth Canadian army-level field artillery regiment that was temporarily attached to the division in June was removed by July. This move immediately subtracted its vehicles and weapons from the division's totals.

As of 31 August, the inventory levels of combat "A" vehicles operated by the 3rd Canadian Infantry Division were satisfactory.[48] A total of 737 "A" vehicles were present within the division versus its authorized war establishment level of 707, making it 4 percent overstrength. The division was significantly overstrength in some "A" vehicles categories, but this was to compensate for shortages in other types. For example, of the 120 T16 gun tractor carriers authorized as antitank gun towers and ammunition carriers, only 13 were present. The nonvehicle weapons state of the division was also satisfactory.[49] The division contained 569 major weapons systems versus an authorized level of 563, making it slightly overstrength in this category. The only significant shortage was in the area of antitank guns as the division was authorized sixteen of the very effective 17-pounder towed antitank guns, but none had been issued. In their place, eighteen extra 6-pounders were on strength.

The division was in good shape in comparison to average German infantry formations. As shown in Figure 6.2, after Normandy, German infantry divisions had very low strengths compared to their wartime establishments. These German formations were burned-out shells because of nonreinforcement. The Canadian Army's competent reinforcement-and-replacement systems for personnel, vehicles, and weaponry had performed to a satisfactory degree. While a complete British infantry division had to be broken up to re-equip and refurbish others in August 1944, this never occurred within the First Canadian Army after Normandy.[50] This is not to say the 3rd Canadian Infantry Division did not suffer severe losses. Following further fighting in the pursuit of the enemy across France, the state of two of its infantry brigades was adequate, and the third was rather weak. Returns for 8 September reflect a division that was still combat capable, but it required reinforcements for its infantry companies.

As of 8 September, post Normandy, the average strength of the three infantry regiments within the 9th Canadian Infantry Brigade was 36 officers and 763 other ranks, 94 percent of the authorized strength of an infantry battalion. The 8th Canadian Infantry Brigade's average battalion strength was even better, standing at 36 officers and 769 other ranks, 95 percent of its authorized strength. The 7th Canadian Infantry Brigade – composed of the Royal Winnipeg Rifles, the Regina Rifle Regiment, and 1st Battalion, the Canadian Scottish Regiment – was the weakest of the three. It had an average battalion strength of 37 officers and 653 other ranks, 81 percent of its war establishments, which meant that three regiments in this brigade were each missing an average of 160 personnel, one and one-third of a complete infantry company.[51]

Figure 6.2

Strength returns versus authorized strengths, 3rd Canadian Infantry Division versus German infantry divisions, August–September 1944

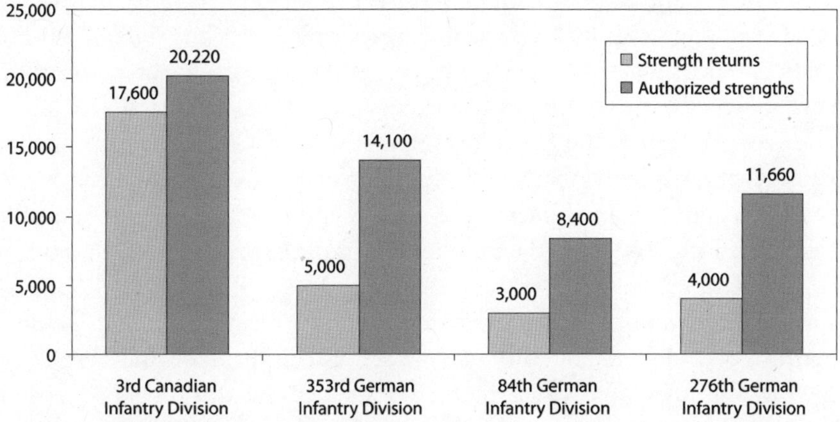

Note: Figures for the Canadian Infantry Division are for 31 August 1944; 353rd German Infantry Division are for 1 September 1944; the 84th German Infantry Division are for 22 August 1944; and the 276th German Infantry Division are for 1 September 1944.
Source: LAC, RG 24, vol. 13,775, "3rd Canadian Infantry Division A&Q War Diary," August 1944; and Niklas Zetterling, *Normandy 1944*, 283, 233, 261.

So, why, at the height of the summer of 1944 "infantry shortage," discussed in Chapter 2, were the 3rd Canadian Infantry Division's infantry brigades in rather good shape compared to those in other Canadian divisions? The answer is that apart from a bad mauling during Operation Spring on 25 July, the division had successfully accomplished tasks delegated to it in August without sustaining heavy losses. Such were the fortunes of war. In the period from 9 July to 8 September, some infantry regiments had taken high levels of casualties, but this had not occurred in a large number of others after 25 July. Had this occurred, the 3rd Canadian Infantry Division would have found itself in a similar state to that of the 2nd Canadian Infantry Division and the 4th Canadian Armoured Division.

Despite its weakened state, on 8 August the 2nd Canadian Infantry Division successfully supported the initial breakthrough of the armoured advance of Operation Totalize. Later that month, the division conducted a successful assault crossing of the Laize River at Bretteville-sur-Laize. It then recrossed the same river at Clair Tizon prior to Operation Tractable.[52] From 27 July to 16 August, the Canadian Army in northwest Europe received 3,589 reinforcements.[53]

Although an impressive number, it was insufficient to cope with the escalating demands of infantry regiments for new personnel, especially those of the 2nd Canadian Infantry Division. And not all reinforcements were infantry – many were artillery and armoured troops. The actual infantry reinforcements were divided among two infantry divisions, an armoured division, multiple smaller units, and headquarters. Nonbattle casualties resulting from battle exhaustion and normal occurrences of accidents, illness, and disease increased the flow of evacuees. In August, the Royal Regiment of Canada's 4th Canadian Infantry Brigade suffered 97 nonbattle casualties. This was in comparison to the 250 battle casualties suffered during the same month.[54] A total of 259 nonbattle casualties occurred within the three regiments of the brigade for the month of August, a significant number.[55]

Combat for noninfantry units within the 2nd Canadian Infantry Division had also been difficult, but they had not suffered similar casualties. While inflicting large losses to enemy armour, the 2nd Anti-Tank Regiment, RCA, had suffered only 187 battle casualties during July and August.[56] The field artillery units also suffered very low casualty rates due to their rear positions on the battlefield. August battle casualties for the 4th Field Regiment, RCA, totalled twenty-two.[57]

For the 2nd Canadian Armoured Brigade, some of the hardest fighting of the campaign occurred during Operation Totalize. The armoured units sought to break through German positions and advance south to Falaise, and they were only partially successful in achieving these goals. During Operation Tractable, it finally met these objectives. In each of these operations, the brigade supported the dismounted infantry units of the 2nd and 3rd Canadian Infantry Divisions. Following these operations, the regiments took an active role in the capture of Falaise and the encirclement of the trapped German forces. Large tank losses occurred within the brigade during these final operations of the Normandy Campaign. A successful repair-and-replacement program, however, ensured adequate tank strengths within the regiments. As of 31 August, the 2nd Canadian Armoured Brigade contained 265 tanks on strength in comparison to its war establishment figure of 199. This return placed the brigade 33 percent over its authorized strength in this category.[58] It should be noted that not all these tanks were operational, and many were being repaired by the LADs or part of the armoured brigade headquarters squadron. Many tanks were lost to mechanical breakdown in late August during rapid advances across northern France after Normandy. During this month, the brigade received seventy-three new and repaired AFVs to maintain its strength.

Arguably among the most powerful Canadian divisions, the 4th Canadian Armoured Division was the last to arrive on the Normandy front and participate in the campaign. The division landed in France in mid-July but did not begin offensive operations until 1 August. As a result, the month of July is not included in the statistical totals and the divisional records. As of 1 August, total divisional strength stood at 829 officers and 14,757 other ranks.[59] At this point, all regiments within the division were at or close to their war establishment personnel strengths. The three armoured regiments within the armoured brigade had high personnel levels. For example, as of 29 July, the 21st Canadian Armoured Regiment, contained 37 officers and 654 other ranks, placing it 1 percent overstrength.[60] The other two armoured regiments had similar returns. The Lake Superior (Motor) Regiment also contained satisfactory personnel levels. Its strength stood at 36 officers and 811 other ranks as of 29 July 1944, 98 percent of its war establishment.[61] The 10th Canadian Infantry Brigade's three regiments were also close to their establishment numbers. To take two regiments as examples, the Lincoln and Welland Regiment contained 37 officers and 810 other ranks, 99 percent of its authorized strength,[62] while the Algonquin Regiment was just as strong, with 37 officers and 803 other ranks, 98 percent of its war establishment.[63] The personnel levels within all four RCA regiments was adequate, with a combined strength of 187 officers and 3,181 other ranks.[64] There were some shortages, however. The strength of the 5th Anti-Tank Regiment stood at 37 officers and 692 other ranks, 93 percent of its authorized strength.[65]

Due to its reduced infantry component, the 4th Canadian Armoured Division did not contain nearly as many personnel as an infantry division. However, it possessed many heavy weapons and AFVs, giving it increased combat power. As of 31 July, there were adequate inventories of combat "A" vehicle within the division.[66] The division contained 830 combat "A" vehicles versus its authorized strength of 783. Of this number, 333 were Sherman medium or Stuart light tanks. A shortage of 17-pounder–equipped Sherman Firefly tanks did exist. Against an authorized strength of forty-five Sherman Vc Fireflies, only eight had been issued. Of the forty-eight Wasp II flamethrower carriers that were authorized, none had been issued to the division. But the division's inventories of heavy weapons were satisfactory.[67] It contained 315 heavy weapons, exactly the number it was authorized. Because it was an armoured division, with much of its strength concentrated in combat "A" vehicles, the division had fewer heavy weapons than an infantry division. This shortage was compensated for by a large number of AFVs, many of which were self-propelled artillery pieces.

Designated as one of the follow-on divisions that formed the 2nd Canadian Corps, the 4th Canadian Armoured Division's first elements landed in Normandy in mid-July 1944. Over the next several days, it concentrated its formations in the area near Caen. Placed under the command of the 2nd Canadian Corps, the division's infantry units relieved those of 3rd Canadian Infantry Division on 31 July.[68] Once it took its place in the line, the 10th Canadian Infantry Brigade continued a chain of costly infantry attacks on the tactically important Verrières Ridge. Two operations to capture the village of Tilly-la-Campagne, on 1 and 5 August, were failures, the attacks bogging down.[69] Following these minor actions, the division prepared itself for further offensive operations. August 1944 would see some of the fiercest combat of the war, at a time when the division's formation and unit commanders lacked combat experience.

The First Canadian Army's aim during this month was to exert pressure on the German's right flank while the enemy's left flank was collapsing under pressure from the First US Army's Operation Cobra and the British Second Army's Operation Bluecoat. To help realize this goal, the division played a major role in Operation Totalize. This armoured assault to break the main line of German resistance, capture Verrières Ridge, and exploit to the south towards Falaise was only partially successful. The 4th Canadian Armoured Division did not capture its objectives on 9 August as part of the second phase of the operational plan. Its advance was halted by traffic jams and strong German opposition, which inflicted a significant amount of personnel and equipment losses. The heaviest of these occurred within the 28th Canadian Armoured Regiment battle group when German armoured forces annihilated the majority of the regiment and part of the Algonquin Regiment.

Despite these challenges during Operation Totalize, the division regrouped for a further push on Falaise. The operational plan for Operation Tractable called for the division to attack on 14 August from Soignolles and then cross the Laizon River and capture the three objectives of Rouvres, Perrières, and Versainville. In the actual attack, Perrières and Rouvres were captured, but Versainville was not reached. It would not be captured because of difficulty crossing the Laizon River and German resistance. At this point, the German forces were weakened and conducting a fighting withdrawal, moving east in large columns to escape the encirclement near Falaise that was being created.

The 4th Canadian Armoured Division continued its drive on 15 August, when the 10th Canadian Infantry Brigade captured Épaney.[70] That same day, the 4th Canadian Armoured Brigade reached the vicinity of Point 159 near Versainville but was driven back by strong German opposition. On the morning of 16 August, the division was ordered to cross the Ante River and then advance east to Trun to meet units of the Third US Army. Attempting to cross the Ante River at Damblainville on 17 August, elements of the 10th Canadian Infantry Brigade were forced back with heavy losses.[71] Diverted to a bridgehead on the Dives River at Couliboeuf on the same day, the 4th Canadian Armoured Brigade successfully crossed the river. It then attacked east, capturing Les Moutiers-en-Auge and Louvières-en-Auge with assistance from other units of the 10th Canadian Infantry Brigade.[72]

From 18 to 21 August the division attempted to block escape routes out of the Falaise Pocket, suffering losses as the German forces tried to fight their way out. Operating with Polish and American forces, the plan was for the division to help secure the line at Chambois–St. Lambert–Trun along the Dives River, blocking German movement east. In chaotic fighting, lead elements of the division captured Trun on 18 August, establishing a blocking position. Because of heavy Allied air attacks and the sheer number of escaping enemy, the division slowly lost contact with the neighbouring 1st Polish Armoured Division.[73]

In the meantime, this division had captured Points 252 and 262 to the east, establishing hilltop blocking positions against fleeing German forces and relief attacks. On the morning of 19 August, the 29th Canadian Armoured Reconnaissance Regiment battle group attacked and captured part of St. Lambert, creating another blocking position. Because of increasing enemy pressure, the often outnumbered Polish and Canadian forces could not maintain a solid defensive perimeter. Despite the efforts of the defenders, on 20 August many German units escaped the pocket. The nearly encircled German forces fought hard to keep viable escape routes open, leading to considerable numbers of Canadian and Polish casualties.[74] After fierce fighting, elements of the isolated 1st Polish Armoured Division were relieved by the 4th Canadian Armoured Brigade on 21 August.[75] The pocket was now firmly closed, and no further German forces escaped.

Nearly continuous combat throughout August took a considerable toll on the division. From the outset, it had been assigned demanding operational tasks that were perhaps excessive for an inexperienced formation. In the 10th Canadian Infantry Brigade, the Argyll and Sutherland Highlanders of Canada took 218 total battle casualties between 27 July and 30 August. In this period, the Algonquin Regiment suffered 244 casualties, the Lincoln and Welland Regiment 258.[76] Nonbattle casualties were less of an issue, with the Algonquin Regiment losing twenty, the Lincoln and Welland Regiment seventy-one, and the Argyll and Sutherland Highlanders of Canada sixty-one.[77] Though these personnel were not killed, wounded, or missing, they were subtracted from the infantry companies just as effectively as combat casualties.

The number of reinforcements dispatched to the infantry regiments was insufficient to cope with the losses. In June, the Canadian reinforcement pool of trained infantrymen had not been strained because only the 3rd Canadian Infantry Division saw action in Normandy. But by 1 August, the infantry components of both the 2nd Canadian Infantry Division and 4th Canadian Armoured Division had joined in combat operations. Faulty planning on casualty rates by Canadian Military Headquarters, London, had led to an insufficient pool of infantry replacements being established. This error was compounded by the performance of a bureaucratic personnel supply system that had a starting point in England. As a result, a large percentage of the infantry replacements that could have been posted to Canadian formations were located across the English Channel during crisis points and not immediately available. The challenge of providing rapid reinforcements of infantry, other ranks, for all three Canadian divisions, at the rate they were demanding them, proved to be impossible. A crash program of remustering took place during summer and early fall 1944, but it could not occur fast enough to solve the problem.

This shortage of infantry replacements for the 4th Canadian Armoured Division occurred at a most inopportune moment. During the critical final August battles to secure the Falaise Pocket, the division was asked to advance in a dynamic fashion using its armoured and infantry forces. For these operations to succeed, the division's infantry strength had to be maintained. The exact opposite occurred, and temporary shortages resulted. The Argyll and Sutherland Highlanders of Canada received twenty-four personnel reinforcements during August.[78] By 30 August, their strength had shrunk to 24 officers and 528 other ranks.[79] The Algonquin Regiment recorded 36 new personnel joining the regiment during the same month. Its strength was reduced to 36 officers and 571 other ranks by the end of August.[80] Luckily, the enemy forces facing the division in late August were on the verge of general disintegration. This offset the weakened state of the divisional infantry regiments and allowed them to accomplish their objectives.

The RCA divisional regiments had suffered considerably fewer casualties, and their personnel levels were still at acceptable levels at the end of the summer. Total consolidated battle casualties for all RCA regiments within the division for the month of August were 257.[81] Most of these losses were concentrated in the front-line 5th Anti-Tank Regiment. Its strength had shrunk to 34 officers and 634 other ranks as of 26 August, 86 percent of its war establishment. Some regiments were largely unaffected by the fighting. The 8th Light Anti-Aircraft Regiment's strength on the same date was 40 officers and 821 other ranks, 99 percent of its authorized strength.[82]

The division's inventories of combat "A" vehicles had been reduced by heavy losses in August but were still large at the end of the month.[83] As of 31 August, the division fielded 809 combat "A" vehicles against a war establishment of 840, 96 percent of its authorized strength. Despite a constant repair-and-replacement effort, some vehicles, missing due to mechanical failure or enemy action, had not been replaced. The number of Mark Vc and Ic 17-pounder Sherman Firefly tanks had increased to twenty-eight by month's end. This was a marked increase from the 31 July totals, but the armoured regiments were still short thirty-two. There was also a shortage of armoured recovery vehicle tanks, with only eight Sherman III ARVs on hand versus the authorized strength of fourteen. There were also shortages of AFVs in the RCA regiments as of 31 August. These regiments were short artillery observation post tanks, having only eighteen Ram II tanks instead of the twenty-seven Sherman III variants that were authorized.[84]

While some ongoing shortages did exist, the division had been extensively resupplied with replacement AFVs and heavy weapons to cover the August losses. "D" Squadron of the 25th CADR delivered 123 Sherman, Sherman Firefly, and Stuart tanks to the division in August. This supply kept the armoured regiments operational in the face of severe losses due to antitank fire and mechanical failures.[85] This figure was enough to nearly re-equip two Canadian armoured regiments and reflects the high rate of losses during this period.

Losses inflicted by enemy action or mechanical failure on nonvehicle weaponry were not severe, and the division contained no shortages in this area as of 31 August. Any weapons systems that had been lost or broken during this period had been replaced. The infantry and artillery regiments continued to contain near perfect levels of all their authorized nonvehicle heavy weapons. Unauthorized overages in antitank guns included one extra 6-pounder and one extra 17-pounder.[86]

Held at the 2nd Canadian Corps level, the 6th Anti-Tank Regiment, RCA; the 18th Canadian Armoured Car Regiment (the Manitoba Dragoons); the 6th Light Anti-Aircraft Regiment, RCA; and the 2nd Survey Regiment, RCA, landed in Normandy in mid-July and became operational shortly afterward.[87] As of mid-July 1944, they were up to strength and contained their full war establishments of combat "A" vehicles and equipment.[88] All four units were committed to operations shortly after their arrival in Normandy. The 6th Anti-Tank Regiment was involved in combat immediately, supporting Canadian forces attacking Verrières Ridge in late July 1944. Given the static nature of the fighting in July, the 18th Canadian Armoured Car Regiment was assigned limited mounted and dismounted reconnaissance duties and suffered continuous losses. The 6th Light Anti-Aircraft Regiment was immediately engaged in combatting a very active

Luftwaffe. The 2nd Survey Regiment supported all RCA units within the beachhead as well as British Army Royal Artillery units in its artillery-survey, flash-spotting, calibration, and sound-ranging role.

Casualties from the summer battles were light for the majority of the 2nd Canadian Corps units, in comparison to those within the Canadian infantry and armoured brigades. As noted previously, an unfortunate side effect of the use of strategic air power as a tactical tool in Normandy was friendly fire, caused by inaccurate bombing runs. It caused many unnecessary losses among rear-deployed 2nd Canadian Corps troops during operations in mid-August. A type of unit that usually had low battlefield casualties, the 2nd Survey Regiment suffered forty-eight battle and twenty-four nonbattle casualties in August.[89] The majority were from inaccurate Allied aerial-bombing runs. The 6th Light Anti-Aircraft Regiment suffered twenty-one battle casualties in July, mainly caused by German air attack and indirect fire.[90] In comparison to the low average monthly casualties experienced by light antiaircraft regiments from September 1944 to May 1945, these figures were high.

Although casualty rates in the summer of 1944 were the heaviest of the war for the Canadian Army, after 31 August all four 2nd Canadian Corps–level units were at adequate personnel levels. For example, the 18th Canadian Armoured Car Regiment's strength was 57 officers and 786 other ranks on 30 August, 98 percent of its war establishment.[91] These personnel totals were taken after its prominent role in pursuing the defeated German Army and Waffen-SS formations across France in late summer. The relatively intact personnel levels of this unit indicate that the German ground forces in late August were involved in an urgent withdrawal, not a fighting retreat. The strength of the 6th Anti-Tank Regiment, RCA, was much weaker. It totalled 37 officers and 690 other ranks as of 26 August.[92] This regiment saw far heavier combat than the other three corps-level units, reducing it to 91 percent of its personnel war establishment. This figure was still significantly better than the average 2nd Canadian Corps infantry regiment in the same period.

With regard to army-level formations and units, upon landing in France, the 2nd Canadian AGRA immediately became involved in artillery programs supporting Anglo-Canadian offensive operations in July and August. The heavy firepower of its units was instrumental in neutralizing German defensive positions throughout the Normandy Campaign. In the final two weeks, the regiments moved continuously to keep their guns in range. During the final Falaise Gap battles, major damage was done to retreating German units by artillery forward observers directing the AGRA's heavy guns. During combat operations from June to mid-August, the four AGRA regiments suffered casualties from

German indirect fire, air strikes, and friendly fire in the form of inaccurate Allied aerial bombing.

This situation changed in mid-August when the German military began its withdrawal from northern France. At this point, German ground forces and the Luftwaffe's ability to attack rear-deployed Allied heavy artillery positions was greatly reduced, and German artillery units lacked the resources and capability to engage in sustained counterbattery fire. The Allied air forces had simultaneously achieved such a level of air superiority that the Luftwaffe had difficulty launching ground attack operations. As a result, the sole unit of the 2nd AGRA in operation in June, the 19th Army Field Regiment, RCA, took few losses during the campaign. From June, this artillery unit had been attached to the 3rd Canadian Infantry Division as a fourth self-propelled field artillery regiment. When the three army-level RCA medium regiments that formed the 2nd AGRA landed in mid-July, the 19th Army Field Regiment was detached to join them.

In conclusion, the Normandy Campaign was arguably the greatest test of Canadian arms in northwest Europe. In the process of besting some of the most powerful panzer and infantry divisions in the German land forces, the units of the First Canadian Army at times sustained catastrophic losses. While the reinforcement system worked continuously, there were limits to the scale of losses it could rapidly make good. The rapid and large number of losses temporarily outstripped the capability of the reinforcement machine in Britain, leading to losses that weakened the front-line infantry companies. However, these shortages were mitigated by the sheer scale of the total and decisive victory of Allied arms in late August.

AEF-AAI-&-UK BATTLE CASUALTY
AEF-AAI-&-UK BATTLE CASUALTY
A TO J

Figure P.1 Personnel working on the index of battle casualties, Canadian Military Headquarters Records Branch, Acton, England, 5 June 1945. The Canadian Army (Active) overseas was extremely well supported in all administrative and record-keeping functions. | LAC 227715

Figure P.2 Regimental aid party treating an infantryman of the South Saskatchewan Regiment who was wounded by sniper fire while crossing a canal north of Laren, Netherlands, 7 April 1945. | LAC 3192271

Figure P.3 Wounded infantrymen of Support Company, the Queen's Own Cameron Highlanders of Canada, being helped to cover south of Kirchhatten, Germany, ca. 22 April 1945. | LAC 3524541

Figure P.4 Tank crew with their Sherman Vc Firefly tank of the 1st Hussars near Zetten, Netherlands, 20 January 1945. | LAC 3207720

Figure P.5 Personnel with the Sherman tank "Bomb" of the Sherbrooke Fusiliers Regiment, which landed in France on D-Day and continued in action through to VE day, Zutphen, Netherlands, 8 June 1945. This tank was rare in that it survived eleven months of combat operations. | LAC 3514141

Figure P.6 Gunners S.S. Lott and J.G. Spear, 17th Field Regiment, Royal Canadian Artillery, overhauling a jeep motor, 11th Infantry Brigade, Royal Canadian Electrical and Mechanical Engineers, Groningen, Netherlands, 28 April 1945. | LAC 3526655

Figure P.7 Brigadier Kenneth Stuart, DSO, MC, stands in the first Canadian-built tank, the Valentine tank, at the Angus Shops of the Canadian Pacific Railway, 1941. As lieutenant-general and chief of the general staff in Ottawa during the summer of 1944, Stuart would preside over the reinforcement shortage of infantry, other ranks, in August and September. | LAC 3195943

Figure P.8 Captain C.H. Davis welcoming an incoming draft to No. 1 Canadian Armoured Corps Reinforcement Unit, Woking, England, 8 August 1944. Armoured troops looked similar to this when they arrived near the front in France to reinforce tank crews. | LAC 3226034

Figure P.9 Infantry, other ranks, reinforcements going ashore from a landing craft assault from HMCS *Prince Henry* off the Normandy bridgehead, June 1944. | LAC 3520621

Figure P.10 W.L. Mackenzie King shaking hands with J.L. Ralston at a banquet celebrating King's twenty-fifth anniversary as leader of the Liberal Party, 7 August 1944. This photo was taken during the beginning of the infantry, other ranks, reinforcement shortage in Normandy. Ralston was just beginning to receive information on the shortage of trained infantry reinforcements. | LAC 3361540

7

Channel Ports, Scheldt, and the River Mass

FOLLOWING THE NORMANDY CAMPAIGN, for the remainder of the month of August and into September, the Allies pursued fleeing German forces across northern France. In the course of the pursuit, perimeters were established around ports on the English Channel that still held German garrisons. Despite the euphoria of victory that marked the closure of the Falaise Gap and the subsequent high-speed pursuit, there were still instances of heavy combat.

The 2nd Canadian Infantry Division's first large offensive operation after Falaise was the clearance of the Forêt de la Londe on the Seine River. Undertaken by the 4th and 6th Canadian Infantry Brigades, this operation lasted from 27–29 August, and the six battalions suffered a total of 577 casualties.[1] For a division already struggling with low strength in its infantry companies, this battle was especially taxing. Luckily for the division, apart from the unopposed liberation of Dieppe on 1 September and some minor actions near Dunkirk, it saw little action in early September. The heavily fortified port of Dunkirk was originally designated to be captured by the division, which, by 9 September, had liberated some of the surrounding towns. As it advanced across France in August and early September, German channel garrisons were its main opposition. During this period, the division continued to carry out operations despite an increasing shortage of infantry, other ranks, replacements. The worst period for the division lasted from late August to mid-September, when all infantry regiments were understrength because of losses in the summer. As illustrated in detail in Appendix 3, the nadir was reached on 3 September, when the division's infantry regiments were short 2,645 other ranks.[2] The division's strength was weaker than that of the 3rd Canadian Infantry Division, even though the latter had been in combat for an additional fifty days.

After some deliberation by 21st Army Group Headquarters, the planned assault on Dunkirk was called off, and the city was to remain surrounded by other Allied forces. This action freed up the division for future operations north of Antwerp, Belgium. By 16 September, most of the division had arrived in its new assembly areas near the city. It had suffered many losses between 15 July and 30 August and needed to rest to receive and train new replacements. This

Figure 7.1

2nd Canadian Infantry Division strengths (thousands), July–September 1944

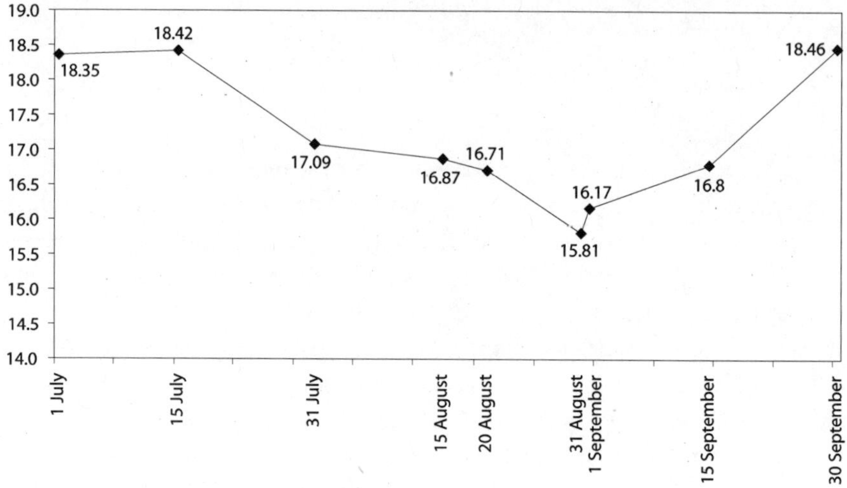

Source: LAC, RG 24, vol. 13,719, "2nd Canadian Corps A&Q War Diaries," July–September 1944, T-1870–71.

unexpected transit and rest period provided an opportunity to carry out this refitting.

During the brief halt in Dieppe in early September, reinforcements equivalent to eight new infantry companies reached the 2nd Canadian Infantry Division's infantry regiments.[3] Further transfers continued all month.[4] Many of these men had been remustered from other trades. This compromise solution to the shortage of readily available other ranks infantry utilized personnel already in the reinforcement stream to increase the speed in which they would reach their new units. These personnel often did not have a high level of infantry training prior to their remustering, and the transformation of a Royal Canadian Artillery (RCA) antiaircraft gunner to an infantryman could not be accomplished instantaneously. Luckily for the division, combat operations north of Antwerp did not begin until early October 1944. Thus by the beginning of the Battle of the Scheldt – operations to clear the approaches to the vital deepwater port of Antwerp – reinforcements accepted early in the month of September had had some time to train and acclimatize themselves.

Figures 7.1 and 7.2 compare the 2nd Canadian Infantry Division's strength against a larger German formation in the months June through September. The

Figure 7.2

German 12th SS Panzer Division strengths (thousands), June–September 1944

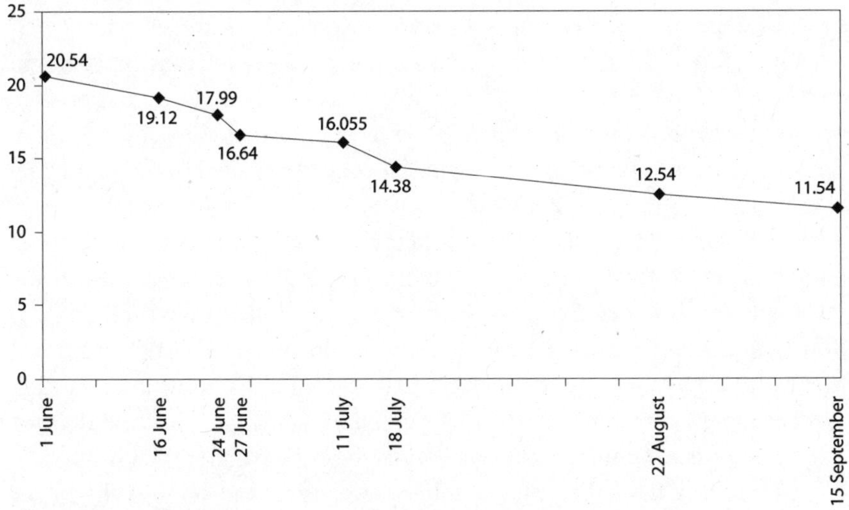

Source: Zetterling, *Normandy 1944*, 355; and Hubert Meyer, *The History of the 12. SS Panzer Division Hitlerjugend* (Winnipeg: J.J. Fedorowicz, 1994), 227.

figure illustrates that despite losses from intensive combat, the 2nd Canadian Infantry Division actually gained strength. The amount of reinforcements had been insufficient at times, but their flow to the division had been continuous. Though there were still some shortages in mid-September, the serious rebuilding effort launched during the halt at Dieppe had helped the division exceed its July strength. On 30 September this strength stood at 988 officers and 17,477 other ranks, making it very combat capable on the eve of the Battle of the Scheldt.[5] As displayed in Figure 7.2, by September the larger German formation's combat elements dwindled away to nearly nothing, leaving mainly rear-echelon troops.

With its new strength, the division plunged into combat operations in eastern Belgium and the southern Netherlands in fall 1944. In late September, initial operations had begun to clear the area west of Antwerp in preparation for a drive north on the left flank of the 4th Canadian Armoured Division. The division crossed the Antwerp-Turnhout Canal on 22 September and regrouped for an advance north. The eventual goal was clearing the northern bank of the Scheldt Estuary to free the port of Antwerp.

Following the Falaise Gap battle, the 3rd Canadian Infantry Division crossed the Seine at Elbeuf, operating with parts of the 4th Canadian Armoured Division.

On 3 September 1944, the division crossed the Somme River and moved northeast towards the channel ports up to the Belgian border. After advancing to the vicinity of Boulogne, France, by 5–6 September, the division embarked on a series of siege operations to capture enemy-held ports. Its first objectives were to overwhelm and force the surrender of the isolated garrisons of Boulogne and Calais.[6] These operations did not involve a large amount of military risk because these ports posed no offensive threat. The biggest challenge to Anglo-Canadian forces at this stage was logistical concerns related to the rapid pace of their advance.

The division managed to eventually take these two ports with support from naval and air assets. From 17 to 22 September, after a short siege, the 8th and 9th Canadian Infantry Brigades, in cooperation with British forces, seized Boulogne and surrounding areas. Because of the concrete fortifications and heavy artillery available to the surrounded German units, some infantry regiments suffered casualties. Between 25 September and 1 October, the division moved onto its next objective, Calais. Aided by Allied aircraft that again conducted multiple air strikes, by 1 October the division had successfully forced the surrender of the German garrison after briefly assaulting some of its fortified defences.[7]

Following the conclusion of the Falaise Gap battles in late August, the 2nd Canadian Armoured Brigade rapidly advanced towards the Belgian border. Operating with the 3rd Canadian Infantry Division, its regiments crossed the Seine and continued to pursue the enemy along the coast. In early September, this rapid advance brought Canadian forces into contact with German garrisons in the occupied channel ports. During these operations, individual armoured squadrons supported infantry regiments as they steadily reduced these challenging fortifications. September was not a period of intense armoured warfare, and the brigade's regiments accepted personnel reinforcements and new tanks without offsetting losses. The three regiments took receipt of forty-four replacement battle tanks during this month to bring them close to their war establishment figures.[8]

Despite heavy infantry losses for the 4th Canadian Armoured Division in the breakthrough battles to Falaise and the Falaise Pocket battles, operations continued without a break into late August and September. The division swept across northern France as part of the 21st Army Group's pursuit of the retreating Germans. Advancing towards the Seine as part of the 2nd Canadian Corps, the division crossed the river at Elbeuf on 26 August. Operating on the right flank of the 2nd Canadian Infantry Division, it liberated St. Omer on 5 September. By 8 September, it had reached Bruges, Belgium, and arrived at the Ghent Canal.

On 13–14 September, the 10th Canadian Infantry Brigade captured a bridgehead over the canal at Moerbrugge, but it was forced to relinquish it after heavy German counterattacks.[9] Further operations led to the liberation of Moerkerke and Eeklo. Subsequent tasks during September included patrolling the Leopold Canal perimeter of the German Breskens Pocket in the southern Netherlands before being redeployed in October to take part in fighting north of Antwerp.[10]

The three infantry regiments of the 10th Canadian Infantry Brigade had been significantly reinforced throughout September.[11] As of 30 September, the strength of the Argyll and Sutherland Highlanders of Canada stood at 37 officers and 834 other ranks. It had received an estimated 579 new personnel, placing it 2 percent over its authorized strength. The Lincoln and Welland Regiment was not as strong, containing 37 officers and 785 other ranks. It had received an estimated 408 replacements, bringing it to 97 percent of its war establishment.

The three regiments of the 4th Canadian Armoured Brigade also received new personnel in September 1944 but not as many as in the infantry regiments. As of 30 September, the 21st Canadian Armoured Regiment contained 36 officers and 563 other ranks. It had received 63 reinforcements in September 1944, bringing it to 91 percent of its authorized strength.[12] The 22nd Canadian Armoured Regiment's strength was 34 officers and 511 other ranks. This was 79 percent of its authorized strength. It had received only 74 new personnel during the month.[13]

As a result of the reduced German ability to attack Canadian units behind the front, the army-level artillery units of the 2nd Canadian Army Group Royal Artillery (AGRA) continued to be highly effective between September 1944 and May 1945 but with far fewer casualties. During the summer, losses in the AGRA units had increased significantly because of friendly fire in the way of inaccurate aerial bombing. These types of operations by Allied four-engined bombers were largely concluded by September. Total battle casualties for all three medium regiments in northwest Europe from 13 July to 4 October had been 250. Nonbattle casualties totalled 115.[14] Recorded monthly battle casualties for the remainder of the war for the three medium regiments totalled 190. Within this regiments, the number of nonbattle casualties that required hospitalization over the same period (October 1944 to May 1945) was an astounding 960.

Personnel replacement data for AGRA units for the period June to September 1944 is inconsistent, but the strength returns indicate that they were adequately resupplied with personnel. Because the Canadian Army's artillery doctrine revolved around these units to a certain degree, they could not be allowed to become weak due to nonreinforcement. As of 26 August, the 7th Medium Regiment, Royal Canadian Artillery (RCA), contained 28 officers and 507 other ranks, 94 percent of its war establishment.[15] The neutralization of the fortified German ports on the English Channel with their coastal gun emplacements was an important task for the 2nd AGRA, and it was fully engaged in these operations throughout late August and September. During the Battle of the Scheldt in October and early November, the 2nd Canadian AGRA delivered effective indirect fire against entrenched German infantry.

The Battle of the Scheldt Estuary began in earnest for the 2nd Canadian Infantry division on 2 October, when it attacked northward towards the South Beveland isthmus. In subsequent combat, the division crossed the isthmus, fought its way west, and linked up with elements of the British 52nd Infantry Division. Soon, all progress made in rebuilding the division was partly erased as infantry losses mounted in the difficult Scheldt Estuary fighting.[16] Forests, flooded fields, canals, rivers, and built-up areas were a challenge for attacking Canadian infantry regiments. These difficult infantry operations in largely flooded terrain ended in early November with the clearance of the north bank of the Scheldt Estuary.[17] Casualties were heavy, and infantry strengths in late October again became an issue. Fall casualty totals for three infantry regiments within the division illustrate the extent of the damage. The Essex Scottish Regiment suffered 396 battle and 134 nonbattle casualties during the September–November phase.[18] Le Régiment de Maisonneuve took 130 battle and 117 nonbattle casualties during the same period.[19] Les Fusiliers Mont-Royal sustained 329 battle and 83 nonbattle casualties.[20] Noninfantry regiments in the division suffered lighter casualties. During these three months, the 8th Canadian Reconnaissance Regiment suffered only 105 battle and 83 nonbattle casualties.[21]

As in Normandy, despite high infantry casualties there was never a shortage of heavy weapons or combat "A" vehicles in the division.[22] The difficult terrain in the Scheldt limited mechanized movement to a large degree and placed the emphasis on dismounted infantry tactics. As of 30 November, the division contained 103 percent of its war establishment strength in combat "A" vehicles and 99 percent of its major weapons systems.

As part of 2nd Canadian Corps, the 3rd Canadian Infantry Division was then ordered to move east to the vicinity of Antwerp, Belgium. From late September onward the division was to take part in operations to clear the Scheldt Estuary. This clearance was necessary so the vital port could be opened for Allied shipping. Strength returns for the infantry regiments during early October reflect the fact that a significant reinforcement of the division had taken place in late September. As of 5 October, the 7th Canadian Infantry Brigade's average battalion strength was 39 officers and 754 other ranks, for a total of 793 personnel. The 8th Canadian Infantry Brigade's average was the strongest at 37 officers and

774 other ranks for a total of 811 personnel. The 9th Canadian Infantry Brigade's average unit strength was the weakest, but still adequate, at 38 officers and 746 other ranks.[23]

The division's main task for October was the liquidation of the Breskens Pocket, an area surrounded by the Leopold Canal forming the south bank of the Scheldt Estuary. The Germans, surrounded in the pocket, were defending the area from prepared positions and were well supplied. On 6 October, the division launched Operation Switchback, which consisted of amphibious assaults across the Leopold Canal to clear the pocket. During land and amphibious assaults in October, it liberated Hoofdplaat, Biervliet, Schoondijke, Groede, Retranchement, and Knocke-sur-Mer, one of the last areas of Belgium to be liberated.[24] Due to the infantry-centric nature of these operations, infantry casualties were high, and the brigades needed considerable reinforcements. The fighting was difficult because of the flooded terrain, dikes, and entrenched enemy.[25] The final German positions fell on 3 November.

The strength and casualty returns for 31 October 1944 illustrate how well the division's infantry regiments had been resupplied with new personnel during the Battle of the Scheldt. The Regina Rifle Regiment of the 7th Canadian Infantry Brigade had suffered 384 battle and 74 nonbattle casualties during the month.[26] It had received 387 reinforcements, the equivalent to three complete new rifle companies, and its strength was 36 officers and 766 other ranks, 94 percent of its authorized personnel strength. The 8th Canadian Infantry Brigade's Queen's Own Rifles of Canada was not as strong. It had suffered 146 battle and 29 nonbattle casualties.[27] It had received 222 reinforcements, bringing its strength at month's end to 34 officers and 721 other ranks, 88 percent of its war establishment.

Casualties among divisional troops and RCA regiments continued to be much lighter than those suffered by the infantry regiments than bore the brunt of German defensive fire during the Battle of the Scheldt. The Cameron Highlanders of Ottawa (Machine Gun) suffered 30 battle and 33 nonbattle casualties. It received 231 reinforcements during the course for the month, rebuilding its machine gun and mortar companies. Suffering 39 battle and 33 nonbattle casualties, the 7th Canadian Reconnaissance Regiment (17th Duke of York's Royal Canadian Hussars) received 83 reinforcements during the course of the month, bringing its strength up to 42 officers and 742 other ranks.[28] RCA casualties within the division were very low because the enemy had a difficult time attacking their gun positions. Massive Canadian retaliation occurred if the Germans made any attempts at sustained counterbattery fire. Because of these conditions, the number of nonbattle casualties in the RCA regiments during October exceeded the number of battle losses: 48 battle and 60 nonbattle casualties. However, 127 reinforcements were dispatched to the RCA regiments, maintaining their strength during the month.[29]

Inventories of combat "A" vehicles and heavy weapons within the 3rd Canadian Infantry Division remained high because operations were focused on infantry-led attacks, some of which were amphibious. Also, there were a limited number of routes and nonflooded terrain that could be used for mechanized warfare in the Breskens Pocket area. Also missing were a viable number of German armoured fighting vehicles (AFVs) or antitank weapons, which could be used to destroy carriers, antitank guns, and tank destroyers within the division. Combat "A" vehicle losses had been light during the October fighting.[30] As of 31 October, 674 vehicles were on strength versus the division's war establishment figure of 612. It was 10 percent overstrength in this category. Unauthorized extra "A" vehicles within the division included four of the invaluable Wasp II flamethrower carriers.

As always, there were some shortages. Against an authorized level of twenty-eight Daimler armoured cars, only twenty-two were present. Of the seventeen M10 17-pounder self-propelled tank destroyers that the division was authorized, none had been issued. The 3rd Anti-Tank Regiment, RCA, was still making do with the older M10 3-inch variants. Of the 120 T16 tracked-gun tractor carriers on the war establishment figures, only twenty-four were on strength. Extra Universal Carriers within the division were assuming their role. Inventories of nonvehicle major weapons within the division were also at high levels as of 31 October.[31] The division contained 96 percent of its heavy weapons, with 536 heavy weapons present compared to its war establishment of 561. Shortages included a total lack of towed 40 mm antiaircraft guns, with more 40 mm antiaircraft self-propelled variants taking up the slack.

The 2nd Canadian Armoured Brigade had a limited role in the Scheldt fighting because the terrain was flooded and criss-crossed with canals and dikes. An armoured squadron would be parcelled off to support a battalion for a limited amount of time, then it would be assigned to another. Tank and crew casualties were considerably lighter in this period because operations were infantry oriented. The regiments lost at total of ninety-five personnel as battle casualties during this month. A total of seventy-two nonbattle casualties were suffered in the same time period, illustrating the constant drain on the regiments, even when they were not involved in combat operations.[32]

Operating under command of the 1st British Corps, the 4th Canadian Armoured Division moved to the vicinity of Antwerp in early October in preparation for combat operations north of the city. On 9 October, its armoured reconnaissance regiment and a company of infantry began operations to support the 2nd Canadian Infantry Division. From 17 October onward, the majority of the division's combat strength was concentrated against the German forces confronting the Canadian Army's right flank in this area. While the 2nd Canadian Infantry Division moved west to attack the South Beveland Peninsula, the 4th Canadian Armoured Division guarded its flank and pushed north. Advancing on the left flank of the 49th British West Riding Division, the division liberated Essen (22 October), Bergen op Zoom (27 October), and Steenbergen and Hollandsch Diep (4 November).

The division's four infantry regiments took heavy losses during the Scheldt fighting.[33] The strength returns at the end of October showcase each regiment's condition during the midpoint of their combat operations, rather than at their start or conclusion. In contrast to August, all infantry units had received constant reinforcements throughout the month. These reinforcements allowed the regiments to retain a higher level of combat effectiveness than in Normandy. The Argyll and Sutherland Highlanders of Canada suffered 186 battle and 64 nonbattle casualties during October and received 118 reinforcements to make up these losses. At the end of the month, this regiment consisted of 29 officers and 649 other ranks, 79 percent of its authorized strength. The Algonquin Regiment took a total of 180 battle and 48 nonbattle losses during the same month. These losses reduced it to 33 officers and 670 other ranks. It had received 164 reinforcements during this period, enough to keep it at 82 percent of its war establishment.

The division had faced determined opposition in the Scheldt in the way of German airborne Fallschirmjäger regiments, but these light-infantry formations were poorly equipped in comparison to the panzer divisions encountered in the summer. As evidence of this difference, total enemy equipment destroyed by the 29th Canadian Armoured Reconnaissance Regiment in October was one 8.8 cm antiaircraft gun, one 8 cm mortar, one 7.5 cm Pak 40 antitank gun, one 7.5 cm L/48 gunned Sturmgeschültz III assault gun, and one obsolete Panzer III medium tank.[34] While the infantry combat was intense, the enemy did not have the same capability to inflict high losses on the noninfantry units. As an example, in October, the 22nd Canadian Armoured Regiment suffered 22 battle and 39 nonbattle casualties and received 129 reinforcements, raising its strength to 37 officers and 577 other ranks, or 89 percent of its war establishment.[35] In reviewing documents on reinforcements allocated to armoured regiments, the totals are often large without a corresponding increase in regimental strength returns. This was due to the practice of dispatching personnel belonging to the regiment to the armoured delivery squadron for further training or to pick up new tanks.

The personnel would then return to the regiment as reinforcements when they had already been part of the regiment.[36]

The four divisional RCA regiments' combined casualty totals for October illustrate a lower casualty rate. All four regiments recorded 36 battle and 49 nonbattle casualties during this month. Against these losses, 102 reinforcements had been dispatched, maintaining the strength of these units.[37] The 8th Light Anti-Aircraft Regiment's strength at the end of the month stood at 35 officers and 559 other ranks, 1 percent above its new September war establishment of 34 officers and 551 other ranks.[38] Compared to Normandy, enemy AFV, artillery, and aerial activity on the Canadian front had dropped off considerably during October and early November. This change led to far fewer battle casualties in the RCA regiments.

On 1 November, midway through its Scheldt combat operations, the division reported a total "fit" AFV strength of 247 medium and light tanks.[39] Returns for 31 October show the division overstrength in combat "A" vehicles: 839 combat vehicles were on strength against an authorized total of 777, placing the division 8 percent over its war establishment.[40] Any shortages in certain vehicles types were made up by extras in others. Some shortages in the armoured and RCA regiments continued to persist. Against a war establishment figure of sixty Mark Vc 17-pounder Sherman Firefly tanks, only eighteen were on strength. Seventeen unauthorized Mark Ic Sherman Firefly variants, which also had the 17-pounder gun, had been issued to partially fill the shortage. This addition gave the division a total of thirty-nine 17-pounder equipped tanks, 65 percent of its authorized war establishment tank strength. A shortage of armoured recovery vehicle tanks was still present at the end of the month. Against the war establishment of twelve Sherman V ARVs, only eight were on hand. None of the twenty-seven authorized Sherman V observation-post tanks had been delivered to the RCA field regiments as of 31 October 1944. Fortunately, seventeen unauthorized Ram observation-post variants had been issued to cover this shortage. As of the end of the month, the twenty-four Crusader gun tractor towers allocated for the antitank regiment had still not been issued. The division had also not received a sizable quantity of Wasp II flamethrower carriers at this point, having only one on strength.

With the division constantly advancing and rarely suffering reverses, few heavy weapons were lost between October and early November. Midway through the Scheldt fighting, the division had excessive inventories.[41] Against an authorized level of 198 heavy weapons, 308 were on strength as of 31 October. These totals indicated a possible change over of equipment for the division or an administrative reporting error. For example, against an authorized total of eighty

2-inch mortars, the infantry regiments contained 142; fifty-one 6-pounder antitank guns were on strength against its authorized war establishment of eighteen.

Following the Normandy Campaign, battle casualties within all 2nd Canadian Corps–level regiments dropped significantly. Although these regiments had roles in the conquest of the channel ports and the Battle of the Scheldt in fall 1944, they did not experience the same levels of combat as they had previously. Due to the enemy's infantry often being entrenched and surrounded, the operations of Canadian antitank, antiaircraft, and long-range reconnaissance forces was limited. As an example, the role of the RCA's 6th Light Anti-Aircraft Regiment had significantly changed due to a lack of actual enemy aircraft to shoot down. In fall 1944, it was available for non-antiaircraft tasks such as engaging ground targets and security sweeps for enemy stragglers. With the enemy's ability to attack its positions on the battlefield significantly reduced, the 2nd Survey Regiment, RCA, suffered only seven battle casualties from September to November.[42] While it recorded eight days of enemy air activity contacts in July and five in August, none were recorded in September 1944.[43]

Despite high infantry casualties between September and November, the 2nd Canadian Infantry Division rapidly rebuilt itself once again after offensive operations ended. As of 30 November, it had few weaknesses apart from a possible lack of training for new replacement soldiers. The formations of the German Fifteenth Army opposing the division in the Netherlands were very weak in comparison. During the fighting in fall 1944, no German panzer divisions had been deployed against Canadian advances, only weak infantry formations.[44] This made a tremendous difference with regard to the number and kind of weapons systems that could be brought to bear by the enemy. If there had been any significant weaknesses within the division during fall 1944, the Germans would have been hard-pressed to exploit them as they had that summer.

In late November, the division held part of the static northern flank of the Nijmegen Salient, a bulge in the line created by the British-American Operation Market Garden in September. Between 10 November 1944 and 31 January 1945, with the First Canadian Army temporarily ceasing offensive operations, the division remained in these positions. During this phase, the infantry regiments were fully rebuilt, the reinforcement shortage having ended by this point. An average Canadian infantry regiment within the 4th Canadian Infantry Brigade, the Essex Scottish Regiment, contained 38 officers and 818 other ranks.[45] These figures placed it 1 percent over its authorized strength. Many other regiments were completely rebuilt in the period from 10 to 30 November and were close to their establishment strengths by month's end. The reinforcement system during this time had been allowed to function without the steady outflow of casualties working against it. The hiatus in offensive operations allowed the infantry regiments to accept reinforcements, rest, and conduct important training and patrolling.[46]

Following the conclusion of Operation Switchback, the 3rd Canadian Infantry Division ceased offensive operations. It assumed a static position on the Maas River as part of the 2nd Canadian Corps' defensive line within the Nijmegen Salient. During this time, the division's activities consisted of manning defensive positions, training, and sending out regular combat patrols.[47] The division suffered few battle casualties between November 1944 and January 1945 as there was limited contact with the enemy. The opposing German forces in the Netherlands were weak, lacking the capability to launch sustained offensive operations. The main German focus on the western front during this time was its offensive operations in Belgium and Luxembourg, where the largest percentage of its divisions and resources were being utilized.

The inventories of Sherman, Sherman Firefly, and Stuart tanks within the 2nd Canadian Armoured Brigade were slightly weaker as of 31 October. The brigade had not lost many tanks during this month, but a number may have been in workshops due to the wear and tear involved in crossing northern France and parts of Belgium. Sherman, Sherman Firefly, and Stuart holdings at this point stood at 161 compared to a new October war establishment figure of 226. This was 71 percent of the new authorized establishment. More Sherman Firefly 17-pounders had become available to the Commonwealth armies in fall 1944, and the total number within the brigade grew to thirty-five by month's end.[48]

Within the 4th Canadian Armoured Division, all three regiments of the 10th Canadian Infantry Brigade were rebuilt following the conclusion of the Scheldt fighting, as reflected in their 30 November strength returns.[49] The Algonquin Regiment, for example, contained 38 officers and 787 other ranks at the end of the month. It had received 278 reinforcements during November, raising it to 97 percent of its authorized strength. The other two regiments within the brigade received even more reinforcements, placing them close to their war establishments. Figure 7.3 shows the strength returns of the Argyll and Sutherland Highlanders of Canada in August and October, which reflected the cost of high-intensity offensive operations in these months. Large losses occurred quickly, often stripping a regiment of a complete company within a day.

Like all formations in the First Canadian Army, the 4th Canadian Armoured Division spent the winter of 1944–45 located in near-static positions. Holding part of the western sector front in depth and conducting regular patrols,

Figure 7.3

Strength returns, the Argyll and Sutherland Highlanders of Canada, August 1944 to April 1945

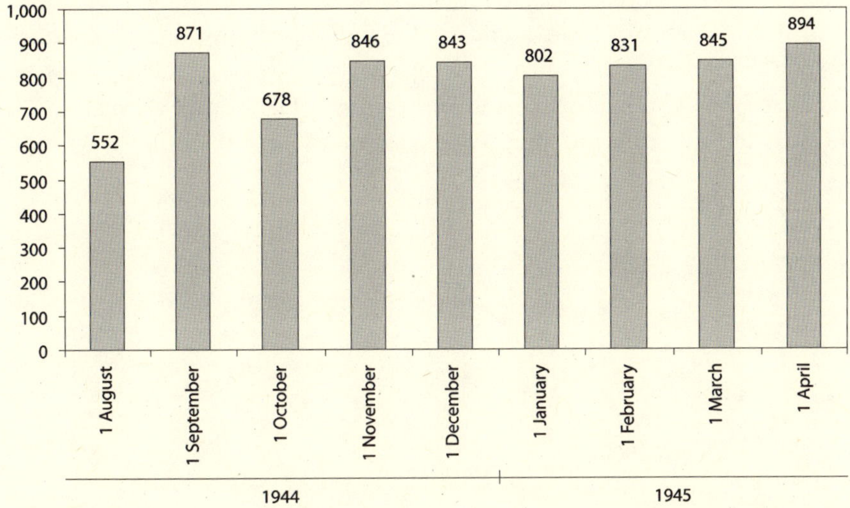

Note: September 1944 war establishment total = 850.
Source: LAC, RG 24, vols. 13,658–65, "First Canadian Army A&Q War Diaries," August 1944 to May 1945, "Consolidated Daily Casualty and Strength Returns."

supported by armoured and artillery assets, it could accept replacements, train, and conduct fire missions against German positions along the Waal River.

Personnel levels for the four 2nd Canadian Corps–level regiments were satisfactory at the end of November and beginning of December 1944, indicating that sufficient reinforcements had been received. For example, on 25 November 1944, the RCA's 6th Light Anti-Aircraft Regiment's strength stood at 38 officers and 746 other ranks, 97 percent of its war establishment. Heavy weapons and combat "A" vehicle inventories were also satisfactory. Troops from 2nd Canadian Corps possessed 271 out of an authorized level of 278 combat "A" vehicles on 30 November 1944.[50] This placed the four regiments at 97 percent of their "A" vehicle war establishments. Nonvehicle equipment levels were also satisfactory. Eighty heavy weapons systems were on strength against the war establishment level of seventy-two on 30 November.[51]

In conclusion, while the First Canadian Army did experience heavy combat during the Battle of the Scheldt in fall 1944, periods of reduced activity before and after this series of operations allowed its infantry regiments to rebuild themselves. Once fully engaged in the battles north and west of Antwerp, a continuous reinforcement effort allowed the infantry regiments involved to maintain their strength. The lack of panzer divisions on their front and a lack of suitable terrain in some phases of the fighting allowed the noninfantry combat arms regiments involved to escape heavy losses. The situation was even better for the RCA's field artillery units, because by fall 1944 the German ability to strike at these units had almost completely disappeared.

8
Veritable, Blockbuster, and War's End

Operations in the new year largely consisted of patrolling and indirect fire missions as formations of the Canadian Army faced the Germans along the Waal and Maas Rivers. Weekly casualties in the winter were low. The time was used wisely for reorganization, integrating new personnel, receiving new vehicles and weapons, and preparing for further offensive operations in the spring.

Prior to its February 1945 deployment to Germany and the battles in the Rhineland, the 2nd Canadian Infantry Division had no obvious weaknesses. Its strength on 31 January 1945 stood at 970 officers and 17,092 other ranks, for a total of 18,062 men, or 99 percent of its authorized establishment.[1] The cutting edge of the division, its infantry regiments, were very strong. The South Saskatchewan Regiment had a strength of 34 officers and 814 other ranks, and the Royal Highland Regiment of Canada (the Black Watch) contained 38 officers and 817 other ranks.[2] Divisional artillery units were also up to strength. On 27 January, the 6th Field Regiment, Royal Canadian Artillery (RCA), had 38 officers and 629 other ranks against an authorized strength of 38 officers and 638 other ranks, while the 2nd Anti-Tank Regiment, RCA, contained 36 officers and 646 other ranks against a war establishment of 35 officers and 614 other ranks.[3]

Near the commencement of Operation Veritable in February, the 2nd Canadian Infantry Division's equipment and combat "A" vehicle state were satisfactory.[4] The division had a large inventory of heavy weapons, 1 percent over what it was authorized. Meanwhile, on 31 January, combat "A" vehicle inventories totalled 745 versus the 638 it was authorized, or 117 percent of its authorized strength. The vehicle return for the end of January records the arrival of some of the most advanced weapons systems operated by the division. The 2nd Anti-Tank Regiment, RCA, received the first six of its authorized Valentine Archer 17-pounder self-propelled antitank guns. With the addition of these armoured fighting vehicles (AFVs), the regiment's antitank capability had never been stronger.

Combat resumed on 8 February with the division's participation in Operation Veritable, designed to clear the western bank of the Rhine in preparation for a deeper invasion of Germany itself. The division was active during this offensive, and between 8 and 19 February its infantry brigades captured Wyler, Kranenberg, and the area near Louisendorf, Germany, the site of bitter combat as German armoured forces counterattacked, battering the division's infantry regiments and causing some local reverses.[5] With armoured support, the division eventually turned the tables on these attacks, and the German forces were forced to withdraw because of heavy losses. By 21 February, the operation was complete. During the fighting, the 2nd Canadian Infantry Division suffered high personnel casualties on several occasions.

Prior to combat operations in the Netherlands and Germany in 1945, the 3rd Canadian Infantry Division had few personnel deficiencies. Its strength as of 31 January stood at 990 officers and 18,346 other ranks.[6] The program of remustering general-duty reinforcements had been successful from September onward.[7] Immediately prior to combat operations in February, there was no lack of combat capability within the division's three infantry brigades and divisional units. Its infantry regiments had suffered few battle casualties and received adequate reinforcements to cover nonbattle losses between November 1944 and January 1945.[8] The number of nonbattle casualties for all combat arms units had increased in the winter months because personnel were living in dugouts or ruined buildings. The Royal Winnipeg Rifles lost 443 personnel to battle and 254 to nonbattle causes in three months. As of 31 January 1945, it received 323 reinforcements, bringing its strength up to 38 officers and 837 other ranks. Le Régiment de la Chaudière suffered 49 battle and 176 nonbattle casualties during the winter period. Over 410 soldiers rejoined the regiment or were posted as reinforcements; on 31 January, its strength was 43 officers and 795 other ranks.

At the end of January, the RCA regiments also contained high levels of personnel. The 3rd Anti-Tank Regiment's strength stood at 36 officers and 632 other ranks, putting it 3 percent over its authorized strength.[9] Casualties were low among the RCA regiments due to the limited capability of the enemy and their battlefield position to the rear of friendly infantry regiments. The artillery regiments were active in supporting the infantry's patrolling activities and in engaging targets of opportunity. The RCA's antiaircraft and antitank crews were also involved in the engagement of enemy positions and occasionally took small infantry roles. Total casualties in January for all RCA regiments within the 3rd Canadian Infantry Division were 3 battle and 156 nonbattle. The regiments received a total of 146 replacements during the month.[10]

As of 31 January, the division's equipment and weaponry inventories were similar to the numbers on strength in October 1944. Little had changed apart from the acquisition of more potent combat "A" vehicles and heavy weapons.[11] New weapons systems on hand included twelve towed 17-pounder antitank guns, acquired at the expense of a similar number of 6-pounders. New combat "A" vehicles included twelve new Valentine Archer 17-pounder self-propelled tank destroyers, received in exchange for M10 3-inch tank destroyers. Unauthorized vehicles held by the division at this point included nineteen Wasp II flame-thrower carriers and fourteen Humber scout cars.

Combat commenced in mid-February. From 8–14 February the division cleared the southern banks of the Waal and Rhine Rivers. Because these areas were flooded, the operations were largely amphibious. Advancing southeast, by 14 February the assaulting infantry brigades reached the Rhine at Emmerich. Between 16–17 February, the division's lead regiments assaulted Moyland Wood in their part of the Hochwald Gap battle. Forest fighting against dug-in enemy positions was difficult, and the progress was slow. Follow-on forces then assaulted west past the German town of Louisendorf, taking heavy casualties when counterattacked by German armoured forces.[12]

In fall and winter 1944–45, the 2nd Canadian Armoured Brigade's regiments accepted personnel reinforcements and more advanced armoured vehicles. As a result, all three regiments had satisfactory personnel levels and sufficient quantities of new and repaired battle tanks at the end of January. Between November 1944 and January 1945, the 27th Canadian Armoured Regiment received 350 personnel.[13] During the same period, the three regiments received 136 new and repaired Sherman, Sherman Firefly, and Stuart light tanks of all marks.[14]

In spring 1945, the brigade played a large role in supporting infantry operations during Operation Veritable. This advance through the Reichswald Forest between the Maas and Rhine Rivers brought the 2nd Canadian Corps to the vicinity of the German city of Goch. These offensive operations were followed up by participation, in late February and early March, in Operation Blockbuster. In these battles, the armoured regiments drove east through the forested areas between the Rhine and Maas Rivers, supporting battalion-level infantry operations. This fighting was challenging as the armoured squadrons had little room to manoeuvre. These engagements brought some of the last armoured encounters of the war for the brigade, and it managed to inflict heavy losses on the German armoured units. Many Sherman Firefly 17-pounder tanks were in action during the fighting, and the well-armed tank was effective against German armour. The regiments suffered a total of 121 battle and 230 nonbattle personnel casualties in February and early March.[15]

The 4th Canadian Armoured Division, as part of forces deployed in the Nijmegen Salient, was subordinated to 1st British Corps. As of 25 December 1944, it was designated an army reserve for the First Canadian Army and redeployed to Breda, the Netherlands. On 26 January 1945, the 10th Canadian Infantry Brigade attacked the German harbour bridgehead of Kapelsche Veer on the southern bank of the Maas River.[16] This limited operation was completed by 30 January, and there were significant infantry casualties because of temporary reverses. After this difficult operation, combat for the division consisted of patrols and raids, often with armoured and artillery support.

Combat "A" vehicle inventories within the 4th Canadian Armoured Division prior to offensive operations in spring 1945 were satisfactory.[17] As of 31 January, the division was overstrength in some categories, had shortages in others, and contained a considerable contingent of unauthorized vehicles. Returns for this date show 741 combat "A" vehicles on strength, 95 percent of its January war establishment of 781. The nonvehicle weaponry inventories of the division was also satisfactory at this time, the totals changing little from their fall 1944 levels.[18] During January, the division received a combined total of forty-seven new and repaired 75 mm Shermans, Sherman Firefly 17-pounders, and Stuart light tanks (all models employed).[19] This number was more than adequate considering the division had been inactive from November 1944 to late January 1945.

From August to December 1944, the division had been adequately reinforced with new and repaired AFVs via "D" Squadron of the 25th Canadian Armoured Delivery Regiment. As illustrated in Figure 8.1, the deliveries of new and repaired tanks for the division were often equal to a third of new German Panzer IV medium tank production for all German land forces. The 7.5 cm L/48 gunned Panzer IV Ausführung H and J models were the backbone of Germany's armoured force in spring and summer 1944, equipping one out of every two battalions in each panzer regiment in the German Army and Waffen-SS. The purpose of this figure is to illustrate the massive superiority of the Allies in their ability to supply large quantities of new and repaired AFVs to front-line units versus the utter collapse of Germany's ability to supply her armed forces.

During the winter, the division had received an adequate number of personnel reinforcements.[20] While the armoured and RCA regiments remained near their October 1944 strengths, as of 31 January the infantry regiments were at much higher levels. The reinforcements dispatched not only replaced battle losses but also mitigated the ongoing drain of nonbattle casualties. The Lake Superior Regiment, for example, lost 146 personnel to nonbattle causes between November 1944 and January 1945. By 31 January, the same regiment had received 351 reinforcements, bringing its strength up to 36 officers and 801 other ranks. The Algonquin Regiment had received 500 replacements over the winter, giving it a strength of 37 officers and 812 other ranks on the eve of combat operations.

Figure 8.1

Comparison of tank replacement and delivery, 4th Canadian Armoured Division, to German Panzer IV medium tank production for all German land forces, August–December 1944

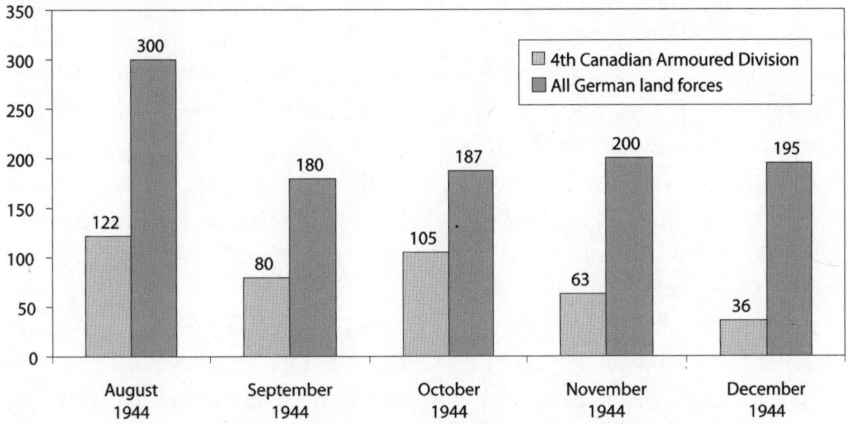

Note: The Canadian tanks were Sherman, Sherman Firefly, and Stuart models.
Source: LAC, RG 24, vol. 14,277, "D Squadron, 25th Canadian Armoured Delivery Regiment, War Diaries," August–November 1944, T-12748; Jentz, *Panzertruppen*, vol. 2, *The Complete Guide*, 283, Appendix B4, "Panzer IV Inventory: Gains and Reported Losses, August–December 1944."

The Lincoln and Welland Regiment was also reinforced significantly, receiving a total of 672 new and returning personnel. Despite this total, it was still weak at month's end, consisting of 28 officers and 764 other ranks. This weakness was the result of heavy casualties in the operation to clear the port village of Kapelsche Veer in late January 1945. Unlike most Canadian divisions, the 4th Canadian Armoured Division was not involved in Operation Veritable, apart from providing support from its divisional artillery.

The winter months of December 1944 and January 1945 were a relatively quiet time for the corps-level units of the 2nd Canadian Corps. They had sufficient time to absorb replacements, conduct training, and support patrolling and artillery activity. On the eve of Operation Veritable, all four regiments contained high personnel levels. The 6th Anti-Tank Regiment, RCA, possessed 37 officers and 724 other ranks, 95 percent of its war establishment. Combat "A" vehicle and equipment returns for 2nd Canadian Corps troops as of 31 January were satisfactory. The units contained 267 combat "A" vehicles against their authorized level of 286, 93 percent of their war establishment. The units were overstrength in their non-"A" vehicle weapons inventories. A total of eighty-four 40 mm antiaircraft guns, 17-pounder antitank guns, and 2-inch mortars were on strength versus a war establishment total of seventy-two.[21]

For the 2nd Canadian Army Group Royal Artillery (AGRA), equipment challenges were not an issue during its campaign in northwest Europe. As shown in Figure 8.2, the operational equipment levels of the three 2nd Canadian AGRA medium regiments were always near 100 percent. If they were to keep delivering the effective indirect fire support that Canadian Army operations revolved around, levels could not drop. These units were in action every day in contrast to the infantry, armoured, antitank, and antiaircraft units. Like the divisional RCA field regiments, the only time they were not in action was when they were in transit to their next gun positions. Strength returns for 2nd Canadian AGRA units on the eve of the February Rhineland battles illustrate that they were constantly reinforced during the winter months. On 27 January, the 7th Medium Regiment, RCA, contained 28 officers and 532 other ranks, 99 percent of its war establishment.[22] The 3rd Medium Regiment, RCA was also strong, consisting of

Figure 8.2

Operational equipment levels of 2nd Canadian AGRA medium regiments, July 1944 to April 1945 (War Establishment = 48 guns)

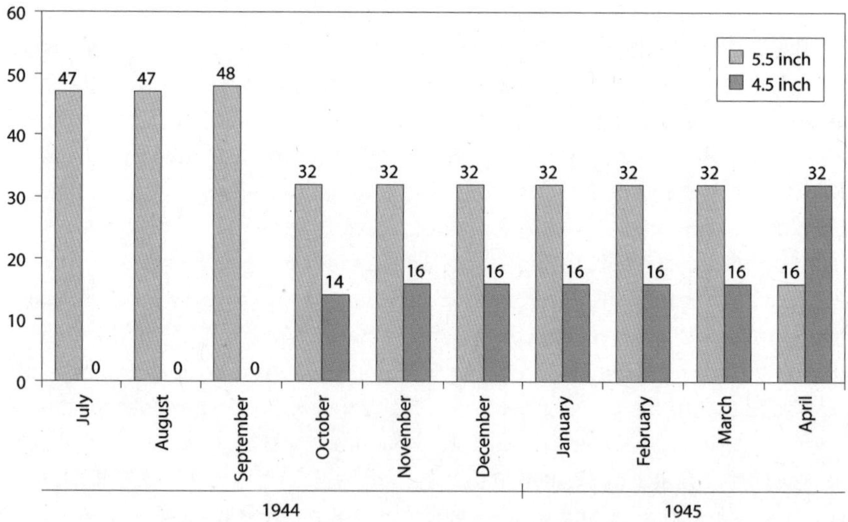

Source: LAC, RG 24, vol. 10,553, "Canadian Army 'A' & 'B' Vehicle Position Report," file 215A21.085 (D1); and LAC, RG 24, vol. 10,670, "Equipment State, Canadian Army, Monthly Report," file 215C1.083 (D6), July 1944 to April 1945.

twenty-nine officers and 516 other ranks. It was only 4 percent understrength compared to its war establishment.[23]

The First Canadian Army encountered heavy resistance during the 1945 Rhineland fighting, which occurred during Operations Veritable and Blockbuster. Both operations were supported by significant artillery programs designed to reduce German defences and inflict a large number of casualties. The 2nd Canadian AGRA, along with other British AGRA formations, played a central role in these programs. The fire of these regiments along with the divisional 25-pounder field regiments was crucial in destroying German positions and repulsing their counterattacks. Casualty totals for the February and March were 67 (battle) and 312 (nonbattle) among the four 2nd Canadian AGRA regiments.[24] The fact that the nonbattle casualties outweighed the battle casualties illustrates Germany's reduced ability that spring to attack or destroy Canadian artillery positions.

Though it had been assembling through the month of March, it was only on 7 April 1945 that returns for the 1st Canadian Infantry Division appeared on the daily "Consolidated Casualty and Strength State" return at First Canadian Army Headquarters. The division's strength was 880 officers and 15,819 other ranks, totalling 16,699 personnel.[25] The transit period from Italy had allowed these regiments to be rested and refitted, and their personnel levels were high. The 48th Highlanders of Canada's strength stood at 38 officers and 830 other ranks, 2 percent overstrength.[26] The Seaforth Highlanders of Canada consisted of 39 officers and 837 other ranks, 4 percent overstrength.[27] The noninfantry regiments within the division were also at satisfactory personnel levels prior to combat operations in mid-April 1945. Take the strengths of two regiments of divisional troops as examples. As of 7 April, the 4th Canadian Reconnaissance Regiment's strength was 42 officers and 759 other ranks, 97 percent of its authorized strength.[28] The Saskatoon Light Infantry's strength on the same date was 34 officers and 693 other ranks, 99 percent of its war establishment.[29]

It is only partially possible to assess how successful the First Canadian Army was in re-equipping the division with vehicles and weapons in March. Its data was not included in the 21st Army Group's consolidated vehicle position report return for 31 March. During this period, its "A" vehicle returns would have been in flux because of the re-equipment process. The division's vehicle return for 30 April is included, but the earlier nonreporting makes it impossible to compare pre- and postcombat "A" vehicle states.[30] The division's data was present on the 21st Army Group's equipment state return of 30 April, which covered all types of nonvehicle major weapons systems such as artillery pieces, mortars, and medium machine guns.[31]

Apart from some minor shortages, as of 31 March the division's inventory levels of authorized major weapons systems was satisfactory.[32] The division contained 527 heavy weapons, 93 percent of its war establishment. Some minor challenges in this area were present. There were only thirty-five medium .303 machine guns against the authorized level of forty. Only 252 infantry 2-inch mortars were on hand against the establishment strength of 283. The division contained only fifty-four 3-inch mortars against its authorized level of sixty.

While the Canadian Army had no major difficulties equipping its units with weapons and vehicles in northwest Europe during spring 1945, the opposing enemy formations facing it did. The state of equipment levels, repair services, fuel supplies, and replacement capability within the enemy units was far below acceptable levels.[33] The 1st Canadian Infantry Division was lavishly equipped in comparison, and this gave it a large degree of superiority over defending German units with regard to the number of weapons systems it could deploy and their effect. Against low-quality entrenched German infantry with little access to heavy weapons, this factor was devastating.[34]

Under the temporary command of 2nd Canadian Corps as of 3 April, the division was deployed in an assembly area in the Reichswald Forest.[35] Its first operation was to attack west into the Netherlands as part of the 2nd Canadian Corp's Operation Cannonshot. The lead elements of the division successfully consolidated a bridgehead over the IJssel River on 11 April.[36] German command and control was disorganized and, on average, the quality of enemy forces facing the division was low. The attacking infantry regiments made rapid progress with minimal casualties. Further advances resulted in the capture of Apeldoorn and the high ground near Arnhem. At the conclusion of this phase of fighting, the division reverted to the command of 1st Canadian Corps. Subsequent advances in mid-April took the division to the vicinities of Amersfoort, Nijkerk, and Harderwijk. Attached units in support of the division aided its rapid advance. The most notable example was 33 Battery, 6th Anti-Tank Regiment, RCA. Its M10 tank destroyers provided mobile fire support throughout the division's April operations.[37] During its brief period of combat operations, the 1st Canadian Infantry Division performed well against an enemy that was disintegrating.

Once these operations were completed on 19 April, the division halted offensive operations in the western Netherlands. The halt at the Grebbe River line was arranged so relief supplies could be delivered to starving Dutch civilians. The German occupation forces allowed these deliveries so long as the Allies advanced no farther west. Given the imminent end of hostilities, this temporary agreement halted the starvation of the civilian populace and spared the country further flooding and destruction.

Despite the short period of time that the division was in combat and the low strength of the defending German formations, the enemy still managed to inflict battle casualties. Divisional casualties were largely confined to the infantry regiments, and their losses were much higher than in the other combat arms. While casualties were at an acceptable level, on occasion they were still severe, with German forces dug in and prepared for a Canadian assault.

In the month of April, the three regiments of the 1st Canadian Infantry Brigade suffered a total of 155 battle casualties. The 2nd Canadian Infantry Brigade suffered 197, and the 3rd Canadian Infantry Brigade suffered a total of 164. The two regiments hardest hit were the Loyal Edmonton Regiment, with 97 battle casualties, and the Royal 22nd Regiment with 67. Although the war was nearly over, small pockets of determined German defenders were encountered; these groups even mounted an occasional counterattack against Canadian positions.

Casualties in April and May were low among noninfantry regiments in the 1st Canadian Infantry Division. For example, the 1st Anti-Tank Regiment, RCA, had only one battle casualty.[38] This points to a scarcity of enemy AFVs in this sector of the front. The Saskatoon Light Infantry suffered only ten battle casualties.[39] While the antitank regiment, the machine-gun battalion, and the reconnaissance regiment were deployed near the infantry positions, the remaining RCA field regiments were deployed to the rear. This grouping encompassed the light antiaircraft regiment and the three RCA field regiments. At this stage in the conflict, there was almost no enemy air activity and little in the way of sustained counterbattery fire on the RCA's field artillery positions. Accordingly, the 1st Field Regiment, Royal Canadian Horse Artillery, suffered only thirteen battle casualties for the months of April and May 1945. The 2nd Light Anti-Aircraft Regiment, RCA, suffered only four. These losses within the RCA regiments were negligible, and these units were never impeded from carrying out their missions.

Like any other formation in the Canadian Army, the 1st Canadian Infantry Division had a constant stream of personnel taken off strength to receive medical care for nonbattle-related causes. Injuries, illness, and battle exhaustion cases were combined within the category of nonbattle casualties. Battle exhaustion cases within the division did occur in spring 1945 but were not heavy because of a decreased level of enemy resistance. The highest levels of divisional nonbattle casualties were in the infantry regiments. If infantry units were living in outdoor dugouts, the soldiers were susceptible to disease and physical injuries. The cold, wet conditions of the flooded landscape provided the worst environment possible for keeping personnel healthy.

Nonbattle casualties were a constant drain on infantry regimental strengths. Take three infantry regiments in April and May as an example. The Princess

Patricia's Canadian Light Infantry suffered fifty nonbattle and fifty-five battle casualties.[40] The Royal 22e Regiment suffered thirty-one nonbattle casualties versus sixty-seven battle casualties.[41] The 48th Highlanders of Canada suffered sixty-two nonbattle casualties in comparison to sixty-two battle casualties.[42] Figure 8.3 reflects the constant wastage of nonbattle casualties within the 1st Canadian Infantry Division's 2nd Canadian Infantry Brigade. These figures were significant over the long term. Rear-deployed RCA units had better living conditions in comparison to the soldiers dug in on the front lines. They were also not subjected to sustained shelling in the form of counterbattery fire in April. The battle and nonbattle casualties of two sample RCA regiments are very low: the 3rd Field Regiment suffered twenty-eight nonbattle and zero battle casualties during the month.[43] The 2nd Light Anti-Aircraft Regiment suffered zero nonbattle casualties and four battle casualties.[44]

Reinforcements were not a concern for the division in spring 1945. All Canadian formations in March and April were recipients of reinforcements drawn from conscripted home defence units raised as a result of the National Resources Mobilization Act (NRMA). The resolution of the Conscription Crisis resulted in large numbers of NRMA personnel being sent overseas to fill the reinforcement pools. These 12,908 new conscripts ensured there was no shortage of personnel in the last stage of the war.[45] Regiments could now send soldiers on compassionate leave to Canada and regular leave on the continent and in the United Kingdom.[46] As an example, three infantry regiments within the division received the following reinforcements over in April and May. The Seaforth Highlanders of Canada received 155 reinforcements against 78 total battle and nonbattle casualties.[47] The Royal 22nd Regiment received 187 new personnel over the same period against 98 battle and nonbattle losses.[48] The Royal Canadian Regiment received 118 reinforcements against 127 losses.[49] The RCA regiments also received regular reinforcements but were not a high priority like the infantry regiments because of their low losses. Replacements for the 1st Anti-Tank Regiment, RCA, consisted of forty new personnel against five losses.[50] The 2nd Field Regiment, RCA, took on seventeen reinforcements in April and May against a loss of five casualties.[51]

On the last day of hostilities, the personnel levels within the division's units were satisfactory. Losses had occurred during operations between 11 and 19 April, but reinforcements fill the gaps. Because of the importance of keeping their units up to strength, a larger effort had been put into reinforcing the infantry at the expense of other regiments. Although not at 100 percent of their war establishment strengths, the noninfantry regiments were at adequate levels. Their strengths were not affected drastically by combat operations in April.

Figure 8.3

Battle and nonbattle casualties, 2nd Canadian Infantry Brigade, April 1945

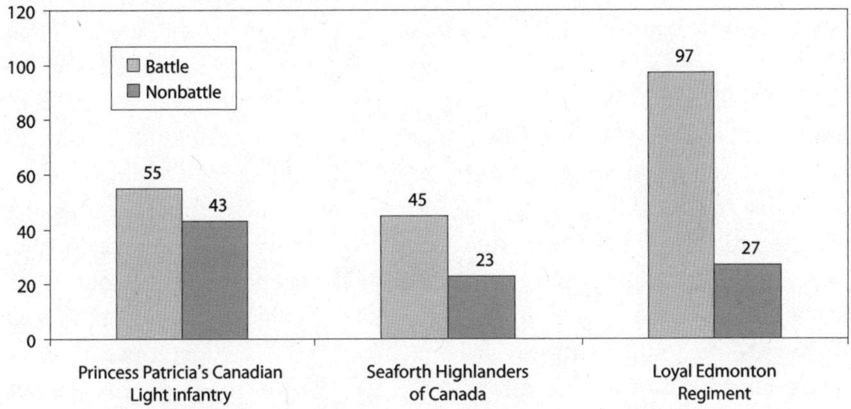

Source: LAC, RG 24, vol. 13,664, "First Canadian Army A&Q War Diary," April 1945.

Evaluating three infantry regimental returns for 5 May, it appears that each was reinforced effectively during April. The Royal Canadian Regiment's strength stood at 35 officers and 781 other ranks, or 4 percent understrength. The West Nova Scotia Regiment's contained 39 officers and 818 other ranks, putting it 1 percent overstrength. The Saskatoon Light Infantry's personnel levels stood at 37 officers and 666 other ranks, which was only 4 percent understrength. Of the noninfantry regiments, the 4th Canadian Reconnaissance Regiment's (4th Princess Louise Dragoon Guards) strength was 36 officers and 758 other ranks, or 3 percent understrength. The 1st Field Regiment, Royal Canadian Horse Artillery, taken as an example of the three field artillery regiments, posted a strength of 37 officers and 596 other ranks. This was 6 percent under its authorized strength. The weakest regiment in the division was the 1st Anti-Tank Regiment, RCA. With a strength of 35 officers and 549 other ranks, it was 10 percent understrength.[52] During combat operations in April, it had only a minimal role, and parts of some batteries were nonoperational.

In reviewing the heavy weapons and combat "A" vehicle returns for the end of April, the division's inventories of heavy weapons were adequate, but those of combat "A" vehicles were low.[53] Against an establishment of 627 combat "A" vehicles, only 427 were on strength, 68 percent of the authorized amount. This was due to two factors. First, a total of 120 T16 tracked gun tractors were listed on the war establishment figures but not issued, the division making do with wheeled gun tractors. Second, the 4th Canadian Reconnaissance Regiment's complete inventory of "A" vehicles is missing from the returns. This regiment was detached from the division to carry out training during April. If these two factors are considered, divisional combat "A" vehicle strengths were much higher.[54]

Most of the units involved in combat operations had adequate inventories of equipment at the end of hostilities, but some shortages did exist. By 5 May, all eleven authorized Valentine Charger command tanks had still not been issued to the 1st Anti-Tank Regiment, RCA. Present but nonfunctioning within the same regiment were eighteen Valentine Archer 17-pounder tank destroyers, whose mechanical issues were never resolved during hostilities. In contrast to these problems, the division did contain some valuable unauthorized tracked "A" vehicles it should not have had. Twenty-four Wasp II flamethrower carriers and twelve Windsor tracked carriers were on strength within the division but not authorized. The division continued to be well supplied with nonvehicle heavy weapons at the end of hostilities. Inventories were similar to the 31 March returns, with 97 percent of authorized heavy weapons present.

In late February and early March, the 2nd Canadian Infantry Division had assaulted the Hochwald Gap in Germany as part of Operation Blockbuster.[55] Severe resistance was encountered in later phases of the fighting. Despite this resistance, the prime objective of Xanten, Germany, fell to the division on 10 March. In late March, the division redeployed west towards the enemy-occupied Netherlands. It attacked out of bridgeheads over the Rhine River (which had been won by the 51st British Highland Division in mid-March) and advanced northwest. In a rapid advance, it liberated the Dutch towns of Silvolde, Terborg, and Doetinchem. These operations led to a further advance in early April that ended with the capture of Groningen on 13 April.[56] In its final operations of the war, the division was moved east into Germany, capturing Grossenkneten, crossing the Hunte River, capturing Oldenburg, and finally taking up positions on the Weser River. These were the last combat actions of the 2nd Canadian Infantry Division before the ceasefire on 5 May.

During this last phase of fighting, from 1 February to 5 May, the division's infantry units again bore the weight of the division's casualties. Battle casualties for three of the division's infantry regiments illustrate the extent of losses. The Essex Scottish Regiment suffered 619 battle casualties. Enduring less fierce combat, Le Régiment de Maisonneuve suffered 367 battle casualties. The Queen's Own Cameron Highlanders of Canada suffered 300 losses.[57] Nonbattle casualties continued unabated at roughly the same rate experienced from July 1944 to January 1945. The closer a unit was to the front lines, the more it suffered from these types of casualties. A rear-deployed regiment's personnel had better mess facilities, shelters, and access to medical care from the regimental aid post in a relaxed environment. From February to May, the 4th Field Regiment, RCA, suffered 55 nonbattle casualties.[58] In the same period the Royal Regiment of Canada infantry regiment suffered 283.[59]

At the war's conclusion, the strength of the 2nd Canadian Infantry Division was 974 officers and 16,947 other ranks, for a total strength of 17,921 men.[60] All regiments in the division had very high personnel levels. The Royal Regiment of Canada of the 4th Canadian Infantry Brigade had a strength of 41 officers and 834 other ranks, 3 percent overstrength. Although strong, the Royal Hamilton Light Infantry was 2 percent understrength with 36 officers and 796 other ranks.[61] Royal Canadian Artillery units were less strong, with the 2nd Anti-Tank Regiment, RCA, fielding 34 officers and 590 other ranks, or 4 percent understrength.[62] The 6th Field Regiment, RCA, was 5 percent understrength with 35 officers and 608 other ranks.[63]

These totals were the result of a sustained effort at reinforcing the division in the February to May phase of the campaign in northwest Europe. In this period, the 2nd Canadian Infantry Division was the recipient of large numbers of infantry reinforcements. Many were newly available NRMA reinforcement personnel from Canada.[64] While the other combat arms were less of a priority, every effort was made to keep Canadian Army infantry regiments at their full authorized strengths. During this period, 417 new personnel were transferred to the South Saskatchewan Regiment.[65] Total reinforcements in the same period for the Le Régiment de Maisonneuve, a regiment that had been weak after Normandy, totalled 669 personnel.[66]

As of 30 April, the division had satisfactory inventories of "A" vehicles and major weapons systems.[67] The division contained 542 combat "A" vehicles against an authorized war establishment of 513, placing the division 6 percent over its war establishment in this category. The returns for the end of April were also satisfactory with regard to the division's nonvehicle major weapons systems.[68] The division contained 102 percent of its authorized number of heavy weapons and had no serious shortages.

Following the conclusion of its participation in Operation Veritable and subsequent fighting in mid March, the 3rd Canadian Infantry Division was redeployed back to the Netherlands to prepare for future operations. Combat recommenced on 5 April, and the following week saw the division capture the Dutch towns of Wehl and Zutphen. It attacked again on 14 April, rapidly liberating the northern Dutch towns of Meppel, Steenwijk, Akkrum, and Leeuwarden. Elements of the division reached the sea at Harlingen during the same period.

The division then switched its advance to the east, relieving the 2nd Canadian Infantry Division and advancing from Groningen to Delfzijl. In what was the division's last significant battle, the Canadian Scottish Regiment of the 7th Canadian Infantry Brigade took the village of Wagenborgen in a two-day battle with armoured support.[69] Crossing into Germany for the last weeks of the war, the division captured the German city of Leer and advanced north to the vicinities of Emden and Aurich against disintegrating opposition. Here, the war ended for the 3rd Canadian Infantry Division.

The German forces' limited capabilities in the last months of the war allowed the divisional RCA regiments to operate within a reduced level of. Field artillery regiments continued to use their full offensive capability to bombard enemy positions with little danger of counterbattery fire occurring. Apart from mined routes and the dangers of infantry combat for their forward observation parties, the enemy had little capacity to retaliate. Antitank and antiaircraft crews utilized their weapons systems on ground targets from long range, also significantly limiting the danger to themselves.

In spring 1945, the number of battle and nonbattle casualties within the division's five RCA regiments had changed little from those suffered in the fall and winter. Totals in February were 44 battle and 108 nonbattle casualties. A total of 116 reinforcements had been dispatched, combatting ongoing attrition.[70] The artillery-based doctrine of the Canadian Army ensured that a constant level of damage was done to the enemy by the division's three field regiments. This was achieved in exchange for few artillery casualties within these regiments. The German forces were bombarded constantly by an unseen enemy, the RCA, which they could do very little about.[71]

The division's infantry brigades had borne the brunt of the fighting between February and April. Two infantry regiments taken as examples reveal that casualties in spring 1945, while heavy, were lighter than those of summer 1944. The 1st Battalion, the Canadian Scottish Regiment of the 7th Canadian Infantry Brigade, sustained a total of 443 battle casualties during these three months, matched with 234 nonbattle casualties. Reinforcements to keep this regiment up to strength totalled 705.[72] Despite receiving reinforcements totalling five and a half complete infantry companies, as of 30 April the regiment could only muster 34 officers and 761 other ranks. Le Régiment de la Chaudière, part of the 8th Canadian Infantry Brigade, suffered 239 battle and 159 nonbattle casualties in the same period. Total reinforcements dispatched to offset losses totalled 416. On 30 April, the regiment's strength was 43 officers and 806 other ranks.[73]

Both regiments received reinforcement personnel from the newly available pool of NRMA conscripts.[74] Reinforcements for all army trades at this stage of the war were plentiful, and leave to the United Kingdom, the Netherlands, and other locations was regularly approved on a rotational basis for soldiers. Deserving long-service members were also eligible for leave to Canada, a welcome respite for soldiers who had been overseas since 1940 or 1941.[75]

Following the difficult battles in the Rhineland, in April and May the 2nd Canadian Armoured Brigade supported units of the 2nd Canadian Corps as they drove northward across the Rhine into the northern Netherlands and Germany. These final operations of the war were mounted against disintegrating German opposition, and casualties were lower than in previous operations. The combined personnel losses of all three armoured regiments during this thirty-five-day period totalled 86 battle casualties and 102 nonbattle losses.[76] The regiments were reinforced with 282 replacements during this period, allowing them to remain close to their war establishment strengths. As an example, the 27th Canadian Armoured Regiment's strength on 5 May was 35 officers and 630 other ranks.[77] These figures placed it at 97 percent of its authorized strength at the end of hostilities.

On 30 April, Sherman, Sherman Firefly, and Stuart strength within the brigade amounted to 227 vehicles against a war establishment of 226. This total placed the brigade at just over 100 percent of its authorized strength.[78] These returns illustrate the constant effort that had gone into reinforcing the brigade to offset the constant drain of AFVs lost to enemy action and mechanical failure. The 2nd Canadian Armoured Brigade's three regiments ended the war in northern Germany, supporting the 2nd Canadian Corps' last infantry operations.

For the 4th Canadian Armoured Division, preparations for a continued drive east in Operation Blockbuster saw it assemble in Cleve, Germany, in mid-February.[79] On 26 February, the division attacked east from the town of Wemmershof between the lines of the 2nd and 3rd Canadian Infantry Divisions. Divided into five battle groups, the division successfully attacked the Calcar-Udem ridgeline.[80] On 27 February, it began a further assault to push through the Tuschen and Balberger Wald forest areas, south of the larger Hochwald Forest. The 10th Canadian Infantry Brigade was relieved on 1 March, after some limited gains. Going back into action the next day, it continued its drive east. Only after bitter fighting and slow progress did the division reach the Sonsbeck-Xanten Road on 3 March.[81] A further advance towards the German city of Veen on 6 March was halted by stiff German resistance. The division was regrouped and then mounted further assaults that encountered additional resistance. On 9 March, the town finally fell when German forces withdrew. The following day, the infantry of the 10th Canadian Infantry Brigade assaulted Winnenthal, successfully capturing the town.

The next operational phase for the division was its role as an exploitation force after the success of Operation Plunder, the 23 March Anglo-American assault crossing of the Rhine River. Operations began on 24 March with the divisional artillery supporting Canadian forces advancing north of the river. Redeploying north into the British bridgehead over the Rhine at Rees, the division prepared to advance into enemy-occupied Netherlands. This assault began with some elements advancing north from Terborg on 1 April. Further advances from Zelhem, as the right flank of 2nd Canadian Corps, resulted in the capture of a bridgehead over the Twente Canal at Delden by 4 April.[82] The Dutch town of Almelo was subsequently liberated by the division the next day after a brief period of fighting. Other parts of the division then advanced north and crossed back into Germany, capturing Emlichheim on 5 April. German resistance at this point was becoming disorganized. Meppen and a bridgehead over the Ems River were subsequently captured by the division on 6 April. Attacking from the vicinity of Sogel, the town of Friesoythe fell to the division on 14 April. German resistance at Edewechterdamm between 15 and 17 April delayed the division's crossing of the Kusten Canal. A bridgehead was eventually secured at the cost of heavy infantry casualties.[83] This fighting was followed by further serious resistance north of the canal. Despite this bitter resistance at the end of the war, the division continued to achieve its objectives and successfully crossed the Aue River on 21 April. The 5 May ceasefire found the 4th Canadian Armoured Division sixteen kilometres north of Oldenburg, Germany.

The losses suffered by the infantry regiments from February to April were not as high as in summer 1944, but they were still considerable.[84] The Argyll and Sutherland Highlanders of Canada suffered 398 battle and 205 nonbattle casualties, and the Lincoln and Welland Regiment had 512 battle and 222 nonbattle casualties. The strength of each regiment at the end of April reflected that an effective reinforcement system was in place. With newly available stocks of NRMA soldiers reaching the division, there were no shortages of personnel.[85] The Argyll and Sutherland Highlanders of Canada's strength as of 30 April 1945 was 40 officers and 854 other ranks, 5 percent over its authorized strength. It had received a total of 707 replacements over the last three months. The Lincoln and Welland Regiment had received 808 replacement personnel during this period. This brought its unit strength to 38 officers and 816 other ranks, 100 percent of its war establishment.

The RCA regiments suffered few casualties between February and April.[86] Total losses in the four regiments within the division were 112 battle and 382 nonbattle casualties. A total of 630 replacements were dispatched to these regiments during this time. As of 30 April, for example, two RCA regiments had each received an adequate number of reinforcements. The 23rd Field Regiment fielded 37 officers and 601 other ranks, 98 percent of its authorized strength. The 5th Anti-Tank Regiment contained 33 officers and 680 other ranks, 92 percent of its effective strength.

The regiments of the armoured brigade and the armoured reconnaissance regiment also suffered low levels of casualties in the last three months of the war.[87] Between February and April, the 28th Canadian Armoured Regiment suffered a total of 132 battle and 21 nonbattle casualties. The 29th Canadian Armoured Reconnaissance Regiment had 60 battle and 102 nonbattle losses during the same period. These low losses indicate a reduced enemy antitank defence capability. Also, a greater number of Canadian tank crews at this stage were equipped with more effective AFVs than had been available in Normandy, giving the crews a fighting chance during tank versus tank engagements and lowering the number of battle casualties.

The division's strength on 5 May was 977 officers and 17,619 other ranks.[88] Its infantry regiments were all near their authorized strengths.[89] During the last three months of the war, an extremely large effort was made to adequately reinforce these units. At the end of hostilities, the Lake Superior (Motor) Regiment contained 34 officers and 830 other ranks, 1 percent over its establishment strength. The armoured and RCA regiments' personnel strength returns were also high. The 21st Canadian Armoured Regiment contained 37 officers and 648 other ranks, 100 percent of its authorized establishment. The 5th Anti-Tank Regiment was the weakest of the divisional RCA regiments. This unit was not a high priority for reinforcements and suffered far lower casualties than the infantry regiments. At the war's conclusion, its strength was 38 officers and 741 other ranks, 92 percent of its war establishment.

The division contained many combat "A" vehicles on 30 April.[90] On this date, it had 909 combat "A" vehicles on strength versus its authorized number of 845. The division was 8 percent overstrength in this category. Despite the excessive total number of vehicles, some shortages persisted. The number of 17-pounder Sherman Firefly tanks within the division had increased, but the numbers still did not match the war establishment figures. Against an authorized strength of ninety-six tanks, only eighty Sherman Mark Ic and Vc Fireflies were present. Unauthorized vehicles on strength included thirteen of the very valuable Wasp II tracked flamethrower carriers. The number of nonvehicle weapons systems within the division was also high as of 30 April.[91] A total of 277 heavy weapons were on strength versus an authorized total of 283, 98 percent of the war establishment figure in this category. There is a significant lack of daily data for the divisional RCA regiments between 22 April and 5 May. Although weekly strength returns exist, data on reinforcements and daily casualties per regiment is incomplete. Daily records are available for each RCA unit in the period from 1 to 21 April.

On arrival in northwest Europe in late February, the 5th Canadian Armoured Division was ordered to conform to the 21st Army Group's staff figures of organization for a Canadian armoured division. These staff figures only allowed for one infantry brigade, and the division had been allocated two during its service in Italy. As a result, the division's 12th Canadian Infantry Brigade was disbanded and its units redistributed.[92] The Lanark and Renfrew Scottish Regiment reverted to its original role and title as a 1st Canadian Corps–level asset, the 1st Light Anti-Aircraft Regiment, RCA. The Westminster Regiment (Motor) rejoined the 5th Canadian Armoured Brigade as its motor battalion. The 4th Princess Louise's Dragoon Guards reverted to its original title, the 4th Canadian Reconnaissance Regiment. This unit then rejoined its original formation, the 1st Canadian Infantry Division. Like the 1st Light Anti-Aircraft Regiment, it had to conduct training and be re-equipped to resume its previous role. While this reorganization was taking place within these units, the remainder of the division continued the process of re-equipping and accepting new personnel reinforcements.

As of 4 April, the division's personnel strength on its third day of combat operations in the Netherlands was 750 officers and 19,659 other ranks.[93] At this point, the division had additional units temporarily attached, and it was 40 percent over the establishment strength of a Canadian armoured division.[94] At the end of March, all combat arms regiments within the division had high personnel levels. The 2nd Canadian Armoured Regiment's strength stood at 38 officers and 679 other ranks, 99 percent of its wartime establishment. The 3rd Canadian Armoured Reconnaissance Regiment had a strength of 38 officers and 644 other ranks, 99 percent of its authorized strength.[95] Units in the infantry brigades also had satisfactory strength levels and had benefitted from an influx of available NRMA conscript reinforcements. The Perth Regiment, as of 31 March, contained 38 officers and 821 other ranks and was 1 percent overstrength.[96] Also 1 percent overstrength, the Irish Regiment of Canada had 37 officers and 822 other ranks. The RCA field artillery regiments of the division were both strong: the 17th Field Regiment contained 38 officers and 625 other ranks, 98 percent of its authorized strength, and the other three RCA regiments were equally close to their authorized strengths.[97]

By 31 March, the division had only just completed its re-equipment process, so the "A" and "B" vehicles situation report at the end of the month did not contain the division's returns. However, the non-AFV equipment report of 31

Figure 8.4

Number of Heavy AFVs delivered to the 5th Canadian Armoured Division versus Panther tanks delivered to all German armoured units, March–May 1945

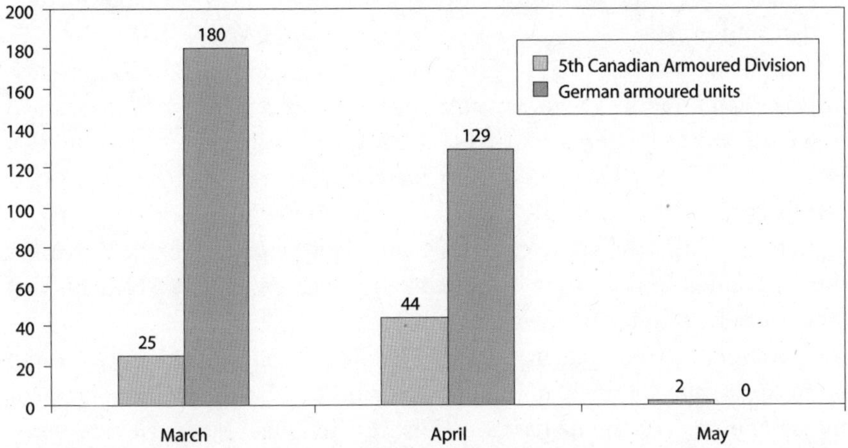

Note: The heavy AFVs were delivered by "G" Squadron, 25th Canadian Armoured Delivery Regiment.
Source: LAC, RG 24, vol. 14,280, "'G' Squadron, 25th Canadian Armoured Delivery Regiment, War Diary," March–May 1945, T-1275; and Martin Block, "Panther Allocation Sorted by Date of Allotment," Panther1944.de, from http://www.panther1944.de/index.php/en/.

March did contain the division's returns, and the totals reflected adequate inventory levels of heavy weapons, which were 5 percent over the authorized amounts.[98] As part of its re-equipment, the division received deliveries of new and repaired AFVs from March through May. Figure 8.4 shows the number of battle tanks delivered to the division in this period versus Panther tank deliveries to the entire German military for the same period. The disparity in these figures is not large, indicating that the Allies' vehicle-replacement system was massively superior. It should be noted that the division was not committed against a sizable formation of German armour during its time in northwest Europe, and it never suffered heavy AFV losses.

On 31 March, the first operational task of the 5th Canadian Armoured Division, newly deployed to northwest Europe, was to relieve the 49th British Infantry Division in its positions in the Oosterhout bridgehead over the Waal River. This bridgehead was within a rectangle of land south of the Nederrijn River. Enclosed by waterways and flooded areas, it formed a temporary island. Beginning offensive operations on 2 April, the division pushed north in cooperation with the British to clear the island area and reach the Nederrijn River.

By 3 April, the area was cleared with relatively few casualties.[99] On 15 April, the division advanced from the British bridgehead over the Nederrijn at Arnhem and attacked west on the left flank of the 1st Canadian Infantry Division. In quick succession the division liberated Deelen and Otterloo, Voorthuizen, Putten, and Ermelo.

Casualties between 1 and 21 April were light and mainly concentrated in the infantry and armoured regiments. Adequate reinforcements were dispatched to replace any losses that occurred. The 22 April strength return for the Irish Regiment of Canada reported 36 officers and 824 other ranks, 1 percent over its establishment strength. The RCA regiments also suffered little in this phase of operations, with four battle casualties and eighty-eight nonbattle casualties during the division's drive into the central Netherlands. Reinforcements dispatched to RCA units in this period totalled 129.[100]

Operations by 1st Canadian Corps to liberate the area west of Utrecht ceased on 19 April. The 1st Canadian Infantry Division relieved the 5th Canadian Armoured Division on this demarcation line, and the latter prepared for redeployment east to the Groningen area of the Netherlands.

On 21 April the division began its move to the eastern part of the Netherlands. On its arrival near the German border, it relieved the 3rd Canadian Infantry Division outside the German occupied port of Delfzijl. The division's assigned task was to clear the port in cooperation with 3rd Canadian Infantry Division operations across the border against Emden, Germany. From 23 April to 2 May, elements of the 5th Canadian Armoured Brigade and the 11th Canadian Infantry Brigade assaulted the port from the north and south, encountering stiff resistance.[101] With the surrender of German forces in the port area on 2 May, combat operations for the division ended, and the ceasefire came into effect three days later.

The 5th Canadian Armoured Division's regiments had adequate personnel levels at the end of hostilities. Its strength return for 5 May was 784 officers and 14,188 other ranks.[102] During its short phase of combat, it was sufficiently resupplied with personnel to keep most of its combat arms regiments above 90 percent of their war establishments. During the March to May period, an adequate number of reinforcements were available because large numbers of NRMA personnel had arrived in Europe. As illustrated in Figure 8.5, the four infantry regiments were slightly weakened by combat but remained over or close to 800 personnel, a satisfactory figure for an infantry battalion engaged in operations. The infantry had suffered the brunt of battle and nonbattle casualties while the division was in combat. The Perth Regiment suffered the highest losses within the infantry brigade with 85 battle and 53 nonbattle casualties, for

Figure 8.5

5th Canadian Armoured Division, infantry regiment strengths, 31 March 1945 and 5 May 1945

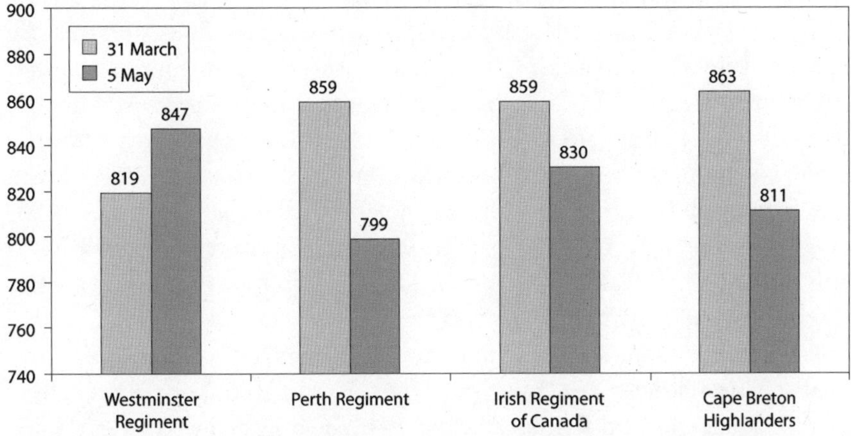

Source: LAC, RG 24, vols. 13,663–65, "First Canadian Army A&Q War Diaries," March–May 1945, T-7094–96, 31 March and 5 May 1945.

a total of 138. It had received 65 replacements during April and May, bringing its strength up to 32 officers and 767 other ranks. This figure was 6 percent under its authorized strength.

The regiments of the armoured brigade and the armoured reconnaissance regiment suffered considerably fewer losses in the same period. The 9th Canadian Armoured Regiment (the British Columbia Dragoons) had 22 battle and 26 nonbattle casualties, for a total of 48 personnel. In this period, it received 37 replacements to bring its strength up to 36 officers and 635 other ranks, 97 percent of its war establishment. RCA casualties had been low for the period of combat operations. The 8th Field Regiment's return on 5 May shows 39 officers and 584 other ranks on strength. In the period of operations from 1 to 21 April, the regiment suffered seven battle and twenty-seven nonbattle casualties.

On 30 April, the 5th Canadian Armoured Division had 849 combat "A" vehicles versus its authorized level of 927, which was 91 percent of its establishment strength, a shortage caused by a failure to issue eighty-three T16 gun tractors and Universal tracked carriers. Instead, the infantry and antitank regiments were making do with trucks and suffered no lack of combat capability during their dismounted operations. The division contained 289 Sherman, Sherman

Firefly, and Stuart battle tanks against a war establishment figure of 261, placing it 11 percent overstrength.[103] Unauthorized combat "A" vehicles held by the division included six Ram Badger flame-throwing tanks and twelve Wasp II tracked flamethrower carriers.[104] Nonvehicle heavy weapon returns for the division on 30 April were just as strong as the previous 31 March returns; the only problem was a shortage of thirteen .303 Vickers medium machine guns.[105]

Once the 1st Canadian Armoured Brigade was declared operational in early April, it was deployed along the Waal River.[106] Throughout March and early April, its regiments were re-equipped with new vehicles and reinforced with new personnel. The brigade's return was not included in the 31 March "A" & "B" vehicle position report for the First Canadian Army as its refitting process was still incomplete.[107] Regimental personnel field returns were recorded in the war diaries, however, and they reflected adequate strengths on the eve of combat operations. For example, on 31 March the 11th Canadian Armoured Regiment contained 39 officers and 644 other ranks, 99 percent of its authorized strength.[108] With Belgian and British units attached to it, the brigade held this line while other 1st Canadian Corps units cleared the temporary island area south of the Nederrijn River during Operation Destroyer. Once this area was cleared, Anglo-Canadian units captured a bridgehead at Arnhem and pushed north of the city. The 11th Canadian Armoured Regiment participated in these operations by supporting units of the 49th British Infantry Division. To facilitate the 5th Canadian Armoured Division's movement to the north of the Nederrijn River, the brigade took over its positions in the island in mid-April. During this phase, it also conducted some successful minor operations with Belgian forces. When hostilities ended, the brigade held positions on the Waal River and north of it near Opheusden.

Casualties and equipment losses for the 1st Canadian Armoured Brigade during its period of operations from 1 to 9 April had been extremely light, and in April and May total personnel losses within the regiments were eleven battle and thirty-seven nonbattle casualties.[109] These figures are low compared to losses within some armoured regiments in summer 1944. In accordance with the artillery-based doctrine, the regiment's squadrons were parcelled off to support British and Belgian infantry operations. In this supporting role, AFV losses were light, and any missing vehicles and equipment were quickly replaced. In its brief period of operations, the brigade's regiments performed well against light opposition.

Although the regiments had begun operations in early April, they were still receiving new combat "A" vehicles to bring them up to strength at the end of the month. The three regiments in the brigade received a total of sixty new

Sherman Firefly 17-pounder variants in March and a further thirty-six battle tanks of various types in April.[110] Since all three of its regiments were armoured, the brigade did not operate any non-"A" vehicle heavy weapons. As of 30 April, the brigade contained 200 battle tanks against its war establishment total of 226, which was 88 percent of its authorized strength.[111] During its time in northwest Europe, the brigade had not been required to fight any major tank battles, nor did its regiments regularly face a well-equipped enemy offering stiff resistance. Any casualties that occurred within the brigade during April and May were quickly replaced, with eighty-three reinforcement personnel joining the three regiments.[112] At the end of hostilities, these regiments were all overstrength in personnel. For instance, the 12th Canadian Armoured Regiment contained 45 officers and 686 other ranks as of 5 May 1945, making it 6 percent overstrength.[113]

In the final phase of the spring 1945 fighting, the four regiments of the 2nd Canadian AGRA followed the advancing 2nd Canadian Corps into the northern Netherlands and Germany. Moving constantly from position to position, they struggled to keep up with the rapid advances of the infantry and armoured brigades. At this stage, German resistance was so weak that by the time the AGRA regiments had reached a firing position, the enemy had been overcome. One of the farthest advancing AGRA medium regiments was the 7th Medium Regiment, RCA, which ended the war in Hesel, Germany, near Leer.

The 1st Canadian AGRA units spent most of their existence in support of 1st Canadian Corps operations in Italy. As mentioned earlier, once redeployed to northwest Europe with the 1st Canadian Corps, the 1st Canadian AGRA units participated in operations in April and May. The 1st Canadian AGRA arrived in Belgium in February and March. This formation consisted of the 1st, 2nd, and 5th Medium Regiments, RCA, and the 11th Army Field Artillery Regiment, RCA. These medium regiments were not equipped in the same manner as those in the 2nd Canadian AGRA medium regiments due to some units fielding 4.5-inch guns. The 11th Army Field Regiment, RCA, was self-propelled, being equipped with the Sexton 25-pounder self-propelled howitzer. The four RCA regiments were deployed to support 1st Canadian Corps operations in the Netherlands during the 2 to 19 April phase of fighting.

In their operational role, 1st Canadian AGRA units supported the Allied crossing of the IJssel River in April and the advance to the Grebbe River, where offensive operations ceased. Because of the enemy forces' limited combat capability, the 1st Canadian AGRA suffered few losses during its operations with the 1st Canadian Corps. While the 1st Canadian AGRA medium regiments were combat-capable, they had not been reinforced to 100 percent of their war establishments for personnel. For example, on 5 May the 1st Medium Regiment, RCA, contained a strength of 29 officers and 493 other ranks, only 92 percent of its war establishment, and the 5th Medium Regiment, RCA, possessed a strength of 29 officers and 501 other ranks, 93 percent of its authorized personnel. It appears that neither of these regiments were a high priority for reinforcements after the 19 April ceasefire in the Netherlands and the imminent end of hostilities. All four 1st Canadian AGRA regiments had adequate inventories of major weapons to complete their missions. The three RCA medium regiments contained all 48 of their authorized number of 4.5- and 5.5-inch guns, and the 11th Army Field Regiment, RCA, contained all 24 of its war establishment number of Sexton 25-pounder self-propelled artillery pieces.[114]

At the conclusion of hostilities in May, the four corps-level regiments of the 2nd Canadian Corps were in various location in northern Germany. In April, all four units had been involved in supporting the Canadian and British forces that crossed the Rhine River and advanced through the northern Netherlands and Germany. The 6th Anti-Tank Regiment, RCA, played a significant role in the fighting to capture Leer in late April.[115] The 18th Canadian Armoured Car Regiment also took a leading role in the final stages of the fighting, advancing with the regiments of the 4th Canadian Armoured Division. This regiment captured Mollberg, Germany, one the farthest points reached by the 2nd Canadian Corps in its advances. The 1945 fighting in the Rhineland, the Netherlands, and northern Germany was often intense, with the German Army occasionally making a determined defensive effort. The four corps units during this period were just as involved in operations as units within Canadian divisions and independent brigades. Casualties were heavy, but not as heavy as the fighting in Normandy. The supply of reinforcements reaching the four regiments during this stage was sufficient to keep their personnel strengths high. From February through May, the 18th Canadian Armoured Car Regiment accepted a total of 120 reinforcements to cover 38 battle and 129 nonbattle casualties.[116] Reflecting the low casualty levels that went with its battlefield role, the 2nd Survey Regiment, RCA, received 111 replacements against 60 nonbattle and 4 battle casualties.[117]

The four corps-level units of the 1st Canadian Corps – the 1st Canadian Armoured Car Regiment (the Royal Canadian Dragoons), the 7th Anti-Tank Regiment (RCA), the 1st Light Anti-Aircraft Regiment (RCA), and the 1st Survey Regiment (RCA) – had all arrived in northwest Europe between February and March 1945 as part of Operation Goldflake. Their travel route to Belgium was the same as the other regiments of the 1st Canadian Corps. On their arrival in Belgium, they began the process of re-equipping, integrating new replacements, and reorganizing their regimental structures to fit 21st Army Group standards. For the most part, they were combat ready at the beginning of April. The one exception was the 1st Canadian Light Anti-Aircraft Regiment, RCA, which had been reorganized during its time in Italy as an infantry unit, the Lanark and Renfrew Scottish Regiment of the 12th Canadian Infantry Brigade.[118] It was not needed in this role on its arrival in Belgium and began a reorganization and retraining program to turn it back into a light antiaircraft unit. Spending April and May in this process, it did not see action in northwest Europe.

As of 1 April, all four 1st Canadian Corps–level units contained adequate personnel levels on the eve of operations in the Netherlands and Germany. As an example, the 1st Canadian Survey Regiment, RCA, contained 31 officers and 546 other ranks, 92 percent of its war establishment. The inventories of heavy weapons and combat "A" vehicles for these four units were satisfactory. On 31 March, the 7th Anti-Tank Regiment, RCA, contained 100 percent of its war establishment of 17-pounder antitank guns and M10 17-pounder (self-propelled) tank destroyers.[119]

Two of the four corps units went on to be involved in 1st Canadian Corps operations on the IJssel River area near Arnhem in April. The 7th Anti-Tank Regiment, RCA, supported 1st Canadian Armoured Brigade operations south of the Nederrijn River, south of Arnhem. Some of its batteries took on an infantry role while its self-propelled elements supported the advance of various Canadian units to the north and west.[120] The 1st Survey Regiment, RCA, in its artillery surveying, flash-spotting, calibration and sound-ranging role supported all RCA regiments within the IJssel River area of operations.[121] Operations for these two units came to a halt on 19 April with the temporary truce between German and Anglo-Canadian forces on the Grebbe River.

In its role as a reconnaissance spearhead, in April and May the 1st Canadian Armoured Car Regiment was placed under command of the 2nd Canadian Corps. In its advance from the Rhine River to the Friesland region in the northern Netherlands, it covered large distances in a short amount of time against disintegrating opposition. Operating in late April and early May with units of the 2nd Canadian Armoured Brigade and the 4th Canadian Armoured Division, by the end of hostilities it had advanced from the Kusten Canal north to Westerstede, Germany.[122] During their period of operations, all three 1st Canadian Corps-level regiments performed to a satisfactory standard in their battlefield roles.

At the end of hostilities, the 1st Canadian Corps–level regiments continued to contain adequate personnel and equipment and vehicle levels. All three operational regiments had received enough replacements to keep them combat effective during this final phase of fighting in the Netherlands and northern Germany. On 5 May, the 1st Canadian Armoured Car Regiment contained 81 officers and 823 other ranks, making it 5 percent overstrength.[123] During the month of April, this regiment had received nineteen replacements and had recorded fourteen battle and thirteen nonbattle casualties.[124] Authorized equipment and vehicle levels were satisfactory, and even the 1st Light Anti-Aircraft Regiment, RCA, which was in the process of retraining and re-equipping, recorded 100 percent of its war establishment of 40 mm antiaircraft guns being on strength.[125] On their arrival in Belgium and the Netherlands in spring 1945, all four corps-level units had been adequately equipped and had no major shortages that would impair their combat capability.

In conclusion, in spring 1945 all Canadian formations involved in operations were adequately reinforced with personnel, vehicles, and weapons. Despite the German military's much reduced offensive and defensive capabilities on the Canadian front, instances of heavy combat did occur. The reinforcement system to maintain each formation's fighting strength performed flawlessly, and any losses suffered were rapidly made good. Regarding personnel, the addition of NRMA conscripts into the reinforcement pool ensured that no deficiencies of any kind were present. On 5 May, at the conclusion of hostilities for the First Canadian Army, each division and independent brigade's units as well as those held at the army and corps level were experienced, battle-hardened, and extremely combat capable, being at or near their war establishment strengths in all relevant categories.

9
An Assessment of Canadian Formations

THROUGHOUT MOST OF THE Canadian Army's campaign in northwest Europe from June 1944 to May 1945, all regiment-sized units at the independent brigade, division, corps, and army level were combat capable. Most units had their full establishment of personnel, vehicles, and equipment. As a result, all formations, those organizations of brigade size or larger, were fully capable of offensive action for nearly all of their combat deployments. At war's end, each of them had largely reached their maximum strength and military capability.

The 1st Canadian Infantry Division was among the most rested and capable of the three Canadian infantry divisions as of May 1945. Infantry and other reinforcements were plentiful, and the number of heavy weapons and "A" vehicles were sufficient for operational units. There were minor equipment challenges, but they were limited to the area of heavy armoured fighting vehicles (AFVs) within the 1st Anti-Tank Regiment, Royal Canadian Artillery (RCA). Combat operations by the division in April 1945 were entirely successful. Any missing assets, such as the 4th Canadian Reconnaissance Regiment (4th Princess Louise Dragoon Guards), had their combat power replaced by attached combat arms units from other formations.[1] On average, enemy opposition during the last month of the war was weak. There was no urgent need to address minor shortages in the division, as the end of the war was imminent. The division finished the war adequately equipped in most equipment categories. Like all Canadian units at this point in the campaign, it was near its authorized strength in personnel.

The 2nd Canadian Infantry Division, though several of its units suffered terrible losses in July 1944, was completely rebuilt and up to strength at war's end. It had endured some difficult reverses at the hands of the Germans during the Normandy Campaign but had emerged as a capable and battle-tested formation. The performance of its infantry regiments was critical in clearing the Seine River crossing at Forêt de la Londe in August 1944, the flooded polders of the Scheldt Estuary in fall 1944, and the Rhineland forests in 1945. By May 1945, the division's field artillery regiments were extremely effective. The division's infantry brigades utilized this strength continually, employing large artillery support programs. However, one area in which the division had significant equipment challenges during 1944 was self-propelled antitank guns and flamethrower carriers.[2] This area of weakness was mitigated by the attachment of Canadian armoured regiments to increase its combat power. Apart from some poor examples of combined arms tactics in July, from August onward Canadian Armoured Corps support was effective.

In order to survive its reverses of July 1944 and the attrition of August and October, the division was rebuilt repeatedly in an efficient manner. The monthly returns from 31 July onward for both heavy weapons and combat "A" vehicles confirm that the formation was adequately resupplied on a regular basis. The shortages it had within its infantry regiments in August and September 1944 were of a temporary nature. The infantry losses of late July had occurred quickly and in such large numbers that the reinforcement system could not keep up because of its temporarily limited resources. As of October, these personnel shortages were no longer a major concern. While comparable German formations were destroyed by attrition and withdrawn for rebuilding, the 2nd Canadian Infantry Division stayed at the front.

The 3rd Canadian Infantry Division was reinforced for part of the Normandy Campaign with an extra Canadian artillery regiment and had self-propelled antitank guns attached to its antitank regiment, providing it with more combat power than a regular Canadian infantry division throughout June and July 1944. For the duration of its operations in northwest Europe, the division never lacked a sufficient number of combat "A" vehicles or heavy weapons.[3] Shortages in personnel did occur, but they were of a temporary nature. Prior to high-intensity offensive operations, the infantry regiments were always above 80 percent of their authorized strengths. Figure 9.1 illustrates that the effective strength of the division never dipped below 17,600 personnel.[4]

This division lost some of its strength in August 1944, but this was largely because of factors other than casualties. The division's authorized strength in summer 1944 was 18,374 personnel.[5] When additional units attached to it during June and July, it was significantly overstrength. In July, the temporarily attached 19th Army Field Regiment, RCA, which was 647 personnel strong, was detached from the division.[6] The 4th Light Anti-Aircraft Regiment, RCA, was also reorganized in summer 1944, reducing its establishment strength from over 866 personnel to 585.[7] As related in earlier chapters, comparable German infantry formations wasted away to nothing after a short exposure to combat. Figure 9.1 illustrates that the exact opposite occurred with the 3rd Canadian Infantry Division. Though the division did suffer significant casualties, it did not lose as many personnel as quickly as did the 2nd Canadian Infantry Division. As a result, the division was not put in a major personnel deficit situation that the

Figure 9.1

3rd Canadian Infantry Division strengths (thousands), 31 July 1944–30 April 1945

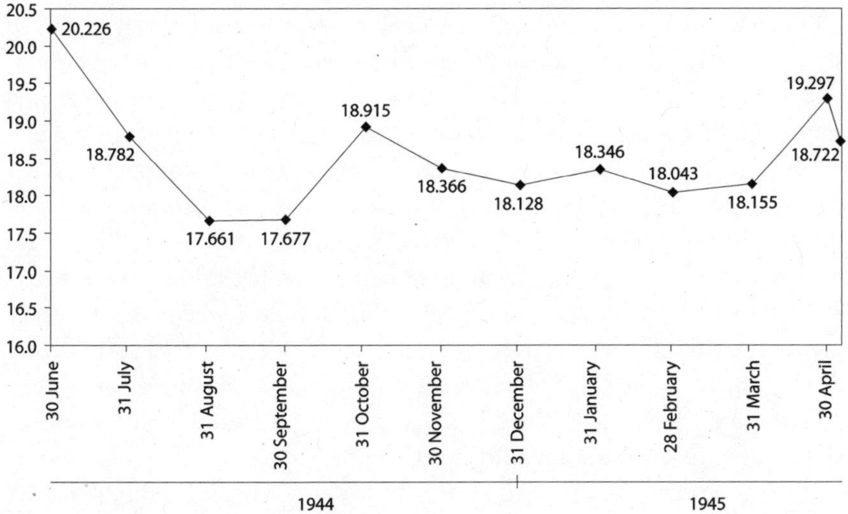

Note: The detachment of the 19th Army Field Regiment, RCA, by August 1944 is reflected in this graph and does not indicate an increased level of casualties.
Source: LAC, RG 24, vol. 13,775, "3rd Canadian Infantry Division A&Q War Diary," June 1944; LAC, RG 24, vols. 13,719–20, "2nd Canadian Corps A&Q War Diaries, July–September 1944," March–May 1945; and LAC, RG 24, vols. 13,660–63, "First Canadian Army A&Q War Diaries," October–December 1944, January–February 1945.

reinforcement system had to rectify while casualties were continuing to mount.

The 4th Canadian Armoured Division, though containing only a single infantry brigade of three regiments, was arguably the most powerful of the Canadian formations in northwest Europe. The only time resupply fell short was in personnel, in August and September 1944. The division's losses shortly after its combat debut were heavy and occurred with such speed that reinforcement fell behind, because Canadian Military Headquarters in London had failed to plan for adequate numbers of replacement infantry. These temporary shortages seriously weakened the infantry component of the division, albeit for a short period, arguably when it needed all its combat capability. The effect of this weakness on battlefield performance was mitigated by a disintegrating enemy in late August 1944.

A successful rebuilding effort coupled with a secondary role during the first two weeks of Scheldt Estuary fighting allowed the division to regain its strength. During this period, the division took on reinforcements and conducted training to incorporate them in the division. Adequate numbers of new "A" vehicles and heavy weapons were also received, bringing the inventory levels considerably closer to their authorized levels.

From mid-October to the beginning of November 1944, improved combined arms tactics and the attrition of the enemy allowed the division to be continuously successful in its operations. The Canadian Army's effective personnel- and equipment-reinforcement processes allowed the division to maintain its strength during this period. When major operations resumed in February 1945, the division had a high level of combat capability due to its being well equipped, well trained, well rested, and experienced. During its advances in the last two months of the war, it captured a large amount of enemy territory. While excellent training, tactics, and operational planning all contributed to the success of the division, its military effectiveness was dependent on more than these factors. Having adequate numbers of personnel and sufficient inventories of vehicles and weaponry provided it with the tools it needed to defeat the enemy consistently during its operations in northwest Europe.

The second division to arrive from Italy, the 5th Canadian Armoured Division, was extremely effective in its short period of combat in northwest Europe. Well supplied with both personnel and equipment, it lacked none of the tools needed to carry out its missions once these assets were in place. The division did face a challenging reorganization and re-equipment process on its arrival in the Netherlands, but it carried these tasks out in a reasonable amount of time. All regiments had satisfactory personnel levels, and reinforcements were rapidly fed into them to counter any shortage because of battle or nonbattle losses. Once it was deemed operational, the division advanced rapidly against an enemy that was disintegrating. During its combat deployment in April and May 1945, the division liberated large portions of territory throughout the eastern Netherlands.

All six armoured regiments of the 1st and 2nd Canadian Armoured Brigades adequately supported infantry operations in northwest Europe during their service within this theatre. During this time, Canadian armoured tactics evolved. The armoured squadron became an integral part of the combined arms team rather than the foremost echelon of the attack. Battalion-level infantry attacks were adequately supported by tank firepower. In this way, vehicle and tank crew losses were reduced, the infantry was adequately supported, and the squadrons preserved their strength to fight off the inevitable German counterattack.

Both independent armoured brigades were constantly reinforced with new and repaired AFVs while they were in the field. Sufficient reserves of replacement tanks and adequate recovery, repair, and delivery systems allowed the regiments to maintain adequate tank strengths. Personnel levels in the armoured units were rarely an issue. Unlike the infantry, there was never a serious deficiency in the number of Canadian Armoured Corps reinforcement personnel.

The army- and corps-level units of the First Canadian Army in northwest Europe were utilized in operations to the same degree as similar units held at the divisional and independent brigade level. Since none of the units were infantry and several were usually deployed to the rear, these units had, on average, lower levels of casualties. But the casualties they did suffer were on par with other regiments of their type. The 6th Anti-Tank Regiment, RCA, saw continuous combat in Normandy and experienced the full force of German armoured counterattacks near Verrières Ridge in July 1944. Its casualties were similar in number to other antitank regiments held at the division level. Though the armoured car regiments did not have prominent roles in some of the most difficult battles, they did lead the pursuit of the German Army across France and kept continuous contact with the retreating enemy. In April and May 1945, these units advanced over large areas of enemy-held territory following the German disintegration in the last weeks of the war. The firepower of the medium regiments of the Army Group Royal Artillery were instrumental in gaining victory in the Normandy Campaign and successfully supported operations to the war's conclusion. Not being part of a division's order of battle, corps- and army-level units were shuffled to divisions where the fighting was the most demanding. Their continuous reinforcement with new personnel, combat "A" vehicles, and heavy weapons kept them operating at a high level that ensured the successful completion of any mission they took on.

In conclusion, what became the First Canadian Army in northwest Europe successfully maintained all its formations, negating the effect of personnel, vehicle, and major weapon systems wastage within its combat arms units engaged in offensive and defensive operations. These formations at all times maintained their integrity, cohesiveness, and a high level of combat capability.

Conclusion

The Canadian Army's ability to reconstitute itself was one of its greatest strengths during the campaign in northwest Europe. While German units became steadily weaker, Canadian combat arms units were continually reinforced to retain their combat capability. In the event that a regiment suffered heavy personnel losses, it would be out of action for half a week at the most.[1] Vehicle and equipment losses could be replaced within days.[2] Although it took some time to rebuild the combat effectiveness of a unit's personnel, actually having the replacement soldiers quickly in place was the crucial first building block. This Canadian capability could not be matched by the enemy and was one of the principal reasons behind its defeat in May 1945. German defences were continuously ground down by a force whose superior resources were mated with an effective artillery-based operational doctrine. This doctrine focused on minimizing Canadian losses while maximizing the ongoing attrition of the enemy, a "compassionate attritionist" approach to warfare. Without replacement resources, German units simply melted away.

While not always efficient, the Canadian Army's approach to the maintenance of its personnel and equipment inventories speaks of a military culture that did not view these items as disposable assets but rather as valuable tools to be maintained. Sophisticated organizations used countless resources to see that equipment remained operational and personnel levels satisfactory. This was very much in contrast to the late war attitude of the German military, which ruthlessly fought formations to destruction in order to achieve dubious objectives, then replaced them with other formations when their usefulness was expended.

Two organizations stood at the forefront of the Canadian Army's effort to constantly maintain its equipment inventories. The processes of the Royal Canadian Electrical and Mechanical Engineers were effective at recovering and repairing unserviceable equipment, and the 25th Canadian Armoured Delivery Regiment was extremely competent at delivering replacement armoured vehicles rapidly. This second organization's whole purpose was to maintain the heavy armoured vehicle strength of all Canadian units, and nothing comparable existed in the German Army or Waffen-SS. The creation of the Royal Canadian Electrical and Mechanical Engineers in 1944 and the earlier adoption of British Army recovery-and-repair methods in 1943 illustrate the constant doctrinal evolution of the Canadian Army during the late war period. The practice of using four staggered maintenance lines produced the maximum number of repaired vehicles and weapons possible in the shortest amount of time. Severely damaged or broken-down vehicles and weapons were stripped from combat units quickly, leaving the Light Aid Detachments to concentrate on small repairs. This allowed Canadian combat arms units to retain their combat effectiveness because they possessed close to totally serviceable inventories of weapons and vehicles. As an example, by 30 April 1945 the Canadian Army contained a total of 4,588 combat "A" vehicles on strength within its combat arms units, close to all that could be assessed as operational.[3] On the same date, the number of Canadian 5.5-inch, 4.5-inch, and 25-pounder artillery pieces in service totalled 510.[4] Any shortages that did occur within the First Canadian Army in northwest Europe were of a temporary nature.

Though most units contained their complete war establishment of equipment by war's end, it was of varying quality within some combat arms units. Though not the responsibility of the repair-and-replacement organizations, a challenge that faced the Canadian Army in northwest Europe was the acquisition of effective types of weapons and armoured vehicle technology for its infantry and armoured units. It is difficult to quantify the limitations inferior technology imposed on successful infantry and armoured offensive tactics, but the widespread use of this equipment certainly did not aid the army's performance, nor did it do much to limit casualties within the infantry.

This was an issue that confronted all British and Commonwealth forces, and there was little the Canadian Army could have done to improve the situation. While the 25-pounder artillery piece of the Royal Canadian Artillery (RCA) was a war-winning ordnance, the 75 mm gunned Sherman tank and the Sten submachine gun were average weapons systems compared to others in the Allied and German arsenals. They did the job but not as effectively as it could be done. As was the case within all British and Canadian units, excellent weapons systems such as the Ram armoured personnel carrier and the Wasp II flamethrower carrier were rare items at the end of hostilities.[5] During June and July 1944, at a time when they were needed the most, no more that twenty-three Sherman Firefly 17-pounders were available to the 2nd Canadian Armoured Brigade.[6]

Having adequate personnel levels within all Canadian combat arms units was a major factor in the successful achievement of their missions. For most of the time that the army conducted combat operations in northwest Europe, its units never lacked for adequate reinforcements to replace battle and nonbattle casualties. Personnel strength was never a problem for artillery and armoured units, and this allowed them to continuously operate their large inventories of weapons and vehicles. Throughout the spring of 1945, infantry regiments could take high losses one day, be rebuilt, and then be strong enough to conduct operations a short time later.[7] But unlike the reinforcement records of the RCA and Canadian Armoured Corps, the history of personnel reinforcement in the Canadian Infantry Corps during 1944 was not without blemish.

During August and September 1944, there were challenges in supplying infantry units with other ranks (nonofficer) replacements. In this two-month period, a shortage of infantry personnel existed within the reinforcement organization's holding units.[8] This was only one trade out of the three combat arms trades, but the infantry was the spearhead of Canadian offensive operations. The shortage lasted only two months out of an eleven-month campaign, but for two weeks of this period it was important for the First Canadian Army to be operating at its highest possible performance level. During the last phases of the Normandy Campaign, each infantry company had large demands placed on it.

While some infantry regiments during August and September 1944 were still reasonably strong, others faced serious shortages that reduced them to two infantry companies rather than four. As an example, Les Fusiliers Mont-Royal on 21 August contained a strength of 37 officers and 516 other ranks, only 65 percent of its war establishment.[9] The lack of a sufficient number of infantrymen at this point in the Normandy Campaign arguably led to a reduction in the First Canadian Army's overall capability. But the strongest Canadian infantry regiments, not the weakest, always led attacks during operations, and by late August the majority of German forces were withdrawing at high speed, not fighting in place. On 21 August, the Falaise Gap battle was largely concluded, and the First Canadian Army was overwhelmingly victorious. It is impossible to determine whether stronger Canadian infantry companies could have concluded this battle sooner or broken through German defences in mid-August more effectively. But it can be noted that in would have been impossible for any army in the Second World War to perfectly maintain its unit establishment strengths during heavy combat against a peer enemy. Modern weapons simply did too much damage at an incredible rate.

A large program to remuster excess personnel in other trades was in effect by August 1944, but the transformation of these personnel into infantry, other ranks, could not occur instantaneously. Significant results were not apparent in formations like the 2nd Canadian Infantry Division until late September.[10] Most deficits were made good by early October, and replacements were not an issue for the remainder of the campaign in northwest Europe. By 30 September, one of the most depleted units, the South Saskatchewan Regiment, contained 32 officers and 703 other ranks, 86 percent of its war establishment.[11] This number would improve before the regiment commenced combat operations in the Scheldt in early October.

RCA units had the fewest problems maintaining personnel strengths. In addition to having the most advanced artillery technology, RCA artillery units suffered consistently lower personnel casualties than armoured and infantry units. The failure of the German Army to effectively use artillery counterbattery fire and the inability of the German Luftwaffe to conduct regular airstrikes meant that RCA operations went largely unhindered. Because the First Canadian Army consistently held the initiative, large numbers of RCA personnel were never lost because of a sudden German advance reaching field artillery and light antiaircraft units. There were instances of batteries losing guns to occasional German counterbattery fire, but their loss was not an everyday occurrence.[12] RCA antitank regiments, with their direct-fire antitank guns and tank destroyers, did suffer significantly higher losses than rear-deployed field artillery regiments, which were somewhat immune to direct fire. A greater effort had to be made to keep these units' personnel levels and equipment inventories up to strength.[13]

For nine months of the eleven-month campaign in northwest Europe, the personnel-reinforcement system operated smoothly for all trades. In June and early July 1944, it had responded effectively to the limited needs of the 3rd Canadian Division and 2nd Canadian Armoured Brigade without difficulty. During this time, both units were involved in challenging combat operations against powerful German units. From October 1944 to May 1945, combat arms units were consistently reinforced, giving them the strength to overpower enemy opposition. The introduction of National Resources Mobilization Act conscripts in spring 1945 erased any remaining shortages within the reinforcement system. The events of August and September 1944 were a temporary blip on an otherwise effective record. Additionally, the fact that a successful personnel reinforcement system was operated within an army composed of an all-volunteer force until early 1945 was an incredible feat.

In conclusion, during most its campaign in northwest Europe in 1944–45, the Canadian Army operated effective, if not efficient, systems to supply its unit equipment inventories and maintain its personnel levels. These twin systems allowed the Canadian Army to continuously maintain its combat effectiveness in comparison to its opponent, whose units were ground down by attrition. The battlefield impact of the First Canadian Army having all its combat arms units constantly at full strength was tremendous. Consistently possessing a superior amount of resources gave Canadian units an undeniable edge before any operation began. When this strength was matched with a superior artillery-based doctrine that caused extreme attrition of the enemy while preserving the strength of Canadian forces, the First Canadian Army became unstoppable.

Senior leadership within the Canadian Army in Europe always understood that there was a direct correlation between adequate personnel levels and combat power. As a result, Canadian Army reinforcement organizations made determined efforts to maintain these levels. What temporary personnel challenges did occur in the late summer of 1944 were due to a failure to predict what infantry reinforcements were required and remuster surplus noninfantry personnel. In spring 1944, there was no overall shortage of reinforcement personnel, just excess numbers in the wrong army trades. Once these problems were ironed out in late September 1944, infantry regiments were consistently kept at high personnel levels for the remainder of the war.

Canadian units in northwest Europe were well equipped combat "A" vehicles and heavy weapons. Little time was needed to replace or repair what losses occurred, and whatever challenges were present in repair turnaround times were minuscule compared to those within the German military. While these vehicles and weapons systems were effective enough to allow the Canadian Army to accomplish its missions, some were more effective than others. Infantry and armoured forces faced challenges in this area, and the inability of the Canadian Army to obtain quantities of the most effective equipment possibly influenced casualty levels and performance. But these weaknesses were compensated for by the superiority of the Canadian artillery arm. The RCA's battlefield dominance allowed the First Canadian Army to relentlessly advance.

Due to the First Canadian Army's massive combat power in 1944–45, it could be slowed down or delayed, but never stopped. In battle after battle, victory after victory was achieved. Though minor tactical reverses did occur, this field army never suffered a major defeat in northwest Europe. What the enemy encountered in the last year of the war was an invincible army, an army of never-ending strength.

Appendices

APPENDIX 1

War Establishments, Canadian Combat Arms Regiments, Late 1944 and Early 1945

In Canadian regimental war diaries, official histories, and operational narratives, there are accounts of units or subunits being "destroyed" or "suffering large losses" in combat. These accounts will often mention the total number of casualties or quantity of equipment lost in a day's fighting.[1] What is not presented is the actual fighting strength of the unit, a figure necessary for understanding the level of damage done to its fighting capability and establishment. If so many tanks or men were lost, could the unit continue operations before reinforcements arrived? To understand how these losses related to the unit's ability to carry out future missions, it is important to comprehend the unit's size and organization. This appendix briefly outlines the structure and size of Canadian combat arms regiments of battalion strength. The second half of this study is largely dedicated to the statistical records of these regiments, what losses they incurred, and the reinforcements they received. Once these organizations are outlined, it is easier to comprehend the significance of losses suffered and how this damage could have affected the army's performance.

Each type of combat arms regiment within the Canadian Army had a different role and was staffed and equipped accordingly. These regiments were structured as battalion-sized units, with their role (infantry, armoured, artillery) influencing how their companies (squadrons, batteries) were titled. This study encompasses nineteen different types of combat arms regiments that served in northwest Europe in 1944–45. Some armour, artillery, antitank, and antiaircraft regiments had up to three different variants at the army, corps, and divisional level. Each was unique because of its role, equipment establishment, or parent organization. Due to these differences, this study includes the organizations of all variants as separate figures, the exception being if the war establishments of two variants were identical but were given different titles. As noted in the Introduction, Canadian units serving within British divisions in northwest Europe are excluded.

Prominent examples are the 1st Canadian Armoured Personnel Carrier Regiment and the 1st Canadian Parachute Battalion. Certain Canadian regiments were rare, with only one or two being raised for overseas service. Others, such as infantry regiments, were plentiful. For example, in May 1945 there were thirty-three lorried Canadian infantry regiments of battalion strength within the First Canadian Army.

The figures that follow provide a basic introduction to Canadian unit war establishments during the Second World War. The war establishment outlined what exactly the unit was supposed to contain in the way of personnel, vehicles, and equipment for it to complete its missions. War establishment personnel and equipment figures depended on economic production levels, troop availability, levels of technology, and fiscal policy. How these war material and personnel were then organized tactically was driven by army doctrine.[2] Establishments for regiments changed regularly as units were reorganized to remedy a deficiency or meet new demands.

The regimental war establishment figures that follow are for late 1944 and early 1945, roughly the midpoint of the campaign in northwest Europe. After this point, there was little in the way of drastic organizational changes. Within the figures provided, the personnel, main weapons systems, and armoured fighting vehicles (AFVs) of the unit are listed. Not included because of space constraints are how the "B" vehicles were dispersed within the "A1" (fighting), "A2," and "B" (supply and administrative) echelons of each regiment. These vehicles were numerous and vital for the logistic, administrative, maintenance, and liaison needs of combat arms regiment in the field. They consisted of everything from jeeps to command caravans to 6 × 4 wheeled drive recovery vehicles. The total number of small arms and how they were distributed are not included. They do include personnel from the Royal Canadian Corps of Signals Corps, the Royal Canadian Army Service Corps, the Royal Canadian Pay Corps, the Royal Canadian Ordnance Corps, and the Royal Canadian Medical Service, among others. These personnel were integral to the medical and administrative performance of the unit and the maintenance of its equipment, and they are categorized as attached in the official war establishment figures. Not included in the regimental establishment personnel totals are the Light Aid Detachment (LAD) personnel of the Royal Canadian Electrical and Mechanical Engineers (RCEME). They were also vital to the maintenance of unit vehicles and AFVs and were with the unit constantly. Their personnel totals are listed at the end of each regiment's description since they were administratively separate.

The 1945 Canadian Armoured Regiment was a battalion-sized Canadian Armoured Corps (CAC) unit, as illustrated in Table A1.1. Its battlefield role was to use its AFVs to defeat the enemy through firepower and manoeuvre. Each armoured division's armoured brigade and independent armoured brigade were authorized three regiments, and there were a total of twelve in northwest Europe by spring 1945. These regiments usually acted independently of one another as part of combined arms teams. Each regiment had three armoured squadrons and a headquarters squadron. These squadrons fielded the Sherman 17-pounder Sherman Firefly tank, the Sherman V 75 mm tank, and the M3 Stuart 37 mm light tank in the reconnaissance role. In early 1945, there was an equal mix of Sherman V 75 mm tanks and Sherman Firefly 17-pounders, totalling sixty-one cruiser tanks. This total was supplemented by eleven M3 Stuart light tanks in the reconnaissance troop and three armoured recovery vehicle tanks. "B" vehicles totalled twenty cars, seventy-three trucks and specialist vehicles, eight motorcycles, and twelve trailers. The antiaircraft troop was deleted as of

Table A1.1

CAC Armoured Regiment (Armoured Brigade or Division), January 1945

Tactical grouping	Subunits, strength officers, and other ranks	Total heavy weapons and AFVs
Regimental HQ	5–16	4 × Sherman V command tanks
Headquarters Squadron	Recce troop Intercommunication troop Admin troop RCEME LAD ("C") 9–172	11 × M3 Stuart Light tanks, 9 × scout cars, 1 × armoured ammunition carrier
"A" Squadron	1 × HQ troop 5 × tank troops 8–153	19 × Sherman Firefly/75 mm Sherman tanks, 1 × ARV tank, 2 × armoured ammo carriers
"B" Squadron	As above	As above
"C" Squadron	As above	As above
Total	38–647	61 × 75 mm Sherman/17-pounder Sherman Firefly tanks, 9 × scout cars, 11 × M3 Stuart tanks, 3 × ARVs tanks, 7 × armoured ammunition carriers

Source: LAC, RG24, vol. 13,662, "First Canadian Army A&Q War Diary," December 1944, "Armoured Division War Establishment Staff Figures, WWE II/151/4, CAC Armoured Regiment and Armoured Reconnaissance Regiment, January 1945."

November 1944. The RCEME LAD type "C" consisted of one officer and fifteen other ranks. Identically equipped, the armoured reconnaissance regiment had the role of aggressive armoured reconnaissance in force as the vanguard of the armoured division. As divisional troops, there was one armoured reconnaissance regiment in each of the two Canadian armoured divisions.

The 1944 Canadian Armoured Car Regiment was a CAC unit employed at the corps level as a reconnaissance unit, as illustrated in Table A1.2. It was placed under the command of armoured and infantry divisions and utilized in this role. As corps troops, there were only two such regiments employed in northwest Europe by the spring of 1945, one for each Canadian corps. This regiment was designed to carry out deep reconnaissance on a wide front during fluid operations, and it used the mobility of its squadrons to carry out this role. Its organization consisted of four squadrons and a regimental headquarters. Each of the squadrons was equipped with a large number of armoured wheeled vehicles of various types. Because of its large pool of vehicles, this regiment could cover a wide area. Armoured vehicles within the regiment consisted of Daimler and Humber scout cars and Daimler, AEC, and Staghound armoured cars. "B" vehicles within the regiment consisted of eight cars, twenty-eight trucks, seventeen M3 White scout cars, thirty-seven specialist vehicles, and twenty-three

Table A1.2

CAC Armoured Car Regiment (Corps Troops), October 1944

Tactical grouping	Subunits, strength officers, and other ranks	Total heavy weapons and AFVs
Regimental HQ	Signals troop RCEME LAD ("C")	13 × scout cars, 4 × armoured cars, 1 × command caravan
"A" Squadron	Squadron HQ troop Heavy troop Support troop 5 × recce troops	13 × scout cars, 17 × armoured cars
"B" Squadron	As above	As above
"C" Squadron	As above	As above
"D" Squadron	As above	As above
Total	7–803	72 × armoured cars, 65 × scout cars, 1 × command caravan

Source: LAC, RG 24, vol. 13,659, "First Canadian Army A&Q War Diary," October 1944, "Corps Troops War Establishment Staff Figures, III/236/2, CAC Armoured Car Regiment, October 1944."

motorcycles. The attached RCEME LAD type "C" consisted of one officer and fifteen other ranks.

The January 1945 Canadian Reconnaissance Regiment was a CAC divisional reconnaissance asset operating within Canadian infantry divisions, as illustrated in Table A1.3. Its organization consisted of a HQ squadron and three reconnaissance squadrons. The reconnaissance regiment differed from an armoured reconnaissance or armoured car regiment because of its combination of infantry heavy weapons and light wheeled armoured vehicles. If need be, it could act as an additional infantry unit while at the same time conducting its primary role as the divisional mobile reconnaissance force. Its AFVs and major weapons systems consisted of the Humber Armoured Car, the Humber Scout Car, the Universal Carrier, the T16 (gun tractor) Carrier, the Universal Mortar Carrier, the 6-pounder antitank gun, and the 3-inch mortar. There were three

Table A1.3

CAC Reconnaissance Regiment (Infantry Division), January 1945

Tactical grouping	Subunits, strength officers, and other ranks	Total heavy weapons and AFVs
Regimental HQ Squadron	Carrier troop Antitank troop Mortar troop RCEME LAD ("A")	1 × armoured cars, 9 × Universal Carriers, 6 × towed 6-pounder A/T guns, 6 × 3-inch mortars, 12 × (gun tractor) Carriers, 6 × Universal Mortar Carriers
Reconnaissance "A" Squadron	Squadron HQ Signal troop Assault troop 3 × scout troops	9 × armoured cars, 18 × Universal Carriers
Reconnaissance "B" Squadron	As above	As above
Reconnaissance "C" Squadron	As above	As above
Total	43–777	6 × 3-inch mortars, 6 × towed 6-pounder A/T guns, 28 × armoured cars, 63 × Universal Carriers, 6 × Universal Mortar Carriers, 12 × T16 (gun tractor) Carriers

Source: LAC, RG 24, vol. 13,662, "First Canadian Army A&Q War Diaries," December 1944, "Infantry Division War Establishment Staff Figures, Reconnaissance Regiment, WE II/251/2, January 1945."

such regiments raised for the Canadian Army, one for each infantry division. "B" vehicles consisted of thirty-six cars, of which twenty-four were light reconnaissance vehicles, and seventy-one trucks in general service and specialist roles. These totals were supplemented by a further fifty-five motorcycles and ten trailers. The RCEME type "A" LAD attached to the regiment consisted of one officer and fifteen other ranks.

Table A1.4

CIC Infantry Regiment, January 1945

Tactical grouping	Subunits, strength officers, and other ranks	Total heavy weapons and AFVs
Regimental HQ	Scout platoon Stretcher bearer group 6–84	1 × Universal Carrier
HQ Company	Company HQ Signals platoon Administration platoon 5–94	
Support Company	Company HQ 3-inch mortar platoon Universal Carrier platoon Antitank platoon Pioneer platoon 7–184	6 × 3-inch mortars, 7 × 3-inch mortar carriers, 14 × Universal Carriers, 6 × towed 6-pounder A/T guns, 12 × T16 (gun tractor) Carriers, 10 × 2-inch mortars
"A" Rifle Company	Company HQ 3 × rifle platoons 1 × light mortar section 5–120	1 × Universal Carrier, 4 × 2-inch mortars
"B" Rifle Company	As above	As above
"C" Rifle Company	As above	As above
"D" Rifle Company	As above	As above
Total	38–812	6 × 3-inch mortars, 6 × towed 6-pounder A/T guns, 26 × 2-inch mortars, 19 × Universal Carriers, 7 × 3-inch mortar carriers, 12 × T16 (gun tractor) Carriers

Source: LAC, RG 24, vol. 13,662, "First Canadian Army A&Q War Diary," December 1944, "Infantry Division War Establishment Staff Figures, Infantry Battalion (Regiment), WE II/233/4, January 1945."

The Canadian Infantry Regiment was a battalion-sized Canadian Infantry Corps (CIC) unit made up of a battalion headquarters and six companies as of January 1945, as illustrated in Table A1.4. These six companies consisted of a headquarters company, a support company, and four rifle companies. Three infantry regiments made up an infantry brigade. The regiment's role was to close with and destroy the enemy. Apart from the carrier platoon, its infantry companies were lorried and went into battle dismounted.[3] Major weapons systems and AFVs consisted of the T16 (gun tractor) Carrier, the Universal Carrier, the Universal 3-inch Mortar Carrier, the 6-pounder antitank gun, and 3-inch and 2-inch mortars. "B" vehicles consisted of fourteen cars and forty-three trucks of various types designed for general service and specialist use. These totals were supplemented by twenty-seven motorcycles, fourteen trailers, and thirty-three bicycles. RCEME support for the three infantry regiments was held at the brigade level with a single brigade electrical- and mechanical-engineer–type LAD.[4]

The 1945 Canadian Motor Infantry Battalion was a mechanized CIC regiment, as illustrated in Table A1.5. It was set up with one fewer company than a regular lorried infantry battalion. In January 1945, it was equipped with armoured trucks to form a mechanized infantry force that would accompany a rapid armoured advance. It consisted of three motor companies, a support company, a HQ company, and a regimental HQ. Its main role was to close with and destroy the enemy, but it used mechanized infantry tactics to do so. Initially, the motor companies were equipped with M3 White half-tracks, but they were replaced in mid-1944 with armoured trucks. Two of these regiments were formed to serve in each of the armoured brigades within the two Canadian armoured divisions. Motor battalions were not present in Canadian independent armoured brigades. The battalion's major weapons systems and AFVs consisted of the Daimler Scout Car, the 6 pounder antitank gun, 3-inch and 2-inch mortars, the Universal Carrier, the Universal 3-inch Mortar Carrier, the T16 (gun tractor) Carrier, and the MMG (machine gun) Carrier. "B" vehicles consisted of eleven cars and ninety-one trucks that were armoured, general service, or specialist types. This vehicle pool was supplemented by forty-nine motorcycles and ten trailers. Unlike nonmechanized infantry regiments, the motor battalion did have an RCEME LAD attached. The attached RCEME LAD type "B" totalled one officer and thirteen other ranks.

The Canadian Machine Gun Battalion as of January 1945 was an independent battalion-sized CIC support regiment, as illustrated in Table A1.6. There was one raised for each of the three overseas infantry divisions. As a divisional unit, this regiment could be split up to support individual infantry regiments within

Table A1.5

CIC Motor Battalion (Armoured Division), January 1945

Tactical grouping	Subunits, strength officers, and other ranks	Total heavy weapons and AFVs
Regimental HQ	5–28	
HQ Company	Company HQ Signals platoon Administration platoon RCEME LAD ("B") 6–96	
Support Company	Company HQ 3 × antitank platoons 2 × medium MG platoons 1 × mortar platoon 7–190	1 × scout car, 12 × towed 6-pounder A/T guns, 24 × T16 (gun tractor) Carriers, 16 × MMG (medium machine gun) Carriers, 6 × 3-inch mortars, 6 × Universal 3-inch Mortar Carriers
"A" Motor Company	Company HQ, Motor platoons 1–3 Scout carrier platoon 7–168	2 × scout cars, 12 × Universal Carriers
"B" Motor Company	As above	As above
"C" Motor Company	As above	As above
Total	39–818	30 × 2-inch mortars, 6 × 3-inch mortars, 6 × Universal 3-inch mortar carriers, 12 × towed 6-pounder A/T guns, 36 × Universal Carriers, 16 × MMG Carriers, 24 × T16 (gun tractor) Carriers

Source: LAC, RG 24, vol. 13,662, "First Canadian Army A&Q War Diary," December 1944, "Armoured Division War Establishment Staff Figures, Motor Battalion (Regiment), WE II/231/3, January 1945."

a brigade.[5] The battalion consisted of a regimental headquarters, three medium machine-gun companies, and a mortar company. The Machine Gun Battalion's battlefield role was that of a combat force multiplier for an infantry brigade or regiment in attack or defence. Major weapons systems apart from its .303 medium machine guns were 4.2-inch mortars, Universal Carriers, MMG (machine gun) Carriers, and T16 Carriers modified to carry the 4.2-inch mortar

Table A1.6

CIC Machine Gun Battalion, January 1945

Tactical grouping	Subunits, strength officers, and other ranks	Total heavy weapons and AFVs
Regimental HQ	Administration platoon Signals platoon RCEME LAD ("B")	
Mortar Company	Company HQ 2 × mortar platoons	14 × 4.2-inch mortars, 32 × T16 4.2-inch mortar carriers
Medium Machine Gun Company	Company HQ Carrier platoon 3 × MMG (medium machine gun) Platoons	12 × Universal Carriers, 12 × MMG Carriers, 12 × .303 MMGs
Medium Machine Gun	As above	As above
Medium Machine Gun Company	As above	As above
Total	37–701	14 × 4.2-inch mortars, 32 × T16 4.2-inch mortar carriers, 36 × Universal Carriers, 36 × MMG Carriers, 36 × .303 MMGs

Source: LAC, RG 24, vol. 13,662, "First Canadian Army A&Q War Diary," December 1945, "Infantry Division War Establishment Staff Figures, Machine Gun Battalion (Regiment), WE II/240/1, January 1945."

and also to act as ammunition carriers. "B" vehicles consisted of eleven cars and seventy-two trucks of various types in the general service and specialist role. This vehicle pool was supplemented by fifty-two motorcycles and nine trailers. The attached RCEME LAD type "B" had the strength of one officer and thirteen other ranks.

The January 1945 Canadian towed RCA Field Regiment infantry division variant was a divisional artillery asset, as illustrated in Table A1.7. It consisted of three batteries and a regimental HQ. Its batteries were equipped with the towed 25-pounder howitzers rather than self-propelled variants. There were three field regiments within each infantry division for a total of nine infantry division variants in northwest Europe by spring 1945. This regiment contained a different war establishment than the self-propelled and towed field regiments within armoured divisions or held at the army level. The most notable difference was the lack of artillery observation post tanks. The forward observation officers

Table A1.7

Towed RCA Field Artillery Regiment (Infantry Division variant), January 1945

Company or platoon	Subunits, strength officers, and other ranks	Total heavy weapons and AFVs
Regimental HQ	Antiaircraft troop RCEME LAD ("B") 8–62	8 × towed 20 mm antiaircraft guns
"A" Battery	2 × field artillery troops 10–192	8 × towed 25-pounder howitzers, 3 × Universal Carriers
"B" Battery	As above	As above
"C" Battery	As above	As above
Total	38–638	24 × towed 25-pounder howitzers, 8 × towed 20 mm antiaircraft guns, 9 × Universal Carriers

Source: LAC, RG 24, vol. 13,662, "First Canadian Army A&Q War Diaries," January 1944, "Infantry Division War Establishment Staff Figures, Field Artillery Regiment, Towed WE II/190B/1, Effective 30.11.44."

of a towed regiment went forward with infantry battalion HQs and were equipped with Universal Carriers. The primary role of the towed field regiment was to provide powerful indirect fire support at the divisional level. It could also provide direct-fire support against infantry or armoured targets by firing over open sights. The regiment also had a troop of 20 mm antiaircraft guns. "B" vehicles as of January 1945 were 21 cars and 103 trucks of general service and specialist designs, including 36 artillery tractors. Supplementing this pool were twenty-six motorcycles and twenty-two trailers. The RCEME LAD type "B" had a total strength of one officer and thirteen other ranks.

The Canadian self-propelled Royal Canadian Artillery (RCA) Field Regiment armoured division variant as of January 1945 contained a very different war establishment from a towed field regiment in an armoured or infantry division, as illustrated in Table A1.8. The main differences were that all its 25-pounder howitzers were self-propelled, and it operated a large number of artillery observation post tanks. The regiment had a total of thirteen of these tanks and a troop of 20 mm antiaircraft guns. The tanks allowed the forward observation officers to keep up with the armoured squadrons. This type of regiment consisted of three batteries and a regimental HQ. It was a divisional artillery asset whose role was to provide powerful, mobile, and indirect fire support. It could also provide mobile direct-fire support against infantry or armoured targets by firing

Table A1.8

Self-Propelled RCA Field Artillery Regiment (Armoured Division), January 1945

Company or platoon	Subunits, strength officers, and other ranks	Total heavy weapons and AFVs
Regimental HQ	Antiaircraft troop RCEME LAD ("D") 9–60	1 × RCA Observation Post (OP) tank, 8 × towed 20 mm antiaircraft guns
"A" Battery	2 × self-propelled field artillery troops 10–183	8 × self-propelled 25-pounder Sexton howitzers, 4 × RCA OP tanks
"B" Battery	As above	As above
"C" Battery	As above	As above
Total	38–609	24 × self-propelled 25-pounder Sexton howitzers, 8 × towed 20 mm antiaircraft guns, 13 × RCA OP tanks

Source: LAC, RG 24, vol. 13,662, "First Canadian Army A&Q War Diary," December 1944, "Armoured Division War Establishment Staff Figures, Field Artillery Regiment, Self-Propelled, WE II/190A/2, January 1945."

over open sights. The two self-propelled RCA Field Regiment's held at the army-level Army Group Royal Artillery (AGRA) groupings had identical war establishment figures to the self-propelled armoured division variant. In late 1944, there was one within each Canadian armoured division and one per each army-level AGRA grouping, for a total of four self-propelled regiments. "B" vehicles as of late 1944 were thirteen cars and ninety-two trucks of general service and specialist types, including thirty-six artillery tractors and thirty-four M14 half-tracks. Supplementing this pool were thirty-two motorcycles and twenty-four trailers. The attached RCEME LAD type "D" strength was one officer and thirty-seven other ranks.

The 1944 armoured division variant of the towed Canadian RCA Field Regiment was a divisional artillery asset, as illustrated in Table A1.9. Like other field regiments, it consisted of three batteries and a regimental HQ. The regiment's primary role was providing indirect fire support at the divisional level. It could also provide direct-fire support against infantry or armoured targets by firing over open sights. There was one regiment of this type established for each Canadian armoured division, for a total of two. They operated in conjunction with the self-propelled RCA field regiments within armoured divisions. The towed field regiment within an armoured division contained a different

Table A1.9

Towed RCA Field Artillery Regiment (Armoured Division), January 1945

Company or platoon	Subunits, strength officers, and other ranks	Total heavy weapons and AFVs
Regimental HQ	Antiaircraft troop RCEME LAD ("B") 8–62	8 × towed 20 mm antiaircraft guns towed
"A" Battery	2 × towed field artillery troops 10–192	8 × towed 25-pounders howitzers, 2 × Observation Post (OP) tanks, 1 × Universal Carrier
"B" Battery	As above	As above
"C" Battery	As above	As above
Total	38–638	24 × towed 25-pounder howitzers, 8 × towed 20 mm antiaircraft guns, 6 × OP tanks, 3 × Universal Carriers

Source: LAC, RG 24, vol. 13,662, "First Canadian Army A&Q War Diary," December 1944, "Armoured Division War Establishment Staff Figures, Field Artillery Regiment, Towed, WE II/190B/1, January 1945."

war establishment than that of a towed field regiment in an infantry division. The most notable difference was a limited allocation of observation post tanks, as its forward observation officers were required to go forward with the armoured squadrons. It only had six observation post tanks on its establishment versus the thirteen of the self-propelled field regiment. It also had a limited number of Universal tracked carriers, having only three. Like all field regiments, its batteries were equipped with a total of twenty-four 25-pounder towed howitzers, and the regimental HQ contained a troop of towed 20 mm antiaircraft guns. "B" vehicles as of January 1945 consisted of 21 cars and 103 trucks of general service and specialist design, including 36 artillery tractors. The regiment also contained twenty-six motorcycles and twenty-two trailers. The RCEME LAD type "B" was one officer and thirteen other ranks.

The Canadian AGRA towed RCA Medium Regiment as of October 1944 was an army-level artillery asset, as illustrated in Table A1.10. It consisted of two batteries of eight 4.5- or 5.5-inch towed guns each, for a total of sixteen guns per regiment. Each battery was divided into two troops of four guns each. The medium regiments were held at the AGRA level and controlled by the army-level AGRA artillery command structure. The primary role of these regiments was to provide flexible, heavy indirect fire support wherever it was needed,

Table A1.10

AGRA RCA Medium Regiment (Army Troops), October 1944

Company or platoon	Subunits, strength officers, and men	Total heavy weapons and AFVs
Regimental HQ	RCEME LAD ("B")	
"A" Battery	2 × towed medium artillery troops	8 × towed 5.5- or 4.5-inch howitzers
"B" Battery	As above	As above
Total	28–540	16 × towed 5.5- or 4.5-inch howitzers, 6 × Universal Carriers

Source: LAC, RG 24, vol. 13,659, "First Canadian Army A&Q War Diary," October 1944, "AGRA War Establishment Staff Figures, AGRA RCA Medium Artillery Regiment, Towed, WE II/10/3, October 1944."

working in close cooperation with field artillery regiments at the divisional level. The Canadian Army in northwest Europe had no superheavy artillery regiments, so these regiments were the most powerful indirect assets the First Canadian Army possessed.

A total of six RCA medium regiments were raised to establish both the 1st and 2nd AGRA formations. These regiments served in both Italy and northwest Europe, three to an AGRA. All six were to come together in spring 1945 because of the redeployment of the 1st Canadian Corps to northwest Europe. Three were equipped with 5.5-inch guns, but the other three were equipped with 4.5-inch variants because of a shortage of 5.5-inch artillery pieces. These regiments did not have an antiaircraft troop. "B" vehicles consisted of eleven cars and eighty-four trucks of various types, including eighteen artillery tractors. This vehicle pool was supplemented by sixteen trailers and nineteen motorcycles. The RCEME LAD type "B" consisted of one officer and thirteen other ranks. As noted previously, there was also one self-propelled field regiment allocated to each of the 1st and 2nd Canadian AGRA organizations. These regiments, designated "Army Field Artillery Regiments," worked in conjunction with the medium regiments to supplement divisional artillery assets. The self-propelled AGRA field regiments were equipped the same as the self-propelled regiments attached to the armoured divisions.[6]

At the corps level, as of October 1944 there were two RCA Survey Regiments of battalion strength, each consisting of two batteries, as illustrated in Table A1.11. The battlefield roles of these units were artillery flash-spotting, sound-ranging,

Table A1.11

RCA Survey Regiment (Corps Troops), October 1944

Company or platoon	Subunits, strength officers, and men	Total heavy weapons and AFVs
Regimental HQ	Regimental HQ airburst-ranging troop RCEME LAD ("A")	
"A" Battery	Flash-spotting troop Sound-ranging troop Survey troop	
"B" Battery	As above	
Total	34–589	

Source: LAC, RG 24, vol. 13,659, "First Canadian Army A&Q War Diary," October 1944, "Corps Troops War Establishment Staff Figures, RCA Survey Regiment, WE III/13/5, October 1944."

and survey duties. They worked closely with army-level AGRA and divisional artillery assets to make indirect fire as accurate as possible. In this role, they operated close to the front lines within the armoured and infantry divisions' areas of operation. These regiments did not have any major weapons systems past small arms and operated sophisticated nongun artillery equipment to accomplish their tasks. "B" vehicles consisted of 39 cars and 117 trucks, of which 12 were M14 half-tracks. Additional vehicles and trailers consisted of forty-five motorcycles and thirty-four trailers. The attached RCEME LAD type "A" consisted of one officer and fifteen other ranks.

The corps-level RCA Anti-Tank Regiment as of October 1944 was an antitank unit whose primary role was to complement divisional antitank units; its organization is illustrated in Table A1.12. It could be deployed at the divisional level where needed. It contained four batteries in late 1944. Two batteries operated towed 17-pounder antitanks guns, and two batteries were self-propelled, operating M10 3-inch gunned tank destroyers. In the spring of 1945, these destroyers were exchanged for Valentine Archer 17-pounder tank destroyers. It was a rare unit in that it also operated tank chassis artillery towers, Universal Carriers, and Valentine Charger artillery command tanks. It also had no antiaircraft guns attached to it. "B" vehicles consisted of twenty-two cars and ninety-four trucks. Of the latter, twenty-four were artillery tractors and four were M14 half-tracks. This vehicle total was supplemented by twenty-five trailers and

Table A1.12

RCA Anti-Tank Regiment (Corps Troops), October 1944

Tactical grouping	Subunits, strength officers, and men	Total heavy weapons and AFVs
Regimental HQ	RCEME LAD ("D")	–
"A" Battery	3 × self-propelled A/T troops	12 × M10 3-inch tank destroyers, 6 × 2-inch mortars, 3 × Universal Carriers, 4 × Valentine Charger Command tanks
"B" Battery	As above	As above
"C" Battery	3 × towed A/T troops	12 × towed 17-pounder A/T guns, 6 × 2-inch mortars, 3 × Universal Carriers, 14 × armoured towers
"D" Battery	As above	As above
Total	38–765	24 × M10 3-inch tank destroyers, 24 × towed 17-pounder A/T guns, 24 × 2-inch mortars, 12 × Universal Carriers, 8 × Valentine Charger Command tanks, 28 × artillery towers

Source: LAC, RG 24, vol. 13,659, "First Canadian Army A&Q War Diaries," October 1944, "Corps Troops War Establishment Staff Figures, RCA Anti-Tank Regiment, WE III/308/1, III/309/1, III/310/10, Effective 23.10.44."

twenty motorcycles. The RCEME LAD type "D" strength was one officer and forty-two other ranks. This high number of personnel in this LAD was due to the large number of specialist vehicles and weapons systems present within the regiment.

The armoured division variant of the RCA Anti-Tank Regiment as of January 1945 was a divisional antitank asset, as illustrated in Table A1.13. It could be deployed where needed to bolster an infantry or armour brigade's antitank capability. It contained four batteries in early 1945. Two batteries operated towed 17-pounder antitanks guns, and two batteries were self-propelled, operating the M10 17-pounder tank destroyers. It also operated Universal Carriers, 20 mm antiaircraft guns, and 2-inch mortars. "B" vehicles consisted of 28 cars and 103 trucks. Of the latter, 26 were artillery tractors. This vehicle total was supplemented by twenty-six trailers and twenty motorcycles. The RCEME LAD type "D" strength was one officer and forty-two other ranks.

Table A1.13

RCA Anti-Tank Regiment (Armoured Division), January 1945

Tactical grouping	Subunits, strength officers, and men	Total heavy weapons and AFVs
Regimental HQ	RCEME LAD ("D") Antiaircraft troop 9–57	5 × towed 20 mm antiaircraft guns
"A" Battery	3 × self-propelled A/T troops 7–169	12 × M10 Achilles 17-pounder tank destroyers
"B" Battery	As above	As above
"C" Battery	3 × towed A/T troops 7–173	12 × towed 17-pounder A/T guns, 3 × 2-inch mortars, 9 × Universal Carriers
"D" Battery	As above	As above
Total	37–741	24 × M10 17-pounder tank destroyers, 24 × towed 17-pounder A/T guns, 12 × 2-inch mortars, 18 × Universal Carriers, 5 × towed 20 mm antiaircraft guns

Source: LAC, RG 24, vol. 13,662, "First Canadian Army A&Q War Diary," December 1944, "Armoured Division War Establishment Staff Figures, RCA Anti-Tank Regiment (Armoured Division), WE II/181/186/188/2, Effective January 1945."

The infantry division variant of the RCA Anti-Tank Regiment as of January 1945 was a divisional antitank asset that was deployed to support the infantry brigades, as illustrated in Table A1.14. As a divisional unit, this regiment was designed to work in conjunction with the antitank platoons at the infantry regiment level. Unlike other antitank regiments, it contained only three batteries in early 1945, the first being equipped with towed 17-pounder antitank guns. The second battery was equipped with self-propelled Valentine Archer 17-pounder tank destroyers. The third battery contained four troops equipped with 6-pounder towed antitank guns. The regiment also operated Universal Carriers, T16 (gun tractor) Carriers, 2-inch mortars, and a single 20 mm antiaircraft gun. "B" vehicles consisted of twenty-six cars and ninety-one trucks of general service and specialist types, sixteen of which were artillery tractors. This vehicle count was supplemented by four trailers and twenty motorcycles. The attached RCEME LAD type "D" consisted of one officer and forty-six other ranks.

Table A1.14

RCA Anti-Tank Regiment (Infantry Division), January 1945

Tactical grouping	Subunits, strength officers, and men	Total heavy weapons and AFVs
Regimental HQ	RCEME LAD ("D")	1 × towed 20 mm antiaircraft gun
"A" Battery	3 × self-propelled A/T troops	12 × Valentine Archer 17-pounder tank destroyers
"B" Battery	3 × towed A/T troops	12 × towed 17-pounder A/T guns, 24 × T16 (gun tractor) Carriers
"C" Battery	4 × towed A/T troops	16 × towed 6-pounder A/T guns towed, 3 × 2-inch mortars, 16 × Universal Carriers
Total	35–614	12 × Valentine Archer 17-pounder tank destroyers, 12 × towed 17-pounder A/T guns, 16 × towed 6-pounder A/T guns, 24 × 2-inch mortars, 16 × Universal Carriers, 24 × T16 (gun tractor) Carriers, 1 × 20 mm antiaircraft gun towed

Source: LAC, RG 24, vol. 13,662, "First Canadian Army A&Q War Diary," December 1944, "Infantry Division War Establishment Staff Figures, RCA Anti-Tank Regiment (Infantry Division), WE II/181/186D/1, January 1945."

The Canadian Corps-level light antiaircraft role was filled by the October 1944 RCA Light Anti-Aircraft (LAA) Regiment corps troops variant, as illustrated in Table A1.15. There were two of these regiments established, one in each Canadian corps overseas. This regiment could have its assets deployed at critical points on the battlefield to bolster the antiaircraft defences of any front-line unit. It could also be deployed to protect line-of-communication rear-area units, headquarters, supply dumps, bridges, and other vital points. As of October 1944, this regiment contained three batteries, each with two troops. One troop was equipped with self-propelled truck-mounted 40 mm antiaircraft guns, and the other was towed. "B" vehicles consisted of twenty-six cars and ninety-five trucks, of which eighteen were the self-propelled mounts for 40 mm antiaircraft guns and eighteen were light artillery tractors. This vehicle pool was supplemented by twenty-six trailers and thirty-eight motorcycles. The RCEME LAA Workshop type "A" personnel consisted of one officer and seventeen other ranks.

Table A1.15

RCA Light Anti-Aircraft Regiment (Corps Troops), October 1944

Tactical grouping	Subunits, strength officers, and men	Total heavy weapons and AFVs
Regimental HQ	RCEME LAA Workshop ("A")	
"A" Battery	1 × self-propelled antiaircraft troop 1 × towed antiaircraft troop	6 × self-propelled 40 mm antiaircraft guns, 6 × towed 40 mm antiaircraft guns
"B" Battery	As above	As above
"C" Battery	As above	As above
Total	34–551	18 × self-propelled 40 mm antiaircraft guns, 18 × towed 40 mm antiaircraft guns

Source: LAC, RG 24, vol. 13,659, "First Canadian Army A&Q War Diary," October 1944, "Corps Troops War Establishment Staff Figures, RCA Light Anti-Aircraft Regiment, WE III/12C/3 III/12A/3, October 1944."

The light antiaircraft role within a Canadian infantry division as of January 1945 was filled by the RCA LAA Regiment infantry division variant, its organization illustrated in Table A1.16. This type of light antiaircraft regiment contained three batteries, each with two troops. Both were equipped with 40 mm antiaircraft guns. One troop was self-propelled with their antiaircraft guns mounted on trucks, and the other was towed. There were three of these regiments established, one for each Canadian infantry division. This regiment could have its assets deployed at critical points on the battlefield to provide effective antiaircraft defence. It could also be deployed to protect headquarters, assembly areas, and other areas of importance. "B" vehicles consisted of 29 cars and 110 trucks, of which 18 were 3-ton self-propelled mounts for 40 mm antiaircraft guns, and 24 were light artillery tractors. Also attached were thirty trailers and thirty-eight motorcycles. The RCEME LAA Workshop type "A" consisted of one officer and seventeen other ranks.

Antiaircraft assets at the armoured division level were provided by the late 1944 RCA LAA Regiment armoured division variant, as illustrated in Table A1.17. There were two of these regiments established, one for each Canadian armoured division. This regiment was entirely self-propelled and consisted of three batteries mounted on 3-ton trucks. Each battery had two troops, both

Table A1.16

RCA Light Anti-Aircraft Regiment (Infantry Division), January 1945

Tactical grouping	Subunits, strength officers, and men	Total heavy weapons and AFVs
Regimental HQ	RCEME LAA Workshop ("A")	
"A" Battery	1 × self-propelled troop of antiaircraft guns 1 × troop of towed antiaircraft guns	6 × self-propelled 40 mm antiaircraft guns, 6 × towed 40 mm antiaircraft guns
"B" Battery	As above	As above
"C" Battery	As above	As above
Total	34–551	18 × self-propelled 40 mm antiaircraft guns, 18 × towed 40 mm antiaircraft guns

Source: LAC, RG 24, vol. 13,662, "First Canadian Army A&Q War Diary," December 1944, "Infantry Division War Establishment Staff Figures, RCA Light Anti-Aircraft Regiment (Infantry Division), WE II/179/180A/1, January 1945."

Table A1.17

RCA Light Anti-Aircraft Regiment (Armoured Division), January 1945

Tactical grouping	Subunits, strength officers, and men	Total heavy weapons and AFVs
Regimental HQ	RCEME LAA Workshop ("A")	
"A" Battery	2 × self-propelled troop of antiaircraft guns	12 × self-propelled 40 mm antiaircraft guns,
"B" Battery	As above	as above
"C" Battery	As above	as above
Total	34–551	36 × self-propelled 40 mm antiaircraft guns

Source: LAC, RG 24, vol. 13,662, "First Canadian Army A&Q War Diary," December 1944, "Armoured Division War Establishment Staff Figures, RCA Light Anti-Aircraft Regiment (Armoured Division), WE II/179/3 and 180/2, January 1945."

equipped with self-propelled 40 mm antiaircraft guns. This regiment would be deployed to provide effective light antiaircraft defence for the divisional area of operations. It could also be deployed to protect headquarters, assembly areas, and other points of importance. "B" vehicles consisted of 29 cars and 128 trucks, of which 36 were the self-propelled mounts for 40 mm antiaircraft guns, and 12 were light artillery tractors. This total was supplemented by thirty trailers and thirty-eight motorcycles. The attached RCEME LAA Workshop type "A" consisted of one officer and twenty-eight other ranks.

Although these war establishment organizational figures set out what the regiments were authorized to contain under 21st Army Group regulations, reality in the field could be different. But in the majority of cases, the organization figures were adhered to. Combat losses often caused temporary organizational changes, such as the reduction of a squadron to three troops or the disbandment of an infantry company. Also, command decisions to replace a unit's vehicles and equipment in the field were often taken before war establishment figures could be amended. This practice often left units with unauthorized items. These figures the underscore the significance (or lack thereof) of unit losses presented in this study.

APPENDIX 2

2nd Canadian Corps Reinforcement Company as an Additional Rehabilitation Tool for Neuro-Psychiatric (Battle Exhaustion) Casualties

Table A2.1

Neuro-Psychiatric (NP) cases in October 1944 within the 3rd Canadian Infantry Division after the Scheldt Estuary battles

Casualties	*N*	NP casualties	*N*	%
Infantry	1,626	Infantry	268	16.4
RCA	93	RCA	3	3.2
Divisional troops	238	Divisional troops	24	10
Total reported	1,957	Total NP cases	295	15

Source: Terry Copp, *Cinderella Army,* Appendix E, 308; LAC, "3rd Canadian Infantry Division Psychiatric Report, October 1944"; LAC, "ADMS 3rd Canadian Infantry Division War Diary, November 1944." These numbers do not include killed and missing casualties, as they are deemed irreversible total losses in personnel.

Table A2.2

Treatment options that were utilized for NP casualties in October 1944 within the 3rd Canadian Infantry Division after the Scheldt Estuary battles

Treatment options	*N*	%
Corps reinforcement centre/company	199	67.5
Reboard and reallocation	52	17.6
Further rehabilitation	28	9.5
General hospital	16	5.4
Total	295	100

Source: Terry Copp, *Cinderella Army,* Appendix E, 308; LAC, "3rd Canadian Infantry Division Psychiatric Report, October 1944." These numbers do not include killed and missing casualties, as they are deemed irreversible total losses in personnel.

APPENDIX 3

Table A3.1

Infantry, other ranks, shortages, by division, northwest Europe, 27 August 1944–28 April 1945

	Canadian Infantry Division			Canadian Armoured Division			
Date	1st	2nd	3rd	4th	5th	Total	No. 2 CBRG holdings
27.08.44	–	1,999	604	522	–	3,125	1,726
29.08.44	–	2,495	836	846	–	4,177	1,306
30.08.44	–	2,522	878	846	–	4,246	1,231
31.08.44	–	2,612	875	831	–	4,318	1,354
3.09.44	–	2,645	752	761	–	4,158	876
4.09.44	–	1,960	736	755	–	3,451	731
5.09.44	–	1,960	737	761	–	3,458	1,785
6.09.44	–	1.450	630	706	–	2,786	954
7.09.44	–	1,478	666	706	–	2,850	882
8.09.44	–	1,478	770	715	–	2,963	987
11.09.44	–	1,794	741	872	–	3,407	1,841
12.09.44	–	1,727	759	865	–	3,351	1,317
13.09.44	–	1,727	788	729	–	3,244	1,141
14.09.44	–	1,550	806	719	–	3,075	1,781
16.09.44	–	1,495	733	713	–	2,941	1,829
18.09.44	–	1,482	814	641	–	2,937	1,710
19.09.44	–	1,553	783	641	–	2,977	2,746
20.09.44	–	1,523	711	707	–	2,941	2,227
22.09.44	–	1,464	621	624	–	2,709	2,492
23.09.44	–	1,299	602	629	–	2,503	1,535
26.09.44	–	1,408	673	282	–	2,363	2,363
27.09.44	–	1,452	802	318	–	2,572	2,363
28.09.44	–	1,442	809	324	–	2,575	2,288
29.09.44	–	1,470	761	180	–	2,411	2,053
2.10.44	–	1,267	816	125	–	2,208	2,814
5.10.44	–	1,165	552	106	–	1,823	2,028
7.10.44	–	1,224	540	112	–	1,876	1,889
10.10.44	–	1,058	464	161	–	1,683	1,160
11.10.44	–	973	624	182	–	1,779	2,124
12.10.44	–	934	646	179	–	1,759	3,053
13.10.44	–	979	749	150	–	1,878	2,181
14.10.44	–	869	851	94	–	1,814	2,234
16.10.44	–	753	747	119	–	1,619	1,947
17.10.44	–	820	793	103	–	1,716	1,858

►

	Canadian Infantry Division			Canadian Armoured Division			
Date	1st	2nd	3rd	4th	5th	Total	No. 2 CBRG holdings
18.10.44	–	852	548	119	–	1,519	3,512
19.10.44	–	681	566	131	–	1,378	1,985
20.10.44	–	652	415	141	–	1,208	2,735
23.10.44	–	478	410	288	–	1,176	2,419
24.10.44	–	474	385	274	–	1,133	2,352
25.10.44	–	548	426	294	–	1,268	2,476
26.10.44	–	657	533	285	–	1,475	2,042
30.10.44	–	679	670	554	–	1,903	1,921
31.10.44	–	679	724	557	–	1,960	1,949
1.11.44	–	755	768	571	–	2,094	2,064
2.11.44	–	815	787	635	–	2,237	2,070
3.11.44	–	858	776	615	–	2,249	2,358
4.11.44	–	798	805	697	–	2,300	2,398
6.11.44	–	803	678	635	–	2,116	2,748
7.11.44	–	803	519	639	–	1,961	2,754
8.11.44	–	803	424	127	–	1,354	2,000
9.11.44	–	632	424	227	–	1,283	2,153
10.11.44	–	530	278	262	–	1,070	1,325
11.11.44	–	579	278	188	–	1,045	1,456
13.11.44	–	424	90	134	–	648	2,323
30.11.44	–	325	125	40	–	490	NIL
29.12.44	–	205	182	36	–	423	20
6.01.45	–	123	104	57	–	284	3,131
13.01.45	–	65	173	51	–	289	3,414
20.01.45	–	105	169	211	–	385	2,650
27.01.45	–	NIL	NIL	95	–	95	2,537
3.02.45	–	NIL	NIL	210	–	210	2,608
10.02.45	–	NIL	NIL	NIL	–	NIL	2,516
17.02.45	–	NIL	NIL	49	–	49	3,768
24.02.45	–	NIL	334	NIL	–	334	4,221
3.03.45	–	244	72	105	–	421	3,704
10.03.45	–	371	62	254	–	687	2,715
17.03.45	–	4	NIL	86	–	90	2,193
24.03.45	132	9	54	8	28	231	3,979
31.03.45	156	48	191	34	NIL	429	5,476
7.04.45	NIL	75	NIL	55	NIL	130	4,036
14.04.45	74	17	50	14	NIL	155	4,022
21.04.45	72	64	25	30	NIL	191	3,473
28.04.45	23	193	225	89	108	638	3,728

Source: LAC, RG 24, vol. 10,699, "Deficiencies and Holdings of Canadian Infantry, Other Ranks, North West Europe, 27 August 1944–28 April 1945."

Notes

Introduction

1 Charles Stacey, *The Official History of the Canadian Army in the Second World War,* vol. 3, *The Victory Campaign: The Operations in North West Europe, 1944–1945* (Ottawa: Queen's Printer and Controller of Stationery, 1960), v–ix.

2 Ibid., Appendix F, "Canadian Army Units in North-West Europe (8 May 1945)," 657–58.

3 Ibid., 271.

4 Russell Hart, *Clash of Arms: How the Allies Won in Normandy* (Norman, OK: University of Oklahoma Press, 2004), 343. The 2nd Canadian Infantry Division's war establishment in the summer of 1944 was 18,376.

5 Stacey, *The Victory Campaign,* 140.

6 Library and Archives Canada (LAC), RG 24, vol. 13,776, "3rd Canadian Infantry Division A&Q War Diary," August 1944. This letter details personnel reinforcements dispatched by the No. 2 Canadian Base Reinforcement Group. A key example of the army's efficient administrative performance was the supply of 6,984 reinforcements to the 3rd Canadian Infantry Division in Normandy up to 4 August 1944.

7 Hart, *Clash of Arms,* 357. Hart notes that Canada's offensive drive was sapped by its lack of infantry.

8 Ibid.

9 LAC, RG 24, vol. 13,658, "First Canadian Army A&Q War Diary," 30 August 1944. The 30 August 1944 return for the Fusiliers Mont-Royal infantry regiment was 37 officers and 485 other ranks, 61 percent of its on-paper establishment strength of 850 personnel. It is important to note that this was at the end of the Normandy Campaign, in August 1944, not the beginning of the month.

10 English, *The Canadian Army and the Normandy Campaign* (Mechanicsburg, PA: Stackpole, 2009), 235. Canadian casualties for the Normandy Campaign totalled 18,444.

11 Terry Copp, *Fields of Fire: The Canadians in Normandy* (Toronto: University of Toronto Press, 2003), 261.

12 LAC, RG 24, vol. 15,061, "The Essex Scottish Regiment War Diary," July 1944, 28 July 1944.

13 Terry Copp, *Cinderella Army: The Canadians in North West Europe, 1944–1945* (Toronto: University of Toronto Press, 2006), 297, Appendix A. The shortage of trained infantry maxed out on this date at 4,318. The total establishment of the twenty-one infantry regiments and one motor battalion was 18,707.

14 Ibid., 302, Appendix 3. Losses for the Canadian Army in northwest Europe during the week of 30 August 1944 totalled 4,574.

15 Niklas Zetterling, *Normandy 1944: German Military Organization, Combat Power and Organizational Effectiveness* (Winnipeg: J.J. Fedorowicz, 2000), 207–8. As of 1 September 1944, Sturmgeschültz-Brigade 394 (Assault Gun) had no operational assault guns following the Normandy Campaign and had to be totally re-equipped.

16 Ibid., 389, citing status report of Panzer Lehr Division sent to the inspector general of Panzer Troops. The German Panzer Lehr Panzer Division suffered nearly 7,411 casualties in Normandy, out of a 1 June 1944 strength of 14,699. These casualties effectively destroyed the infantry component of this elite division. The division was withdrawn and rebuilt in fall 1944.

17 Robert Engen, *Strangers in Arms: Combat Motivation in the Canadian Army, 1943–1945* (Montreal/Kingston: McGill-Queens University Press, 2016); and Dan Byers, *Zombie Army: Canadian Conscription in the Second World War* (Vancouver: UBC Press, 2016). Both works have large segments on the issues of conscription and reinforcements.

18 LAC, RG 24, vol. 12,448, "Organization and Administration of No. 2 CBRG, 03/44–02/46," and Stacey, *The Victory Campaign*, 630–31. The reinforcement battalion was itself an administrative holding organization for reinforcements rather than an army battalion trained in a specific trade or mission. It usually comprised several hundred transient personnel, controlled and administered by a permanent battalion command structure.

19 LAC, RG 24, vol. 10,663, "Figure 2: First Canadian Army Plans Diagram of Personnel Replacement and Releases," file 215C1.045 (D12); and Stacey, *The Victory Campaign*, 630–32.

20 Ibid., "Figure 2: First Canadian Army Plans Diagram of AFV 'A' Vehicle Recovery, Repair and Replacement," file 215C1.045 (D12). See also Tanya Grodzinski, *Operational Handbook for the First Canadian Army, 1944–45: Formation Organization, Staff Technique and Administration*, rev. ed. (Lower Sackville, NS: Regimental Historian, 2017), 87, Appendix D.

21 Stacey, *The Victory Campaign*, Appendix F, "Canadian Army Units in North-West Europe (8 May 1945)," 657–62. Within the Normandy beachhead, two specialized reinforcement organizations were present by August 1944. The No. 2 Canadian Base Reinforcement Group, which had five replacement battalions, existed to replace personnel. The 25th Canadian Armoured Delivery Regiment, with four squadrons, existed to replace heavy armoured vehicles.

22 Angelo Caravaggio, "The Human Dimension of Compromised Command: Major General George Kitching and the 4th Canadian Armoured Division in Normandy" (research paper, Royal Military College, Kingston War Studies Course 504, 2002), 45. On 8 August 1944, the air attack for the first phase of Operation Totalize included dropping 3,500 tonnes of bombs by four-engine bombers.

23 E.L.M. Burns, *Manpower in the Canadian Army, 1939–1945* (Toronto: Clarke, Irwin, 1956), 89–90. This work looks at the larger strategic direction taken by the Canadian Army in the Second World War.

24 LAC, RG 24, vol. 14,276, "C Squadron, 25th Canadian Armoured Delivery Regiment War Diary," October 1943 to December 1944. This forward-delivery squadron was tasked with transporting repaired armoured vehicles to armoured units at the front.

25 Burns, *Manpower in the Canadian Army*.

26 Stacey, *The Victory Campaign*, Appendix F, "Canadian Army Units in North-West Europe (8 May 1945)," 657. There were other Canadian units serving with the 6th British Airborne Division, the 79th British Armoured Division, and the 107th British Anti-Aircraft Brigade, but they are excluded.

27 John Ellis, *Brute Force: Allied Strategy and Tactics in the Second World War* (London: Andre Deutsch, 1990), 556, Appendices, Figure 50, "Allied Crude Oil Production." It is a given that these items in 1944 were extremely plentiful on the Allied side.

Chapter 1: Personnel Reinforcements

1 Charles Stacey, *The Official History of the Canadian Army in the Second World War*, vol. 3, *The Victory Campaign: The Operations in North West Europe 1944–1945* (Ottawa: Queen's Printer and Controller of Stationery, 1960), 284–85. Despite evidence of higher infantry-casualty rates in Italy and totally different geographical terrain, North African level wastage rates were utilized by CMHQ for northwest Europe. Using these projections, it appeared that enough Canadian reinforcements were present in the United Kingdom during the spring of 1944.

2 Stacey, *The Victory Campaign*, 623.

3 Ibid., 630.

4 Ibid., "General Order 297, 21 June 1944, relating to the Establishment of No. 2 CBRG."

5 R.B. Oglesby, "Canadian Organization in the Theatres of Operations, 1939–1945," Canadian Historical Section, Army Headquarters Reports, 1948–59, no. 53, http://publications.gc.ca/collections/collection_2016/mdn-dnd/D63-5-53-1952-eng.pdf, para 23.

6 Ibid., para. 24. Effective 27 March 1944, No. 2 CBRG was formed by GO 297/44.

7 Stacey, *The Victory Campaign*, 631. Library and Archives Canada (LAC), RG 24, vol. 12,448, "Organization and Administration of No. 2 CBRG, 03/44–02/46."

8 Oglesby, "Canadian Organization in the Theatres of Operations," para. 24.

9 Ibid.

10 Ibid., para. 27.

11 Tanya Grodzinski, *Operational Handbook for the First Canadian Army, 1944–1945: Formation Organization, Staff Techniques and Administration*, rev. ed. (Halifax, NS: Regimental Historian, 2018), 96–97.

12 "Organization and Administration of No. 2 CBRG." Stacey, *The Victory Campaign*, 630–31. The reinforcement battalion itself was an administrative holding organization for reinforcements rather than an army battalion trained in a specific trade or mission. It usually consisted of several hundred transient personnel, controlled and administered by a permanent battalion command structure.

13 LAC, RG 24, vol. 15,001, "Algonquin Regiment War Diary," April 1945. One diary entry refers to only 25 percent of the reinforcements having combat experience, illustrating the mix the army received in way of replacements.

14 Oglesby, "Canadian Organization in the Theatres of Operations," para. 27.

15 Stacey, *The Victory Campaign*, 632; and "Organization and Administration of No. 2 CBRG."

16 Ibid.

17 Oglesby, "Canadian Organization in the Theatres of Operations, 1939–1945," para. 31.

18 LAC, RG 24, vol. 12,448, "Organization and Administration of No. 3 CBRG, 04/45–05/45;" and Stacey, *The Victory Campaign*, 632.

19 LAC, RG 24, vol. 10,663, "Figure 2: First Canadian Army Plans Diagram of Personnel Replacement and Releases," file 215C1.045 (D12); and Stacey, *The Victory Campaign* 630–32.

20 Terry Copp, *Cinderella Army: The Canadians in Northwest Europe, 1944–1945* (Toronto: University of Toronto Press, 2006), 294–95. Copp relates the story of the infantry's remustering and retraining of Lieutenant Walter Keith, a Signals Corps officer, in the United Kingdom over the winter of 1944–45.

21 "Echelon," Canadiansoldiers.com, http://www.canadiansoldiers.com/glossary/glossarye.htm. Combat arms regiments consisted "F," "A," and "B" Echelons. "F" was the fighting component of the unit, containing everything needed for the combat mission while "A" and "B" Echelons filled supply and administrative roles.

22 LAC, RG 24, vol. 18,616, "Reinforcement Drafts from UK by Date and Amount." The 2 September 1944 draft from the United Kingdom, SP INF 4, consisted of 91 officers and 562 other ranks. Divided among the infantry regiments of the 2nd and 3rd Canadian Infantry Divisions and the 4th Canadian Armoured Division, it was not a huge amount.
23 Stacey, *The Victory Campaign*, 631–33. Reinforcements coming through took an average of three to four days transit to show up on the nominal rolls of the receiving regiment. In October 1944, before the Port of Antwerp opened, reinforcements took seven days to arrive. This delay was due to the increased distance from the Normandy beachhead to the front line in the Scheldt.
24 Terry Copp and Bill McAndrew, *Battle Exhaustion: Soldiers and Psychiatrists in the Canadian Army, 1939–1945* (Montreal/Kingston: McGill-Queen's University Press, 1990), 57.
25 Copp, *Cinderella Army*, 308–11, Appendix E, "Third Division Psychiatric Report, October 1944."
26 Ibid. Appendix 9 in Copp's *Cinderella Army* breaks down neuropsychiatric casualties in the 3rd Canadian Infantry Division in fall 1944. It illustrates that the corps' reinforcement company was utilized as the treatment option for 67.5 percent of all battle exhaustion casualties within the division. These neuropsychiatric casualties constituted 15 percent of total divisional casualties, a large percentage that highlights the importance of the reinforcement company in this additional role.
27 LAC, RG 24, vol. 18,616, "17 March 1945 Report on Canadian Reinforcements Dispatched to 21st Army Group in North West Europe, 5 August 1944–28 February 1945," file 133.035 (D92).

Chapter 2: The Sixty-Day Shortage

1 Library and Archives Canada (LAC), RG 24, vol. 10,517, "Daily Record of Casualties for the 3rd Canadian Infantry Division from 6 June 1944," file 215A21.009 (D167). The 3rd Canadian Infantry Division suffered 564 battle casualties from 1 August to 16 August 1944.
2 Charles Stacey, *The Official History of the Canadian Army in the Second World War*, vol. 3, *The Victory Campaign: The Operations in North West Europe, 1944–1945* (Ottawa: Queen's Printer and Controller of Stationery, 1960), 633–35.
3 Ibid., 634.
4 Charles Stacey, *Arms, Men and Governments: The War Policies of Canada, 1939–1945* (Ottawa: Queen's Printer, 1970), 473.
5 Tanya Grodzinski, *Operational Handbook for the First Canadian Army, 1944–1945: Formation Organization, Staff Techniques and Administration*, rev. ed. (Lower Sackville, NS: Regimental Historian, 2018), 4–6.
6 Stacey, *Arms, Men and Governments*, 39.
7 Ibid., 43; and John Rickard, *The Politics of Command: Lieutenant General A.G.L. McNaughton and the Canadian Army, 1939–1943* (Toronto: University of Toronto Press, 2010), 39–40. Prime Minister Mackenzie King was apprehensive regarding Canadian participation in intensive combat operations in the first year of the war.
8 J.L. Granatstein, *Conscription in the Second World War, 1939–1945* (Toronto: Ryerson Press, 1969), 9.
9 Stacey, *Arms, Men and Governments*, 449.
10 Richard Walker, "The Political Management of Army Leadership: The Evolution of Canadian Civil-Army Relations 1898–1945" (PhD diss., University of Western Ontario, 2003), 332.

11 Paul Dickson, *A Thoroughly Canadian General: A Biography of General H.D.G. Crerar* (Toronto: University of Toronto Press), 162.
12 Walker, "The Political Management of Army Leadership," 334.
13 Ibid., 364.
14 Dickson, *A Thoroughly Canadian General*, 175.
15 Ibid., 176–77. Some of the additional Canadian formations would also be armoured divisions, and they had a limited requirement for infantry within them. This factor was seen to limit potential future casualties.
16 Ibid., 182.
17 Walker, "The Political Management of Army Leadership," 329.
18 Ibid., 341.
19 Rickard, *The Politics of Command*, 41.
20 Ibid., 152. Because of equipment shortages, what eventually evolved into the 5th Canadian Armoured Division was impaired in all aspects of formation-level training in the United Kingdom during 1941. In February 1942, it finally received forty M3 Lee tanks. By the end of 1942, it only had 75 percent of its authorized armour.
21 Dickson, *A Thoroughly Canadian General*, 159. This was particularly the case for the 5th Canadian Armoured Division, which lacked tanks.
22 Ibid., 332.
23 E.L.M. Burns, *Manpower in the Canadian Army, 1939–1945* (Toronto: Clarke, Irwin, 1956), Figure 2, 17. The percentage allocated to the Canadian Army overseas was the problem, even though 11.6 percent of the total US Army equalled 737,697 personnel.
24 Dickson, *A Thoroughly Canadian General*, 353.
25 Ibid., 383.
26 Stacey, *Arms, Men and Governments*, 400–1.
27 Granatstein, *Conscription in the Second World War*, 47–48.
28 Laurier Military History Archive, Terry Copp Papers, Colonel C.P. Stacey, Canadian Army Historical Report No. 134, "Historical Sketch: Rates of Wastage of Personnel, Canadian Army, 1939–1945, Canadian Military Headquarters, London, United Kingdom, 5 April 1945," 3, 4.
29 Rickard, *The Politics of Command*, 47.
30 Stacey, "Historical Sketch," 5, figure depicting projected wastage by army trades.
31 Ibid., 6.
32 Ibid., 10.
33 Stacey, *The Victory Campaign*, 630.
34 Burns, *Manpower in the Canadian Army*, 91. They were based on July 1943 assumed wastage rates.
35 Ibid., 90.
36 Ibid., 91.
37 Ibid., 92.
38 Ibid., 91, Figure 3.
39 LAC, RG 24, vol. 13,581, "Canadian Section, GHQ 1st Echelon, 21st Army Group; CMHQ Correspondence to Canadian Section, 1st Echelon, 21st A.G. Headquarters Dated 16 March 1944."
40 LAC, RG 24, vol. 12,295, "Rates of Wastage and Policy of Reserves–Personnel," file 1/Wastage/2 Correspondence of General Stuart to Secretary D.N.D., 16 March 1944.
41 Stacey, *Arms, Men and Governments*, 427. There was a shortage of 8,777 infantry, other ranks, against an authorized total of 23,000.
42 Ibid., 428.

43 Stacey, *Arms, Men and Governments,* 425–27; Burns, *Manpower in the Canadian Army,* 91, Figure 13; and Russell Hart, *Clash of Arms: How the Allies Won in Normandy* (Norman, OK: University of Oklahoma Press, 2004), 190.
44 Stacey, *Arms, Men and Governments,* 428.
45 Ibid., 451.
46 Caroline D'Amours, "Reassessment of a Crisis: Canadian Infantry Reinforcements during the Second World War," *Canadian Army Journal* 14, 2 (2012): 73–89.
47 Burns, *Manpower in the Canadian Army,* 88–89.
48 Stacey, *Arms, Men and Governments,* 425–27.
49 Ibid., 434; and LAC, RG 24, vol. 10,517, "Daily Record of Casualties for the 3rd Canadian Infantry Division from 6 June 1944," file 215A21.009 (D167). As of 30 June, the 3rd Canadian Infantry Division recorded 2,978 battle casualties.
50 Burns, *Manpower in the Canadian Army,* 92.
51 Stacey, *Arms, Men and Governments,* 435.
52 Dickson, *A Thoroughly Canadian General,* 325–26.
53 Burns, *Manpower in the Canadian Army,* 96–97.
54 Stacey, *The Victory Campaign,* 194.
55 LAC, RG 24, vol. 13,719, "2nd Canadian Corps A&Q War Diary," 31 July 1944.
56 Stacey, *Arms, Men and Government,* 437.
57 Ibid., 438; and Dickson, *A Thoroughly Canadian General,* 323. General Crerar at this stage understood that current reinforcements on hand would not be enough.
58 Dickson, *A Thoroughly Canadian General,* 323.
59 LAC, RG 24, vol. 18,616, "Reinforcement Drafts Sent to North West Europe from UK Reinforcements Dispatched to 21 AG from UK, UKAG, 1 to 30 Inclusive, August 1944," file 44/Svy Rfts/1 AG Stats, 17 March 1945.
60 LAC, RG 24, vol. 10,699, "Deficiencies and Holdings of Canadian Infantry, Other Ranks, North West Europe, 27 August 1944–28 April 1945."
61 Ibid.
62 Stacey, *Arms, Men and Governments,* 439.
63 Stacey, *The Victory Campaign,* 631–32.
64 Andrew Brown, "North West Europe Men in the Line: An Assessment of the Reinforcements of the 48th Highlanders in Italy, January–October 1944," *Canadian Military History* 21, 3 (2015): 1.
65 Ibid., 8.
66 Daniel Byers, *Zombie Army: Canadian Conscription in the Second World War* (Vancouver: UBC Press, 2016), 237.
67 Brown, "North West Europe: Men in the Line," 9.
68 Carlo D'Este, *Decision in Normandy* (New York: Konecky and Konecky, 1983), 260.
69 Ibid., 262.
70 Ibid., 268.
71 John R. Peaty, "British Army Manpower Crisis, 1944" (PhD diss., Kings College, University of London, 2000), 343, Figure 11, "Training Establishment and Training Stream." This figure indicates that British Army reinforcements on 30 September 1944 numbered 44,726. On that same day, there were 134,003 British Army trainers, cadres, and administrators in the United Kingdom.
72 D'Este, *Decision in Normandy,* 267.
73 Peter Mansoor, *The GI Offensive in Europe: The Triumph of American Infantry Divisions, 1941–1945* (Lawrence: University of Kansas Press, 1999), 155.

74 Ibid., 115.
75 Stacey, *Arms, Men and Governments*, 442.
76 Ibid., 442.
77 LAC, RG 24, vol. 10,699, "Deficiencies and Holdings of Canadian Infantry, Other Ranks, North West Europe, 27 August 1944–28 April 1945." In October 1944, daily casualties continued to be high. On this date, there was no way of knowing that the casualty figures for November, December, and January would be very low.
78 Stacey, *The Victory Campaign*, 633; and Walker, "The Political Management of Army Leadership," 391.
79 Stacey, *The Victory Campaign*, 633.
80 Stacey, *Arms, Men and Governments*, 482.
81 Ibid., 482.

Chapter 3: Vehicles and Weapons

1 Library and Archives Canada (LAC), RG 24, vol. 10,553, "21st AG, 'A' & 'B' Canadian Vehicle Position Report," file 215A21.085 (D1). Monthly returns from May 1944 to May 1945 detail exactly what was considered an "A" or "B" vehicle and how many were held at the divisional, corps, and army level. Within the British Army, all combat vehicles were classified as "A" vehicles while noncombat soft-skinned vehicles were classified as "B" vehicles.
2 Charles Stacey, *Arms, Men and Governments: The War Policies of Canada, 1939–1945* (Ottawa: Queen's Printer, 1970), 486.
3 Ibid., 487. A total of 815,729 soft-skinned vehicles were produced in Canada for Allied militaries; in terms of material contribution, this was Canada's crowning achievement in the Allied war effort.
4 Ibid., 488.
5 Ibid.
6 "4th Canadian (Armoured) Division," Canadiansoldiers.com, http://www.canadiansoldiers.com/organization/fieldforces/casf/4thdivision.htm. By October 1942, the 4th Canadian Armoured Division only had 255 Universal Bren Gun Carriers for training. It did not receive tanks until later.
7 John English, *The Canadian Army in the Normandy Campaign: A Study in the Failure of High Command* (Mechanicsburg, PA: Stackpole, 2009), 104.
8 Family of Captain Proctor Clifford Neil, "Captain Neil's Story: Bio and Military Cross Award," Captain Proctor Clifford Neil: Honouring the Life and Accomplishments of a WWII Hero, http://www.captainpcneil.com/holy-roller.html.
9 Tanya Grodzinski, *Operational Handbook for the First Canadian Army, 1944–45: Formation Organization, Staff Technique and Administration*, rev. ed. (Lower Sackville, NS: Regimental Historian, 2018), 88–89.
10 Ibid., 92–93.
11 Ibid., 92. Second-line transport was corps and army-level transport, and first-line transport was attached to divisional units.
12 Charles Stacey, *The Official History of the Canadian Army in the Second World War*, vol. 3, *The Victory Campaign: The Operations in North West Europe, 1944–45* (Ottawa: Queen's Printer and Controller of Stationery, 1960), Appendix F, "Canadian Army Units in North-West Europe (8 May 1945)", 661.
13 Grodzinski, *Operational Handbook*, 88.
14 "21st AG, A&B Canadian Vehicle Position Report," 31 January 1945.

15 LAC, RG 24, vol. 13,793, "4th Canadian Armoured Division, A&Q War Diary," November 1944, "Return on AFVs within the Division, 1 November."

16 LAC, RG 24, vol. 10,670, "Equipment State, Canadian Army, Monthly Report," file 215C1.083 (D6). The final report at the army level was the monthly returns of all controlled stores (see above), such as 25-pounder howitzers and 17-pounder antitank guns on a divisional basis.

17 LAC, RG 24, vol. 14,276, "C Squadron, 25th Canadian Armoured Delivery Regiment, War Diary," June 1944. The 25th CADR squadron war diaries are very detailed regarding actual deliveries of tanks to the units. The only caveat is that there are often discrepancies between the numbers reported being delivered to a regiment and the receiving regiment's strength increase. This was largely because of breakdowns in transit, delays in reporting, and tanks being sent back to the delivery squadron to correct kit deficiencies. Early in the campaign, because of a shortage of AFVs, there was also some "borrowing" between armoured regiments. Also, when a regiment was in action, it often did not have time to report strengths and losses. It would take a day or two for all tanks and crews to be accounted for.

18 Leonard Curchin, *The Elgins: A Regimental History* (St. Thomas: Sutherland Press, 1977), 78. These regiments had suffered large losses on 6–7 June 1944.

19 Ibid. Once "D" Squadron disembarked, it immediately turned over twenty-two tanks with full crews to the 4th Canadian Armoured Brigade to cover losses suffered on 9–10 August 1944.

20 Grodzinski, *Operational Handbook, 87–88.*

21 LAC, RG 24, vol. 14,279, "F Squadron, 25th Canadian Armoured Delivery Squadron, War Diary," October 1944. On 2 October, several Kangaroo armoured personnel carriers slated for delivery to the 1st Canadian Armoured Personnel Carrier Regiment by "F" Squadron, 25th CADR, were instead rerouted back to the Royal Canadian Electrical and Mechanical Engineers maintenance units because of mechanical issues.

22 LAC, RG 24, vol. 10,457, "Tank Replaces and Releases," file 212C1 (D28), figure detailing the actions of a rear delivery squadron of the 25th Canadian Armoured Delivery Regiment.

23 LAC, RG 24, vol. 14,277, "'D' Squadron, 25th Canadian Armoured Delivery Regiment, War Diary," 9 August 1944 (hereafter "D" Squadron War Diary).

24 LAC, RG 24, vol. 14,292, "28th Canadian Armoured Regiment, War Diary," 9 August 1944.

25 "D" Squadron War Diary, 12 August 1944.

26 LAC, RG 24, vol. 14,287, "27th Canadian Armoured Regiment Tanks State Report," file 1044.

27 Niklas Zetterling, *Normandy 1944: German Military Organization, Combat Power and Organizational Effectiveness* (Winnipeg: J.J. Fedorowicz, 2000), 386.

28 Zetterling, *Normandy 1944*, 390.

29 "D" Squadron War Diary, October 1944. End of month statistics.

30 Stacey, *The Victory Campaign*, Appendix F, "Canadian Army Units in North-West Europe (8 May 1945)," 661.

31 Ibid.

32 LAC, RG 24, vol. 13,661, "First Canadian Army, A&Q, War Diary," December 1944, "Ammunition Usage and Receipts Return, 1st British Corps and 2nd Canadian Corps, 16 December 1944." The "Guns State" was also needed to calculate the required amount of ammunition needed to keep a regiment combat capable.

33 LAC, RG 24, vol. 14,472, "14th Field Regiment, RCA, War Diary," 7 August 1944. The British field ordnance park in question for this exchange was designated a "Royal Artillery re-organization centre."

34 "21st AG, A&B Canadian Vehicle Position Report," 31 August 1944, "'B' Vehicle State for the 2nd Canadian Infantry Division as of 31 August 1944."

35 Russell Hart, *Clash of Arms: How the Allies Won in Normandy* (Norman, OK: University of Oklahoma Press, 2004), 225. This state of affairs reduced the division's mobility in Normandy drastically.

36 Murray Johnston, *Canada's Craftsmen at 50: The Story of Electrical and Mechanical Engineering in the Canadian Armed Forces* (Borden, ON: Guild of the Electrical and Mechanical Engineering Branch Charitable Trust, 2008), 267.

37 Ibid., 268.

38 Murray Johnston, *Canada's Craftsmen: The Story of the Corps of Royal Canadian Electrical and Mechanical Engineers and of the Land Ordnance Engineering Branch* (Ottawa: RCEME Corps History, 1983), 167.

39 R.H. Hodgson, *The RCEME History*, vol. 1, *The Formation of the Corps of Royal Canadian Electrical and Mechanical Engineers*, ed. Doug Knight (Ottawa: RCEME Corps Fund, 2016), 21.

40 Johnston, *Canada's Craftsmen at 50*, 269.

41 Ibid., 42.

42 Ibid.

43 Ibid., 327, Appendix 5.

44 Ibid., 65.

45 "21st AG, 'A' & 'B' Canadian Vehicle Position Report," 30 November 1944 to 31 January 1945. Divisional vehicles strengths went down in this period, but this was not due to enemy action but rather mechanical repairs.

46 LAC, RG 24, vol. 14,278, "E Squadron, 25th Canadian Armoured Delivery Regiment, War Diary," December 1944. There are multiple entries on the delivery of RCA self-propelled artillery pieces and Ram tracked-gun tractors (towers).

47 Grodzinski, *Operational Handbook*, 89–90.

48 Ibid., 74.

49 Ibid., 89–90.

50 Johnston, *Canada's Craftsmen at 50*, 62.

51 Hart, *Clash of Arms*, 187.

Chapter 4: Army Doctrine and Losses

1 Terry Copp, *Fields of Fire: The Canadians in Normandy* (Toronto: University of Toronto Press, 2006), 195. Canadian Army operations in Normandy such as Totalize and others were preceded by massive artillery bombardments that supressed and destroyed the enemy's front-line positions.

2 I.C.B. Dear and M.R.D. Foot, eds., *The Oxford Companion to the Second World War* (Oxford: Oxford University Press, 1995), 566–67.

3 Ibid., 1102–3.

4 Richard Holmes, ed., *The Oxford Companion to Military History* (Oxford: Oxford University Press, 2001), 92. A quarter of the Anglo-Commonwealth Armies were composed of artillery units.

5 Niklas Zetterling, *Normandy 1944: German Military Organization, Combat Power and Organizational Effectiveness* (Winnipeg: J.J. Fedorowicz, 2000), 360. As an example, the 12th SS Panzer Division was one of the strongest German panzer divisions; on 1 June 1944, it had over 146 panzers in its Panzer Regiment. In comparison to other German Panzer divisions on the eastern front, this was a sizable amount.

6 Doug Delaney, *The Imperial Army Project* (Oxford: Oxford University Press, 2017), 230–31; and John English, *The Canadian Army in the Normandy Campaign* (Mechanicsburg, PA: Stackpole, 2009), 123–24.
7 Michael M. Postan, *History of the Second World War Civil Series: British War Production* (London: Her Majesty's Stationery Office, 1952), 184.
8 Ibid.
9 Ibid, 186.
10 Ibid., 238.
11 Dear and Foot, *The Oxford Companion*, 328.
12 Library and Archives Canada (LAC), RG 24, vol. 14,213, "6th Canadian Armoured Regiment War Diary," 11 June 1944 (hereafter 6th CAR War Diary). Large tank losses were suffered by the 1st Hussar's (6th Canadian Armoured Regiment) "B" Squadron in the 11 June 1944 attack on Le Mesnil-Patry, France.
13 Brian A. Reid, *No Holding Back: Operation Totalize, Normandy, August 1944* (Mechanicsburg, PA: Stackpole, 2009), 329. On 9 August 1944, the 21st Canadian Armoured Regiment's (the Governor General's Foot Guards) No. 1 Squadron alone lost twelve tanks, destroyed or knocked out.
14 Roman J. Jarymowycz, "The Quest for Operational Maneuver in the Normandy Campaign: Simonds and Montgomery Attempt the Armoured Breakout" (PhD diss., McGill University, 1997), 107–10.
15 Ibid., 314.
16 English, *The Canadian Army in the Normandy Campaign*, 160.
17 LAC, RG 24, vol. 13,712, "2nd Canadian Corps General Staff War Diary," August 1944, "Operation Totalize Operation Order No. 4." Exploitation roles of Canadian armoured units were designed to be flexible and guided by the corps commander once a breakthrough was achieved. The initial armoured breakthrough had to occur first, though.
18 LAC, RG 24, vol. 14,260, "22nd Canadian Armoured Regiment War Diary," 8 August 1944 (hereafter 22nd CAR War Diary). Near Rocquancourt-Cintheaux, the destruction of the No. 3 Squadron command tanks of Major Smith, Lieutenant Smith, and Lieutenant Fisher significantly influenced command and control.
19 Ibid., 8 August 1944; and Jarymowycz, "The Quest for Operational Maneuver," 208–10. Because of traffic jams, the 22nd Canadian Armoured Regiment advanced exceedingly slowly, from 0900 to 1500 without contact.
20 Jarymowycz, "The Quest for Operational Maneuver," 316.
21 Ibid., 280.
22 LAC, RG 24, vol. 13,661, "First Canadian Army A&Q War Diary," December 1944. Because of a lack of offensive operations, there were no recorded battle casualties for the 21st Canadian Armoured Regiment for the month of December 1944.
23 Copp, *Fields of Fire*, 76.
24 Jarymowycz, "The Quest for Operational Maneuver," 278.
25 6th CAR War Diary, 9 June 1944. On this day, all operational tanks were involved in defensive tasks and inflicted heavy casualties on the enemy. One Sherman 17-pounder Firefly knocked out five German 75 mm L71-gunned Panther tanks.
26 Ibid. The most successful tank commander for the 1st Hussars, with five kills, commanded a Firefly on 9 June 1944. He was twenty-six-year-old Lieutenant Gordon Henry: Marc Milner, *Stopping the Panzers: The Untold Story of D-Day* (Lawrence: University Press of Kansas, 2014), 92–244.
27 English, *The Canadian Army in the Normandy Campaign*, 312.

28 22nd CAR War Diary, 8–10 August 1944. On 8–10 August, the regiment was occupied in anti-infantry actions rather than focusing on bypassing opposition to advance south. Its movement was inhibited by losses from mines and long-distance antitank fire. While it was successful against infantry opposition, a breakthrough by the regiment was not achieved.
29 Stacey, *The Victory Campaign*, 487–89.
30 LAC, RG 24, vol. 13,662, "First Canadian Army A&Q War Diary," November 1944, "Infantry Division War Establishment Staff Figures, Infantry Battalion (Regiment), WE II/233/4 October 1944." Total strength per battalion was 38 officers and 812 other ranks.
31 Stacey, *The Victory Campaign*, 189–207. There were four failed major assaults on this village from 25 July to 5 August 1944.
32 LAC, RG 24, vol. 15,122, "The North Nova Scotia Highlanders War Diary," 25 July 1944. Normandy, a dismounted night attack without tanks or heavy artillery support on Tilly-la-Campagne, failed because of intense machine-gun and tank main gun fire with high explosive rounds. Stacey, *The Victory Campaign*, 190.
33 John Marteinson and Michael McNorgan, *The Royal Canadian Armoured Corps: An Illustrated History* (Toronto: Robin Brass Studio, 2000), 250. One of the 7th Canadian Reconnaissance Regiment's "B" Squadron troops, with fifteen Universal Carriers, charged through a Waffen-SS panzer grenadier position during Operation Charnwood, turning the tide of a battle near Gruchy, France.
34 LAC, RG 24, vol. 15,020, "The Calgary Highlanders War Diary," 1 August 1944. The Canadian infantry who, in pitch darkness, assaulted Tilly-la-Campagne on the evening of 31 July and 1 August were badly shelled on their dismounted approach. On the first failed assault, the British Scots Greys' armour squadron did not advance in support and only committed three tanks (one troop) to the second failed assault, losing two of the three tanks.
35 Russell Hart, *Clash of Arms: How the Allies Won in Normandy* (Norman, OK: University of Oklahoma Press, 2004), 367.
36 Jean Bouchery, *From D-Day to V-E Day: The Canadian Soldier* (Paris: Histoire and Collections, 2003), 152–53.
37 1st Canadian Armoured Personnel Carrier Regiment, *1st Armoured Personnel Carrier Regiment: History of the Kangaroos* (St. Thomas, ON: Elgin Regiment Association, 1962).
38 LAC, RG 24, vol. 10,553, "21st Army Group 'A' & 'B' Vehicle Position Report," file 215A21.085 (D1), 31 August 1944. In August 1944, the 3rd Canadian Infantry Division had one vehicle on strength.
39 LAC, RG 24, vol. 13,663. "First Canadian Army A&Q War Diary," February 1945. The consolidated strength-and-casualty report's daily returns for February 1945 identify two days of intensive combat for the Algonquin Regiment.
40 Rudolf Lehmann and Ralf Tiemann, *The Leibstandarte IV/1* (Winnipeg: J.J. Fedorowicz, 1993), 181. A German Waffen-SS panzer grenadier company inflicted heavy losses on the Royal Highland Regiment of Canada (the Black Watch) in this action.
41 LAC, RG 24, vol. 15,009, "The Royal Highland Regiment of Canada (the Black Watch) War Diary," 5 August 1944. Attempting to keep in contact with the enemy, the regiment advanced to May-sur-Orne. There, it suffered heavy casualties from German tank and infantry defensive fire. David R. O'Keefe, "'Pushing Their Necks Out': Ultra, the Black Watch, and Command Relations, May-sur-Orne, Normandy, 5 August 1944," *Canadian Military History* 15, 1 (2006): http://scholars.wlu.ca/cmh/vol15/iss1/3; and Stacey, *The Victory Campaign*, 207. Stacey states that the 10th Canadian Armoured Regiment was slated to support the Black Watch in this operation.

42 English, *The Canadian Army and the Normandy Campaign*, 193; and LAC, RG 24, vol. 10,527, "Canadian Section, GHQ, 2 Echelon," file 215.921.009 (D203), "Return Showing Battle and Non-battle Casualties: Total Battle and Non-battle Casualties, 1 June–30 August, 1944," 29 June–2 August 1944.

43 David, O'Keefe, "'Pushing Their Necks Out': Ultra, the Black Watch, and Command Relations, May-sur-Orne, Normandy, 5 August 1944," *Canadian Military History* 15, 1 (2006): http://scholars.wlu.ca/cmh/vol15/iss1/3. On 5 August 1944, the Black Watch suffered another reverse near May-sur-Orne, losing seventy personnel in the process.

44 Hart, *Clash of Arms*, 357–58. At times during the Normandy Campaign, poor Canadian tactical leadership resulted in high levels of casualties.

45 Peter Mansoor, *The GI Offensive in Europe: The Triumph of American Infantry Divisions, 1941–1945* (Lawrence: University of Kansas Press, 1999), 253.

46 Stephen Hart, *Colossal Cracks: Montgomery's 21st Army Group in North West Europe, 1944–1945* (Mechanicsburg, PA: Stackpole, 2007), 84–85; and Mansoor, *The GI Offensive in Europe*, 56.

47 LAC, RG 24, vol. 13,708, "1st Canadian Corps A&Q War Diary," April 1945. On 22 April 1945, the total indirect artillery assets attached to RCA Headquarters, 1st Canadian Infantry Division, included the 1st, 2nd, 3rd, and 11th RCA Field Regiments; the 68th Medium Regiment, Royal Artillery; and the 3rd Medium Regiment, Royal Canadian Artillery. This was a tremendous amount of indirect firepower.

48 English, *The Canadian Army in the Normandy Campaign*, 123–24; and Hart, *Colossal Cracks*, 84.

49 English, *The Canadian Army in the Normandy Campaign*, 61.

50 Ibid., 56.

51 Ibid., 126.

52 Ibid., 1102–3.

53 LAC, RG 24, vol. 13,712, "2nd Canadian Corps General Staff War Diary," August 1944, "Operation Totalize Air Programme." The operational phases (I and II) of Operation Totalize were anchored by massed four-engined bomber attacks.

54 Stacey, *The Victory Campaign*, 658. Within the First Canadian Army order of battle during September 1944, there were three medium AGRA regiments and a rocket battery of captured German Nebelwerfers on strength.

55 LAC, RG 24, vol. 13,708, "1st Canadian Corps A&Q War Diary," April 1945; and LAC, RG 24, vol. 14,412, "1st Field Regiment, RCHA, War Diary," April 1945.

56 Terry Copp, *Fields of Fire: The Canadians in Normandy* (Toronto: University of Toronto Press, 2003), 159.

57 LAC, RG 24, vol. 14,445, "5th Field Regiment, RCA, War Diary," October 1944. On 8 October 1944, the Canadian infantry saw eighty-two rounds per gun fired; 9 October 1944 saw ninety-two fired, crushing German counterattacks. These are average daily numbers.

58 Nigel F. Evans, "British Artillery in WWII: Artillery Methods," British Artillery World War 2, http://nigelef.tripod.com/maindoc.htm#Basic.

59 Dear and Foot, *The Oxford Companion to the Second World War*, 61.

60 Ibid.

61 Michael Bechthold, "Air Support in the Breskens Pocket: The Case of the First Canadian Army and the 84 Group Royal Air Force," *Canadian Military History* 3, 2 (1994): http://scholars.wlu.ca/cmh/vol3/iss2/6, 2.

62 Ibid., 4.

63 Tanya Grodzinski, *Operational Handbook for the First Canadian Army, 1944–45: Formation Organization, Staff Technique and Administration*, rev. ed. (Lower Sackville, NS: Regimental Historian, 2018), 113–15.

64 LAC, RG 24, vol. 14,287, "27th Canadian Armoured Regiment War Diary," July 1944. On 23 July 1944, a large grouping of German armour was spotted by this regiment east of May-sur-Orne. Two hours later, the message was received that air support was not available.

65 Grodzinski, *Operational Handbook*, 113–15.

66 LAC, RG 24, vol. 15,000, "The Algonquin Regiment War Diary," 9 August 1944. As the combined arms "Worthington Force" (28th Canadian Armoured Regiment and a company of the Algonquin Regiment) was being destroyed in its isolated position on Hill 140, there were no RAF or RCAF forward air controllers present. Armour and infantry personnel were reduced to signalling Typhoon ground-support aircraft with yellow smoke and ground panels. This type of fighter-bomber aircraft provided excellent ground support.

67 LAC, RG 24, vol. 13,789, "4th Canadian Armoured Division, War Diary," 14–15 August 1944; and Grodzinski, *Operational Handbook*, 60. On 14 August 1944, friendly aerial bombing destroyed the 4th Canadian Armoured Division Headquarters' communications equipment and vehicles, inhibiting command and control.

68 Stacey, *The Victory Campaign*, 559. As an example, a medium bomber strike (requested three days prior) on a significant rail junction and military barracks in Oldenburg, Germany, was cancelled en route by the 2nd Tactical Air Force. RAF leadership was convinced that the barracks would be needed postwar by the occupation forces. First Canadian Army Headquarters staff officers were embittered by this, despite successful strikes later.

69 Zetterling, *Normandy 1944*, 355. Total personnel losses from 27 June to 11 July 1944 are estimated to be at least six hundred personnel, from a regiment that was already at 60 percent strength.

70 LAC, RG 24, vol. 10,553, "21st AG, 'A' & 'B' Canadian Vehicle Position Report," file 215A21.85 (D1), 31 May 1944. At this point, the 4th Canadian Armoured Division held none of its forty-five authorized 17-pounder Firefly tanks. It was authorized thirty-six Wasp II flamethrowers but had only obtained two. These weapons systems would become some of the most effective for the Canadian Army in northwest Europe. The formation still contained 102 obsolete Ram II tanks.

71 Hart, *Clash of Arms*, 186.

72 English, *The Canadian Army in Normandy*, 104.

73 Ibid., 160.

74 Grodzinski, *Operational Handbook*, 48, "5th Canadian Armoured Division Order of Battle."

75 English, *The Canadian Army in the Normandy Campaign*, 54.

76 Ibid., 251.

77 Ibid., 133.

78 Hart, *Clash of Arms*, 361.

79 LAC, RG 24, vols. 14,237–38, "11th Canadian Armoured Regiment War Diary," December 1942 to August 1944. This regiment, one of three within the 1st Canadian Armoured Brigade, performed at a very high level in all its operations in Italy and Sicily.

80 Hart, *Clash of Arms*, 361.

81 Terry Copp, "The Bite and Hold Approach: Army, Part 80," *Legion Magazine*, February 2009, https://legionmagazine.com/en/2009/02/the-bite-and-hold-approach-army-part-80/.

82 Milner, *Stopping the Panzers*, 301.
83 Jarymowycz, "The Quest for Operational Maneuver," 285.
84 Stacey, *The Victory Campaign*, 547.
85 LAC, RG 24, vol. 13,711, "2nd Canadian Corps General Staff War Diary," July 1944. During Operations Atlantic and Spring, no less than eighteen Canadian infantry battalions and two machine-gun battalions of the 2nd and 3rd Canadian Infantry Divisions were active or present near the area of Verrières Ridge. This is not counting CAC or RCA forces.
86 LAC, RG 24, vol. 13,708, "1st Canadian Corps A&Q War Diary," April 1945; and LAC, RG 24, vol. 14,437, "3rd Field Regiment, RCA, War Diary," April 1945. April 1945 casualties for the 3rd Field Regiment, RCA, consisted of eleven nonbattle casualties and no battle casualties, despite the intensity of constant indirect fire missions to support the 1st Canadian Corps. The regiment received thirteen replacement personnel during this month.
87 LAC, RG 24, vol. 13,664, "First Canadian Army A&Q War Diary," April 1945. In April 1945, the Loyal Edmonton Regiment suffered ninety-seven battle casualties and twenty-seven nonbattle casualties despite offensive operations throughout the month.

Chapter 5: Formations and Their Units

1 Charles Stacey, *The Canadian Army, 1939–1945: An Official Historical Summary* (Ottawa: Edmond Cloutier/King's Printer, 1948), 14–17.
2 Ibid., 30.
3 Ibid., 90.
4 Charles Stacey, *The Official History of the Canadian Army in the Second World War*, vol. 3, *The Victory Campaign: The Operations in North West Europe, 1944–45* (Ottawa: Queen's Printer and Controller of Stationery, 1960), 529–30.
5 Historical Section, Canadian Military Headquarters, Report No. 181, "Operation GOLDFLAKE: The Move of the 1 Canadian Corps from Italy to North-West Europe, February–March 1945," http://www.cmp-cpm.forces.gc.ca/dhh-dhp/his/rep-rap/doc/cmhq/cmhq181.pdf.
6 Stacey, *The Victory Campaign*, Appendix F, "Canadian Army Units in North-West Europe (8 May 1945)," 657–62.
7 Terry Copp, *The Brigade: The 5th Canadian Infantry Brigade, 1939–1945* (Willowdale, ON: Fortress, 1992), 32. Losses to the division during the Dieppe Raid had totalled 214 officers and 3,153 other ranks. Units in the 4th and 6th Canadian Infantry Brigades had to be completely rebuilt.
8 Stacey, *The Victory Campaign*, Appendix F, "Canadian Army Units in North-West Europe (8 May 1945)," 657.
9 Library and Archives Canada (LAC), RG 24, vol. 10,553, "21st AG, 'A' & 'B' Canadian Vehicle Position Report," file 215A21.085 (D1), 31 May 1944.
10 Stacey, *The Victory Campaign*, Appendix F, "Canadian Army Units in North-West Europe (8 May 1945)," 657–62.
11 John English, *The Canadian Army in the Normandy Campaign: A Study in the Failure of High Command* (Mechanicsburg, PA: Stackpole, 2009), 104.
12 Russell Hart, *Clash of Arms: How the Allies Won in Normandy* (Norman, OK: University of Oklahoma Press, 2004), 182. The 3rd Canadian Infantry Division and the 2nd Canadian Armoured Brigade began to train together in April 1944.
13 Stacey, *The Victory Campaign*, Appendix F, "Canadian Army Units in North-West Europe (8 May 1945)," 657–62.

14 LAC, RG 24, vol. 10,670, "Equipment State, Canadian Army, Monthly Report," file 215C1.083 (D6), LAC, RG 24, vol. 10,670, "Equipment State, Canadian Army, Monthly Report," file 215C1.083 (D6); and "21st AG, 'A' & 'B' Canadian Vehicle Position Report," 31 May 1944. The divisional RCA field artillery regiments had an authorized level of ninety-six M7 105 mm Priest self-propelled howitzers in accordance with the war establishment figures. Marc Milner, *Stopping the Panzers: The Untold Story of D-Day* (Lawrence: University Press of Kansas, 2014), 67–69.
15 English, *The Canadian Army in the Normandy Campaign*, 98, 104. In the United Kingdom, the spring 1943 exercise Spartan did not include the 4th Canadian Armoured Division because of its lack of advanced training.
16 Ibid., 177, Figure 9.2, "2nd Canadian Corps Order of Battle."
17 Stacey, *The Victory Campaign*, Appendix F, "Canadian Army Units in North-West Europe (8 May 1945)," 661.
18 Historical Section, Canadian Military Headquarters, Report No. 181.
19 "1st Canadian Armoured Brigade," Canadiansoldiers.com, http://www.canadiansoldiers.com/organization/1stcanadianarmouredbrigade.htm.
20 Stacey, *The Victory Campaign*, Appendix F, "Canadian Army Units in North-West Europe (8 May 1945)," 657. The Royal Canadian Electrical and Mechanical Engineers' 1st Armoured Brigade Workshop supported the 1st Canadian Armoured Brigade in its operations. "A" Squadron, 25th Canadian Armoured Delivery, supported the 1st Canadian Armoured Brigade in the tank delivery role.
21 Ibid., Appendix F, "Canadian Army Units in North-West Europe (8 May 1945)"; and Historical Section, Canadian Military Headquarters, Report No. 181.
22 Stacey, *The Victory Campaign*, Appendix F, "Canadian Army Units in North-West Europe (8 May 1945)," 657. The Royal Canadian Electrical and Mechanical Engineers' 2nd Armoured Brigade Workshop supported the 2nd Canadian Armoured Brigade in its operations.
23 Ibid., Appendix G, "Officers Holding Principal Appointments," 663.
24 Ibid., Appendix F, "Canadian Army Units in North-West Europe (8 May 1945)," 657.
25 Ibid., Appendix F, "Canadian Army Units in North-West Europe (8 May 1945)," 657; and G.W.L. Nicholson, *The Gunners of Canada: The History of the Royal Regiment of Canadian Artillery*, vol. 2, *1919–1967* (Toronto: McClelland and Stewart, 1972), Appendix C, "RCA Order of Battle," 647.

Chapter 6: The Normandy Campaign

1 Charles Stacey, *The Official History of the Canadian Army in the Second World War, Volume III, The Victory Campaign: The Operations in North West Europe, 1944–1945* (Ottawa: Queen's Printer and Controller of Stationery, 1960), 37.
2 LAC, RG 24, vol. 10,670, "Equipment State, Canadian Army, Monthly Report," file 215C1.083 (D6); and LAC, RG 24, vol. 10,553, "21st AG, 'A' & 'B' Canadian Vehicle Position Report," file 215A21.085 (D1), 31 May 1944. The division had fifteen M10 3-inch gunned tank destroyers on charge.
3 Stacey, *The Victory Campaign*, Appendix B, "Canadian Army Casualties, Normandy D-Day, 6 June 1944," 650.
4 Ibid., 130–40.
5 Russell Hart, *Clash of Arms: How the Allies Won in Normandy* (Norman, OK: University of Oklahoma Press, 2004), 344.
6 Stacey, *The Victory Campaign*, 139.

7 LAC, RG 24, vol. 15,233, "The Royal Winnipeg Rifles War Diary," 30 June 1944, strength return. Calculated by taking strengths at certain dates and subtracting casualties for the month of June 1944.

8 "21st AG, 'A' & 'B' Canadian Vehicle Position Report," 31 May 1944.

9 LAC, RG 254, vol. 14,233, "10th Canadian Armoured Regiment War Diary," 3 June 1944.

10 LAC, RG 24, vol. 10,517, "Canadian Army Casualties," file 215A21.009 (D167), "Battle Casualties, 2nd Canadian Armoured Brigade, 6–30 June 1944."

11 John Marteinson and Michael McNorgan, *The Royal Canadian Armoured Corps: An Illustrated History* (Toronto: Robin Brass Studio, 2000), 244.

12 Stacey, *The Victory Campaign*, 152–64.

13 Terry Copp, *Fields of Fire: The Canadians in Normandy* (Toronto: University of Toronto Press, 2003), 180.

14 LAC, RG 24, vol. 15,270, "The Stormont, Dundas and Glengarry Highlanders War Diary," 28 July 1944.

15 LAC, RG 24, vol. 15,122, "Nova Scotia Highlanders War Diary," 29 July 1944.

16 LAC, RG 24, vol. 14,276, "C Squadron, 25th Canadian Armoured Delivery Regiment War Diary," June 1944.

17 "21st AG, 'A' & 'B' Canadian Vehicle Position Report," 31 July 1944.

18 LAC, RG 24, vol. 13,719, "2nd Canadian Corps A&Q War Diary," July 1944. Casualties had occurred at this point, but the division had yet to embark on its first offensive operation.

19 LAC, RG 24, vol. 15,065, "Les Fusiliers Mont-Royal War Diary," 1 July 1944.

20 LAC, RG 24, vol. 15,020, "The Calgary Highlanders War Diary," 9 July 1944.

21 LAC, RG 24, vol. 14,441, "4th Field Regiment, RCA, War Diary," 15 July 1944.

22 LAC, RG 24, vol. 14,591, "3rd Light Anti-Aircraft Regiment, RCA, War Diary," July 1944. July would see the regimental war establishment of a light antiaircraft regiment drastically reduced.

23 "21st AG, 'A' & 'B' Canadian Vehicle Position Report," 31 May 1944. The war establishment for a division was constantly changing as its regiment's establishments constantly changed.

24 "Equipment State, Canadian Army, Monthly Report," This series of returns states the inventory of all major nonvehicle weapons systems within each Canadian formation.

25 LAC, RG 24, vol. 10,527, "Canadian Section, GHQ, 2 Echelon," file 215.921.009 (D203), "Return Showing Battle and Non-battle Casualties: Total Battle and Non-battle Casualties, 1 June–30 August, 1944." Battle casualties for the Essex Scottish Regiment totalled 22 officers and 326 other ranks up to 2 August 1944.

26 Stacey, *The Victory Campaign*, 188.

27 LAC, RG 24, vol 13,719, "2nd Canadian Corps A&Q War Diary," 31 July 1944 return, minus 16 July.

28 Stacey, *The Victory Campaign*, 194. The Black Watch's casualties totalled 307 for 25 July 1944: 123 killed, 101 wounded, and 83 missing: "Canadian Section, GHQ, 2 Echelon." The Royal Highland Regiment of Canada totals from 29 June to 2 August 1944 show 291 battle casualties, obviously an error.

29 LAC, RG 24, vol. 15,009, "The Royal Highland Regiment of Canada (the Black Watch) War Diary," 27 July 1944.

30 2nd Canadian Corps A&Q War Diary," July 1944, "Letter to GOC 2nd Canadian Corps Regarding 2nd Canadian Infantry Division Reinforcement Shortages"; and Stacey, *The Victory Campaign*, 630–31. Each division had a forward battalion that received replacements from the No. 2 Canadian Base Reinforcement Group advance reinforcement battalion.

31 "Letter to GOC."
32 "2nd Canadian Corps A&Q War Diary," "25 July 1944 Report of 2nd and 3rd Canadian Division Equipment Losses, 20–23 July, 1944, during Operation Atlantic."
33 "21st Army Group Consolidated Vehicle Position Report," 31 August 1944; and "Equipment State, Canadian Army, Monthly Report," Return for 31 August 1944.
34 Stacey, *The Victory Campaign,* 223. The North Shore Regiment suffered heavy casualties in one infantry company.
35 Ibid., 242.
36 Ibid., 256–65.
37 LAC, RG 24, vol. 13,776, "3rd Canadian Infantry Division A&Q War Diary," July 1944, "Divisional Report on Casualties to D+49."
38 LAC, RG 24, vol. 13,658, "First Canadian Army A&Q War Diary," 30 August 1944.
39 "Canadian Section, GHQ, 2 Echelon," file 215.921.009 (D203), "Return Showing Battle and Non-battle Casualties: Total Battle and Non-battle Casualties, 1 June–30 August, 1944."
40 Estimated figures taking strengths at certain dates and subtracting casualties for months June to September 1944.
41 "Canadian Section, GHQ, 2 Echelon," "Return Showing Battle and Non-battle Casualties: Total Battle and Non-battle Casualties, 1 June–30 August, 1944;" and LAC, RG 24, vol. 13,658, "First Canadian Army A&Q War Diary," 30 August 1944.
42 LAC, RG 24, vols. 13,659–65, "First Canadian Army A&Q War Diaries," October 1944 to May 1945. Estimated figures taking strengths at certain dates and subtracting casualties for months June to September 1944.
43 LAC, RG 24, vol. 13,176, "3rd Canadian Infantry Division A&Q War Diaries," June–August 1944.
44 LAC, RG 24, vol. 14,461, "12th Field Regiment, RCA, War Diary," During 8–12 August 1944 there was one battle casualty. There is a lack of surviving data for the RCA artillery regiments. Casualties for RCA regiments were very low in comparison to the monthly totals in the infantry and some armoured regiments. To save space within reports, the division- and corps-level adjutant and quartermaster war diaries recorded only consolidated figures for all RCA units within the division. These consolidated records are the only reliable source of data for RCA battle and nonbattle casualties as well as reinforcements for the months June 1944 to May 1945.
45 LAC, RG 24, vol. 13,776, "3rd Canadian Infantry Division A&Q War Diary," August 1944, "Report of Reinforcements Despatched to the Division to 6 June to 4 August 1944."
46 "Equipment State, Canadian Army, Monthly Report"; and "21st AG, 'A' & 'B' Canadian Vehicle Position Report," "31 August 1944 Divisional Returns for Both Weapons Systems and 'A' Vehicles."
47 "21st AG, 'A' & 'B' Canadian Vehicle Position Report," 31 July and 31 August 1944; and "12th Field Regiment, RCA, War Diary," August 1944. Entries for 1 and 2 August 1944 relate that all self-propelled equipment and observation post tanks had been turned in by the regiment for 25-pounders and Quad towing vehicles.
48 "21st AG, 'A' & 'B' Canadian Vehicle Position Report," 31 August 1944 return.
49 "Equipment State, Canadian Army, Monthly Report," 31 August 1944 divisional returns.
50 Copp, *Fields of Fire,* 154. The 59th British Infantry Division was broken up to refurbish other weakened British divisions.
51 LAC, RG 24, vol. 13,659, "First Canadian Army A&Q War Diary," September 1944, 8 September 1944.
52 Stacey, *The Victory Campaign,* 234.

53 LAC, RG 24, vol. 18,616, "Canadian Reinforcements Dispatched to 21st Army Group, 8 June 1944–9 February 1945." Total for 16 August 1944 minus the total as of 27 July 1944.
54 "Canadian Section, GHQ, 2 Echelon," "Return Showing Total Non-battle and Battle for the Royal Regiment of Canada 3–30 August 1944."
55 Ibid.
56 LAC, RG 24, vol. 14,559, "2nd Anti-Tank Regiment, RCA, War Diary," July 1944.
57 LAC, RG 24, vol. 14,441, "4th Field Regiment, RCA, War Diary," August 1944.
58 "21st AG, 'A' & 'B' Canadian Vehicle Position Report," 31 August 1944 return.
59 Hart, *Clash of Arms*, 343; and PRO War Office 179/2574, "Composition of the CANADIAN ARMY," War Diary, General Staff, Canadian Army GHQ, November 1944. Comparing this figure to the division's total war establishment figures for November 1944 of 750 officers and 14,069 other ranks, we can see that the division was powerful.
60 LAC, RG 24, vol. 14,255, "21st Canadian Armoured Regiment War Diary," 29 July 1944. War establishment strengths are provided in Appendix 1.
61 LAC, RG 24, vol. 15,098, "The Lake Superior (Motor) Regiment War Diary," 29 July 1944.
62 LAC, RG 24, vol. 15,104, "The Lincoln and Welland Regiment War Diary," 29 July 1944.
63 LAC, RG 24, vol. 15,000, "The Algonquin Regiment War Diary," 29 July 1944.
64 LAC, RG 24, vol. 13,793, "4th Canadian Armoured Division, A&Q War Diary," 1 August 1944.
65 LAC, RG 24, vol. 14,567, "5th Anti-Tank Regiment, RCA, War Diary," 29 July 1944.
66 "21st AG, 'A' & 'B' Canadian Vehicle Position Report," "31 July 1944: Divisional Return for 'A' Vehicles."
67 "Equipment State, Canadian Army, Monthly Report," 31 July 1944.
68 Stacey, *The Victory Campaign*, 206.
69 Ibid.
70 Ibid., 248.
71 Ibid., 252.
72 Copp, *Fields of Fire*, 236–37.
73 Stacey, *The Victory Campaign*, 259.
74 Hart, *Clash of Arms*, 357.
75 Copp, *Fields of Fire*, 250.
76 "Canadian Section, GHQ, 2 Echelon," "Return Showing Battle and Non-battle Casualties: Total Battle and Non-battle Casualties, 27 July–30 August 1944."
77 Ibid.
78 LAC, RG 24, vol. 15,005, "The Argyll and Sutherland Highlanders of Canada War Diary," August 1944, "Pt I, Orders Detailing North West Europe Personnel Posting Details."
79 LAC, RG 24, vol. 13,658, "First Canadian Army A&Q War Diary," 30 August 1944.
80 "The Algonquin Regiment War Diary," August 1944. Estimated figure for reinforcements came from taking strength returns and subtracting casualties. LAC, RG 24, vol. 13,658, "First Canadian Army A&Q War Diary," 30 August 1944.
81 "4th Canadian Armoured Division, A&Q War Diary," August 1944, "Consolidated Divisional Strength and Casualty Return."
82 LAC, RG 24, vol. 14,609, "8th Light Anti-Aircraft Regiment, RCA, War Diary," August 1944. This regiment, along with all of its type, was restructured to an establishment of 34 officers and 551 other ranks as of September 1944.
83 "21st AG, 'A' & 'B' Canadian Vehicle Position Report," "31 August 1944 Divisional Return for Combat 'A' Vehicles."
84 Ibid.

85 LAC, RG 24, vol. 14,277, "D Squadron, 25th Canadian Armoured Regiment, War Diary," August 1944.
86 "Equipment State, Canadian Army, Monthly Report," 31 August 1944 return.
87 Stacey, *The Victory Campaign,* Appendix F, "Canadian Army Units in North-West Europe (8 May 1945)," 657.
88 "21st AG, 'A' & 'B' Canadian Vehicle Position Report"; and "Equipment State, Canadian Army, Monthly Report."
89 LAC, RG 24, vol. 14,649, "2nd Survey Regiment, RCA, War Diary," August 1944.
90 LAC, RG 24, vol. 14,601, "6th Light Anti-Aircraft Regiment, RCA, War Diary," July 1944.
91 LAC, RG 24, vol. 13,658, "First Canadian Army A&Q War Diary," 30 August 1944.
92 LAC, RG 24, vol. 14,570," 6th Anti-Tank Regiment, RCA, War Diary," 26 August 1944.

Chapter 7: Channel Ports, Scheldt, and the River Mass

1 Charles Stacey, *The Official History of the Canadian Army in the Second World War,* vol. 3, *The Victory Campaign: The Operations in North West Europe, 1944–1945* (Ottawa: Queen's Printer and Controller of Stationery, 1960), 290, 292.
2 Library and Archives Canada (LAC), RG 24, vol. 10,699, "Deficiencies and Holdings of Canadian Infantry, Other Ranks, North West Europe, 27 August 1944–28 April 1945," 3 September 1944.
3 Terry Copp, *Cinderella Army: The Canadians in North West Europe, 1944–1945* (Toronto: University of Toronto Press, 2006), 55. During the division's halt at Dieppe, it received more than one thousand reinforcements, but they were not sufficient and proved to be merely a first installment. See Figure 7.1.
4 LAC, RG 24, vol. 13,718, "2nd Canadian Corps A&Q War Diary," September 1944, "Consolidated Strength and Casualty Daily Returns."
5 Ibid.
6 Stacey, *The Victory Campaign,* 326.
7 Ibid., 352.
8 LAC, RG 24, vols. 14,276–77, "C Squadron, 25th Canadian Armoured Delivery Regiment, War Diary," September 1944.
9 Mark Zuehlke, *Terrible Victory: First Canadian Army and the Scheldt Estuary Campaign: September 13–November 6, 1944* (Toronto: Douglas and McIntyre, 2014), 7, 12–27.
10 Stacey, *The Victory Campaign,* 367.
11 LAC, RG 24, vol. 13,659, "First Canadian Army A&Q War Diary," September 1944, Strength Returns for 30 September 1944; and LAC, RG 24, vol. 10,527, "Canadian Section, GHQ, 2 Echelon," file 215.921.009 (D203), "Return Showing Battle and Non-battle Casualties by Week: Totals for 10th Canadian Infantry Brigade Units for Weeks 31 August–4 October 1944." Reinforcements were estimated by subtracting casualty figures from strength returns at the end of August and September.
12 "First Canadian Army A&Q War Diary," 30 September 1944; and LAC, RG 24, vol. 14,255, "21st Canadian Armoured Regiment War Diary," September 1944, "Part I Orders, September 1944."
13 "First Canadian Army A&Q War Diary," 30 September 1944; LAC, RG 24, vol. 14,261, "22nd Canadian Armoured Regiment War Diary," September 1944, "Part I Orders, September 1944."
14 "Canadian Section, GHQ, 2 Echelon," "Return Showing Battle and Non-battle Casualties."
15 LAC, RG 24, vol. 14,401, "7th Medium Regiment, RCA, War Diary," 26 August 1944.

16 Copp, *Cinderella Army,* 140–41. The Royal Highland Regiment of Canada (the Black Watch) suffered 145 casualties on 13 October 1944.
17 Stacey, *The Victory Campaign,* 424.
18 "Canadian Section, GHQ, 2 Echelon," "Return Showing Battle and Non-battle Casualties," The Essex Scottish Regiment returns, 31 August–1 November, 1944.
19 Ibid., "Return Showing Battle and Non-battle Casualties: Le Régiment de Maisonneuve returns, 31 August–1 November 1944."
20 Ibid., Les Fusiliers Mont-Royal returns, 31 August–1 November 1944.
21 LAC, RG 24, vols. 13,659–60, "First Canadian Army A&Q War Diaries," September–October 1944; and LAC, RG 24, vol. 14,225, "8th Canadian Reconnaissance Regiment War Diary," September 1944.
22 LAC, RG 24, vol. 10,553, "21st Army Group Consolidated Vehicle Position Report," file 215A21.085 (D1), 31 May 1944; and LAC, RG 24, vol. 10,670, "Equipment State, Canadian Army, Monthly Report," file 215C1.083 (D6), 30 November 1944.
23 "First Canadian Army A&Q War Diary," October 1944, 3rd Canadian Infantry Division Regimental Returns.
24 Stacey, *The Victory Campaign,* 424–25, battle map.
25 Copp, *Cinderella Army,* 113.
26 "First Canadian Army A&Q War Diary," October 1944, "Consolidated Strength and Casualty Returns for October 1944."
27 Ibid.
28 Ibid.
29 LAC, RG 24, vol. 13,776, "3rd Canadian Infantry Division A&Q War Diary," October 1944, "Consolidated Strength and Casualty Returns, October 1944."
30 LAC, RG 24, vol. 10,553, "21st AG, 'A' & 'B' Canadian Vehicle Position Report," file 215A21.085 (D1), "31 August 1944 Divisional Returns for Both Weapons Systems and 'A' Vehicles."
31 "Equipment State, Canadian Army, Monthly Report."
32 "First Canadian Army War Diary," October 1944, "Consolidated Daily Casualty and Strength Returns."
33 Ibid. These are difficult to calculate since they took place over the course of two months.
34 LAC, RG 24, vol. 14,295, "29th Canadian Armoured Reconnaissance Regiment War Diary," 31 October End of Month Entry.
35 "First Canadian Army A&Q War Diary," October 1944, "Consolidated Daily Casualty and Strength Returns."
36 LAC, RG 24, vol. 14,292, "28th Canadian Armoured Regiment War Diary," September 1944.
37 LAC, RG 24, vol. 13,793, "4th Canadian Armoured Division, A&Q War Diary," October 1944, "Consolidated Daily Casualty and Strength Returns."
38 LAC, RG 24, vol. 14,609, "8th Light Anti-Aircraft Regiment, RCA, War Diary." 31 October 1944 entry.
39 "4th Canadian Armoured Division, A&Q War Diary," AFV State for 1 November 1944.
40 LAC, RG 24, vol. 10,553, "21st AG, 'A' & 'B' Canadian Vehicle Position Report," file 215A21.085 (D1), "31 October 1944 Divisional Return for Both 'A' and 'B' Vehicles."
41 "Equipment State, Canadian Army, Monthly Report," 31 October 1944.
42 LAC, RG 24, vol. 14,649, "2nd Survey Regiment, RCA, War Diary," September–November 1944.
43 LAC, RG 24, vols. 14,601–2, "6th Light Anti-Aircraft Regiment, RCA, War Diary," July–September 1944.

44 "15. Armee (A.O.K. 15)," Die Deutsche Wehrmacht, http://www.diedeutschewehrmacht.de/15%20armee.htm, accessed 17 August 2020. The German Fifteenth Army consisted of ten infantry divisions on this date; it was later supplemented with self-propelled assault gun and parachute infantry units.
45 LAC, RG 24, vol. 13,660, "First Canadian Army A&Q War Diary," November 1944.
46 LAC, RG 24, vol. 14,448, "6th Field Regiment, RCA, War Diary," November 1944 to January 1945. Troops regularly saw films and took trips to Antwerp.
47 Copp, *Cinderella Army*, 178.
48 "21st AG, 'A' & 'B' Canadian Vehicle Position Report," 31 October 1944.
49 "First Canadian Army A&Q War Diary," "October 1944 Consolidated Casualty and Strength Returns."
50 "21st AG, 'A' & 'B' Canadian Vehicle Position Report," 30 November 1944.
51 LAC, RG 24, vol. 10,670, "Equipment State, Canadian Army, Monthly Report," file 215C1.083 (D6), November 1944.

Chapter 8: Veritable, Blockbuster, and War's End

1 Library and Archives Canada (LAC), RG 24, vol. 13,719, "2nd Canadian Corps A&Q War Diary," 31 January 1945.
2 LAC, RG 24, vol. 13,664, "First Canadian Army A&Q War Diary," January 1945.
3 LAC, RG 24, vol. 14,448, "6th Field Regiment, RCA, War Diary," 27 January 1945; and LAC, RG 24, vol. 14,559, "2nd Anti-Tank Regiment, RCA, War Diary," 27 January 1945.
4 LAC, RG 24, vol. 10,553, "21st AG, 'A' & 'B' Canadian Vehicle Position Report," file 215A21.085 (D1), 31 January 1945; and LAC, RG 24, vol. 10,670, "Equipment State of Canadian Units in the First Canadian Army," 21st Army Group, file 215C1.083 (D6), "Monthly Equipment States, 31 January 1945."
5 Charles Stacey, *The Official History of the Canadian Army in the Second World War*, vol. 3, *The Victory Campaign: The Operations in North West Europe, 1944–1945* (Ottawa: Queen's Printer and Controller of Stationery, 1960), 490, 484.
6 LAC, RG 24, vol. 13,778, "3rd Canadian Infantry Division A&Q War Diary," 31 January 1945, "Consolidated Strength and Casualty Return."
7 Terry Copp, *Cinderella Army: The Canadians in North West Europe, 1944–1945* (Toronto: University of Toronto Press, 2006), 178.
8 LAC, RG 24, vols. 13,660–62, "First Canadian Army A&Q War Diaries," November 1944 to January 1945, "Daily Consolidated Casualty and Strength Returns."
9 LAC, RG 24, vol. 14,562, "3rd Anti-Tank Regiment, RCA, War Diary," 26 January 1945.
10 LAC, RG 24, vol. 13,778, "3rd Canadian Infantry Division A&Q War Diary," "January 1945 Consolidated Strength and Casualty Returns."
11 "Equipment State, Canadian Army, Monthly Report"; and "21st AG, 'A' & 'B' Canadian Vehicle Position Report," "31 January 1945 Divisional Returns for Both Major Weapons Systems and 'A' Vehicles."
12 Copp, *Cinderella Army*, 221.
13 LAC, RG 24, vols. 13,660–62, "First Canadian Army War Diary," November 1944 to January 1945.
14 LAC, RG 24, vol. 14,277, "C Squadron, 25th Canadian Armoured Delivery Regiment, War Diary," November 1944 to January 1945.
15 LAC, RG 24, vol. 13,664, "First Canadian Army A&Q War Diary," February–March 1945, "Consolidated Daily Casualty and Strength Returns."
16 Stacey, *The Victory Campaign*, 450–54.

17 “21st AG, ‘A’ & ‘B’ Canadian Vehicle Position Report,” “31 January 1945 Divisional Return for ‘A’ Vehicles.”
18 LAC, RG 24, vol. 10,670, “Equipment State, Canadian Army, Monthly Report,” file 215C1.083 (D6), 31 January 1945.
19 LAC, RG 24, vol. 14,277, “‘D’ Squadron, 25th Canadian Armoured Delivery Regiment, War Diary,” January 1945.
20 LAC, RG 24, vol. 13,660–62, “First Canadian Army A&Q War Diaries,” November 1944 to January 1945, “Consolidated Strength and Casualty Returns November 1944–January 1945.”
21 LAC, RG 24, vol. 10,670, “Equipment State of the Canadian Army in North West Europe (Non-Vehicle/AFV),” file 215C1.083 (D6), January 1945.
22 LAC, RG 24, vol. 14,401, “7th Medium Regiment, RCA, War Diary,” 27 January 1945.
23 LAC, RG 24, vol. 14,389, “3rd Medium Regiment, RCA, War Diary,” 27 January 1945.
24 LAC, RG 24, vol. 13,663. “First Canadian Army A&Q War Diaries,” February–March 1945.
25 LAC, RG 24, vol. 13,664, “First Canadian Army A&Q War Diary,” 7 April 1945.
26 Ibid. The war establishment of a Canadian Infantry Corps battalion at the war’s conclusion was 38 officers and 812 other ranks, for a total of 850 personnel.
27 Ibid.
28 LAC, RG 24, vol. 12,649, “4th Canadian Reconnaissance Regiment War Diary,” 7 April 1945.
29 LAC, RG 24, vol. 13,664, “First Canadian Army A&Q War Diary,” 7 April 1945.
30 “21st A.G. Canadian ‘A’ & ‘B’ Vehicle Position Report,” 30 April 1945.
31 LAC, RG 24, vol. 10,670, “Equipment State of Canadian Units in the First Canadian Army,” file 215C1.083 (D6), 31 March 1945.
32 Ibid.
33 Martin Block, “Panther Allocations 1945,” Panther1944.de, http://www.panther1944.de/index.php/en/sdkfz-171-pzkpfwg-panther/truppenteile/panther-zuweisungslisten/panther-zuweisungsliste-1945. In February 1945, 180 Panther tanks were issued to German units. A mere 20 were issued to a formation that faced the Canadian Army in that month, the Panzer Lehr panzer division.
34 G.W.L. Nicholson, *The Gunners of Canada: The History of the Royal Regiment of Canadian Artillery,* vol. 2, *1919–1967* (Toronto: McClelland and Stewart, 1972), 431. There were no German AFVs present to combat the amphibious assault.
35 Stacey, *The Victory Campaign,* 529. The division began to deploy to the area on 1 April.
36 Ibid., 551–52.
37 LAC, RG 24, vol. 14,556, “1st Anti-Tank Regiment, RCA, War Diary,” April 1945. Eighteen Valentine Archer 17-pounder tank destroyers were delivered on 10 April 1945. All eighteen had defective recoil buffers and saw extremely limited, if any, action.
38 LAC, RG 24, vol. 14,556, “1st Anti-Tank Regiment, RCA, War Diaries,” April–May 1945.
39 LAC, RG 24, vol. 13,664–65, “First Canadian Army A&Q War Diaries,” April–May 1945.
40 Ibid.
41 Ibid.
42 Ibid.
43 LAC, RG 24, vols. 13,708–9, “1st Canadian Corps A&Q War Diaries,” April–May 1945; and LAC, RG 24, vol. 14,437, “3rd Field Regiment, RCA, War Diary,” April 1945.
44 LAC, RG 24, vols. 13,708–9, “1st Canadian Corps A&Q War Diaries,” April–May 1945; and LAC, RG 24, vol. 14,589, “2nd Light Anti-Aircraft Regiment, RCA, War Diary,” April 1945.
45 Stacey, *The Victory Campaign,* 633.

46 LAC, RG 24, vol. 14,206, "4th Canadian Reconnaissance Regiment War Diary," April 1945. On 1 April 1945, the officer commanding headquarters squadron and fourteen other ranks left for rotational leave in Canada.
47 LAC, RG 24, vols. 13,664–65, "First Canadian Army A&Q War Diaries," April–May 1945.
48 Ibid.
49 Ibid.
50 RG 24, vol. 13,708–9, "1st Canadian Corps A&Q War Diaries," April–May 1945; and LAC, RG 24, vol. 14,556, "1st Anti-Tank Regiment, RCA, War Diary," April–May 1945.
51 RG 24, vol. 13,708–9, "1st Canadian Corps A&Q War Diaries," April–May 1945; and LAC, RG 24, vol. 14419, "2nd Field Regiment, RCA, War Diary," April–May 1945.
52 LAC, RG 24, vol. 13,665, "First Canadian Army A&Q War Diary," 5 May 1945.
53 "Equipment State of Canadian Units in the First Canadian Army," 30 April 1945; and "21st A.G. Canadian 'A' & 'B' Vehicle Position Report," 30 April 1945.
54 "21st A.G. Canadian 'A' & 'B' Vehicle Position Report," 30 April 1945. The 4th Canadian Reconnaissance Regiment war establishment figures show twenty-eight armoured cars, sixty-three Universal Carriers, six 3-inch mortar carriers, and twelve T16 antitank gun tracked gun tractors as "A" (combat) vehicles. See Appendix 1 for January 1945 infantry division reconnaissance regiment figures for equipment and vehicles.
55 Stacey, *The Victory Campaign*, 496–97.
56 Ibid., 555.
57 LAC, RG 24, vols. 13,663–65, "First Canadian Army A&Q War Diary," February–May 1945.
58 LAC, RG 24, vol. 14,442, "4th Field Regiment, RCA, War Diary," February–May 1945.
59 LAC, RG 24, vols. 13,663–65, "First Canadian Army A&Q War Diary," February–May 1945.
60 "2nd Canadian Corps A&Q War Diary," 5 May 1945.
61 LAC, RG 24, vol. 13,665, "First Canadian Army A&Q War Diary," May 1945.
62 "2nd Anti-Tank Regiment, RCA, War Diary," May 1945.
63 "6th Field Regiment, RCA, War Diary," 5 May 1945.
64 Stacey, *The Victory Campaign*, 633. These conscripts were formerly only eligible for service in Canada.
65 LAC, RG 24, vols. 13,662–65, "First Canadian Army A&Q War Diaries," February–May 1945.
66 Ibid.
67 "21st AG Consolidated Vehicle Position Report," 30 April 1945; and "Equipment State of Canadian Units in the First Canadian Army," 21st Army Group, 30 April 1945.
68 "Equipment State of Canadian Units in the First Canadian Army," 21st Army Group, 30 April 1945.
69 Stacey, *The Victory Campaign*, 561–62.
70 LAC, RG 24, vols. 13,779, "3rd Canadian Infantry Division A&Q War Diary," February 1945, "Consolidated Strength and Casualty Returns for All RCA Regiments."
71 Copp, *Cinderella Army*, 210. The 13th Field Regiment, RCA, subdued the village of Zandpol with a five-minute bombardment, which allowed it to be taken without a fight on 8 February 1945.
72 LAC, RG 24, vols. 13,662–64, "First Canadian Army A&Q War Diaries," February–April 1945, "February, March, and April 1945 Consolidated Strength and Casualty Daily Returns."
73 Ibid.
74 Charles Stacey, *Arms, Men and Governments: The War Policies of Canada, 1939–1945* (Ottawa: Queen's Printer, 1970), 479. Following the Conscription Crisis in fall 1944, a small number of NRMA conscripts had been sent overseas to serve as reinforcements.

75 "3rd Anti-Tank Regiment, RCA, War Diary," January–April 1945. The entries are filled with information on personnel going on leave to the United Kingdom, the Continent, and Canada.
76 LAC, RG 24, vol. 13,664–65, "First Canadian Army A&Q War Diary," April–May 1945.
77 LAC, RG 24, vol. 13,665, "First Canadian Army A&Q War Diary," 5 May 1945.
78 "21st AG, 'A' & 'B' Canadian Vehicle Position Report," 30 April 1945.
79 Stacey, *The Victory Campaign*, 494.
80 Ibid., 500.
81 Copp, *Cinderella Army*, 241–42.
82 Ibid., 262.
83 Stacey, *The Victory Campaign*, 557–60.
84 LAC, RG 24, vols. 13,663–64, "First Canadian Army A&Q War Diaries," February–April 1945, "Consolidated Casualty and Strength Returns."
85 E.L.M. Burns, *Manpower in the Canadian Army, 1939–1945* (Toronto: Clarke, Irwin, 1956), 125.
86 LAC, RG 24, vol. 13,793, "4th Canadian Armoured Division, A&Q War Diary," February–April 1945, "Consolidated Casualty and Strength States February–April 1945."
87 Ibid.
88 Ibid.
89 LAC, RG 24, vol. 13,665, "First Canadian Army A&Q War Diary," 5 May 1945.
90 "21st AG, 'A' & 'B' Canadian Vehicle Position Report," "30 April 1945 Divisional Return for 'A' Vehicles."
91 "Equipment State, Canadian Army, Monthly Report," 30 April 1944.
92 "5th Canadian Armoured Division," Canadiansoldiers.com, http://www.canadiansoldiers.com/organization/fieldforces/casf/5thdivision.htm.
93 LAC, RG 24, vol. 13,708, "1st Canadian Corps A&Q War Diary," March 1945, "Divisional Strength Return, 4 April 1945." The division at this point had the 7th Anti-Tank Regiment, RCA, and 15 Anti-Tank Battery, RCA, under command.
94 LAC, RG 24, vol. 13,661, "First Canadian Army A&Q War Diary," December 1944. Staff figures organization for a standard Canadian Armoured Division in January 1945.
95 LAC, RG 24, vol. 13,708, "1st Canadian Corps War Diary," 30 March 1945.
96 LAC, RG 24, vol. 13,663, "First Canadian Army A&Q War Diary," 31 March 1945.
97 LAC, RG 24, vol. 13,708, "1st Canadian Corps A&Q War Diary," 31 March 1945, RCA return.
98 "Equipment State of Canadian Army in North West Europe," 31 March 1945.
99 Stacey, *The Victory Campaign*, 567–68.
100 LAC, RG 24, vol. 13,708, "1st Canadian Corps A&Q War Diary," April 1945. Entries for the 5th Canadian Armoured Division stop abruptly on 21 April 1945.
101 Copp, *Cinderella Army*, 282.
102 LAC, RG 24, vol. 13,665, "First Canadian Army A&Q War Diary," "Consolidated Casualty and Strength Return," 5 May 1945; and LAC, RG 24, vol. 13,661, "First Canadian Army A&Q War Diary," December 1944. The January 1945 war establishment of a Canadian Armoured Division was 744 officers and 13,879 other ranks.
103 "21st AG, 'A' & 'B' Canadian Vehicle Position Report," 30 April 1945.
104 Ibid.
105 "Equipment State of Canadian Army in North West Europe," "5th Canadian Armoured Division, 30 April 1945."
106 Stacey, *The Victory Campaign*, 529.

107 "21st AG, 'A' & 'B' Canadian Vehicle Position Report," 31 March 1945.
108 LAC, RG 24, vol. 14,240, "11th Canadian Armoured Regiment War Diary," 31 March 1945.
109 LAC, RG 24, vol. 13,664, "First Canadian Army A&Q War Diaries," April 1945, "Consolidated Daily Casualty and Strength Returns."
110 LAC, RG 24, vol. 14,269, "'A' Squadron, 25th Canadian Armoured Delivery Regiment, War Diary," March–April 1945.
111 "21st AG, 'A' & 'B' Canadian Vehicle Position Report," 30 April 1945.
112 LAC, RG 24, vols. 13,664–65, "First Canadian Army A&Q War Diary," April–May 1945.
113 LAC, RG 24, vol. 13,665, "First Canadian Army A&Q War Diary," 5 May 1945.
114 "Equipment State of Canadian Army in North West Europe," April 1945.
115 Stacey, *The Victory Campaign*, 593–94.
116 LAC, RG 24, vols. 13,662–65, "First Canadian Army A&Q War Diaries," February–May 1945.
117 LAC, RG 24, vol. 14,649, "2nd Survey Regiment, RCA, War Diary," February–May 1945.
118 Nicholson, *The Gunners of Canada*, 214–15.
119 "21st AG, 'A' & 'B' Canadian Vehicle Position Report"; and "Equipment State of Canadian Army in North West Europe."
120 Nicholson, *The Gunners of Canada*, 430.
121 LAC, RG 24, vol. 14,646, "1st Survey Regiment, RCA, War Diary," April 1945.
122 Stacey, *The Victory Campaign*, 600.
123 LAC, RG 24, vol. 13,665, "First Canadian Army A&Q War Diary," 5 May 1945.
124 Ibid., "April 1945 Consolidated Casualty and Strength Returns."
125 "21st AG, 'A' & 'B' Canadian Vehicle Position Report"; and "Equipment State of Canadian Army in North West Europe," 30 April 1945.

Chapter 9: An Assessment of Canadian Formations

1 Library and Archives Canada (LAC), RG 24, vols. 13,664–65, "First Canadian Army A&Q War Diaries," April–May 1945; and LAC, RG 24, vol. 14,205, "4th Canadian Reconnaissance Regiment War Diary," April–May 1945. Battle and nonbattle casualties for the unit in April–May 1945 totalled twenty-three losses.
2 LAC, RG 24, vol. 10,670, "Equipment State Canadian Army Monthly Report (Non-Vehicle/AFV)," file 215C1.083 (D6); and LAC, RG 24, vol. 10,553, "21st AG, 'A' & 'B' Canadian Vehicle Position Report," file 215A21.085 (D1), 31 July 1944 divisional returns. As of 31 July 1944, the 3rd Canadian Infantry Division contained fifteen of its sixteen authorized M10 3-inch tank destroyers, while the 2nd Canadian Infantry Division was authorized none. On 31 July 1944, the division was authorized sixty-six Wasp II flamethrower carriers yet had none.
3 "21st AG, 'A' & 'B' Canadian Vehicle Position Report," "30 April 1945 returns for 'A' vehicles." The 4th Canadian Armoured Division possessed a battery of the M10 17-pounder tank destroyers as of 31 August 1944.
4 LAC, RG 24, vol. 13,776, "3rd Canadian Infantry Division A&Q War Diary," August 1944, letter to General Officer Commanding, 3rd Canadian Infantry Division. Up to 7 July 1944, the Stormont, Dundas, and Glengarry Highlanders had taken a total of 470 battle casualties. This equalled a loss of 55 percent of the division's effective strength and did not include nonbattle casualties.
5 Russell Hart, *Clash of Arms: How the Allies Won in Normandy* (Norman, OK: University of Oklahoma Press, 2004), 343; PRO War Office 179/2574, "Composition of the CANADIAN

ARMY," WD GD, Canadian GHQ, November 1944. Authorized levels of personnel in all Canadian formations in Normandy during summer 1944 are listed.

6 LAC, vol. 13,662, "First Canadian Army A&Q War Diaries," January 1944, "Armoured Division War Establishment Staff Figures for a Field Artillery Regiment, (Self-Propelled), RCA, War Establishment II/190A/22, Effective January 1945."

7 LAC, RG 24, vol. 14,591, "3rd Light Anti-Aircraft Regiment, RCA, War Diary," July 1944. This 2nd Canadian Infantry Division unit's war establishment was identical to that of the 4th Light Anti-Aircraft Regiment, RCA. It was reduced to 585 by September 1944.

Conclusion

1 David O'Keefe, "'Pushing Their Necks Out': Ultra, the Black Watch, and Command Relations, May-sur-Orne, Normandy, 5 August 1944," *Canadian Military History* 15, 1 (2006): http://scholars.wlu.ca/cmh/vol15/iss1/3. The Royal Highland Regiment of Canada returned to the front lines on 4 August 1944, ten days after the battle on Verrières Ridge, which destroyed its infantry companies.

2 Library and Archives Canada (LAC), RG 24, vol. 14,277, "C" Squadron, 25th Canadian Armoured Delivery Regiment War Diary," April 1945. This squadron delivered fifty-six new and repaired AFVs to 2nd Canadian Armoured Brigade units in April 1945, an average of 1.86 AFVs per day to the three armoured regiments.

3 LAC, RG 24, vol. 10,553, "21st AG, 'A' & 'B' Canadian Vehicle Position Report," file 215A21.085 (D1). This did not include vehicles in the repair or delivery systems, but only those within combat arms units.

4 Ibid.; and LAC, RG 24, vol. 10,670, "Equipment State of Canadian Army in North West Europe," file 215C1.083 (D6), July 1944–April 1945.

5 "21st AG, 'A' & 'B' Canadian Vehicle Position Report." As of 30 April 1945, there were 104 Ram Kangaroo armoured personnel carriers on strength within the entire Canadian Army.

6 Roman J. Jarymowycz, "The Quest for Operational Maneuver in the Normandy Campaign: Simonds and Montgomery Attempt the Armoured Breakout" (PhD diss., McGill University, 1997), 275.

7 LAC, RG 24, vol. 15,009, "The Royal Highland Regiment (the Black Watch) War Diaries," July–August 1944. After the complete destruction of its infantry companies on 25 August 1944, the entire battalion conducted a heavy attack on May-sur-Orne on 5 August 1944.

8 LAC, RG 24, vol. 10,669, "Deficiencies and Holdings of Canadian Infantry, Other Ranks, Northwest Europe, 27 August 1944–28 April 1945."

9 LAC, RG 24, vol. 13,658, "First Canadian Army A&Q War Diary," 30 August 1944.

10 LAC, RG 24, vol. 10,669, "Deficiencies and Holdings."

11 LAC, RG 24, vol. 13,659, "First Canadian Army A&Q War Diary," 30 September 1944.

12 LAC, RG 24, vol. 14,461, "12th Field Regiment, RCA, War Diary," August 1944.

13 LAC, RG 24, vols. 13,708–9, "1st Canadian Corps A&Q War Diaries," April–May 1945; and LAC, RG 24, vol. 14,556, "1st Anti-Tank Regiment, RCA, War Diaries," April–May 1945. The regiment had forty recorded personnel reinforcements during April 1945.

Appendix 1

1 Terry Copp, *Cinderella Army: The Canadians in North West Europe, 1944–1945* (Toronto: University of Toronto Press, 2006), 216–17. In his description of the Moyland Wood fighting near Louisendorf in February 1945, Copp lists the casualties of the 7th Canadian Infantry Brigade's Royal Winnipeg Rifles at one hundred, with twenty-six killed.

2 Tanya Grodzinski, *Operational Handbook for the First Canadian Army, 1944–45: Formation Organization, Staff Technique and Administration*, rev. ed. (Lower Sackville, NS: Regimental Historian, 2018), 8.

3 As noted earlier, the 1st Canadian Armoured Personnel Carrier Regiment could only support a regiment or certain elements of a brigade at one time. During its existence, it supported the British Army as much as the Canadian Army.

4 Data on its composition was not found.

5 Charles Stacey, *The Official History of the Canadian Army in the Second World War*, vol. 3, *The Victory Campaign: The Operations in North West Europe, 1944–45* (Ottawa: Queen's Printer and Controller of Stationery, 1960,) Appendix F, "Canadian Army Units in North-West Europe (8 May 1945)," 657. Overseas, the Canadian Armoured Division had an independent machine-gun company, but because of its nonbattalion strength status, it is not included in this study.

6 LAC, RG 24, vol. 13,659, "First Canadian Army A&Q War Diary," October 1944, "AGRA War Establishment Staff Figures, AGRA, RCA, Field Artillery Regiment, Self-Propelled, WE II/190A/2, October 1944."

Selected Bibliography

Archival Sources

Laurier Military History Archive (LMH), Waterloo, ON

Library and Archives Canada (LAC), Ottawa, ON

No. 2 Operational Research Section Papers

RG 24, Department of National Defence Fonds

Other Sources

Barbe, Dominque. *Charnwood: La Bataille de Buron-Saint-Contest.* Conde-Sur-Noireau, FR: Editions Charles Corlet, 1994.

Battistelli, Pier. *Panzer Divisions, 1944–45.* Oxford: Osprey Publishing, 2009.

Bechthold, Michael. "Air Support in the Breskens Pocket: The Case of the First Canadian Army and the 84 Group Royal Air Force." *Canadian Military History* 3, 2 (1994): http://scholars.wlu.ca/cmh/vol3/iss2/6.

Block, Martin. "Panther Allocations 1945." *Panther 1944,* http://www.panther1944.de/index.php/en/sdkfz-171-pzkpfwg-panther/truppenteile/panther-zuweisungslisten/panther-zuweisungsliste-1945, accessed August 2019.

–. "Panther Allocation Sorted by Date of Allotment." *Panther 1944,* http://www.panther1944.de/index.php/en/sdkfz-171-pzkpfwg-panther/truppenteile/panther-zuweisungslisten/panther-zuweisungsliste-1945, accessed August 2019.

Bouchery, Jean. *From D-Day to V-E Day: The Canadian Soldier.* Paris: Histoire and Collections, 2003.

Brown, Andrew. "New Men in the Line: An Assessment of Reinforcements to the 48th Highlanders in Italy, January–October 1944." *Canadian Military History* 21, 3 (2015): http://scholars.wlu.ca/cmh/vol21/iss3/4.

Buckley, John. *British Armour in the Normandy Campaign, 1944.* London: Frank Cass, 2004.

Burns, E.L.M. *Manpower in the Canadian Army, 1939–1945.* Toronto: Clarke, Irwin, 1956.

Byers, Daniel. *Zombie Army: Canadian Conscription in the Second World War.* Vancouver: UBC Press, 2016.

Caravaggio, Angelo. "Commanding the Green Centre Line in Normandy: A Case Study of Divisional Command in The Second World War." PhD diss., Wilfrid Laurier University, 2009.

–. "The Human Dimension of Compromised Command: Major General George Kitching and the 4th Canadian Armoured Division in Normandy." Research paper, Royal Military College of Canada, War Studies Course 504, 2002.

Citino, Robert M. *The Wehrmacht Retreats: Fighting a Lost War, 1943.* Lawrence: University of Kansas Press, 2012.

Curchin, Leonard. *The Elgins: A Regimental History.* St. Thomas, ON: Sutherland Press, 1977.

Copp, Terry. "The Bite and Hold Approach: Army, Part 80." *Legion Magazine*, 16 February 2009: https://legionmagazine.com/en/2009/02/the-bite-and-hold-approach-army-part-80/.
–. *The Brigade: The 5th Canadian Infantry Brigade, 1939–1945*. Willowdale, ON: Fortress, 1992.
–. *Cinderella Army: The Canadians in North West Europe, 1944–1945*. Toronto: University of Toronto Press, 2006.
–. *Fields of Fire: The Canadians in Normandy*. Toronto: University of Toronto Press, 2003.
Copp, Terry, and Bill McAndrew. *Battle Exhaustion: Soldiers and Psychiatrists in the Canadian Army, 1939–1945*. Montreal/Kingston: McGill-Queens University Press, 1990.
D'Amours, Caroline. "Reassessment of a Crisis: Canadian Infantry Reinforcements during the Second World War." *Canadian Army Journal* 14, 2 (2012): 73–89. Dear, I.C.B, and M.D.R. Foot, eds. *The Oxford Companion to the Second World War*. Oxford: Oxford University Press, 1995.
Delaney, Doug. *The Imperial Army Project*. Oxford: Oxford University Press, 2017.
D'Este, Carlo. *Decision in Normandy*. New York: Konecky and Konecky, 1983.
Dickson, Paul. *A Thoroughly Canadian General: A Biography of General H.D.G. Crerar*. Toronto: University of Toronto Press, 2007.
Edgerton, David. *Britain's War Machine: Weapons, Resources and Experts in the Second World War*. Oxford: Oxford University Press, 2011.
Ellis, John. *Brute Force: Allied Strategy and Tactics in the Second World War*. London: Andre Deutsch, 1990.
Engen, Robert. *Strangers in Arms: Combat Motivation in the Canadian Army, 1943–1945*. Montreal/Kingston: McGill-Queens University Press, 2016.
English, John. *The Canadian Army in the Normandy Campaign: A Study in the Failure of High Command*. Mechanicsburg, PA: Stackpole, 2009.
Evans, Nigel F. "British Artillery in WW II: Artillery Methods." http://nigelef.tripod.com/maindoc.htm#Basic Procedures for Opportunity Targets.
Family of Captain Proctor Clifford Neil. "Captain Neil's Story: Bio and Military Cross Award." Captain Proctor Clifford Neil: Honouring the Life and Accomplishments of a WWII Hero. http://www.captainpcneil.com/holy-roller.html.
1st Canadian Armoured Personnel Carrier Regiment. *1st Armoured Personnel Carrier Regiment: History of the Kangaroos*. St. Thomas, ON: Elgin Regimental Association, 1962.
Fort Garry Horse. *Vanguard: The Fort Garry Horse in the Second World War*. Doetinchem, NL: Regimental Association History, 1945.
French, David. *Raising Churchill's Army: The British Army in the Second World War*. Oxford: Oxford University Press, 2000.
Granatstein, J.L. *Conscription in the Second World War, 1939–1945*. Toronto: Ryerson Press, 1969.
Granatstein, J.L., and J.M. Hitsman. *Broken Promises: A History of Conscription Canada*. Toronto: Oxford University Press, 1977.
Grodzinski, Tanya. *Operational Handbook for the First Canadian Army, 1944–45: Formation Organization, Staff Technique and Administration*. Rev. ed. Lower Sackville, NS: Regimental Historian, 2018.
Gullachsen, A.W. "The Defeat and Attrition of the 12th SS Panzer Division: 'Hitlerjugend,' a Case Study, June 6th–July 12th, 1944." Master's thesis, University of New Brunswick, 2005.

Hart, Russell. *Clash of Arms: How the Allies Won in Normandy.* Norman, OK: University of Oklahoma Press, 2004.

Hart, Stephen. *Colossal Cracks: Montgomery's 21st Army Group in North West Europe, 1944–1945.* Mechanicsburg, PA: Stackpole, 2007.

Holmes, Richard, ed. *The Oxford Companion to Military History.* Oxford: Oxford University Press, 2001.

Huffman, M.B. "Operation GOLDFLAKE: The Move of the 1 Canadian Corps from Italy to North-West Europe, February–March 1945." Canadian Military Headquarters Reports, 1940–48, no. 181. http://www.cmp-cpm.forces.gc.ca/dhh-dhp/his/rep/rap/doc/cmhq/cmhq181.pdf.

Jarymowycz, Roman J. "The Quest for Operational Maneuver in the Normandy Campaign: Simonds and Montgomery Attempt the Armoured Breakout." PhD diss., McGill University, 1997.

Jentz, Thomas. *Panzertruppen.* Vol. 2, *The Complete Guide to the Creation and Combat Employment of Germany's Tank Force, 1943–1945.* Atglen, PA: Schiffer Publishing, 1996.

Johnston, Murray C. *Canada's Craftsmen at 50: The Story of Electrical and Mechanical Engineering in the Canadian Armed Forces.* Borden, ON: Guild of the Electrical and Mechanical Engineering Branch Charitable Trust, 2008.

Kennedy, Gary. "The German Grenadier Battalion, 1943–1945." *Battalion Organization during the Second World War.* http://www.bayonetstrength.uk/GermanArmy/GerInfBn/Org%20of%20the%20German%20Inf%20Bn%201938-45.pdf.

Keshen, Jeffery A. *Saints, Sinners, and Soldiers: Canada's Second World War.* Vancouver: UBC Press, 2004.

Lehmann, Rudolf, and Ralf Tiemann. *The Leibstandarte IV/1.* Winnipeg: J.J. Fedorowicz, 1993.

Liddell-Hart, B.H. *History of the Second World War.* London: Konecky and Konecky, 2007.

Mansoor, Peter R. *The GI Offensive in Europe: The Triumph of American Infantry Divisions, 1941–1945.* Lawrence: University of Kansas Press, 1999.

Marteinson, John, and Michael R. McNorgan. *The Royal Canadian Armoured Corps: An Illustrated History.* Toronto: Robin Brass Studio, 2000.

Meyer, Hubert. *The History of the 12. SS-Panzerdivision Hitlerjugend.* Winnipeg: J.J. Fedorowicz, 1994.

Milner, Marc. *Stopping the Panzers: The Untold Story of D-Day.* Lawrence: University Press of Kansas, 2014.

Nicholson, G.W.L. *The Gunners of Canada: The History of the Royal Regiment of Canadian Artillery.* Vol. 2, *1919–1967.* Toronto: McClelland and Stewart, 1972.

O'Brien, Phillips P. "East versus West in the Defeat of Nazi Germany." *Journal of Strategic Studies* 23, 2 (2000): 89–113.

Oglesby, R.B. "Canadian Organization in the Theatres of Operations, 1939–1945." Canadian Historical Section, Army Headquarters Reports, 1948–59, no. 53. http://publications.gc.ca/collections/collection_2016/mdn-dnd/D63-5-53-1952-eng.pdf.

O'Keefe, David. "'Pushing Their Necks Out': Ultra, the Black Watch, and Command Relations, May-sur-Orne, Normandy, 5 August 1944." *Canadian Military History* 15, 1 (2006): http://scholars.wlu.ca/cmh/vol15/iss1/3.

Ose, Deiter. *Entscheidung im Westen 1944: Der Oberbefelshaber West und die Abwehr der Allierten Invasion.* Stuttgart: Deutsche Verlags-Anstalt, 1982.

Overy, Richard. *The Bombing War: Europe, 1939–1945.* London: Allen Lane, 2013.

Peaty, John R. "British Army Manpower Crisis, 1944." PhD diss., Kings College, University of London, 2000.

Perry, F.W. *The Commonwealth Armies: Manpower and Organization in the Two World Wars.* Manchester: Manchester University Press, 1988.

Postan, Michael M. *History of the Second World War Civil Series: British War Production.* London: Her Majesty's Stationery Office, 1952.

Reid, Bryan. *No Holding Back: Operation Totalize, Normandy, 1944.* Mechanicsburg, PA: Stackpole, 2009.

Rickard, John. *The Politics of Command: Lieutenant-General A.G.L. McNaughton and the Canadian Army, 1939–1943.* Toronto: University of Toronto Press, 2010.

Spilling, Michel, ed. *Battles That Changed Warfare, 1457–1991.* London: Amber Book, 2008.

Stacey, Charles. *Arms, Men and Governments: The War Policies of Canada, 1939–1945.* Ottawa: Queen's Printer, 1970.

–. *The Canadian Army, 1939–1945: An Official Historical Summary.* Ottawa: King's Printer, 1948.

–. *The Official History of the Canadian Army in the Second World War.* Vol. 3, *The Victory Campaign: The Operations in North West Europe, 1944–45.* Ottawa: Queen's Printer and Controller of Stationery, 1960.

–. *Six Years of War: The Army in Canada, Britain, and the Pacific.* Ottawa: Queen's Printer and Controller of Stationery, 1955.

Számvérber, Norbert. *Waffen-SS Armour in Normandy: The Combat History of SS Panzer Regiment 12 and SS-Panzerjäger Abteilung 12, Normandy 1944, Based on Their Original War Diaries.* Solihull: Helion and Company, 2012.

Van Crefeld, Martin. *Supplying War: Logistics from Wallenstein to Patton.* Cambridge: Cambridge University Press, 1977.

"Veritable 1945: The Canadian Finale (Moyland Wood and Goch-Calcar Road)." WW2Talk. http://ww2talk.com/index.php?threads/veritable-1945-the-canadian-finale-moyland-wood-goch-calcar-road.47307/.

Walker, Richard J. "The Political Management of Army Leadership: The Evolution of Canadian Civil-Army Relations, 1898–1945." PhD diss., University of Western Ontario, 2003.

Whitaker, Shelagh, and Denis Whitaker. *Tug of War: The Canadian Victory that Opened Antwerp.* Toronto: Stoddart, 1984.

Wilmot, Chester. *The Struggle for Europe.* London: Wordsworth Military Library, 1998.

Zetterling, Niklas. *Normandy 1944: German Military Organization, Combat Power and Organizational Effectiveness.* Winnipeg: J.J. Fedorowicz, 2000.

Zuehlke, Mark. *Terrible Victory: First Canadian Army and the Scheldt Estuary Campaign: September 13–November 6, 1944.* Toronto: Douglas and McIntyre, 2014.

Index

Note: an "f" following a page number indicates a figure; "t" indicates a table.

Adjutant and Quartermaster (A&Q) war diaries, 10
Adjutant General: 2nd ("A") Echelon, 13, 14f, 16–17; personnel matters, 13
Afrika Korps, 66, 82
AFV Support Unit, 3rd Canadian, 51
AGRA. *See* Army Group Royal Artillery (AGRA)
air support, 71, 85–87, 90. *See also* Royal Air Force (RAF); Royal Canadian Air Force (RCAF)
Airborne Division, 6th British, 201*n*26
Akkrum, 153
Algonquin Regiment: within 10th Canadian Infantry Brigade, 96; losses/casualties, 114, 115, 135–36, 212*n*66; in Normandy Campaign, 113, 114, 115, 116, 210*n*39, 212*n*66; reinforcements, 116, 135, 144; at Scheldt, 135–36; strength, 113, 116, 144
Almelo, 156
Amersfoort, 148
"Ammunition Usage" report, 54
Ante River, 114–15
Anti-Aircraft Brigade, 107th British, 201*n*26
Anti-Aircraft Regiment, Heavy (RCA) (Mobile), 2nd, 100
antiaircraft units: in 3rd Canadian Infantry Division, 95, 142; in 4th Canadian Armoured Division, 96; in 5th Canadian Armoured Division, 97; in Canadian Armoured Regiment, 179–80; equipment status reporting, 54–55; in Netherlands/Germany, 154. *See also* light anti-aircraft (LAA) regiments (RCA)
Anti-Tank Brigade (RCA), 101
antitank forces: 3rd Canadian Infantry Division, 95, 142; in 4th Canadian Armoured Division, 96; in 5th Canadian Armoured Division, 97; brigade workshops working on ordnance, 61; in combined arms tactics, 67–68, 71, 73–75; coordination with infantry/armour/artillery, 78, 80; German, 70–71; in Netherlands/Germany, 154; in rolling barrage, 73
Anti-Tank Regiment (RCA), 1st: about, 94; battle/nonbattle casualties, 150; casualties, 149; heavy AFVs, 167; personnel reinforcements, 150; strength, 151
Anti-Tank Regiment (RCA), 2nd: about, 94, 95; casualties, 112; in Normandy Campaign, 112; personnel strength, 141; strength, 153; vehicles/weaponry, 141
Anti-Tank Regiment (RCA), 3rd: about, 95; personnel strength, 142; weaponry, 134
Anti-Tank Regiment (RCA), 5th: about, 96; casualties/losses, 116, 157; in Normandy Campaign, 113, 116; personnel strength, 113, 157
Anti-Tank Regiment (RCA), 6th: 33 Battery, 148; about, 100; casualties, 171; at Leer, 164; in Normandy Campaign, 117, 118, 171; personnel strength, 117, 145–46; vehicles/equipment, 145–46
Anti-Tank Regiment (RCA), 7th: about, 99; in Nederrijn area, 165; in northwest Europe, 164–65; vehicle/weapon strength, 165

antitank regiments: Armoured Division (RCA), 191–92; Corps Troops (RCA), 190–91; equipment status reporting, 54–55; Infantry Division (RCA), 192–93; losses, 175; role, 65
antitank weapons: concentrated artillery and, 82; guns, 73, 108, 110; M10 tank destroyers, 101, 134, 143, 148, 191, 224*n*2; SPM M10, 82; tank vulnerability to, 69; Valentine Archer tank destroyers, 141, 143, 152, 190, 192, 221*n*37
Antwerp, 3, 16, 127, 129, 131, 132, 134, 139
Antwerp-Turnhout Canal, 129
Apeldoorn, 148
Argyll and Sutherland Highlanders of Canada: about, 96; casualties, 115, 135–36, 156; in Normandy Campaign, 115, 116; reinforcements, 116, 135, 156; at Scheldt, 135–36; strength, 116, 131, 138, 139f, 156
Armoured Brigade, 1st Canadian (earlier 1st Canadian Army Tank Brigade): about, 97–98; armoured regiments, 170; casualties, 162, 163; combat "A" vehicles, 162–63; equipment losses, 162; personnel strength, 163; regiments, 98; and Royal Canadian Electrical Mechanical Engineers workshop, 98; support for infantry operations in northwest Europe, 170; vehicle strength, 162–63; at Waal River, 162
Armoured Brigade, 2nd Canadian: 2nd Canadian Army Tank Brigade renamed as, 99; and 3rd Canadian Infantry Division, 130; about, 97–98; advance from Rhine to Friesland, 165; armoured regiments, 170; armoured vehicles, 143; in Battle of the Scheldt, 134; casualties, 21, 103, 134, 143, 155; D-Day landing, 102–3; formerly 4th Canadian Infantry Division, 98; in Germany/Netherlands, 155; headquarters squadron, 99; LADs, 60; in Normandy Campaign, 14, 33, 50, 102, 104; in northern Netherlands/Germany, 155; in Operation Blockbuster, 143; in Operation Overlord, 3; in Operation Totalize, 112; in Operation Tractable, 112; in Operation Veritable, 143; personnel reinforcements, 33, 103, 143, 175; regiments, 99; replacement tanks, 130; strength, 102, 155; support for infantry operations in northwest Europe, 170; tank losses, 112; tank strength, 49; training for Operation Overlord, 213*n*12; vehicles/weaponry, 138, 155, 173; workshop, 60–61, 99
Armoured Brigade, 4th Canadian: 25th CADR "D" Squadron and, 50; about, 96; equipment, 76; in Operations Totalize and Tractable, 69; personnel reinforcements, 131
Armoured Brigade, 5th Canadian: about, 97; in Delfzijl, 160; equipment, 76
armoured brigades: in 5th Canadian Armoured Division, 97–98; motor battalions, 77; Motor Infantry Battalions in, 183
armoured brigades (independent): within Canadian Corps, 3; reinforcement, 170–71
Armoured Car Regiment, 1st Canadian (Royal Canadian Dragoons): about, 99; advance from Rhine to Friesland, 165; casualties, 166; under command of 2nd Canadian Corps, 165; equipment/vehicle levels, 166; in northwest Europe, 164–65; personnel strength, 166; reinforcements, 166
Armoured Car Regiment, 18th Canadian (12th Manitoba Dragoons): with 4th Canadian Armoured Division, 164; about, 100; casualties, 164; at Mollberg, 164; in Normandy Campaign, 117, 118; personnel strength, 118; reinforcements, 164
armoured car regiments: about, 180–81; components, 180; LAD, 181; in northwest Europe, 171; role, 180; vehicles, 180–81
armoured cars: Daimler, 134; Fox, 106; Humber, 106, 181
Armoured Corps, Canadian (CAC): and German armour/antitank guns, 70–71; noninfantry casualties, 91; personnel reinforcement, 174; recce units, 65; reinforcement personnel attached to

25th Canadian Armoured Delivery Regiment (CADR), 16; role of, 64–65; weaponry compared to RCA, 87–88; weapons systems, 64–65
Armoured Delivery Regiment, Canadian (CADR), 25th: about, 50; administrative complications, 8; AFV floats/balances to draw from, 51–52; "B" Squadron, 61; "C" Squadron, 61, 104, 225*n*2; corps delivery squadron, 51; "D" Squadron, 50, 51–52, 61, 144; delivery of AFVs, 55, 61; "E" Squadron, 50, 61; "F" Squadron, 50–51; "G" Squadron, 61; in Normandy Campaign, 104; purpose, 201*n*21; rapidity of delivery, 172; reinforcement CAC personnel attached to, 16; repaired AFVs shipped back to, 63; resupply of all units operating heavy AFVs, 52; squadrons, 50; supply of new/repaired AFVs, 50; tank circuits, 51; in tank delivery procedure, 51; war diaries, 207*n*17
Armoured Division, 1st Canadian (later 5th Canadian Armoured Division), 97, 98
Armoured Division, 1st Polish, 115
Armoured Division, 4th Canadian: with 1st British Corps, 143; 2nd Canadian Infantry Division and, 135; 3rd Canadian Infantry Division and, 129–30; 18th Armoured Car Regiment with, 164; about, 96–97; advance from Rhine to Friesland, 165; AFV deliveries to, 52; antitank/antiaircraft assets, 96; armoured brigade, 96; as army reserve for First Canadian Army, 143; in Breda, 144; brigade workshops, 61; casualties, 20–21, 115–16, 135–36, 156–57; combat capability, 170; combat formations, 96; as exploitation force, 156; field artillery, 96–97; friendly aerial bombing destruction of headquarters' communications, 212*n*67; in Germany/Netherlands, 155–56; infantry, other ranks shortage, 33; infantry component, 96; Kusten Canal crossing, 156; losses vs. reinforcement, 169; M10 17-pounder tank destroyers, 224*n*3; in Nijmegen Salient, 143; in Normandy Campaign, 113–17; in northern France/Belgium, 130–31; numbers of armoured vehicles, 206*n*6; numbers of tanks/scout cars, 50; in Operation Blockbuster, 155; in Operation Plunder, 156; in Operation Totalize, 114; in Operation Tractable, 108, 114; as part of 2nd Canadian Corps, 114; personnel reinforcements, 135–36, 138, 144–45, 156–57; personnel shortage, 169; personnel strength, 111, 113, 116, 138–39, 156, 157, 169–70; and Ram II tanks, 212*n*70; rebuilding, 169–70; reconnaissance within, 96; reinforcements, 116, 170; relieving 1st Polish Armoured Division, 115; at Scheldt, 134–37, 169; Sherman Firefly 17-pounder tanks, 212*n*70; shortage of replacements, 116; tank reinforcements, 144, 145f; tank replacement/delivery vs. German Panzer IV production, 144, 145f; vehicles/weaponry, 87, 113, 117, 135, 136–37, 144, 157–58, 169–70; Wasp II flamethrowers, 212*n*70; winter of 1944–45, 138–39. *See also* 4th Canadian Infantry Division
Armoured Division, 5th Canadian (formerly 1st Canadian Armoured Division): with 1st Canadian Corps, 17; 4th Canadian Infantry Division units in, 96; about, 97; AFV losses, 159; antitank/antiaircraft assets, 97; armoured brigades, 170–71; casualties, 160; combat capability, 170; diversion of 4th Canadian Infantry Division units to, 96; in eastern Netherlands, 170; effectiveness, 170; equipment shortages, 161–62, 204*n*20; field artillery regiments, 97; fighting components, 97; in Groningen area, 160; heavy AFVs delivered, vs. Panther tank deliveries to German armoured units, 159; at Nederrijn River, 159–60; in Netherlands, 159–60; new infantry brigade, 34; in northwest Europe, 97, 158; at Oosterhout bridgehead over Waal River, 159; ordnance depots, 54; Ordnance Field Park, 54; as part of 1st Canadian Corps, 97;

personnel strength, 158, 160–61, 170; reconnaissance, 97; reinforcements, 160–61, 170–71; relief by 1st Canadian Infantry Division, 160; relief of 3rd Canadian Infantry Division, 160; relief of 49th British Infantry Division, 159–60; vehicles/weaponry, 158–59, 161–62
Armoured Division, 79th British, 77, 201*n*26
armoured divisions: anti-tank regiments, 190–91; armoured reconnaissance regiments, 180; within Canadian Corps, 3; light anti-aircraft regiments, 194, 195t, 196; other ranks, shortages, in northwest Europe, 198–99; self-propelled field artillery regiments, 186–87; towed field artillery regiments, 187
armoured fighting vehicles (AFVs): and 2nd Canadian Infantry Division, 95; 3rd Canadian AFV Support Unit, 51; 4th Canadian Armoured Division and, 96; 4th Canadian Armoured Division reinforcement, 144; 25th CADR resupply of all units, 52; brigade workshops and, 61; completion of repairs to, 62–63; concentrated artillery and, 82; delivery of, 8; German forces repair/replacement process, 52; as major systems in armoured/artillery regiments, 11; in Normandy Campaign, 104; RCA regiments, 55; reception/inspection, 50–51; replacement system, 49f; replacement/transport system for, 48; shortages, 50; strength, vs. German units, 52, 53f; strength reports, 49–50; tank circuits, 51; transportation of, 48–52, 54; US production, 67; Windsor carriers, 152. *See also* antitank weapons; tanks
Armoured Ordnance Sub-park, 205th Canadian, 54
Armoured Personnel Carrier Regiment, 1st Canadian, 77, 207*n*21, 226*n*3
armoured personnel carriers, 64; about, 76–77; Kangaroos, 77, 88, 207*n*21, 225*n*5; Ram, 88, 173, 225*n*5; SPW 251, 76; White M3, 76, 77; White M3 half-track, 76, 77. *See also* Universal Carriers
Armoured Regiment, 2nd Canadian (Lord Strathcona's Horse) (Royal Canadians), 97, 158
Armoured Regiment, 5th Canadian (8th Princess Louise's [New Brunswick] Hussars), 97
Armoured Regiment, 6th Canadian (1st Hussars): about, 99; attack on Le Mesnil-Patry, 68, 70; LAD, 60; in Normandy Campaign, 104; Sherman tank strength, 53f; tank losses, 4, 46–47, 209*n*12; tank reinforcements, 103
Armoured Regiment, 9th Canadian (British Columbia Dragoons), 97, 161
Armoured Regiment, 10th Canadian (Fort Garry Horse): about, 99; LAD, 60; at Louisendorf, 71, 72f; in Normandy Campaign, 102–3
Armoured Regiment, 11th Canadian (Three Rivers Regiment), 98, 162
Armoured Regiment, 12th Canadian (Ontario Regiment), 98, 163
Armoured Regiment, 14th Canadian (Calgary Regiment), 98
Armoured Regiment, 21st Canadian (Governor General's Foot Guards): about, 96; in Normandy Campaign, 113; reinforcements, 131; strength, 113, 131, 157; tank losses, 209*n*13
Armoured Regiment, 22nd Canadian (Canadian Grenadier Guards): about, 96; destruction of command tanks, 69; losses, 135; in Normandy Campaign, 69, 209*n*19, 210*n*28; personnel strength, 131; reinforcements, 131, 135; at Scheldt, 135
Armoured Regiment, 27th Canadian (Sherbrooke Fusiliers): about, 99; AFV replace/repair process for, 52; at Carpiquet/Caen, 68–69; at Falaise Pocket, 52; LAD, 52, 60; in Operation Charnwood, 74–75f; in Operation Totalize, 52; in Operation Tractable, 52; personnel reinforcements, 143; strength, 155; tank reinforcements, 103
Armoured Regiment, 28th Canadian (British Columbia Regiment): about, 96; casualties/losses, 114, 157, 212*n*66; vehicles/equipment, 51–52

armoured regiments: about, 178–80; anti-aircraft troop, 179–80; antiank weapons vs., 65; armoured reconnaissance regiment, 180; attachment to 2nd Canadian Infantry Division, 168; and combat capability, 168; components, 179; LADs, 52, 60, 180; numbers of attacks led by, 68; as offensive vanguard, 68; personnel losses in Normandy Campaign, 104; personnel reinforcement system and, 16; role, 178–79; and Sherman tanks, 65; vehicles/weaponry, 11, 179

armoured troop carriers. *See* armoured personnel carriers

Armoured Troops (third-line maintenance) Workshop, 4th Canadian, 51

armoured units, 170; British Army changes in tactical employment of, 66; casualties, 69–70, 175; in combined arms tactics, 67–68, 71, 72f, 73–75, 89, 91–92; concentrated artillery and, 82; coordination with antitank forces/infantry/artillery, 78, 80; flexible exploitation roles, 209*n*17; role of, 64–65; in rolling barrage, 73; at Scheldt, 90; unsupported, as vanguard, 67; vehicles/weapons system, vs. in artillery/infantry, 176. *See also* armoured brigades; armoured divisions; armoured regiments

armoured vehicles: CAC "contact cars," 86; Lend-Lease program and, 67; supply of, 45–46. *See also* armoured fighting vehicles (AFVs); armoured personnel carriers

Army Group, 21st: 1st Canadian Echelon, 14f, 47–48; 2nd Canadian Echelon, 13, 14f, 15, 17; "'A' & 'B' Consolidated Vehicle Position Report," 105; administrative system, 7; advanced divisional reinforcement control officer, 16–17; "B" vehicle release, 55; Canadian reinforcements dispatched to, 19–20; consolidated vehicle position report, 147; echelons, 13, 14f; No. 1 Advanced Base Workshop, 62; No. 2 Advanced Base Workshop, 62; and No. 2 CBRG, 15; personnel deficits listing, 16–17; pursuit of retreating Germans in northern France, 130; regulations for combat arms group establishment, 88; standards, 165

Army Group Royal Artillery (AGRA), 81; army-level units, 100; medium regiments, 100, 171, 188–89; in Normandy Campaign, 118–19, 171; in northwest Europe, 146–47; personnel reinforcements, 131–32; self-propelled RCA Field Regiments, 187; and Yoke target, 85

Army Group Royal Artillery (AGRA), 1st Canadian: with 1st Canadian Corps, 163; about, 100; in Belgium, 163; components, 100; at Grebbe River, 163; at IJssel River, 163; in Italy, 163; losses, 163; monthly returns, 106; in Netherlands, 163–64; reinforcement, 163–64; vehicles/weapons, 163; weapons, 164

Army Group Royal Artillery (AGRA), 2nd Canadian: about, 100; artillery programs in Rhineland, 147; casualties, 118–19, 131–32, 147; components, 100; equipment levels, 146; medium artillery regiments grouped in, 83; neutralization of channel ports, 132; in Normandy Campaign, 118–19; in northern Netherlands/Germany, 163; in northwest Europe, 146–47; operational equipment levels, 146; personnel replacement, 131–32; at Scheldt, 132; strength, 146–47

Army Programme, 1942–1943, 26

Army Tank Brigade, 1st Canadian (later 1st Canadian Armoured Brigade), 98

Army Tank Brigade, 2nd Canadian: about, 98; regiments broken up for reinforcements, 98–99; renaming as 2nd Canadian Armoured Brigade, 99; training for Operation Overlord, 99

Army Tank Brigade, 3rd Canadian: about, 98–99; regiments in 2nd Canadian Army Tank Brigade, 99

army-level units: about, 99, 100; combat capability, 131; in First Canadian Army, 99; in Normandy Campaign, 118–19

Arnhem, 148, 160, 162, 165

artillery: barrage fire plans, 83, 84f, 89; at Carpiquet/Caen, 68–69; in combined arms tactics, 67–68, 71, 73–75,

89; concentrated fire, 81, 82; coordination with infantry/armour/antitank forces, 78, 80; creeping/standing barrage, 81–82; decentralization of command/control, 81; divisional ordnance parks, 54; equipment status reporting, 54–55; field ordnance parks/subparks, 55; fire plans, 90; forward observation officers, 82; and infantry casualties, 71; mechanization of Commonwealth units, 82; moving fire, 81–82; in North Africa, 81; in northwest Europe, 83–84; ordnance delivery organization recordkeeping, 10; Ordnance Maintenance Company and equipment, 54; role, 81; rolling barrage, 72–73, 89; "Uncle"/"Victor"/"Yoke"/"Mike" fire-plan tactics, 83–84, 85. *See also* medium regiments; Royal Canadian Artillery (RCA); vehicles/weaponry; weaponry

artillery observation post tanks, 185

artillery regiments: "Ammunition Usage" reports, 54; "Gun State of Ordnance Holdings" reports, 54; gun status reporting, 54; in Normandy Campaign, 83; vehicles/weapons systems, 11; weaponry, 87–88. *See also* field regiments (RCA); medium regiments

artillery units: 1st Canadian Infantry Division, 94; 2nd Canadian Infantry Division, 94–95; 3rd Canadian Infantry Division, 95; antitank regiments, 65; as building blocks in operational plans, 83–84; within Canadian Corps, 3; casualties, 175; components, 65; field regiments, 65; light antiaircraft regiments, 65; medium regiments, 65; vehicles/weapons system, vs. in infantry/armoured forces, 176

artillery-based operational doctrine, 91; AGRA and, 100; corps-/army-level combat arms units and, 99; and full personnel/equipment strengths, 176; German armies vs., 172

Atlantic, Battle of the, 24, 46

Atlantic, Operation, 103, 104, 106, 107, 213*n*85

Atlantic Wall defence, 3

attrition: "compassionate," 9, 172; enemy, 9, 11, 172, 176; German forces and, 6, 90, 168; during Normandy Campaign, 4, 91; US Army and, 38

Aue River, 156

Aurich, 154

Authie, 87

"**B**" echelons, 17, 18, 19, 46, 48, 50

Balberger Wald forest area, 155

battle exhaustion, 112, 149; 2nd Canadian Corps Reinforcement Company rehabilitation tool, 197; treatment options, 197t

battlegroups: regiments and, 64. *See also* combined arms tactics

Beament, A.W., 13, 30, 33–34

Bergen op Zoom, 71, 135

Beveland, South, 132, 135

Beveridge Report, 56

Biervliet, 133

Blockbuster, Operation, 143, 147, 152, 155

Bluecoat, Operation, 114

Borden, Robert, 24

Boulogne, 130

Breda, 144

Breskens Pocket, 131, 133–34

Bretteville-l'Orgueilleuse, 102

Bretteville-sur-Laize, 111

brigades, size/composition, 11

British Army: Canadian war production for, 45; changes after North African campaign, 66; changes in tactical employment of armour, 66; junior infantry officer casualties, 22; in Normandy Campaign, 39; ordnance field parks, 54; personnel management, 39; pressure on CMHQ, 31–32; recovery/repair/replacement systems, 38–39, 56, 173; reinforcement practices, 14; reinforcements, 39

British Corps, 1st: 4th Canadian Armoured Division with, 143; reinforcement company, 15

British Scots Greys, 210*n*34

Bruges, 130

Burns, E.L.M., 13, 27

Buron, 74–75f

Cabinet War Committee. *See* War Committee
Caen, 68–69, 103, 104, 114
Calais, 130
Calcar-Udem ridgeline, 155
Calgary Highlanders: about, 94; in Normandy Campaign, 105; at Tilly-la-Campagne, 210*n*34
Calgary Regiment, 98
Cameron Highlanders of Ottawa (Machine Gun), 95, 96, 133
Can Loan scheme, 22
Canadian Army: acceptance standards for recruits, 25–26; artillery-based doctrine, 154; composition, 93; equipment sources, 46; expansion, 23–24, 25, 26–27, 42; infantry orientation, 90; as last to receive resources, 45; maximization of strengths/minimization of weaknesses, 91–92; NRMA creation of twin armies, 25; personnel reinforcements in northwest Europe, 111–12; personnel utilization, 27; reconstitution of self, 172; size of, 23–24; total number of combat "A" vehicles, 173
Canadian Army (Active): adoption of British Army practices, 63; as all-volunteer, 42, 43; and infantry, other ranks shortage, 43; in Italian campaign, 63; as later name of Canadian Army Active Service Force, 25; new divisions raised from members of, 28; and personnel reinforcements, 40; uninvolvement in continuous combat operations, 45; volunteers for Army expansion, 28
Canadian Army Active Service Force, as home defence, 25
Canadian Corps, 1st: 1st Canadian AGRA with, 100, 163; 1st Canadian Infantry Division as part of, 93; 1st Canadian Infantry Division under command of, 148; 5th Canadian Armoured Division as part of, 97; formations within, 3; headquarters, 99; at IJssel River, 165; in Italy, 95; in Netherlands, 17; in northwest Europe, 164–65; personnel strength, 165; reunion with 2nd Canadian Corps, 3; vehicles/weapons strength, 165. *See also* corps-level units
Canadian Corps, 2nd: 1st Canadian Armoured Car Regiment under, 165; 1st Canadian Infantry Division under command of, 148; 2nd Canadian Infantry Division as part of, 94; 4th Canadian Armoured Division as part of, 114; and 25th Canadian Armoured Delivery Regiment (CADR), 50; becoming operational, 15; casualties, 118, 164; combat "A" vehicles, 139; corps-level units, 99–100; "E" Squadron responsibility for tank delivery to, 50; under First Canadian Army, 15; formations within, 3; headquarters, 99; losses, 12; in northern Netherlands/Germany, 155, 163, 164; in Operation Cannonshot, 148; in Operation Veritable, 143; reinforcement company, 19; reunion with 1st Canadian Corps, 3; under Second British Army, 15; strength, 145–46; training for invasion of France, 66; Troops Workshop, 61; during winter 1944–45, 145–46. *See also* corps-level units
Canadian Corps of Electrical and Mechanical Engineers. *See* Royal Canadian Electrical and Mechanical Engineers (RCEME)
Canadian Echelon, 1st, 13–14; "A1" (Fighting) Echelon, 46; "A2" Echelon, 46; equipment/weaponry for First Canadian Army, 46
Canadian Echelon, 2nd, 13, 14f, 15, 17
Canadian Engineering Institute, 57
Canadian Military Headquarters (CMHQ), London: and 4th Canadian Armoured Division's personnel shortage, 169; and 21st Army Group echelons, 14f; British Army pressure on, 31–32; and casualties, 31–32; casualty-projection planning, 10; and creation of RCEME, 57; on defensive vs. offensive role for forces in UK, 29; forecasting of casualties, 42; and infantry, other ranks shortage, 33; and infantry reinforcement miscalculations, 30; and

personnel replacement system, 13; and sixty-day shortage, 22
Canadian Scottish Regiment: about, 95, 110; casualties, 154; reinforcements, 154–55; in Wagenborgen, 154
Cannonshot, Operation, 148
Cape Breton Highlanders, 97
Carleton and York Regiment, 94
Carpiquet, 102, 103
Carpiquet airfield, 68–69, 102, 103, 104
casualties/losses: absence of combined arms tactics and, 73, 76; air support and, 86–87; among antitank vs. field artillery regiments, 175; of armoured regiments during Normandy Campaign, 104; armoured regiments as offensive vanguard and, 68; in armoured units, 69–70; army-/corps-level units in northwest Europe, 164, 171; army-level units in Normandy Campaign, 118–19; artillery, and infantry, 71; in artillery vs. armoured/infantry units, 175; battle vs. nonbattle, 151f; "bite and hold" tactics and, 91; British Army, 22, 38, 39; causes of, 21; combat capability vs., 12; in D-Day landings, 33; in Dieppe Raid, 9; dismounted infantry, 76–77, 78; estimations, for size of personnel reinforcement system, 29; field artillery units, 83, 112; First Canadian Army headquarters returns regarding, 10; forecasting, 34f, 42–43; friendly, 9, 86–87, 118, 119, 131; within German armies on eastern front, 9; at Hong Kong, 26; infantry projection rates, 36, 37f, 40; at Juno Beach, 101–2; from lack of coordination of infantry/artillery with armour/antitank forces, 78, 80; medium regiments, 83, 131; neuropsychiatric, 203*n*26; nonbattle, 112, 115, 118, 132, 133–34, 142, 144, 147, 149–50, 152–53, 154; during Normandy Campaign, 3–4, 33, 34f, 68, 69, 104, 110, 112, 118–19; in North Africa, 10, 29, 30; NRMA conscripts, 41; numbers, vs. personnel reinforcement, 20–21; numbers, vs. personnel reinforcements, 150; offensive operations and, 65; in Operation Spring, 35; at Operation Totalize, 77; personnel reinforcement system vs., 119; projections, 10, 29–30, 31, 42–43; rate, vs. projected figures, 30; RCA regiments, 136; in Rhineland/Netherlands/northern Germany, 164; at Scheldt, 37, 132, 133–34, 135–36, 137; in Sicilian/Italian campaigns, 29–30; tank design, and, 67; timeframe for mitigation, 172; US Army, 39–40; during winter 1944–45, 142, 144. *See also* battle exhaustion; *and under names of individual military units*
Chambois, 115
channel ports, 130, 132
Charnwood, Operation, 68–69, 74–75f, 87, 103, 104, 210*n*33
Chevrolet trucks, 76
Clair Tizon, 111
Clash of Arms (Hart), 4–5, 63
Cleve, 155
Cobra, Operation, 114
combat capability: 2nd AGRA army-level artillery units, 131; 3rd Canadian Infantry Division, 110; 4th Canadian Armoured Division, 170; 5th Canadian Armoured Division, 170; Canadian vs. German armies, 172; at conclusion of hostilities, 166; corps-level regiments (1st Canadian Corps), 165–66; of First Canadian Army in northwest Europe, 171; full strength and, 176; infantry shortage and, 174; losses vs., 12; in Normandy Campaign, 22; in northwest Europe, 167; perpetual state of, 12; personnel levels and, 173–74, 176; personnel reinforcements and, 19; personnel/equipment supply systems and, 175–76; recovery-and-repair system and, 173; reinforcement for, 172; training/integration of replacement personnel and, 80; and victories, 176; weapons/vehicles losses and, 88–89
combined arms tactics: about, 67–68; absence of, 73, 76; air support, 71, 85–87, 90; armour in, 91–92; artillery support, 89; at Bergen op Zoom, 71; emphasis on, 91–92; exercises, 87; in

infantry attack, 73–75; infantry in battlegroups, 82; infantry-led, 71, 91–92; at Louisendorf, 71, 72f; naval support, 90; tank-infantry cooperation, 87; training, 87
conscription: army expansion and, 27–28; avoidance of, 10; crisis, 9–10, 23, 40–42, 150; during First World War, 24, 25; for home defence, 25; of home defence for overseas, 10, 15, 25; for infantry reinforcements, 23; NRMA and, 15, 150, 166, 175; political attitudes toward, 24–26, 27–28, 42; volunteers vs., 23
Copp, Terry, 5
Corps Administrative Area, 47
Corps of Royal Canadian Electrical and Mechanical Engineers (RCEME). *See* Royal Canadian Electrical and Mechanical Engineers (RCEME)
Corps of Royal Electrical and Mechanical Engineers (REME). *See* Royal Electrical and Mechanical Engineers (REME)
Corps Troops Area, 47
corps-level units: 1st Canadian Corps, 99; 2nd Canadian Corps, 99–100, 117–18, 137, 145–46; with 4th Canadian Armoured Division, 164; about, 99; casualties, 137, 164; combat capability, 165–66; in First Canadian Army, 99; and Grebbe River truce, 165; in Netherlands/Germany, 164; in Normandy Campaign, 117–18; in northwest Europe, 164–65; personnel reinforcements, 164; personnel strengths, 139, 145, 164; at Scheldt, 137; vehicle/weapon strengths, 145–46; during winter 1944–45, 145–46
Couliboeuf, 115
Crerar, H.D.G., 4–5, 26, 27, 34–35, 99
Crerar, T.A., 25

Damblainville, 115
Deelen, 160
Delden, 156
Delfzijl, 154, 160
D'Este, Carlo, 39
Destroyer, Operation, 162
Dieppe (1944): halt at, 128, 129; liberation of, 127
Dieppe Raid (1942): 2nd Canadian Infantry Division at, 94, 95; 2nd Canadian Infantry Division in, 95; Calgary Regiment in, 98; losses at, 94; personnel losses at, 9
Dill, Sir John, 29
Dives River, 115
Divisional Administrative Area, 47
divisions, size/composition, 11
doctrine: artillery-based, 91, 99, 100, 154, 172, 176; defined, 64; equipment/firepower use, vs. human capital expenditure, 9; indirect fire in artillery-based, 99; Montgomery's training in, 66
Doetinchem, 152
Dunkirk, 127

Edewechterdamm, 156
Eekloo, 131
Eighth Army (British Army): 1st Canadian Infantry Division serving with, 93; casualties in North Africa, 10, 30; defeat by Afrika Korps, 66
El Alamein, 82
Elbeuf, 129, 130
Emden, 154, 160
Emlichheim, 156
Emmerich, 143
Ems River, 156
English, John, 70
Épaney, 114
equipment: 2nd Canadian Infantry Division challenges, 167–68; 3rd Canadian Infantry Division, 101; 21st Army Group 1st Canadian Echelon and, 46; 25th Canadian Armoured Delivery Regiment and inventories of, 172; access to, 46; inventory maintenance in Canadian vs. German military cultures, 172; Lend-Lease, 10, 46, 67; RCEME and inventories of, 172; recovery/repair/replacement system, 44; status reporting, 54–55; stockpiling for invasion of Europe, 46; temporary nature of shortages, 173; transportation to fighting units, 52, 54–55; varying

quality of, 173; war establishment figures, 101; wastage incidence, 10. *See also* vehicles/weaponry
equipment losses: 1st Canadian Armoured Brigade, 162; about, 44; accidents, 44, 59; First Canadian Army headquarters returns regarding, 10; during Normandy Campaign, 46–47; and strength levels, 44; strength vs., 44; wear and tear, 44, 138
equipment recovery/repair/replacement system. *See* recovery/repair/replacement system
equipment strengths: 2nd Army Group Royal Artillery (AGRA), 146; artillery-based doctrine and, 176; establishment-level inventories, 44; losses vs., 44. *See also* personnel strengths; vehicle/weapon strength
Ermelo, 160
Essen, 135
Essex Scottish Regiment: about, 94; casualties, 132, 152, 215*n*25; at Scheldt, 132; strength, 5, 137

Falaise, 130; 4th Canadian Armoured Division at, 130
Falaise Gap/Pocket, 6, 127; 3rd Canadian Infantry Division at, 108; 4th Canadian Armoured Division at, 114–15, 116, 130; 27th Canadian Armoured Regiment at, 52; about battle at, 4–5; armoured regiments at, 112; Army Group Royal Artillery (AGRA) at, 118; German forces at, 3, 108, 115; infantry regiment effectiveness at, 5, 174; recovery/repair/replacement system and closure of, 63
field artillery regiments: in 4th Canadian Armoured Division, 96–97; in 5th Canadian Armoured Division, 97; armoured division variant (self-propelled), 186–87; armoured division variant (towed), 187–88; as army-level units, 100; brigade workshops working on ordnance, 61; casualties/losses, 83, 112, 175; equipment status reporting, 54–55; forward observation officers, 185–86; infantry division variant (towed), 185–86, 187–88; in Netherlands/Germany, 154; observation post tanks/forward observation officers, 188; role, 65; weaponry, 87–88
field regiments (RCA): 1st (Royal Canadian Horse Artillery), 83, 94, 149, 151; 2nd, 94, 150, 211*n*47; 3rd, 94, 150, 211*n*47, 213*n*86; 4th, 94, 105, 112, 153; 5th, 94; 6th, 94, 141, 153; 8th (self-propelled), 97, 161; 11th, 100, 163, 164, 211*n*47; 12th, 95, 109; 13th, 95, 222*n*71; 14th, 95; 15th (self-propelled), 96–97; 17th, 97, 158; 19th, 100, 101, 119, 168; 23rd, 97, 157
Fifteenth Army (German), 137
firebase tactic, 71–73, 89
First Canadian Army: 1st Canadian Echelon dealing with equipment/weaponry for, 46; and 2nd Canadian Corps, 15; 4th Canadian Armoured Division as army reserve for, 143; and 25th Canadian Armoured Delivery Regiment (CADR), 50; army-/corps-level units, 99; becoming operational, 15; British Army standard doctrine/equipment, 66; Canadian corps in, 3; combat capability at conclusion of hostilities, 166; combat capability in northwest Europe, 171; combat power, 176; components, 93; at conclusion of hostilities, 166; deputy director of mechanical engineering, 61–62; “F” Squadron responsibility for vehicle delivery to, 50; headquarters, 99; lack of reinforcement plan for sustenance of, 26–27; laying of foundations of, 26; near all-volunteer status, 43; in Normandy Campaign, 22, 114; numbers of reinforcement personnel dispatched to, 21; and Operation Goldflake, 93; organization, 3; personnel deficit, 35; re-equipping of 1st Canadian Infantry Division, 147; repair-and-replacement services, 44; in Rhineland, 147; road-head staging area, 15; at Scheldt, 139; sixty-day shortage and, 22; strengths/weaknesses, 64; sufficiency of replacement personnel to cope with ongoing

battle losses, 20–21; units/formations, 11t; during winter of 1944–45, 137, 139
First World War: "bite and hold" tactics, 90; concentrated artillery, 81; infantry casualties, 76
Ford trucks, 76
Forêt de la Londe, 127, 167
Fort Garry Horse. *See* Armoured Regiment, 10th Canadian (Fort Garry Horse)
Forward Maintenance Area, 47
Foster, H.W., 93
Foulkes, Charles, 94, 99
France: allied invasion, 3; fall of, 29, 45. *See also* Normandy Campaign
Francoeur, G., 15
Friesland, 165
Friesoythe, 156
Les Fusiliers Mont-Royal: about, 94; casualties, 132; establishment strength, 200*n*9; losses, 36; in Normandy Campaign, 36, 105; reinforcements, 36; at Scheldt, 132; strength, 174

Gauntlet, Operation, 93
German Army: 6th Anti-Tank Regiment pursuit of, 171; AFV repair/replacement process, 52; and artillery counter-battery fire, 175; "B" combat vehicles, 55; combat capability, 142; Normandy Campaign and, 101; panzer divisions, 65; in Sicilian/Italian campaigns, 30; during spring 1945 fighting, 164; tank losses, 52; in USSR, 68
German forces: 2nd Canadian Corps corps-level units and, 118; AFV strength, vs. Canadian, 52, 53f; antitank defence, 70–71; attrition, 6, 90, 168, 170, 172, 176; attrition, and withdrawal for rebuilding, 168; Canadian artillery-based doctrine vs., 172; Canadian combat capability vs., 172; combat employment system, 6; combined arms/air support in defeat of, 87; counterattacks vs. offensive operations, 65–66; on eastern front, 9; equipment upkeep/replacement system, 44, 144, 145f, 159; at Falaise Gap, 108, 115; focus on dismounted infantry, 78; and Grebbe River halt, 148, 165; infantry strengths, vs. Canadian, 110, 111f; lack of artillery counterbattery capability, 83; mid-August 1944 collapse, 3; in Netherlands/Germany, 138, 154, 163; after Normandy Campaign, 65–66; in Normandy Campaign, 104, 116; in Operation Veritable, 142; personnel losses and replacements, 20, 21f; and reinforcement, 6; repair turnaround times, 176; at Scheldt, 137; during spring 1945 fighting, 166; at Stalingrad, 9; Sturmgeschütz assault guns, 70, 135, 200*n*15; surrender, 160; weakened state, 65–66, 92, 163, 166, 167, 169, 170; during winter 1944–45, 138; withdrawal for rebuilding, 168; withdrawal from northern France, 119, 174. *See also* German Army; Luftwaffe; tanks; Waffen-SS
Ghent, 16
Ghent Canal, 130
Goch, 143
Goldflake, Operation, 93, 97, 98, 164
Goodwood, Operation, 103
Gostling (Brigadier), 15
Grebbe River, 148, 163, 165
Groede, 133
Groningen, 152, 154, 160
Grossenkneten, 152
Gruchy, 87
"Gun State of Ordnance Holdings" report, 54
guns, 77–78, 79t; carriers/tractors, 55, 76, 77, 106, 108, 110, 134, 151–52, 161, 181, 183, 184, 192, 206*n*6; Lee-Enfield Mark 4 rifle, 77; machine, 77, 108, 173; maintenance, 54–55; MP 40, 77; RCA state of, 50; status reporting, 54; Sturmgeschütz III assault, 70, 135; submachine gun, 77, 173

Harderwijk, 148
Harlingen, 153
Hart, Russell, *Clash of Arms*, 4–5, 63
Hastings and Prince Edward Regiment, 93
Henry, Gordon, 209*n*26

Hesel, 163
Highland Division, 51st British, 152
Highland Light Infantry of Canada, 73, 74–75f, 95
Highlanders of Canada, 48th, 37–38, 93, 147, 150
Hochwald Gap, 143, 152, 155
Hoffmeister, Bertram, 97
Hollandsch Diep, 135
home defence: Canadian Army Active Service Force as, 25; conscription for, 25; conscription for overseas service, 10, 15, 23; conscripts as personnel reinforcements, 10; disbandment of 7th/8th Canadian Infantry Divisions for, 22; NRMA establishment of, 25
Hong Kong: losses at, 26; personnel losses at, 9
Hoofdplaat, 133
howitzers, 55, 81, 108, 163, 164
Hunte River, 152
Husky, Operation, 14
Hussars, 1st. *See* Armoured Regiment, 6th Canadian (1st Hussars)

IJssel River, 90, 148, 163, 165
Independent Machine Gun Company, 10th (New Brunswick Rangers), 96
Independent Machine Gun Company, 11th (Princess Louise Fusiliers), 97
indirect fire, 69–70, 73, 76, 81, 99, 141, 186–87, 188–89, 211*n*47
infantry: alone, vs. in combined arms team, 73; armoured transport, 76–77; casualties in Normandy Campaign, 33, 34f, 65; casualties in northwest Europe, 65; casualties vs. artillery/armoured units, 175; casualty projection rates, 36, 37f; in combined arms tactics, 67–68, 71, 73–75, 82, 89; concentrated artillery and, 82; coordination with antitank forces/armour/artillery, 78, 80; dismounted, 76–776; Normandy Campaign demands on, 174; orientation in Canadian Army, 90; reinforcements, 23, 36–37, 116; remustering for, 32, 33; role of, 64; in rolling barrage, 73, 89; understrength, 4–5; in vanguard, 67–68; vehicles/weapons system, vs. in artillery/armoured forces, 176; weapons, 77–78, 79t
infantry, other ranks: casualty projections for, vs. other trades, 29–30; casualty rates, 30; deficiency in, 5; francophone, 36; lack of replacements, and Conscription Crisis, 9–10
infantry, other ranks shortages: 2nd Canadian Infantry Division, 128; failure to heed, 42; during Normandy Campaign, 22, 116; in northwest Europe, 198–99; of reinforcements, 22, 31–32, 33–34, 35, 43; remustering program for, 22, 30, 43; retraining for, 22; sixty-day duration, 22–23
Infantry Brigade, 1st Canadian, 93, 149
Infantry Brigade, 2nd Canadian: about, 93; battle casualties, 149; nonbattle vs. battle casualties, 150, 151f; regiments comprising, 93–94
Infantry Brigade, 3rd Canadian, 94, 149
Infantry Brigade, 4th Canadian: about, 94; clearance of Forêt de la Londe, 127; at Louisendorf, 71; nonbattle casualties, 112; rebuilding after Dieppe Raid, 213*n*7; strength, 153
Infantry Brigade, 5th Canadian, 94, 106
Infantry Brigade, 6th Canadian, 94, 127, 213*n*7
Infantry Brigade, 7th Canadian: about, 95; casualties, 133; in Normandy Campaign, 102; at Scheldt, 132, 133; strength, 110, 132
Infantry Brigade, 8th Canadian: about, 95; casualties, 133; and channel ports, 130; at Quesnay Wood, 108; at Scheldt, 132–33; strength, 110, 132–33
Infantry Brigade, 9th Canadian: about, 95; casualties, 102; and channel ports, 130; in Normandy Campaign, 102, 103; at Scheldt, 133; strength, 110, 133
Infantry Brigade, 10th Canadian: about, 96; in Belgium, 131; casualties, 115, 144; at Épaney, 114; formation of, 32; in Germany, 155; at Kapelsche Veer, 144; in Normandy Campaign, 113, 114, 115; personnel reinforcements, 131;

rebuilding, 138; reinforcements, 138; strength, 113, 131
Infantry Brigade, 11th Canadian, 97, 160
Infantry Brigade, 12th Canadian: about, 94; creation of, 32; disbandment of, 17, 158; headquarters for 1st Canadian Corps replacements, 17
infantry brigades: 1st Canadian Infantry Division, 93–94; 2nd Canadian Infantry Division, 94, 167; 3rd Canadian Infantry Division, 95; 4th Canadian Armoured Division, 96; 5th Canadian Armoured Division, 97; infantry regiments and, 64, 183
Infantry Corps, Canadian (CIC): composition, 64; infantry, other ranks shortage, 22, 43; majority of casualties within, 16; personnel reinforcements, 109, 174; regiments, 64; role of, 64; tactics with armoured forces, 71; weaponry compared to RCA, 87–88. *See also* Machine Gun Battalion, Canadian; Motor Infantry Battalion, Canadian
Infantry Division, 1st Canadian: 1st Canadian Corps command, 148; 2nd Canadian Corps command, 148; about, 93–94; artillery assets, 211*n*47; artillery units, 94; casualties, 149–50; combat capability, 167; divisional troops, 94; equipment, 101, 167; equipping from British stocks, 45; First Canadian Army re-equipping of, 147; halt at Grebbe River, 148; in Italy, 93, 147; move to Belgium, 93; in Netherlands, 148; in Operation Cannonshot, 148; in Reichswald Forest, 148; reinforcements, 150, 167; relief of 5th Canadian Armoured Division, 160; strengths, 147, 149–51; weapons/vehicles, 147–48, 151–52, 167
Infantry Division, 2nd Canadian: 3rd Canadian Infantry Division relieving, 154; 4th Canadian Armoured Division and, 135; about, 94–95; armoured regiments attachment to, 168; artillery units, 94–95; "B" vehicle return vs. 12th SS Panzer Division vehicles, 55; battle casualties, 152; casualties, 20–21, 106–7, 127–28, 132, 137, 142, 152–53, 168; clearance of Forêt de la Londe, 127; combat capability, 129; at Dieppe, 94, 95; divisional units, 94; equipment, 101, 167–68; field artillery regiments, 167–68; in France, 167; at Hochwald Gap, 152; infantry, other ranks shortage, 33, 35, 36f, 127; infantry brigades, 94, 167–68; infantry shortage, 5; in Netherlands/Germany, 152; at Nijmegen Salient, 137; in Normandy Campaign, 94, 103–8, 111–12, 116, 167; in Operation Atlantic, 106, 107; in Operation Blockbuster, 152; in Operation Totalize, 108; in Operation Veritable, 141–42; personnel shortages, 107, 174; personnel strength, 141, 153; rebuilding of, 167, 168; reinforcements, 106–8, 111–12, 127–28, 129, 137–38, 153, 168, 174; in Rhineland, 152, 167; at Scheldt, 127–28, 129, 132, 135, 167; strength, 104–5, 106–7, 111, 127, 128f, 132, 137; strength compared to 12th SS Panzer Division, 128–29; vehicles/weaponry, 87, 105–6, 108, 132, 141, 153, 167–68
Infantry Division, 3rd Canadian: 2nd Canadian Armoured Brigade and, 130; and 4th Canadian Armoured Division, 129–30; 4th Canadian Armoured Division infantry units relieving, 114; 5th Canadian Armoured Division relieving, 160; 19th Army Field Regiment detached from, 168; about, 95–96; antitank/antiairdraft units, 95; artillery units, 95, 109–10, 142; battle exhaustion/neuropsychiatric casualties, 197, 203*n*26; casualties, 20–21, 103, 108–9, 110, 130, 133–34, 138, 142, 143, 154, 168; channel ports to Belgian border, 129–30; combat capability, 110, 142; equipment, 101, 142–43, 168; field artillery regiments, 101, 109–10, 119; infantry formations, 95, 110; Juno Beach assault, 101–2; losses, 168; mass equipment draw by, 55; in Netherlands/Germany, 153–54; nonartillery divisional units, 95–96; nonbattle casualties, 142, 154; in Normandy Campaign, 33, 102, 103, 105, 108–11, 116, 168; and Normandy

landing, 14, 101; in Operation Charnwood, 87; in Operation Overlord, 3, 95; in Operation Spring, 111; in Operation Switchback, 133, 138; in Operation Totalize, 108; in Operation Tractable, 108; in Operation Veritable, 143; RCA units, 109, 133–34, 142–43; reinforcements, 33, 102, 109, 110, 132–33, 134, 142, 154–55, 168, 175, 200*n*6; relieving 2nd Canadian Infantry Division, 154; at Scheldt, 132–33, 197t; strength, 109, 110–11, 127, 132–33, 142, 168–69; strength vs. German infantry divisions, 111f; training for Operation Overlord, 213*n*12; vehicle strength, 210*n*38; vehicles/weaponry, 105, 134, 142–43, 168, 224*n*2; weaponry shortages, 134; weapons/vehicles losses/replacements, 109–10

Infantry Division, 4th Canadian: and 2nd Canadian Army Tank Brigade, 98; about, 96; renamed 2nd Canadian Armoured Brigade, 98; reorganization as armoured division, 98. *See also* 4th Canadian Armoured Division

Infantry Division, 7th Canadian, disbandment of, 22

Infantry Division, 8th Canadian, disbandment of, 22

Infantry Division, 49th British: 5th Canadian Armoured Division relief of, 159–60; 11th Canadian Armoured Regiment supporting, 162

Infantry Division, 50th (British Army), 39

Infantry Division, 52nd (British), 132

Infantry Division, 59th (British Army), 39, 216*n*50

infantry divisions: anti-tank regiments, 192–93; within Canadian Corps, 3; Canadian Machine Gun Battalions, 183; Canadian Reconnaissance Regiments, 182; field artillery regiments, 185; light anti-aircraft regiments, 194; other ranks, shortages, in northwest Europe, 198–99; strength of 3rd Canadian vs. German, 110, 111f

infantry regiments: about, 64, 182–83; Canadian Machine Gun Battalions, 183–84; components, 64; and infantry brigades, 183; LADs, 183; organization, 182t, 183; power of, 64; reinforcement battalions and, 16; role, 183; strength of, 23; vehicles/weapons systems, 12; weaponry/AFVs, 182t, 183

infantry shortages: 2nd Canadian Division, 5; 2nd Canadian Infantry Division, 112; 3rd Canadian Infantry Division, 110; vs. average infantry strength, 6; casualties/losses and, 4–5; and Falaise Gap battle, 174; nadir at August 31, 35; and Normandy Campaign, 27, 116; and reinforcements, 10; of reinforcements, 36, 116; as remedied by mid-September, 5–6; remustering/training for, 35, 101, 174–75; sixty-day, 174; strength vs., 6. *See also* infantry, other ranks shortages

Irish Regiment of Canada, 97, 158, 160

Italian Campaign: 1st Canadian AGRA units in, 163; 1st Canadian Infantry Division in, 93; 5th Canadian Armoured Division in, 97; armoured operations in, 68; and British Army influence on Canadian, 66; Canadian Army (Active) in, 63; casualties, 30; casualty rate estimations for, 29–30; expeditionary force in, 8–9; infantry casualty rates, 202*n*1; replacement systems during, 8–9

Jubilee, Operation, 94. *See also* Dieppe Raid (1942)

Juno Beach, 62, 101–2, 103. *See also* Overlord, Operation

Kangaroos (armoured personnel carriers), 77, 207*n*21; Ram, 88, 225*n*5

Kapelsche Veer, 144, 145

Keller, Rodney, 95

King, William Lyon Mackenzie: and "Big Army," 27–28; and conscription, 10, 24–26, 41; and deployment of conscript personnel overseas, 23; and expansion of army, 24, 26; infantry shortage and, 10; and limitation of involvement in direct front-line combat, 45

Kitching, George, 96

Knocke-sur-Mer, 133
Kranenberg, 142
Kusten Canal, 156, 165

Laing, H.V.D., 107
Laize River, 111
Laizon River, 114
Lake Superior (Motor) Regiment: about, 96; nonbattle casualties, 144; reinforcements, 144; strength, 113, 144, 157
Lanark and Renfrew Scottish Regiment, 158; reorganization of 1st Light Anti-Aircraft Regiment (RCA) as, 165
Laurier, Wilfrid, 24
Le Mesnil-Patry, 68, 70, 102, 209*n*12
Leer, 154, 163, 164
Leeuwarden, 153
Left Out of Battle grouping, 17, 19, 51
Leopold Canal, 131, 133
Les Moutiers-en-Auge, 115
Light Aid Detachments (LADs): 27th Canadian Armoured Regiment, 52; about, 60; anti-tank regiments (Armoured Division) (RCA), 191; anti-tank regiments (Corps Troops) (RCA), 191; anti-tank regiments (Infantry Division) (RCA), 192; armoured regiments, 180; "F" Squadron, 51; field artillery regiments (armoured division variant) (self-propelled), 187; field artillery regiments (armoured division variant) (towed), 188; field artillery regiments (infantry division variant) (towed), 186; gun repairs, 54–55; infantry regiments, 183; machine gun battalions, 185; medium regiments, AGRA towed, 189; motor infantry battalions, 183; in Normandy Campaign, 104; personnel, 178; reconnaissance regiments, 182; in recovery/repair/replacement system, 59, 63. 57; small repairs by, 173; survey regiments (RCA), 190
light anti-aircraft (LAA) regiments (RCA), 65; 1st, 99, 158, 164–65, 166; 2nd, 94, 149, 150; 3rd, 94–95, 105; 4th, 95, 97, 168; 5th, 96, 97; 6th, 100, 117–18, 137, 139; 8th, 116, 136; Armoured Division, 194, 195t, 196; Corps Troops, 193–94; Infantry Division (RCA), 194, 195t; workshops, 194, 195t, 196
Lincoln and Welland Regiment, 131; about, 96; battle/nonbattle casualties, 156; casualties, 115, 145; at Kapelsche Veer, 145; personnel strength, 113; reinforcements, 131, 156; strength, 131, 156
Line of Communications Area, 47, 48, 62
Louisendorf, 71, 72f, 142, 143, 225*n*1
Louivières-en-Auge, 115
Loyal Edmonton Regiment, 93–94, 149, 213*n*87
Luftwaffe: Fallschirmjäjer regiments, 135; ineffectiveness, 83; lack of replacement of losses, 20, 21f; in Normandy Campaign, 119; power in 1941, 24; regular airstrike inability, 175

Maas River, 3, 138, 141, 143, 144
machine gun battalions: in 4th Canadian Armoured Division, 96; about, 183–85
machine guns: Bren light, 77, 108; tracked carriers, 106
Market Garden, Operation, 137
materiel. *See* equipment; vehicles/weapon systems
May-sur-Orne, 78, 80, 225*n*7
McClenaghan, V.S.C., 13
McNaughton, Andrew G.L., 26, 41, 56
medium regiments: as army-level units, 100; artillery, 100; casualties, 83, 131; equipment status reporting, 54–55; role, 65
medium regiments (RCA): 1st, 100, 163, 164; 2nd, 100, 163; 3rd, 100, 146–47, 211*n*47; 4th, 100; 5th, 100, 163, 164; 7th, 100, 131–32, 146, 163
medium regiments, AGRA towed, 188–89; Army Field Artillery Regiments and, 189; LADs, 189
Meppel, 153
Meppen, 156
MG 42 machine guns, 78
"Mike" fire-plan tactics, 84, 85, 90
Military Services Act, 24
MMG (machine gun) Carriers, 183, 184
Moerbrugge, 131

Moerkerke, 131
Mollberg, 164
Montague, P.J., 34, 35
Montgomery, Bernard, 31–32, 33, 66
mortars, 108; carriers, 106, 108
motor infantry battalions, 183, 184t
Moyland Wood, 143, 225*n*1
Murchie, J.C., 34
Murphy, W.C., 98

National Defence Headquarters (NDHQ): and army program, 26, 27; and Beament on reinforcement miscalculations, 30; and casualty estimations, 29; forecasting of casualties, 42; and reinforcements, 42
National Resources Mobilization Act (NRMA): about, 24–25; casualties, 41; conscripts, and personnel reinforcement, 40–42, 43, 150, 153, 154–55, 160, 166, 175; home defence conscripts, 15, 23; training of conscripts, 38; twin armies established under, 25
Nederrijn River, 159–60, 162, 165
Nijkerk, 148
Nijmegen Salient, 137, 138, 143
No. 1 Canadian Base Reinforcement Group (No. 1 CBRG), 14, 30
No. 2 Canadian Base Reinforcement Group (No. 2 CBRG): and 12th Base Reinforcement Battalion, 16; under 21st Army Group, 15; about, 7–8, 14–15; float of personnel, 18; infantry, other ranks shortages, in northwest Europe, 198–99; and infantry shortage, 35; personnel reinforcement organization, 14; purpose, 201*n*21; reinforcement battalions, 15, 17–18; reinforcements during Normandy Campaign, 33; reorganization of, 16; replacement system, 7–8; and sixty-day shortage, 22; unit strength, 15. *See also* reinforcement battalions
No. 2 Tank Troops Workshop, 62
No. 3 Canadian Base Reinforcement Group (No. 3 CBRG), 14, 17
Normandy Campaign: 2nd Canadian Armoured Brigade in, 102–3, 104; 2nd Canadian Corps corps-level units in, 117–18; 2nd Canadian Corps headquarters and, 99; 2nd Canadian Infantry Brigade in, 102; 2nd Canadian Infantry Division in, 94, 103–8, 111–12, 116, 167; 3rd Canadian Infantry Division in, 102, 103, 105, 108–11; 4th Canadian Armoured Division in, 96, 113–17; 6th Anti-Tank Regiment in, 171; 7th Canadian Infantry Brigade in, 102; 9th Canadian Infantry Brigade in, 102, 103; 25th CADR in, 104; armoured regiments as offensive vanguard in, 68–69; Army Group Royal Artillery (AGRA) in, 171; army-level units in, 118–19; artillery bombardments preceding operations, 208*n*1; artillery regiments in, 83; attrition in, 4, 91; British Army in, 39; casualties, 3–4, 33, 34f, 68, 69, 104, 106–7, 108–9, 110, 112, 174; combat capability in, 22; condition of German forces following, 65–66; coordination of armour/antitank forces with infantry/artillery, 78, 80; equipment losses during, 46–47; equipment replacements during, 4; First Canadian Army headquarters and, 99; German forces during, 101, 104, 116; German forces strengths, vs. Canadian, 110, 111f; infantry shortage, 22, 27, 112 (*see also* infantry shortages); LADs in, 104; personnel strengths during, 114; reinforcement shortages, 116; reinforcement systems in, 4, 15, 101, 110, 112; reinforcements, vs. Sicily, 14; and specialized recovery assets, 62; tactics in, 90; tank losses, 112; troop density in, 91; vehicles/weapons losses in, 4; vehicles/weapons strength, 105–6, 114. *See also* Overlord, Operation
North African campaign: British Army changes after, 66; casualties, 29, 30; Commonwealth casualties in, 10; dilution of artillery force in, 81; Eighth Army casualties in, 10; infantry casualty rates, 202*n*1
North Nova Scotia Highlanders: casualties, 109; in Normandy Campaign, 95, 103–4;

strength, 109; at Tilly-la-Campagne, 73, 76, 104
North Shore Regiment, 95, 109

offensive operations: and casualties, 65; combat experience, and performance levels, 89; defensive transition phase, 89–90; German counterattacks vs., 65–66; overwhelming force, and success of, 71; personnel/equipment levels for, 4
Oldenburg, 152, 156, 212*n*68
Oosterhout bridgehead, 159
Opheusden, 162
Ordnance Field Park, 48
Ordnance Maintenance Company (OMC), 47–48, 49, 54; Tank Railhead Section, 50
Otterloo, 160
Overlord, Operation: 2nd Canadian Army Tank Brigade training for, 99; 3rd Canadian Infantry Division in, 95, 101; amphibious landing phase, 3; and creation of RCEME, 57; equipment on eve of, 101; projected casualties, 31. *See also* Normandy Campaign

Panzer Lehr Division, 71, 201*n*16, 221*n*33; Regiment 130, 52
Penhale, M.H.S., 35
Perrières, 114
personnel reinforcement system: 1st Canadian Corps, 17; 2nd Canadian Corps, 17; 25th CADR squadrons in, 16; acclimatization in, 19; administrative structure/system, 8; advanced divisional reinforcement control officer, 16–17; all-volunteer force and, 27, 175; and August 1944 personnel deficit, 19; British Army, 38–39; bureaucratic layers, 13; Canadian Armoured Corps and, 16; Canadian control of, 15; casualty estimations and, 29, 31; categories of, 15–16; CMHQ and, 13; as continuously productive, 21; delivery system, 17–20, 21; design, 13; flexibility of, 21; in German forces vs. Canadian Army, 20, 21f; ignoring of need for, 42; and infantry shortage during Normandy Campaign, 116; Left Out of Battle contingents, 17, 19; losses vs., 119; management of pool, 31; No. 2 CBRG and, 14, 18; during Normandy Campaign, 4, 15; Normandy Campaign and, 101; numbers of battalions, 14; personnel deficits lists, 16–17; personnel destinations, 16; personnel redirection in, 17–18; psychiatric/battle exhaustion cases in, 19; quality of remustered, 37–38; rapid mass transfers, 18–19; recovered medical casualties in, 19; regimental "B" echelons in, 17; remustering of other trades into infantry, 30, 116; training/retraining, 14, 18, 35, 37–38; transport time, 16; US Army, 39–40; during winter 1944–45, 20, 137–38. *See also* reinforcement battalions
personnel reinforcements: army expansion plan and, 26–27; from Canadian Army (Active), 40; Canadian Army as whole, 111–12; Canadian Infantry Corps (CIC), 109; casualty projections and numbers of, 31, 40, 42–43; for casualty replacements, 173–74; for combat capability, 172; Conscription Crisis and infantry, other ranks, 9–10; and constant front-line deployment, 6; corps-level regiments (2nd Canadian Corps), 164; for D-Day landings losses, 33; divisional breakups for, 39; efficiency of, 4; failure to predict, and personnel shortages, 176; as functioning, vs. losses, 5; home defence conscripts as, 10; infantry, other ranks, 9–10, 31–32, 33–34, 35, 116; infantry, other ranks shortage and, 22, 43; infantry, other ranks vs. other trades, 22; infantry casualties and, 16; infantry shortage in, 116; infantry shortages and, 10; during Italian campaign, 8–9; miscalculations of numbers available, 30–31; No. 2 CBRG system, 7–8; during Normandy Campaign, 112; for Normandy vs. Sicily, 14; NRMA conscripts and, 40–42, 43, 150, 153, 154–55, 160 175, 175; numbers, vs. casualties, 20–21, 35, 150; numbers of

all trades, 31; personnel shortages vs., 169; projected casualty rates and number of, 29, 30; remustering program for, 32, 33–34, 35, 101, 142; shortages of, 35, 42, 43; shortages of, and army personnel resource management, 27; shortages vs., 150; sixty-day shortage vs., 5; smooth operation of, 175; subalterns, 22; for subalterns, 22; training/acclimatization, 80–81, 169. *See also under names of individual military units*

personnel shortages: 2nd Canadian Infantry Division, 107–8; 3rd Canadian Infantry Division, 168; 4th Canadian Armoured Division, 113, 169; excess numbers in wrong trades, and, 176; failure to predict infantry reinforcements and, 176; reinforcement vs., 169. *See also* infantry, other ranks shortages; infantry shortages

personnel strengths: artillery-based doctrine and, 176; and combat capability, 173–74, 176; corps-level units, 139, 145, 164, 165–66; establishment levels of, 200*n*9; independent armoured brigades, 170–71; infantry regiments at, 23; maintenance of infantry vs. noninfantry regiments, 150; in Normandy Campaign, 114; NRMA conscripts and, 166; RCA units and, 175; South Saskatchewan Regiment, 175; under-, of infantry, 4–5; and weapon/vehicle inventory maintenance, 174. *See also under names of individual military units*

Perth Regiment, 97, 158, 160–61

Plunder, Operation, 156

Priest: M7 howitzers, 55; M7 self-propelled artillery, 77, 100, 101

Princess Patricia's Canadian Light Infantry, 93, 149–50

Putot, 102

Putten, 160

Quartermaster General ("Q") Branch: 1st ("Q") Echelon, 13, 14f, 16; logistics "Q" matters, 13

Queen's Own Cameron Highlanders of Canada, 94, 152

Queen's Own Rifles of Canada, 95, 102, 133

Quesnay Wood, 108

Ralston, J.L., 23, 25, 26, 34, 37–38, 40–41

Ram: armoured personnel carriers, 88, 173, 225*n*5; Badger flame-throwing tank, 162; Kangaroos, 88, 225*n*5; observation-post tank, 136; tanks, 77, 212*n*70; II tanks, 117, 212*n*70

rebuilding: 2nd Canadian Infantry Division, 129, 137, 167, 168; 4th Canadian Armoured Division, 138–39, 169–70; Canadian Army's ability for, 172; following Scheldt Battle, 19; following sixty-day shortage, 19; German forces and, 168; and victory, 6; during winter 1944–45, 138–40, 141. *See also* recovery/repair/replacement systems; reinforcement(s)

reconnaissance: Daimler Scout Cars, 183; Humber Scout cars, 143; scout cars, 50

reconnaissance regiments: 1st Canadian Infantry Division, 94; 3rd Canadian Armoured (Governor General's Horse Guards), 97, 158; 4th Canadian (Princess Louise's Dragoon Guards), 94, 147, 151, 152, 158, 167, 222*n*54; in 4th Canadian Armoured Division, 96; in 5th Canadian Armoured Division, 97; 7th Canadian (17th Duke of York's Royal Canadian Hussars), 95–96, 133, 210*n*33; 8th Canadian (14th Canadian Hussars), 94, 132; 29th Canadian Armoured (South Alberta Regiment), 96, 115, 135, 157; about, 181–82; armoured, 65; LAD, 182; organization, 181; role, 65, 181; weaponry/vehicles, 181–82

recovery/repair/replacement systems: 3rd Canadian Infantry Division, 109–10; 25th CADR and delivery of replacement armoured vehicles, 172; administrative structure/system, 8, 47–54; armoured vehicle rapid-response capability, 51–52; armoured vehicles, 25th CADR and, 50; armoured/infantry ordnance subparks, 54; brigade workshops, 60–61, 62; British Army methods, 173; British

influence on, 56–57; combat "A" vehicles, 48; combat "B" vehicles, 48, 57f; and combat capability, 173; common stock depots, 10; delivery of armoured vehicles, 172; divisional ordnance field parks, 54; division-level field/subfield parks, 48, 52, 54; division-level ordnance field parks, 56; effectiveness of, 44; equipment, 44; and Falaise Gap closing, 63; German Army, 52; during Italian campaign, 8–9; maintenance lines, 58–63, 173; No. 1 Advanced Base Workshop, 62; No. 2 Advanced Base Workshop, 62; during Normandy Campaign, 4; ordnance field parks, 48; Ordnance Maintenance Company (OMC), 47–48, 49; rail-/roadheads, 48; RCEME and, 56–58, 172; RCOC and, 56–57; rebuilding/reconditioning equipment, 62; repair units as separate from combat arms units, 44; specialized recovery assets, 62; turnaround times, 176
Red Army. *See* USSR
Rees, 156
Le Régiment de la Chaudière: about, 95; casualties, 36, 154; reinforcements, 36, 142, 154–55; strength, 142, 154
Le Régiment de Maisonneuve: about, 94; casualties, 36, 132, 152; reinforcements, 36, 153; at Scheldt, 132
regiments (battalions): about, 64; size/composition, 11
Regina Rifle Regiment, 95, 102, 110, 133
Reichswald Forest, 143, 148
reinforcement battalions: 12th Base, 16; categories of personnel, 15–16; forming No. 3 CBRG, 17; landing in Normandy, 15; No. 2 advanced, 17; No. 3 CBRG, 17; personnel drafts, 17; replacement stocks, 30; roles, 16
reinforcement(s): 3rd Canadian Infantry Division, 143; Canadian vs. German system, 110; constant, 6; effective, 7; effective, defined, 4; effectiveness/efficiency of system, 7–8; efficiency in, 4, 7; German forces and, 6; independent armoured brigades, 170–71. *See also* personnel reinforcements; recovery/repair/replacement systems; vehicle/weapon reinforcements
Retranchement, 133
Rhine River, 141, 143, 152, 156, 164, 165
Rhineland, 146, 147, 152, 164, 167
Rocquancourt-Cintheaux, 69
rolling barrage, 72–73, 89
Rommel, Erwin, 82
Rouvres, 114
Royal 22nd Regiment, 94, 149, 150
Royal Air Force (RAF): 2nd Tactical Air Force, 85, 86, 212*n*68; 83 Group, 85; 84 Group, 85; air support, 85–87; Air Support Signal Unit, 86; Air Support Squadron Unit, 85; production resource allocation to, 66–67; surplus personnel, 39
Royal Armoured Corps, 68
Royal Artillery, 73–75, 81–83, 118. *See also* Army Group Royal Artillery (AGRA)
Royal Canadian Air Force (RCAF), 24, 45, 85–87
Royal Canadian Army Service Corps, 34
Royal Canadian Artillery (RCA): casualties, 136, 175; combat forces, 65; corps-/army-level combat arms units and, 99; gun state, 50; heavy AFVs, 55; non-infantry casualties, 91; personnel reinforcement, 174; personnel strength maintenance, 175; regimental combat effectiveness increasing over time, 88–89; and remustering as other ranks infantry, 34; Royal Artillery reforms mirrored within, 83; at Scheldt, 133–34; weaponry compared to CAC/CIC, 87–88. *See also* antitank regiments; field regiments; light antiaircraft (LAA) regiments; medium regiments; survey regiments
Royal Canadian Electrical and Mechanical Engineers (RCEME): 1st Canadian Armoured Brigade workshop, 98; about, 44, 56–58; "B" vehicle repair, 56; and British Army recovery-and-repair methods, 173; capability of, 63; creation of, 23, 57, 172–73; effectiveness of, 172; formerly Canadian Corps of Electrical and Mechanical Engineers,

57; maintenance/repair lines, 58–63, 173; No. 2 Recovery Company, 62; numbers of units/subunits, 63; projected intense rate losses for, 31; RCOC "E" branch rebadged to, 57; reinforcement personnel for, 31; remustering from, 38; repaired AFVs sent to, 63; repaired vehicles sent to 25th CADR squadrons, 51; separation from combat arms units, 44; transporting of repaired/reconditioned equipment to division field ordnance parks/subparks, 54
Royal Canadian Navy, 24, 45
Royal Canadian Ordnance Corps (RCOC): "E" branch, 57, 58; "O" branch, 57; personnel roles, 56–57; projected intense rate losses for, 31; reinforcement personnel for, 31; remustering from, 38
Royal Canadian Regiment, 93, 150, 151
Royal Electrical and Mechanical Engineers (REME), 56–57
Royal Hamilton Light Infantry, 94, 153
Royal Highland Regiment of Canada (Black Watch): about, 94; casualties, 78, 80, 106; at May-sur-Orne, 78, 80, 225*n*7; in Normandy Campaign, 106; personnel strength, 141; at Verrières Ridge, 78, 225*n*1
Royal Navy, 39, 66–67
Royal Ordnance Corps (British), 56
Royal Regiment of Artillery. *See* Royal Artillery
Royal Regiment of Canada, 94, 112, 153
Royal Winnipeg Rifles: about, 95, 110; battle/nonbattle casualties, 142; casualties, 225*n*1; in Normandy Campaign, 102; reinforcements, 102, 142; strength, 102, 142

St. André-sur-Orne, 78
St. Lambert, 115
St. Omer, 130
Saskatchewan Light Infantry (Machine Gun), 94
Saskatoon Light Infantry: casualties, 149; personnel strength, 147; strength, 151
Scheldt, Battle of the, 3, 132–37, 139–40; 2nd Canadian Armoured Brigade, 134; 2nd Canadian Army Group Royal Artillery (AGRA) in, 132; 2nd Canadian Infantry Division at, 127–28, 129, 132, 167, 175; 3rd Canadian Infantry Division at, 132–33; 4th Canadian Armoured Division at, 134–36, 169; armour in, 90; battle exhaustion casualties, 197; casualties, 132, 133–34, 135–36, 137; flooding of estuary, 85, 90, 167; and freeing of Antwerp port, 129; German forces at, 135, 137; infantry shortages and, 5, 107; losses in, 37; rebuilding of unit strengths after, 19, 129
Schoondijke, 133
scout cars: Daimler, 183; Humber, 143, 181
Seaforth Highlanders of Canada, 93, 147, 150
Second British Army: 2nd Canadian Corps under, 15; Operation Bluecoat, 114
Seine River, 127, 129, 130, 167
Sexton artillery pieces, 163, 164
Sherbrooke Fusiliers. *See* Armoured Regiment, 27th Canadian (Sherbrooke Fusiliers)
Sherman Firefly tanks, 143; 17-pounder, 4, 69, 70, 113, 117, 138, 143, 144, 157, 163, 173, 179, 212*n*70; about, 70; Mark Ic, 117, 136, 157; Mark Vc, 113, 117, 136, 157; shortages, 70
Sherman tanks, 67, 143; 6th Canadian Armoured Regiment losses, 46–47; 6th Canadian Armoured Regiment strength, 53f; 75 mm, 144, 173, 179; abundance of, 65; adoption of, 45; armoured recovery vehicles (ARVs), 117, 136; armoured regiments and, 65; medium, 113; observation-post, 136
Sicilian Campaign: 1st Canadian Army Tank Brigade in, 98; adoption of REME processes at time of, 57; armoured operations in, 68; and British Army influence on Canadian, 66; Canadian Army in, 28; casualty rate estimations for, 29–30; invasion/Operation Husky, 14; numbers of personnel reinforcements, vs. Normandy, 14
Silvolde, 152

Simonds, Guy G., 66, 83, 99, 107
Sinclair-Weeks-Dunkly Report, 56
Sogel, 156
Soignolles, 114
Somme River, 130
Sonsbeck-Xanten Road, 155
South Saskatchewan Regiment: about, 94; personnel strength, 141, 175; reinforcements, 153; at Scheldt, 175
Spitzbergen, 93
Spragge, J.G., 15
Spring, Operation, 35, 103, 104, 106, 111, 213*n*85
Stalingrad, 9
Steenbergen, 135
Steenwijk, 153
Sten submachine gun, 77, 173
Stonk (standard regimental concentration), 85
Stormont, Dundas, and Glengarry Highlanders, 95, 103, 224*n*3
strength(s): of Corps formations in April 1945, 3; First Canadian Army headquarters returns regarding, 10; full, and combat capability, 176; German infantry vs. Canadian, 110, 111f; maximum, 167; in northwest Europe, 167. *See also* equipment strengths; personnel strengths; vehicle/weapon strengths; *and under names of individual military units*
Stuart, Kenneth, 26, 28, 31–32, 34, 40, 42
Stuart tanks, 117; light, 113, 143, 144; Recce, 51
Sturmgeschütz assault guns, 70, 135, 200*n*15
survey regiments (RCA), 189–90; 1st, 99, 164–65; 2nd, 100, 117, 118, 137, 164
Switchback, Operation, 133, 138
Sword Beach, 62

tactics: and armoured forces, 71; artillery "Uncle"/"Victor"/"Yoke"/"Mike" fireplan, 83–84, 85; "bite and hold," 90–91; British Army changes in employment of armour, 66; combined arms, 67–68, 71, 72f, 73–75, 87, 89; defined, 64; on eastern front, 91; firebase, 71–73, 89; grind, 91; indirect fire, 82, 91–92, 141, 186–87, 188–89; in Normandy Campaign, 90; set-piece operations, 5, 82, 90, 92
tank destroyers. *See* antitank weapons
tanks: adoption of Sherman, 45; Allied vs. German, 70–71; British production of, 66; Cromwell, 67; Cruiser-type, 67; Crusader antiaircraft, 51; design, and losses, 67; in direct-fire firebase, 71–73; German compared to British, 66; German replacement/delivery system, 144, 145f; German superiority, 70–71; German use of terrain, 68; infantry-type, 67; M3 Stuart light, 179; M3 White half-tracks, 183; M14 half-tracks, 190; Panther tank deliveries vs. heavy AFVs delivered to 5th Canadian Armoured Division, 159; Panzer III, 135; Panzer IV, 52, 53f, 66, 70, 144, 145f; Panzer IV production vs. 4th Canadian Armoured Division tank replacement/delivery, 144, 145f; Panzer V A/G, 70; Panzer VI, 70; production expansion, 66–67; Ram, 77, 117, 136, 162, 212*n*70; Sherman (*see* Sherman tanks); T-34, 91; terrain and, 68; vulnerability to antitank weapons, 69
Terborg, 152, 156
Third US Army, 115
Thompson submachine gun, 77
Tilly-la-Campagne, 73–76, 103, 104, 114, 210*n*32, 210*n*34
Toronto Scottish (Machine Gun) Regiment, 94
total war, 9, 26, 28
Totalize, Operation: 2nd Canadian Infantry Division in, 111, 112; 3rd Canadian Infantry Division in, 108, 109; 4th Canadian Armoured Brigade in, 69; 4th Canadian Armoured Division in, 114; 27th Canadian Armoured Regiment in, 52; air attack for first phase, 201*n*22; bomber attacks in operational phases, 211*n*53; and infantry losses/shortages, 4–5; Kangaroos at, 77; maintenance of artillery pieces prior to, 62; and need for reinforcements, 35

Tractable, Operation: 2nd Canadian Infantry Division in, 111, 112; 3rd Canadian Infantry Division in, 108; 4th Canadian Armoured Brigade in, 69; 4th Canadian Armoured Division in, 114; 27th Canadian Armoured Regiment in, 52; and infantry losses/shortages, 4–5
Trun, 114–15
Tuschen forest area, 155
Twente Canal, 156

"Uncle" fire-plan tactics, 84, 85, 90
United States: Army Air Force, 86; Canadian adoption of standard equipment/weaponry, 45; entry into war, 45, 67; First US Army Operation Cobra, 114; headquarters units compared to Canadian, 27; Lend-Lease program, 67; neutrality of, 45; Sherman tank, 45; war production, 67
United States Army: replacement of losses, 38, 39–40; training/integration of replacement personnel, 80–81
Universal Carriers: 2nd Canadian Infantry Division loss replacements, 108; 3rd Canadian Infantry Division, 134, 224*n*2; as "A" vehicle, 55; anti-tank regiments and, 190, 191, 192; Bren Gun, 76, 77, 206*n*6; disadvantages of, 64; forward observation officers using, 82; infantry regiments and, 183; machine gun battalions and, 184; Mortar, 181, 183; Reconnaissance Regiment and, 181; self-propelled field regiment armoured division variant and, 186; T16, 55, 184–85; tracked, 64, 82, 108, 161, 162, 188; transport/delivery of, 55; Wasp II flamethrowers, 77, 78, 88, 106, 113, 134, 136, 143, 152, 162, 173, 212*n*70, 224*n*2
USSR: armoured battle tactics by, 91; German armour in, 68; infantry, 91; Stalingrad, 9
Utrecht, 160

Valentine Archer tank destroyers, 141, 143, 152, 190, 192, 221*n*37
Valentine Charger artillery command tanks, 152, 190
Veen, 155
vehicles: 21st Army Group administrative echelons and, 46; attrition causes, 46; classifications, 144; field artillery regiments (armoured division variant) (self-propelled), 186, 187t; general service, 55, 56; monthly returns, 206*n*1; scout cars, 50, 143, 181, 183. *See also* recovery/repair/replacement system
vehicles, "A" combat: 1st Canadian Armoured Brigade, 162–63; 1st Canadian Infantry Division, 147, 151–52; 2nd Canadian Infantry Division, 106, 108; 3rd Canadian Infantry Division, 109, 110, 142; 4th Canadian Armoured Division, 113, 117, 139, 144; Canadian Army total number, 173; defined, 144; delivery, 55; maintenance lines, 58f; recovery/repair/replacement system, 59–60; replacement/repair system, 48; variety of, 48
vehicles, "B" combat: about, 55; defined, 144; in German vs. Canadian forces, 55; maintenance lines, 58f; path for replacement, 57f; recovery/repair/replacement system, 48, 55–56, 57f, 59f; release/delivery, 55–56; repaired by RCEME units, 56; transportation/delivery of, 55–56; variety of, 48
vehicles/weaponry: 1st Canadian AGRA, 163; 1st Canadian Infantry Division, 147–48, 151–52; 2nd Canadian Armoured Brigade, 155; 2nd Canadian Infantry Division, 105–6, 108, 153; 3rd Canadian Infantry Division, 105, 134, 168; 4th Canadian Armoured Division, 113, 117, 135, 136–37, 144, 157–58, 169–70; 5th Canadian Armoured Division, 158–59, 161–62; AGRA medium regiments, 171; anti-tank regiments (Armoured Division) (RCA), 191, 192t; anti-tank regiments (Corps Troops) (RCA), 190–91; anti-tank regiments (Infantry Division) (RCA), 192, 193t; armoured regiments, 11; artillery regiments, 11; British standards for, 45; comparative effectiveness of, 176; corps-level regiments, 139; efficiency of reinforcement, 4; field

artillery regiments (armoured division variant) (towed), 188; field artillery regiments (infantry division variant) (towed), 186; independent armoured brigades, 170; infantry regiments, 12; light anti-aircraft (LAA) regiments (RCA), 193, 194, 194t, 195t, 196; losses, and combat effectiveness, 88–89; losses in Normandy Campaign, 4; in machine gun battalions, 184–85; medium regiments, AGRA towed, 189; motor infantry battalions, 183, 184t; personnel strengths and inventory maintenance, 174; reasons for losses, 47; reconnaissance regiments, 181–82; survey regiments (RCA), 190. *See also* recovery/repair/replacement system; vehicles; weaponry

vehicle/weapon strengths: 1st Canadian Armoured Brigade, 162–63; 3rd Canadian Infantry Division, 110, 142–43; 4th Canadian Armoured Division, 136–37; corps-level regiments (1st Canadian Corps), 165–66; corps-level units (2nd Canadian Corps), 145–46; in northwest Europe, 176

Veritable, Operation, 49, 83, 84f, 141–48

Verrières Ridge, 68, 78, 103, 104, 114, 117, 171, 213*n*85, 225*n*1

Versainville, 114

Vickers machine guns, 78, 162

"Victor" fire-plan tactics, 84, 85

Voorthuizen, 160

Vyler, 142

Waal River, 139, 141, 143, 159, 162

Waffen-SS: German II/SS Panzer Regiment Panzer IV tank strength, 53f; lack of replacement of losses, 20, 21f; panzer divisions, 65; Panzer Grenadier Regiment, 25th, 87; Panzer IV tank strength, 53f; tank replacement/delivery, 144, 145f. *See also* German forces

Waffen-SS Panzer Division, 12th, 55, 129f; "B" combat vehicles, 55; Hitlerjugend, 90; strength compared to 2nd Canadian Infantry Division, 128–29; strength of, 208*n*5

Wagenborgen, 154

Walford, A.E., 27

Walker, Richard, 25, 42

Walker-Robinson report, 26

War Committee: and "Big Army," 27–28; and conscription, 25, 28, 40–41; and expansion of Canadian Army, 42; infantry, other ranks shortage, and, 9–10; and maintenance of reserve, 23; proconscription camp in, 26; and reinforcements, 42

war production: for British Army, 45; equipment/vehicles, 45; for equipping/resupplying of military, 46; resource allocation to navy/air force, 66–67; weapons systems, 67

weaponry: 1st Canadian AGRA, 164; 3rd Canadian Infantry Division shortages, 134; 21st Army Group 1st Canadian Echelon and, 46; artillery regiments, 87–88; Canadian Armoured Corps, 64–65; Canadian arms industry and, 27; Commonwealth dependency on Britain/US for design, 88; field artillery regiments (armoured division variant) (self-propelled), 186, 187t; infantry, 77–78, 79t; Lend-Lease program and, 67; transportation to fighting units, 52, 54–55; war production, 67. *See also* recovery/repair/replacement system; vehicles/weaponry

Wehl, 153

Wemmershof, 155

Weser River, 152

West Nova Scotia Regiment, 94, 151

West Riding Division, 49th (British), 135

Westerstede, 165

Westminster Regiment (Motor), 97, 158

Windsor, Operation, 68–69, 103, 104

Winnenthal, 155

winter 1944–45: 4th Canadian Armoured Division, 138–39; casualties, 141; hiatus in offensive operations over, 137–38; personnel reinforcement demand during, 20; rebuilding during, 137–38, 139–40, 141; training/integration of replacement personnel during, 80

Wyman, R.A., 99

Xanten, 152

"Yoke" fire-plan tactics, 84, 85

Zandpol, 222*n*71
Zelhem, 156
Zutphen, 153

Studies in Canadian Military History

John Griffith Armstrong, *The Halifax Explosion and the Royal Canadian Navy: Inquiry and Intrigue*
Andrew Richter, *Avoiding Armageddon: Canadian Military Strategy and Nuclear Weapons, 1950–63*
William Johnston, *A War of Patrols: Canadian Army Operations in Korea*
Julian Gwyn, *Frigates and Foremasts: The North American Squadron in Nova Scotia Waters, 1745–1815*
Jeffrey A. Keshen, *Saints, Sinners, and Soldiers: Canada's Second World War*
Desmond Morton, *Fight or Pay: Soldiers' Families in the Great War*
Douglas E. Delaney, *The Soldiers' General: Bert Hoffmeister at War*
Michael Whitby, ed., *Commanding Canadians: The Second World War Diaries of A.F.C. Layard*
Martin F. Auger, *Prisoners of the Home Front: German POWs and "Enemy Aliens" in Southern Quebec, 1940–46*
Tim Cook, *Clio's Warriors: Canadian Historians and the Writing of the World Wars*
Serge Marc Durflinger, *Fighting from Home: The Second World War in Verdun, Quebec*
Richard O. Mayne, *Betrayed: Scandal, Politics, and Canadian Naval Leadership*
P. Whitney Lackenbauer, *Battle Grounds: The Canadian Military and Aboriginal Lands*
Cynthia Toman, *An Officer and a Lady: Canadian Military Nursing and the Second World War*
Michael Petrou, *Renegades: Canadians in the Spanish Civil War*
Amy J. Shaw, *Crisis of Conscience: Conscientious Objection in Canada during the First World War*
Serge Marc Durflinger, *Veterans with a Vision: Canada's War Blinded in Peace and War*
James G. Fergusson, *Canada and Ballistic Missile Defence, 1954–2009: Déjà Vu All Over Again*

Benjamin Isitt, *From Victoria to Vladivostok: Canada's Siberian Expedition, 1917–19*

James Wood, *Militia Myths: Ideas of the Canadian Citizen Soldier, 1896–1921*

Timothy Balzer, *The Information Front: The Canadian Army and News Management during the Second World War*

Andrew B. Godefroy, *Defence and Discovery: Canada's Military Space Program, 1945–74*

Douglas E. Delaney, *Corps Commanders: Five British and Canadian Generals at War, 1939–45*

Timothy Wilford, *Canada's Road to the Pacific War: Intelligence, Strategy, and the Far East Crisis*

Randall Wakelam, *Cold War Fighters: Canadian Aircraft Procurement, 1945–54*

Andrew Burtch, *Give Me Shelter: The Failure of Canada's Cold War Civil Defence*

Wendy Cuthbertson, *Labour Goes to War: The CIO and the Construction of a New Social Order, 1939–45*

P. Whitney Lackenbauer, *The Canadian Rangers: A Living History*

Teresa Iacobelli, *Death or Deliverance: Canadian Courts Martial in the Great War*

Graham Broad, *A Small Price to Pay: Consumer Culture on the Canadian Home Front, 1939–45*

Peter Kasurak, *A National Force: The Evolution of Canada's Army, 1950–2000*

Isabel Campbell, *Unlikely Diplomats: The Canadian Brigade in Germany, 1951–64*

Richard M. Reid, *African Canadians in Union Blue: Volunteering for the Cause in the Civil War*

Andrew B. Godefroy, *In Peace Prepared: Innovation and Adaptation in Canada's Cold War Army*

Nic Clarke, *Unwanted Warriors: The Rejected Volunteers of the Canadian Expeditionary Force*

David Zimmerman, *Maritime Command Pacific: The Royal Canadian Navy's West Coast Fleet in the Early Cold War*

Cynthia Toman, *Sister Soldiers of the Great War: The Nurses of the Canadian Army Medical Corps*

Daniel Byers, *Zombie Army: The Canadian Army and Conscription in the Second World War*

J.L. Granatstein, *The Weight of Command: Voices of Canada's Second World War Generals and Those Who Knew Them*

Colin McCullough, *Creating Canada's Peacekeeping Past*

Douglas E. Delaney and Serge Marc Durflinger, eds., *Capturing Hill 70: Canada's Forgotten Battle of the First World War*

Brandon R. Dimmel, *Engaging the Line: How the Great War Shaped the Canada–US Border*

Meghan Fitzpatrick, *Invisible Scars: Mental Trauma and the Korean War*

Patrick M. Dennis, *Reluctant Warriors: Canadian Conscripts and the Great War*

Frank Maas, *The Price of Alliance: The Politics and Procurement of Leopard Tanks for Canada's NATO Brigade*

Geoffrey Hayes, *Crerar's Lieutenants: Inventing the Canadian Junior Army Officer, 1939–45*

Richard Goette, *Sovereignty and Command in Canada–US Continental Air Defence, 1940–57*

Geoff Jackson, *The Empire on the Western Front: The British 62nd and Canadian 4th Divisions in Battle*

Steve Marti and William John Pratt, eds., *Fighting with the Empire: Canada, Britain, and Global Conflict, 1867–1947*

Steve Marti, *For Home and Empire: Voluntary Mobilization in Australia, Canada, and New Zealand during the First World War*

Peter Kasurak, *Canada's Mechanized Infantry: The Evolution of a Combat Arm, 1920–2012*

Sarah Glassford and Amy Shaw, eds., *Making the Best of It: Women and Girls of Canada and Newfoundland during the Second World War*

George Belliveau and Graham W. Lea, eds., *Contact! Unload: Military Veterans, Trauma, and Research-Based Theatre*

Alex Souchen, *War Junk: Munitions Disposal and Postwar Reconstruction in Canada*

Tim Cook and Jack Granatstein, eds., *Canada 1919: A Nation Shaped by War*

STUDIES IN CANADIAN MILITARY HISTORY
Published by UBC Press in association with the Canadian War Museum.